INGMAR BERGMAN

Also by Peter Cowie:

THE CINEMA OF ORSON WELLES (1978)
DUTCH CINEMA (1979)
EIGHTY YEARS OF CINEMA (1977)
FINNISH CINEMA (1976)
INTERNATIONAL FILM GUIDE (ANNUAL)

INGMAR BERGMAN

A Critical Biography

PETER COWIE

CHARLES SCRIBNER'S SONS · NEW YORK

Library of Congress Cataloging in Publication Data

Cowie, Peter.
  Ingmar Bergman: a critical biography.

  Bibliography: p.
  Filmography: p.
  Includes index.
  1. Bergman, Ingmar, 1918–   . 2. Moving-picture
producers and directors—Sweden—Biography. I. Title.
PN1998.A3B46147   1982   791.43'0233'0924 [B] 82–10346
ISBN 0–684–17771–4

1 3 5 7 9 11 13 15 17 19   F/C   20 18 16 14 12 10 8 6 4 2

Printed in the United States of America.

This book is for Monica

Acknowledgments

The author wishes to thank the following individuals and organizations for their time and help in the preparation of this book:

Kjell-Albin Abrahamson
Jan Aghed
Bibi Andersson
Harriet Andersson
Ornólfur Árnason
Paul Britten Austin
Yngve Bengtsson
Ingmar Bergman
Margareta Bergman
Gunnar Björnstrand
Jacob Boëthius
Gudrun Brost
Peter Darvill
Jörn Donner
Allan Ekelund
Arne Ericsson
Kenne Fant
Gunnar Fischer
Else Fisher-Bergman
Bengt Forslund
Christer Frunck
Herbert Grevenius
Ann-Marie Hedwall
Claes Hooglund
Kerstin Högvall
Gun Hyltén-Cavallius
Erland Josephson

Hauke Lange-Fuchs
Käbi Laretei
Lars-Olof Löthwall
Veronica Lucas
Torborg Lundell
Mago
Aito Mäkinen
Birger Malmsten
Maj-Britt Nilsson
Erik Nordgren
Lennart Olsson
Måns Reuterswärd
Olle Rosberg
Ulla Ryghe
Maud Sandvall
Alf Sjöberg
Henrik Sjögren
Nils Petter Sundgren
Ove Svensson
Max von Sydow
Sven Tollin
Hartvig Torngren
Liv Ullmann
Rune Waldekranz
Gertrud Wincrantz
Dieter Winter

Also my agent, Gerald Pollinger, my editor, Michael Pietsch, and the staff at the Swedish Film Institute.

Photographs are reproduced by courtesy of Svensk Filmindustri, the Swedish Film Institute, Sveriges Radio, Malmö Stadsteater, Kungl. Dramatiska Teater (Beata Bergström), Lennart Nilsson, Sandrews, Nordisk Tonefilm, Cinematograph, ABC Pictures Corporation, Personafilm, Dino De Laurentiis.

Contents

Preface

To write a biography of a living person arouses conflicting emotions. On the one hand, there is the sense of exasperation at being unable, by virtue either of fastidiousness or of a certain fear of the laws of libel, to pry too keenly into the intimate ways of the subject; on the other, the stimulus that comes from personal contact with the artist and all his works, the recognition perhaps of a career still vibrant rather than cold and rigid in outline and achievement.

From childhood on, Ingmar Bergman has been assailed by pressures and stimuli of uncommon strength; where these have affected his accomplishments as an artist, they have been described without inhibition. I leave the task of pursuing more dramatic or licentious revelations to my successors in the decades to come.

Bergman has recently announced his departure from the rigors of the film studio. After the manner of many an athlete or entertainer, however, he is unlikely to abandon his craft until infirmity demands it. This book must therefore be accounted an interim report on the life and skills of a major director.

INGMAR BERGMAN

The cinema is not a craft. It is an art. It does not mean teamwork. One is always alone; on the set as before the blank page. And, for Bergman, to be alone means to ask questions. And to make films means to answer them. Nothing could be more classically romantic.

Jean-Luc Godard

CHAPTER ONE

Childhood Shows the Man

ALL ARTISTS ARE TO SOME EXTENT MARKED BY THEIR CHILDHOOD experience. While some are influenced in their work by the reality of the world about them, others prove susceptible to the fantasies that germinate at will in the first few years of life. Ingmar Bergman, like Eugene O'Neill, Edvard Munch, and Federico Fellini, belongs to the latter category. His childhood was enclosed to such a degree, and his imagination was from the very beginning so fertile, that he created a world of his own to which he has returned for inspiration throughout his adult life. As he has aged, his memories have grown more, rather than less, distinct, and his early resentment of his parents and the world they typified has mellowed into affection. "When I think back to it," he told me in 1980, "it must have been a very happy and very beautiful childhood."

Ingmar Bergman was born on July 14, 1918, at the Academic Hospital in Uppsala, about fifty miles north of Stockholm, and christened Ernst Ingmar Bergman. He had a caul over his head at birth—a sign of future success and prosperity—and he was a Sunday child, a token of grace in the eyes of his parents. Because his mother had been recommended to a doctor in Uppsala, Ingmar was reared in the home of his maternal grandmother there.

The Sweden into which Bergman was born was by no means calm. Although the nation had stood neutral since the close of the nineteenth century, the cost of living had doubled during the years of World War I,

3

and the harvest of 1917 was catastrophic in the wake of exceptionally
dry weather. Dairy, produce, meat, fuel, and other essentials were in
short supply. Lenin's revolution to the east exacerbated these problems,
spurring the militant left wing in Swedish politics to cry for a general
strike to overcome the entrenched power of the bourgeoisie. There was
severe unemployment, many strikes took place, and poverty prevailed.

While Ingmar's father, a chaplain, was never without a position after
1918, the family suffered from financial inconvenience, if not outright
poverty, in the early years of Bergman's life. During Ingmar's first years,
his father was busy from morning to night burying victims of a Spanish
flu epidemic. Whortleberries were a staple of the family's diet, and the
Bergmans found it difficult to scrape together the ingredients for a
christening cake for their new son. According to his sister Margareta,
young Ingmar is said to have nearly died from sheer inanition.

In the cinemas in the late summer of 1918, Chaplin's *The Pawnshop*
was enjoying its premiere run, and at the famous Röda Kvarn theater
(where many of Ingmar Bergman's films would open), *The Birth of a
Nation* was being presented. In the studios, Mauritz Stiller was shooting
The Song of the Blood-Red Flower, and his friend and colleague, Victor
Sjöström, directed and starred in *The Sons of Ingmar*. The golden age
of Swedish silent cinema was at its zenith.

Bergman's lineage is significant for the insights it gives to the themes
and characters in his work as a film director. The Bergman family
consisted of pastors and farmers right back to the sixteenth century;
piety, diligence, and an innate conservatism were passed to each new
generation. Henrik, Ingmar's great-grandfather, was a pastor, and his
wife, Augusta Margareta Agrell, was the daughter of the rector of the
Jacob's School in Stockholm. Ingmar's grandfather, Axel, was a chemist
on the island of Öland in the Baltic. He died very young, and his wife
had to care alone for Erik, Ingmar's father, who also suffered the death
of his two-year-old sister, Margareta. Erik Bergman was brought up in
the town of Gävle, in a household composed of women: his mother,
Alma; her sister, Emma (a somewhat difficult person who never married
and tended to miss trains); and his mother's mother. Forced in the
manner of the times to "say farewell to the dead" by bowing beside the
open coffin of deceased relatives, Erik became fond of dressing up as a
clergyman and pretending to be at a funeral, an experience that led him
toward his life's work.

Karin Åkerblom, Ingmar's mother, was an upper-class girl from the
bourgeoisie that had gradually displaced the landed class predominant
in Swedish society until the nineteenth century. Her mother's father,
Dr. Ernst Gottfrid Calwagen, came of pure Walloon stock (from the

French-speaking part of Belgium originally) and enjoyed a reputation as a linguist and grammarian. His father in turn had been a rural dean and doctor of theology; the roots of devotion lie deep in Bergman's family. Dr. Calwagen's wife, Charlotta Margareta Carsberg, was fascinated by the arts and by music in particular, and their daughter Anna (Karin's mother) was very intellectual. Anna Calwagen traveled, practiced several languages, and taught French at a school in Uppsala. She married a man twenty years older than herself, Johan Åkerblom, who built the Southern Dalarna Railroad.

The Bergmans and the Åkerbloms were related, so while applying himself to theology at the University of Uppsala, Erik called on the family to pay his respects. He promptly fell head over heels in love with his second cousin, Karin. The ardor was not at first entirely reciprocal, but over the years the couple grew to love each other.

Erik Bergman was not permitted by his mother to marry Karin Åkerblom until he had secured a proper job. He was ordained and soon found a post as chaplain of a small mining community, Söderhamn, outside Gävle. He flung himself into his work without reserve, living with Karin in his primitive vicarage, an old wooden house beside a lake. With considerable reluctance, the couple moved to Stockholm when the curacy at the celebrated church of Hedvig Eleonora was offered to Erik. Hedvig Eleonora, with its immense dome grown green with verdigris, is the most perfect church in Stockholm. It stands foursquare in its own grounds on the slope of Östermalm, and its bell tower includes a clock with four faces, which can be seen in both *Prison* and *Woman Without a Face* (a film Bergman scripted for Gustaf Molander). Accepting the post, Erik took a miserable little apartment in Skeppargatan, in the Östermalm district.

The Bergmans' first child was Dag, four years ahead of Ingmar; Margareta, the last child of the Bergman–Åkerblom marriage, was born in 1922. Dag has achieved a distinguished career as a diplomat, serving as consul in Hong Kong and as ambassador in Athens during the Colonels' regime. Margareta has had considerable success as a novelist.

Bergman's parents were in reality decent people, if also prisoners of their class and their beliefs. His mother was a handsome woman, short of stature, with extremely dark hair worn in a bun and an intense gaze that suggested her Walloon ancestry. She was, according to Ingmar, "awfully intelligent and gifted." Karin's mother did not like girls, as Bergman's sister recalls, so Karin had been taught as she grew up to repress "feminine" behavior. Nevertheless, those who knew her felt her to be a passionate woman. Although there were those who were intimidated by her striving after truth, the fact remains that in Ingmar's eyes his mother was a warm and glowing materfamilias.

In her short book *Karin by the Sea,* Margareta Bergman has evoked the personality of her parents:

> After spending half the night indulging one of her few vices—reading—and having in its second half managed to scrape together a few hours' sleep for herself, [mother] would come stumbling in to breakfast only half awake and in a state of extreme nervous irritability, to find her freshly washed, matitudinally cheerful spouse, already hungry as a hunter, standing by the breakfast table with his gold watch in his hand.

Pastor Erik's day would start with his

> splashing, whistling, jubilantly singing fragments of hymns. . . . He would take an ice-cold shower, shave, and brush his teeth with the same frenzy because year in and year out poor Father, clergyman of the State Lutheran Church as he was, lived on the borderline of minimum erotic subsistence.[1]

Erik Bergman was tall, well groomed, and good looking in a Scandinavian way; women always wanted to do things for him, particularly in his later years. He had a special passion for those domestic screen comedies that so charmed Swedish audiences during the thirties—frothy, inconsequential capers that diverted the mind from the impact of the Depression years. Although he was quite nervous and prone to insomnia, his comparative weakness vanished the instant he ascended the steps of his pulpit. It was as though he could find in the church a place of unquestionable command such as the wiry personality of Karin Åkerblom denied him at home.

The couple would talk together at the dinner table in a calm, controlled, pleasant manner, but beneath this decorum Ingmar could sense the enormous tension between them, and an undeclared aggression. In part this was due to a basic conflict of personalities, Karin's willfulness posing a block to Erik's authoritarianism. During one phase of the marriage, Karin's repressed passion for another man made her even more angry and withdrawn. But both kept up with the times, which meant that feelings were not displayed—especially when punishing the children, which had to be done with utter objectivity. As a result, Bergman's villains are always devoid of feeling. Funerals, which Ingmar had to attend, were conducted in the same idiom: candles, flowers, proper costumes, and then the slow disappearance of the coffin. No tears.

Looking back now, in his sixties, Bergman believes that it would have been extremely difficult for his parents to have behaved any other way. "They lived completely officially, observed if you like, as a priest and his wife. Like politicians, they had no privacy." The house was always open to guests, except for Sunday evenings, which were dedicated to the family. Karin Bergman jealously guarded that single interlude of pleasure, when the children and their parents would play games together, or make models, or listen to a novel read aloud by Karin.

Karin's father was so attached to the railroad he had built that he had a villa constructed overlooking the line at Duvnäs so that he could watch the trains go by in his old age. It was to this picturesque setting that the baby Ingmar was brought every summer of his life, and his friends assert that a Dalarna accent is still discernible in his speech. As a child, he adored the blithe summers at "Wåroms" ("our place") near Gagnef, and he would sit daydreaming on a bridge near the Åkerblom house for hours on end, gazing into the water below. (Daydreaming, like rising at six o'clock every morning, is a habit he has carried with him into adulthood.) He also liked to sit on the veranda with his grandfather, who suffered from paralysis in both legs, a condition that eventually afflicted both Erik Bergman and his elder son, Dag.

But the environment that left the greatest impact on the young Ingmar was his grandmother's apartment in Uppsala. Uppsala has a history second to none in Scandinavia. It is frequently mentioned in the Icelandic–Norwegian sagas as being of vital significance in religious and political matters, and Adam of Bremen described the town as being at the center of bloodcurdling sacrifices during certain periods of the year. "Old" Uppsala, which lies a few miles north of the modern city, was the residence of the ancient royal family, the Ynglings. From atop the grassy burial mounds of the old city, the huge Wasa castle is visible, squat and dominant in the surrounding plain. A twin-towered cathedral could be seen from the two-story house at no. 12 Trädgårdsgatan, where Bergman spent his early years, as could the square where Sweden's mad King Erik XIV had one of his adversaries put to death. Uppsala implanted a dramatic sense of Nordic history in Bergman, who would turn to medieval times for his backdrop in *The Seventh Seal* and *The Virgin Spring*.

There were fourteen rooms in the apartment itself, each arranged exactly as it had been in 1890 when Anna Calwagen had come there as a bride. In *Bergman on Bergman*, the director recalls that there were "lots of big rooms with ticking clocks, enormous carpets and massive furniture . . . the combined furniture of two upper middle-class families, pictures from Italy, palms."[2] Here Ingmar's imagination flourished: "I used to sit under the dining table there, 'listening' to the sunshine which came in through the cathedral windows."[3] "The cathedral bells went ding-dong, and the sunlight moved about and 'sounded' in a special way." One day at the end of winter, when Bergman was five, he heard a piano being played in the neighboring apartment,

> waltzes, nothing but waltzes, and on the wall hung a large picture of Venice. As the sunlight moved across the picture, the water in the canal began to flow, the doves flew up from the square, gesticulating people were engaged in inaudible conversation. The bells were not those of Uppsala Cathedral but came from the very picture itself as did the piano music.[4]

On another occasion, he imagined that the statue of the Venus de Milo standing beside one of the windows began suddenly to move. "It was a kind of secret terror that I recognized again in Cocteau's *Blood of a Poet*."[5]

About the same time, Bergman discovered the latent magic of the nursery window blind, which when drawn down became a source of strange figures:

> No special little men or animals, or heads or faces, but *something for which no words existed*. In the fleeting darkness they crept out of the curtains and moved toward the green lampshade or to the table where the drinking water stood. They . . . disappeared only if it became really dark or quite light, or when sleep came.[6]

In the early twenties, the family moved to rather more commodious quarters in Floragatan (the elegant street where, incidentally, Bergman's own film company, Cinematograph, still has its offices). Then in 1924 their lives changed even more, due to the intervention of the wife of King Gustav V, Victoria. One Sunday the queen heard Erik Bergman deliver his sermon in eloquent and lyrical style and appointed him chaplain to the Royal Hospital, Sofia-hemmet. So at last the Bergmans were installed in a decent vicarage, a yellow-faced villa in the parkland belonging to the hospital, with a huge rustic kitchen on the ground floor.

In the woods behind Sofia-hemmet, Bergman recalls, "I played very much alone. . . . There was a small chapel in that park, where the dead patients were brought and placed until they were taken for burial." He made friends with the gardener, whose duty it was to take the corpses from the hospital to the mortuary. "I found it fascinating to go with him; it was my first contact with the human being in death, and the faces looked like those of dolls. It was scary but also very fascinating."

Ingmar Bergman's father in the pulpit of Hedvig Eleonora Church. Photo courtesy Swedish Film Institute.

In the boiler room beneath the hospital, he watched orderlies carrying boxes full of limbs and organs removed during surgery, which were burned in the gigantic, coal-fired furnaces. "For a child," says Bergman, "it was traumatic, and I loved it!"

Although the legend has developed of Bergman's being at odds with his parents from earliest youth, the truth is not so harsh. He would accompany his father on bicycle excursions to churches in the Uppland district just north of the capital. On these "festive journeys" through the Swedish countryside, Bergman's father taught him the names of flowers, trees, and birds. "We spent the day in each other's company," wrote Bergman in a program note to accompany the opening of *The Seventh Seal* in 1957, "without being disturbed by the harassed world around us."

All three Bergman children were made to go to church on Sunday to hear their father preach. Religion was "something to get hold of, something substantial." Saturday was quiet, for father was composing his sermon. On Sunday morning, a psalm would be read aloud, or brief prayers said, before breakfast. This immersion in religious routine would influence many of Bergman's films, and he once asked, rhetorically, how writers could assess his work if they had not even read Luther's shorter catechism.

But the pressures of organized religion goaded Bergman. Although he abided by the rules of the house and attended his father's sermons, he loathed confession as he would an allergy. He disliked the trappings and dogma that went in train with Swedish Lutheranism, and he found his father's fortnightly sermons in the hospital chapel an interminable bore. Immediately afterward, there was a ritual known as the church coffee in the parsonage for the elderly nursing "sisters" who lived at a home in the Sofia-hemmet park. The boys had to be present, but they escaped as soon as they could because on Sundays there were matinee performances at the Stockholm cinemas.

Although it was certainly not without its lighter moments, Bergman's childhood was clouded by a terrible fear of punishment and humiliation. Being the elder, Dag may have been punished more severely than Ingmar—after a beating from his father Dag would seek out his mother, who bathed his back and seat where the weals flushed red—but Ingmar was made to suffer considerably. When he had wet his bed—and incontinence was a regular affliction—he was forced to wear a red skirt throughout the day, in front of the family. "I was always babbling out excuses, asking forgiveness right, left, and center. And I felt unspeakably humiliated."[7]

Margareta recalls that Ingmar's charm could occasionally be turned to good effect. Sometimes he would be told to wait in his father's room for punishment, and then, when Erik arrived, Ingmar would melt his anger with a childish plan to build a hut out of cushions or some such scheme. To justify himself in paternal eyes was vital: "I remember from early childhood a need to show what I had achieved; progress in drawing, the ability to bounce a ball against the wall, my first strokes in the water."[8]

The most notorious incident of Ingmar's childhood, when he was locked in a closet, has been embellished and distorted over the years.

A picture has emerged of Ingmar's father imprisoning him in a closet on several occasions as a form of vindictive punishment. In fact, it was Ingmar's beloved grandmother, who had come from Uppsala to look after the children, who shut him into a wardrobe in the nursery. Ingmar shouted with shock and anger, and Margareta rushed away searching for the key to the white closet. She was back in a few moments, but in that interval Ingmar had in panic torn the hem of his mother's dress with his teeth. In *Hour of the Wolf*, Johan Borg tells his wife of such a traumatic experience and how he was afraid that a "little man" lurking in the dark would gnaw his feet.

As Bergman grew up during the twenties and thirties, Sweden's economic situation improved. Kreuger, the Swedish match king, established an international financial empire, and Swedish industrial names such as Electrolux and SKF began to appear abroad. In 1921 Parliament enfranchised women, and in 1932 the Social Democrats came to power with a wide-ranging program of social reform.

In his teens, Ingmar attended Palmgren's School in Kommendörs-gatan, a short morning scamper from Storgatan, where his parents lived from 1934 onward, after Erik had been appointed head pastor at Hedvig Eleonora. The school still stands, five stories high, its frontage a dull ochre and its echoing stairways so clearly the inspiration for *Torment*, one of Bergman's first screenplays. There was short shrift at Palmgren's for the pupil who might arrive late for morning prayers, and Ingmar's inhibited manner and rather weedy physique was a favorite butt for the mockery of many teachers. At this time, Bergman was thin and puny looking, with green eyes that would soon turn darker and that from the earliest years evinced an intensity remembered by everyone who met him. From infancy onward he suffered from stomach upsets, which led to a recurrent ulcer in adulthood.

Two apartments were at the disposal of the Bergmans on the top floor of no. 7 Storgatan. They were linked by a small staircase and a corridor, and Ingmar was given a tiny room behind the kitchen, down the staircase. His mother and sister missed the park at Sofia-hemmet and placed potted plants in the windows to mask the street view, but Ingmar liked his quarters because he could see far out over central Stockholm and because he was removed from the activity of the household. His father did not come back there often, and Ingmar became fast friends with Laila, the aged cook from Småland who had been with the family for nearly half a century by the time Ingmar was in his teens. (Jullan Kindahl recreates this character memorably in *Wild Strawberries* and *Smiles of a Summer Night*.) Bergman recounts,

Ingmar Bergman (second from left) in school, circa 1926. Photo courtesy Swedish Film Institute.

"She was supposed to control my moral life, but she didn't. So I could come and go, which was very good for me, because we were so controlled in every other way."

The young Bergman was a tender plant, and no evidence points to his having pursued a scandalous existence. He was probably more interested in playing his records of *The Threepenny Opera* than in entertaining the female sex. But he did meet one girl in her mid-teens with whom he had a rewarding and very liberating relationship, a "big and fat and terribly nice" girl who helped to release him from the emotional strictness of his domestic environment and the lack of any feminine company outside the family circle.

The Bergmans inherited a bulky Victorian doll's house early on. Spurred by his sister Margareta and her friend Lillian, who was virtually adopted by the family, Ingmar—or Putte ("little chap"), as he was called—began to indulge his incipient love of theater. In 1930 he saw Alf Sjöberg's production of a Swedish fairy tale, *Big Klas and Little Klas,* at the Royal Dramatic Theater, and this inspired him to build his own puppet playhouse in the nursery at home. He created a revolving stage, moving scenery, and an elaborate lighting system. The stage was formed by turning a large white table upside down, and Ingmar's mother was prevailed upon to make a curtain. One of the first fantasies that Ingmar and Margareta presented was called *When the Ice Troll Melts.* Gramophone records were used to establish a mood, the scenery was carefully sketched, and there were endless discussions between brother and sister as to which dolls should be assigned to each role.

When he was ten, Ingmar started accompanying his brother to screenings at the Östermalm Grammar School. They were mostly documentaries, nature films, and features edited for children's consumption. But the addiction was beginning. If his father remained rather uninterested in Ingmar's love of films, he fostered it indirectly by showing lantern slides on themes such as the Holy Land in the congregation room of Hedvig Eleonora. Ingmar was allowed to sit among the parishioners, watch the spectacle, and listen to Pastor Bergman's discourses.

Before long, Ingmar became a confirmed film buff. The theater held pride of place among his interests, but the capacity for creating illusionary effects, for gripping an audience by the scruff of the neck, was common to both arts, and film had fascinated him ever since he had been taken to see *Black Beauty,* with its vivid fire sequence, at the age of six. So excited by the experience, he stayed in bed for three days with a temperature.

There were matinees every Sunday, the first at one o'clock and the second at three. Admission was twenty-five öre when Ingmar started attending, but that soon increased to thirty-five öre, which was more than Ingmar's allowance. Ingmar soon found that his father's small change was kept in his coat pocket in the study, and the necessary coins were filched. His grandmother was keen on films and used to accompany him to the cinema in Nedre Slottsgatan. "She was in every way my best friend," recalls Bergman.

One of Ingmar's earliest ambitions was to be a projectionist, like the man at the Castle Cinema in Uppsala. Bergman says that he regarded him as someone who ascended to heaven every evening. The projectionist sometimes let the boy join him in the booth, but his effusive cuddling in due course discouraged Ingmar.

Then, circa 1928, a munificent aunt sent Dag a movie projector as a Christmas present. On Boxing Day, Ingmar swapped half his army of lead soldiers for the precious contraption. "He beat me hollow in every war ever afterward," Bergman recalls. "But I'd got the projector, anyway."⁹ It was a rickety apparatus with a chimney and a lamp and a band of film that circulated endlessly. Soon Ingmar was assembling his own films from lengths of material that he purchased by the meter from a local photography store. The first subject he bought was called *Frau Holle*, even though the "Frau" herself did not appear. A girl in national costume was seen asleep in a meadow. She awoke, stretched, pirouetted, and then exited right. And again, and again, ad infinitum, as long as the projector handle was turned. Three meters of paradise.

Learning to splice film marked a critical stage. Ingmar devised plots to suit the montage of various strips that he joined to one another and wound on a primitive film spool that he had built out of Meccano. Pocket money was hoarded whenever possible until an even larger projector could be purchased. From there, it was but a step to the essential acquisition of a box camera. "[I] then made a cinema out of cardboard with a screen, on which I glued up the photos I'd taken. I made whole series of feature films and ran them through on that screen and made believe it was a cinema."¹⁰ Although he sold off his collection of films before he went to the university, he reconstructed one of them to form the farce watched by the young lovers in *Prison*.

During his teens, Ingmar visited the cinema whenever he could, sometimes several evenings in succession. Monster movies, such as *The Mummy*, were among his favorites, and the 1931 version of *Frankenstein* was a memorable experience. In 1935 or 1936 he saw Gustav Machaty's *Ecstasy*, which left a deep impression on him. ("And then of course there was that naked woman one saw suddenly, and that was beautiful and disturbing.") His sense of wonder at the sleight of hand of cinema was enhanced by a visit to the "film town" at Råsunda in the suburbs of Stockholm, around 1930. His father had christened the son of some important personality, and in lieu of payment Erik suggested that his son be allowed to glimpse Råsunda, where the man worked. "It was just like entering heaven," recalls Bergman. These were the studios where Victor Sjöström and Mauritz Stiller had made films. The word *Filmstaden* was printed in large, illuminated letters on an arched sign, just like at the Hollywood studios. The rows of terracotta red buildings were a repository of magic, the factory from which movies emerged full blown as if by some wondrous alchemy. Bergman has always responded to the sights, smells, and sounds of the studios: "For me," he wrote in the fifties, "[filmmaking] is a dreadfully exacting work, a broken back, tired eyes, the smell of makeup, sweat, arc-lights, eternal tension, and waiting, a continuous struggle between choice and necessity, vision and reality, ambition and shiftlessness."

Music, too, was a prime element of Bergman's youth. His father played the piano, and many family friends were adept on violin and cello. There were those who sang, and chamber music gatherings were frequent. An old piano of the Hammerflügel kind stood in his grandmother's home, and Ingmar would sit at it, listening to the casual tunes his fingers could pick out. Later he would go to the opera, where he returned to the gallery week after week, following each production with score in hand. In his room at Storgatan he played 78 rpm discs at a thunderous volume and would be angry if anyone dared interrupt the storm of melody. He was delighted by Wagner and saw *Tannhäuser* at the age of eight.

His tastes changed as he matured. Bach, Handel, Mozart, Beethoven, Brahms, Bartók, and Stravinsky joined his pantheon, and he fostered a particular affection for the French composer Paul Dukas.

Literature never became quite as vital to him. His passion for Strindberg is significant (see Chapter 3), as is his admiration for the novels of Agnes von Krusenstjerna, whose view of women influenced his own attitudes. He enjoyed "huge Russian novels," and as he grew he turned to such rewarding writers as Shakespeare, Maupassant, Balzac, George Bernanos, and the Swede Hjalmar Bergman. But he has always found reading a laborious process and likes best to listen to books read aloud (see, for example, the passage from *Pickwick Papers* read in *Cries and Whispers*).

In the summer of 1934, Ingmar went to Germany for the first time, on an exchange visit involving some two thousand youngsters. The Swedes would go to Germany for the first part of the summer, and then their German counterparts would return home with them to spend the final weeks of sunshine in Swedish homes. Germany and its history already intrigued Ingmar, who was assigned to a pastor's family in the village of Heine, between Weimar and Eisenach. It was a large household, with five sons and two daughters. Hannes, the teenage son designated to look after Ingmar, was in the Hitler Youth, and the girls belonged to the German Girls' League. Ingmar attended Hannes's school, and he was soon subjected to heavy indoctrination about the might and right of the Nazi cause. The pastor had a tendency to use extracts from *Mein Kampf* for his sermon texts, and Hitler's portrait hung everywhere.

The family made an excursion to Weimar, first to a rally celebrating the anniversary of the Party and attended by Hitler, and then to the opera for a performance of Wagner's *Rienzi*. When he asked his host at what point during the rally he should say "Heil Hitler!" the pastor replied gravely, "That's considered as more than mere courtesy, my dear Ingmar." On another trip, to the house of a neighboring banker, Ingmar met a girl named Renata. "I was in love with her," he says. He discovered only later that her family was Jewish. This explained the sudden and ominous silence the following year when, after a correspondence in German, letters no longer came from Renata. On going back to Germany the next summer, for the exchange experiment was a success, Ingmar heard that the banker and his family had vanished.

When Hannes in turn came to spend some weeks with the Bergmans, he found himself in a much less regimented milieu than his own. Out at the summer villa on Smådalarö (in the southern sector of the famous Stockholm archipelago), the Bergman family led a lazy existence free from the commands of city routine. There was tennis, swimming, dancing, even lovemaking. Hannes was thrilled by the presence of Margareta, Ingmar's sister, and the two soon became seriously attached. There were eventually plans for them to marry, but Hannes was shot down as a pilot on the first day of the German invasion of Poland.

After the war, when the newsreels of the concentration camps began to be shown in Sweden, Bergman realized the horror he had brushed shoulders with. "My feelings were overwhelming . . . and I felt great bitterness toward my father and my brother and the schoolteachers and everybody else who'd let me into it. But it was impossible to get rid of the guilt and self-contempt."[11] In the 1970s, after almost thirty-five years of reticence, Bergman was able to admit to having been affected by the Nazi propaganda. "When I came home I was a pro-German fanatic," he has said, although none of his contemporaries recall any pronounced political leanings in him at that period. One of the most meaningful consequences of this episode was that Bergman turned his back on politics in every form. For years he did not vote in elections, did not read political leaders in the papers, and did not listen to speeches.

The visits to Germany may have scarred Bergman as far as politics were concerned, but the experience also heightened his predilection for the Gothic and for supernatural elements. Many of his films, including *The Serpent's Egg*, owe their sense of the macabre to Bergman's immersion in Nazi life and culture at that impressionable age.

In 1937 Bergman took what is known in Sweden as the student examination, which is an equivalent of the English advanced level and a prerequisite for anyone intending to go to college. He passed with quite a respectable grade, although he failed Latin. The day before that particular paper, he had been compelled to attend the funeral of one of his father's fellow clergymen, and the incident upset him so much that he made a mess of a subject he had previously enjoyed. He considered himself "totally, completely devoid of any talent for math."[12] He also found geography difficult, whereas history and religion were more engaging. To study Latin, though, "was a combination of detective work and a kind of intuition. It was terribly exciting to figure out those old texts."

Before proceeding to Stockholm High School, as the University of Stockholm was known in those times, Bergman did compulsory military service in two stretches, amounting officially to five months each. He was soon sent home, however, thanks to a doctor's amiable assertion that his stomach was in need of more delicate sustenance than the army could offer. "I don't think I was a very good soldier," he recalls. His most arduous obligation was to manage a machine gun with six other youths. The weapons were obsolescent, and the machine guns, which dated from 1914, were as unwieldy as small cannon, mounted on carriages but lacking the horses of yore to drag them along. The officers refused permission for the recruits to wear earplugs during shooting practice, and Bergman maintains that he became partially deaf in his right ear. To this day he is aware of a faint singing sound that reminds him of his days at the military camp in Strangnäs.

At the university, his chosen subjects were literature and the history of art. Like many another genius, though, he could not be pinned down to the precise demands of a curriculum. He did not complete the degree course, although he was stimulated by the lectures of Martin Lamm and managed to hand in a paper on Strindberg's *The Keys of Heaven*. His determination to pursue a career in the theater (and Kerstin Högvall, an acquaintance at the time, remembers his saying with intensity, "I *will* be a great director. I *want* to be!") coincided with a decisive break with his home life. When Bergman, like so many teenagers, rebelled against his parents, it was not over politics, or money, or even a girlfriend, but because at root Bergman loathed the "iron caskets of duty" in which his parents were caught fast. His father had long been exasperated by Ingmar's failure to toe the traditional path through youth and the tension between them erupted one day the year after Ingmar had left school. The pastor slapped his son during the course of an argument, and Ingmar retaliated violently, knocking the older man to the floor. When his mother attempted to mediate, Ingmar dealt her a slap for her pains, ran to his room, packed a case, and left no. 7 Storgatan.

The break with Ingmar's parents was severe, although once or twice a week a friend of the family would trek across town to bring him a bottle of red wine and some decent food and to retrieve the dirty socks for washing at home. He was not the first son to revolt against his father, but one may speculate as to why this particular rupture was so decisive. For some years Ingmar had rankled under the cloak of good decorum that the Bergman family laid over its activities. "It was as though they were from another planet," he said of his parents in later years. Sex and money were taboo subjects in the Bergman household, and for a young man whose reading and schoolboy experiences opened up new vistas, the situation was stifling. Punishment was a frequent ritual, and grown-ups would not speak to the offending child until he had shown contrition. This form of punishment led to Ingmar's developing a stammer and even impeded his writing. "I couldn't draw, I couldn't sing. . . . I couldn't dance. I was shut in in every way."

"That really was God's silence," remarked Bergman. "Even today, I can still lose my temper for no apparent reason when someone consistently keeps silent and turns away from me—then I kick and keep at them until I get an answer."

Ingmar did not see his parents for four years, although he was in touch with them through a respectable go-between, Sven Hansson, who ran the Christian settlement for young people known as Mäster-Olofsgården in the Old Town area of Stockholm. Ingmar had often requested publications on the theater at Sandberg's Bookshop, where Hansson worked, and the acquaintance led to Ingmar's being asked to teach a course on stage matters at Mäster-Olofsgården. Bergman shared digs with Hansson in the Old Town, which, with its narrow streets, restaurants, and buildings dating back to medieval times was a perfect refuge for the incipient bohemian. He frequented the Opera and the Royal Dramatic Theater, and also threw himself into the minutiae of successive amateur theatricals at the settlement.

Mäster-Olofsgården afforded Bergman his first opportunity to develop his stage talents. "When I began at Mäster-Olofsgården," he told Henrik Sjögren, "all theater was for me suggestions, atmosphere, situations. But I came much later to the notion that a stage play has an intellectual aspect. And the idea that I myself could have an intellectual attitude to a production came still later."[13] He did work outside Hansson's tiny auditorium as well: Erland Josephson (later to star in such Bergman films as Scenes from a Marriage and Face to Face) remembers the young Ingmar coming to the Norra Real High School and directing The Merchant of Venice with a cast of pupils, Josephson playing Antonio. "He was so absolutely clear what he wanted," Josephson recalls. The two men became friends at university, and a few years later Josephson followed Bergman down to Helsingborg and took up acting as a professional.

In the spring of 1938, Bergman directed Sutton Vane's Outward Bound in Mäster-Olofsgården, he himself playing the Reverend Frank Thomson, and on May 24 there appeared a factual if also favorable notice in the morning newspaper Svenska Dagbladet. His next production was a Strindberg play, Lucky Peter's Journey.

Bergman's labor at Mäster-Olofsgården continued for two more years, and his team grew to love him. His demands were onerous, but he never spared himself. Daily rehearsals were essential just before a premiere, and there was a Sunday morning rehearsal whatever the state of the production. The climax of this phase of Bergman's career came in April 1940 with his production of *Macbeth*. Maud Sandvall, who played Lady Macbeth, recalls that confusion raged when news broke of the Nazi invasion of Denmark and Norway on April 9; with the opening only four days away, all the male actors were called up for military service. Sven Hansson quickly contacted officials in high places and was able to get most of the actors released from duty. *Macbeth* opened as scheduled, and, in the shadow of the Occupation, the play assumed an additional symbolic force. Bergman himself played Duncan.

Meanwhile, Pastor Erik Bergman uttered a powerful sermon against the Nazi threat and was making tremendous efforts to secure the safe passage to Sweden of German refugees.

Although Sweden was fated to preserve her neutrality once again, the advent of war in Europe signified the end of the most formative part of Bergman's youth. In 1941 he would already be considering a career in films. The life at Storgatan belonged to the past. Years later, when he visited the apartment and found his parents surrounded by the same belongings and the same habits, he felt it was "a petrified world, something [he] no longer had any contact with."[14] Erik and Karin remained immured in the Sweden of the nineteenth century, unable to grasp or accept the new ideas and nihilist attitudes of Ingmar's generation in the forties.

Bergman now credits his family for much of his development: "That strict middle-class home gave me a wall to pound on, something to sharpen myself against. At the same time they taught me a number of values—efficiency, punctuality, a sense of financial responsibility—which may be 'bourgeois' but are nevertheless important to the artist. He had become a rebel both in spite of, and because of, his parents.

CHAPTER TWO

The Road Through Torment *and* Crisis

ONCE ESTRANGED FROM HIS FAMILY, INGMAR BERGMAN SOON BECAME everyone's favorite neophyte director. He snatched work when and where he could find it and worked backstage at the Opera to help make ends meet; he lived with a young sophisticate whose voracious personality he would analyze in the screenplay for *Woman Without a Face* in 1947; and he placed his involvement in theater above all other considerations.

During the next five years he would establish the ways of his working life: furious activity in both theater and cinema, an intuitive talent that fixed on certain themes and shook them until they let fall their fruit; and a self-conscious, often egotistical attitude toward friends and colleagues, although this did not impede his popularity among those working with him. Even if the opportunities that opened up before him seem fortuitous, the fact is that Bergman's ambition was powerful and insistent. Even without the good luck he had, sooner or later he would have reached the top in his chosen profession.

Lars-Eric Kjellgren, a prominent director of the day, describes Bergman in his early twenties as a living *perpetuum mobile*. Carl Anders Dymling, head of Svensk Filmindustri, recalls him as "tall, thin, with black hair and burning black eyes."[1] Maud Sandvall was also struck by the dark, intense gaze. During this period, he was prone to tears and full of inchoate fury at himself and the world in general. "Everything revolved around myself and my senses," he admitted later. Nerves drove him to shut himself up in the toilet for long spells, leaving friends like the actor Stig Olin to wonder if he was alive or dead—or just sulking.

By 1940, Bergman was producing plays at the Student Theater in Stockholm as well as at Mäster-Olofsgården. His pace was hectic. He had managed to persuade those in charge of various organizations that he would produce to order for them and, moreover, keep to a tight budget and time schedule. Since the leading directors of the period were reluctant to involve themselves with small Stockholm amateur groups, Bergman's talent and enthusiasm were welcomed. Rehearsals frequently lasted into the night, to the consternation of residents on the upper floors of the student building. The auditorium was a restaurant by day, and Bergman once stopped the dishwashing machines because the noise interrupted his run-throughs. He hated first nights, taking refuge in the projectionist's booth above the auditorium.

Strindberg's *The Pelican* was Bergman's first production at the Student Theater. An earlier production of the play by one of Bergman's gods, Olof Molander, had convinced him that this dream-play could and should become "a vision of toiling, weeping, evil-smitten humanity . . . strange, muted chamber music . . . in all its grotesqueness, its terror, and its beauty."[2]

In the fall season of 1941, Bergman was embroiled in a series of productions at the Medborgarhuset (Civic Center), among them *A Midsummer Night's Dream* and one of Strindberg's most taxing plays, *The Ghost Sonata*. The ninety-nine-seat library was designed as a place where children might be entertained, and Bergman cheerfully put on plays for younger audiences, using professional, adult actors for the leading roles and dubbing his endeavor the Sagoteater (literally, "Fairy-tale Theater").

By 1942 Bergman was anxious to see his own work performed, and the premiere of his *The Death of Punch* (*Kaspers död*) at the Student Theater in September was a momentous occasion, not by virtue of the play's brilliance but because of what ensued. Early the next morning, Stina Bergman was reading her newspapers at the headquarters of Svensk Filmindustri, where she was in charge of the script department. This portly woman was the widow of one of Sweden's greatest writers of the century, Hjalmar Bergman, and as soon as she had digested Sten Selander's notice in *Svenska Dagbladet* ("No debut in Swedish has given such unambiguous promise for the future"), she rang the Student Union and asked for Bergman's home number. She was told that Ingmar was still asleep. When he returned the call, he was suspicious and offhand. Stina Bergman invited him to come up for a chat that afternoon.

He came, according to Stina Bergman, looking "shabby and discourteous, coarse and unshaven. He seemed to emerge with a scornful laugh from the darkest corner of Hell; a true clown, with a charm so deadly that after a couple of hours' conversation, I had to have three cups of coffee to get back to normal."[3] She suggested on the spot that he should join Svensk Filmindustri as an assistant in the screenwriting division. He was delighted, not only because the job presented a fresh challenge but also because the salary amounted to a princely five hundred crowns a month for "a poor, confused young man"—Bergman's own description of himself.

So he was given a desk and a tiny office—there were six people there— and he "washed and polished" scripts. The regimen was tough, and if one of her young men had finished editing a screenplay ten minutes before the close of work, Stina Bergman expected him to plunge at once into another manuscript or novel synopsis. Erland Josephson reflects: "Stina Bergman had been in a very complex symbiosis with her late husband and could see in Ingmar someone extremely talented who also belonged to the same tradition as Hjalmar. And of course Ingmar was fascinated by that sort of link with Hjalmar Bergman."[4]

Gunnar Fischer, Bergman's cameraman from 1948 on, remembers being in Stina Bergman's office looking over a screenplay. "A young man came in, didn't say hello or anything, but promptly lay down on the floor with his hands behind his head. Poorly dressed, with rubber boots. He shut his eyes and didn't say a word for about half an hour or so, and then he left without saying goodbye. That was Ingmar."[5]

It is difficult to establish when Bergman began writing plays. He spent the summer of 1942, for sure, in a concentrated burst of energy that yielded a dozen plays; yet only seven of all his dramas seem to have seen the light of day. He once told a French critic that he had written in toto some twenty-three or twenty-four. None has become a staple of the Swedish repertoire and, with the exception of pieces written for television and radio, none has been revived since the fifties.

Bergman's plays are not a rewarding source for those wishing to understand his films. Certainly, *Painting on Wood* (1954) forms the nucleus of *The Seventh Seal,* but the works of the forties are interesting mostly for their concentration on the struggle between Good and Evil, a conflict that suffuses such early films as *A Ship Bound for India* and *Prison.* "What I believed in those days—and believed in for a long time—was the existence of a virulent evil, in no way dependent on environmental or hereditary factors. Call it original sin or whatever you like—anyway an active evil, on which human beings, as opposed to animals, have a monopoly."[6]

The Death of Punch, scribbled in a frenzied twenty-four-hour stint during July 1942, describes a man's sardonic attempt to elude the staid decorum of bourgeois marriage. He gets drunk at an inn, is forced to dance on the table by the other revelers (a foretaste of the scene in *The Seventh Seal* where Jof is tormented by the taverners), and borne off by Death. Punch begs to be excluded from Heaven, which appears identical to the crass serendipity of his marriage. The genesis of the piece lay in a fairy story by Hans Christian Andersen, but Bergman's Punch figure is an embittered Everyman who pops up in practically every script and play written by the Swede during the decade. Their protest as yet lacking in form, his Punch and his "Jack" character seek a higher power, a Creator responsible for the world's tribulations. As will the Knight in *The Seventh Seal*, Jack Kasparsson in *Jack Among the Actors* (1947) addresses the darkness: "Is there no one there who can help me? Dear God, help me. Yes, dear God in Heaven, help me, God, you who are somewhere, who must be somewhere, you must help me!"[7] *The Station* (1942), in a railroad milieu, was offered to the Student Theater and rejected. *Tivoli*, portraying the denizens of an amusement park, was accepted, however, and performed the following year. *The Lonely Ones* (1942), featuring a father-figure as a schoolteacher, was not published.

The paradox remains, however, that the clues to Bergman's art (if not to his obsessions) are more clearly defined in his productions of plays by other authors (Strindberg, Molière, Ibsen, Tennessee Williams) than in his own apprentice works as a playwright.

The choreographer on *The Death of Punch* was a pert, wide-eyed woman named Else Fisher. Bergman had met her in April 1942 and had asked her to supervise a pantomime program at the Civic Center. She called it "Beppo the Clown," and with it she revealed her gifts for both dancing and choreography. Else had been born in Australia, the daughter of a Norwegian–Swedish marriage. The same age as Ingmar, she was only twenty-one when she took a prize at the International Dance Competition in Brussels; during the forties and fifties she went on to become secretary of the Swedish Dramatists' Association.

In October Else and Ingmar became engaged. Their relationship was founded in work and romance. By day, Ingmar immersed himself in novels and screenplays at Svensk Filmindustri; by night, he rehearsed plays and—somehow—continued to write. (By nature, he is a slow writer and slow reader, and there was no typewriter at home.)

On March 25, 1943, Ingmar and Else Fisher were married with pleasant pomp at Hedvig Eleonora. Else wore the gold crown of the church itself, and Ingmar (who had chosen the hymns and the organ music) was in white tie and tails. There was a reception at no. 7 Storgatan and then a mere two days' honeymoon in Gothenburg. Dieter Winter, who had emigrated from Germany with the help of the Swedish

Church in Berlin and had been given accommodation by the Bergmans, was best man. Another guest was Max Goldstein, who had also escaped from Hitler's clutches thanks to the efforts of Erik Bergman and who would later become Mago, the brilliant set and costume designer.

The newlyweds coped with the exigencies of married life in a two-room apartment. Ingmar still felt uncertain about his career: "You have a profession, and I have none," he would tell Else, who was committed to her dancing. He could not yet envision himself sharing the same arena as Alf Sjöberg or Olof Molander, two giant figures in the triumvirate that held sway over the Swedish theater. (The third was Per Lindberg, whose productions left Bergman unmoved.) Sjöberg's Shakespearian productions appeared so flawless, so invincible, that to this day Bergman has not tried to match them, and the interpretations of Strindberg staged by Olof Molander during the mid-thirties set a standard not seen since the days of Max Reinhardt. Bergman queued to watch Molander's production of *A Dream Play*: "Night after night I stood in the wings and sobbed and never really knew why."[8] In October 1942 he witnessed Molander's version of *The Ghost Sonata*, and it stunned him. Years later, when he staged that play in Malmö, he had the sincerity to admit in the program,

> No cockerel, I suppose, has ever found his own crowing-stick so emphatically in his gullet as I did that evening. Walking home through a black and rainy park, I decided to quit the theatrical bandwagon altogether, obey my good parents' wishes, and go back to college. What I'd seen in the theater that evening seemed so absolute as to be beyond achieving. And it still is.[9]

Ingmar was not entirely the manic bohemian, although he was certainly aware of his own image. He made a point, when attending the cinema, of sitting in the front row with his feet on a bench beside the piano. Letters and articles would be signed with a flourish accompanied by the insignia of a little devil. He took a liking to Else's beret and soon adopted it as a badge of artistic courage. (He remained addicted to berets until Käbi Laretei, his fourth wife, put a stop to the habit.) A beard was of course *de rigueur* for the times, and Bergman sported a small pointed variety that gave him the guise of a Mephistopheles. More often than not, no doubt, the beard was grown less at fashion's dictate than to avoid the sheer bother of shaving. But he could be generous as well. He laughed a great deal—huge explosions of laughter— and on one occasion, after raging at Maud Sandvall when she refused to attend a rehearsal of Bach's *Matthew Passion* with him, he sent her a bunch of roses the next day even though he was short of money.

Ingmar Bergman and Else Fisher, newly married outside Hedvig Eleonora Church on March 25, 1943. Photo courtesy Else Fisher-Bergman.

At one point he was smoking several packs of cigarettes a day and could often be found at his favorite restaurant, Sturehof, in the center of Stockholm, his feet up on the table and friends and admirers in attendance. Ulcer symptoms soon persuaded him to abandon smoking, and he was never—even in youth—tempted by the bottle. A small glass of wine or beer was sufficient, and a *Ramlösa* (the Swedish equivalent of club soda) would be his habitual accompaniment to food or conversation.

Birger Malmsten, who would personify Bergman in films of the forties and fifties, recalls the director in the war years as "small and skinny, wearing a pair of worn-out suede pants and a brown shirt. . . . He directed the play holding a hammer in his hand, and he threw it from time to time at the young actors." Another image of Bergman at this time is conjured up by an incident involving Gunnar Björnstrand. Bergman offered him a part in his production of *The Ghost Sonata* at the Civic Center. The rehearsals dragged on, and Bergman had guaranteed that there would be a minimum of ten performances for each of which Björnstrand would be paid ten crowns. Although the critics were generous, the public ignored the play, and after three performances Bergman declared that he would shut up shop. Björnstrand was offered thirty crowns for his pains and was shocked. "I need to eat!" he protested. "Food!" cried Bergman. "Who in hell says you've a right to food? Live on coffee and cookies, like me!" The two men did not speak to each other for several years.

When Brita von Horn offered Bergman an assignment with her Playwrights' Studio (Dramatikerstudion) in 1943, it was not so much the chance to rail at Nazi Germany that appealed to him as the opportunity to express his own theatrical ideas. (Horn was the leader of several Swedish playwrights who had banded together in 1940 as a means of tacit resistance to any kind of sympathy toward the Nazis.) The primary aim of the Playwrights' Studio was to give vent to the work of Swedish authors, and Ingmar Bergman's aid was welcomed; he already enjoyed a reputation for stagecraft among the cognoscenti. When Per Lindberg (incidentally the brother-in-law of Hjalmar Bergman) fell sick while preparing Rudolf Värnlund's U-Boat 39, the Playwrights' Studio turned to Bergman for help. The play was pacifist in tone and described the sinking of a British submarine on the very threshold of the war; the doomed vessel became a metaphor for Europe herself as she was overwhelmed by German aggression. Bergman's production was praised, and by coincidence a submarine was sunk off the west coast of Sweden a few days after the premiere. It was usual for presentations of the Playwrights' Studio to be repeated no more than once or twice, but the catastrophe at sea gave U-Boat 39 a topical twist, and there were several additional performances.

Some months later, Bergman was involved in an even more significant and poignant production: the premiere of *Niels Ebbesen*, by the Danish priest and author Kaj Munk. Although the action unfolded during the Middle Ages, as the Danes rebelled against their German ravagers, the Counts of Holstein, the parallels with the present were unmistakable. Swedish intellectuals felt a keen sympathy with the courageous Munk, who would be murdered by the Nazis within a year. Toivo Pawlo and Anders Ek, two young actors who became friends with Bergman and appeared in many film and stage productions with him over the years, had the leading roles, and Else Fisher contributed her customary choreographic interlude with some dancing peasant maids. Vilgot Sjöman, later famous as director of *I Am Curious (Yellow)*, flourished in a tiny part. He and Bergman had become friends after Sjöman solicited Bergman's opinion of his own fledgling work as a dramatist.

Yet Bergman's passions were still devoted to the cinema, followed closely by theater and classical music. By March of 1943 he was accepted at Svensk Filmindustri as a scriptwriter (his contract ran initially from January 16 for one year), and Allan Ekelund, producer of all Bergman's films until the 1960s, remembers his first effort, entitled *Scared to Live*. "We discussed it quite seriously at the studio; it was based on a novel, and it showed considerable talent." Other suggestions put forward by Bergman were his stories "Prison," "The Fish," and "The Fog," and he adapted Astrid Väring's novel, *Katinka*. According to Jörn Donner, these scripts were often prefaced by short essays from Bergman's pen. His basic salary was good, and on his twenty-fifth birthday he went to spend a week in the country with Else and appeared with five thousand crowns that he had saved from his remuneration.

Svensk Filmindustri was, and remains, the country's largest film company by virtue of its huge chain of cinemas. Sweden was unusual in that its three leading studios produced, distributed, and exhibited movies, and although the efforts of Anders Sandrew and Gustav Scheutz created two viable alternatives to Svensk Filmindustri in the late thirties, there was no doubting the preeminence of "SF," as the place was known. Charles Magnusson had founded Svensk Filmindustri in 1919, when he absorbed the assets of his chief rival, AB Skandia, into his own company, Svenska Bio, to which he had already signed Mauritz Stiller and Victor Sjöström. Most of the talented personalities in Swedish cinema had worked at the SF studios in Råsunda, and the administrative head-quarters (where Bergman had begun working in the script department) were at no. 36 Kungsgatan, in the very heart of Stockholm. Carl Anders Dymling, a former head of Swedish Radio, assumed responsibility for SF in 1942 and immediately brought an enlightened mind to bear on the problems of film production. One of his first decisions was to appoint Victor Sjöström artistic director of SF.

Sjöström liked Bergman and his work, and when Kaj Munk's death was announced in January 1944 he asked the younger man to help him write a tribute for publication in the papers.[10] He was also impressed by the treatment for *Torment*, which Bergman had written while recovering from an illness the previous winter, and urged SF to make it into a film. At first the studio's "house directors" refused to direct it, and the screen-play landed on the desk of Alf Sjöberg. "It was Dymling who told me I should read it because he thought there could be something in it. I read the script and found that it mirrored exactly my own experience as a boy. The atmosphere at my school was very Germanic and full of spiritual pressure. Ingmar Bergman and I had had the same teacher—I for eight or nine years!" Their mutual bête noir had been known to boys at both schools as the "Coachman," driving his class along with cracks of the whip and frequent tongue-lashings.

Alf Sjöberg was then forty. At the age of twenty-seven he had become a director at the Royal Dramatic Theater and was to remain on the staff there as an elder statesman until his death in a street accident in 1980. In 1929 he made one of the last and finest of Swedish silent films, *The Strongest One*, shot on location in the region around Spitzbergen and Tromsö and dealing with whale hunters. But during the thirties, Sjöberg was ostracized by the film industry. So keen was the public appetite for frivolous domestic comedies that a director of Sjöberg's serious intent was incongruous at the studios. By 1939 the atmosphere had changed, and he was able to return to the screen with *They Staked*

Their Lives, a disturbing allegory in modern dress, set in an unidentified Baltic state and describing the anxiety and confusion experienced by the members of an underground movement opposed to the regime. Sjöberg attained even greater heights with *The Road to Heaven* (1942), based on the morality play by Rune Lindström. Here, for the first time since Sjöström and Stiller, was a director who could reconcile the alfresco scope of the cinema with the visual effects and concentrated acting born of the stage.

The notion for the screenplay of *Torment* had germinated since the late thirties, and Bergman had written the gist by hand in a blue exercise book. The idea of expanding it into a full-length treatment came when SF asked him to write an original synopsis of his own. The first draft was edited by Stina Bergman; Sjöberg developed it from that point on. Shooting began on February 21, 1944.

For Bergman, the opportunity of seeing one of his scripts converted into film by the most respected Swedish director of the forties was thrilling, even though he had to be content with the unlikely (and unsuitable) role of "script girl," in charge of continuity from scene to scene and from shot to shot. He must have learned much from observing a craftsman of Sjöberg's caliber, but there were occasions when he forgot a small detail. Sjöberg would be vexed, and Bergman would leave the set and weep tears of exasperation, so excited was he by the whole enterprise. To be present on a film set for the first time, with its air of artifice and calculation, was an experience as significant as his first visit to the "film town" as a boy of twelve.

Torment (*Hets*) opens in the school where Jan-Erik (Alf Kjellin) is studying hard for his matriculation exam. His Latin master, known hatefully as "Caligula," humiliates his pupils and preys on Jan-Erik in particular. At first the teacher's position appears impregnable. Caligula is, however, as unstable and sadistic as his classical nickname suggests. Subtle details betray his Nazi sympathies; he reads *Dagsposten*, a Swedish Nazi newspaper, for instance. These details were added by Sjöberg who, in his own words, "changed Caligula to a political portrait because the war was on. Of course he is based on Himmler. It tied in with the anti-Nazi plays I was staging at the Royal Dramatic Theater by writers like Pär Lagerkvist."

Jan-Erik meets a girl, Bertha (Mai Zetterling), who works in a nearby tobacconist's, and shares his misery with her. His parents are aloof and incapable of understanding his problems; a schoolmaster could not, they imply, be aught but a model of integrity. Bertha tells Jan-Erik that she is terrified of a nocturnal visitor, who follows her insistently and is so delicate in his movements, so swift in his disappearances, that she wonders if he is a ghost. This of course is Caligula,

Expressionist shadows in Torment, *scripted by Bergman and directed by Alf Sjöberg. Photo courtesy Svensk Filmindustri.*

although Bergman's early leaning toward dramatic irony ensures that Jan-Erik is ignorant of the torturer's identity until it is too late. One night he discovers Bertha dead in her room. A quick search of the apartment uncovers Caligula, trembling, concealed behind some coats in the lobby. He is transformed into a pathetic creature obsessed by his inferiority and a coward outside the realm of his classroom.

The police dismiss Bertha's death as the result of a combination of alcoholism and heart failure. But Jan-Erik knows that Caligula is responsible and denounces him to the headmaster so passionately that he is disqualified from taking his matriculation exam. His friends pass, and Jan-Erik lives alone in Bertha's old room. The headmaster visits him and proffers help, but there is no optimism at the end of the film. Only one friend, Sandman (Stig Olin), dares to accuse Caligula in public. Jan-Erik's love is dead; his academic career is wrecked; and although he survives the struggle with Caligula, he is scarred for life by the experience.

In his introduction to the screenplay, Bergman warns against the danger of dubbing Caligula's behavior pathological, even though his villain pleads sickness to both Bertha and the police: "All that stems from an undisciplined gratification of the instincts of one kind or another is not necessarily pathological; but Caligula's gradual petrification, his deliberate, perverse desire to confess his sin and expose himself, his malicious attitude toward the suffering of his fellow men, are probably pathological."[11]

With the passage of time, Bergman's interpretation of Caligula has outlasted Sjöberg's, which was more deeply anchored in the period. But Sjöberg brought to *Torment* a brilliant pictorial flair. Every composition is tightly compressed and shut in with heavy, menacing shadows. When people are talking, there is the sense of other, unseen things happening in the room. The school scenes were shot in the Östra Real School attended by Sjöberg and by Bergman's brother Dag. The opening sequence, showing a boy who is late for class being hounded with fiendish concentration by a teacher (Gunnar Björnstrand, no less), sets the mood of persecution. The echoing stairways and the harsh shouts of the teacher smack of the concentration camp. The school is a microcosm of the hell that Bergman's later figures will regard as symbolic of the world in general.

With few interior sets and virtually no exteriors (only ten days' worth, at the beginning of May), *Torment* was an inexpensive gamble for Svensk Filmindustri, and the film found a wide audience. A responsive chord was struck by Bergman's seething rebellion against his family background, only now discernible, which could easily be heard as a more profound cry of exasperation against the lethargy of Swedish society in the face of World War II. Because *Torment* was not just a drama perfunctorily contrived to suit the disposition of the hour but rather surged up from the personal anguish of Bergman himself, it has endured longer than the more overt political films of the forties in Sweden. Yngve Bengtsson, who was later to become involved in the Swedish Film Society movement, recalls that he and other movie buffs noted how different *Torment* was from Sjöberg's earlier films and that they assumed this to have owed something to Bergman's contribution.

The film triggered quite a debate in the Swedish press. The headmaster of Palmgren's School protested in the pages of *Aftonbladet* the day after the premiere (October 3, 1944), saying that Bergman's father, brother, and Ingmar himself had all been satisfied with their education there. Bergman responded immediately in captious tones, saying outright at one point that he abhorred school as a principle, a system, and an institution.

Certainly the film was a success, and Alf Kjellin and Mai Zetterling were soon sought by foreign producers. Even Bergman, according to one report, was wooed by the British company Two Cities Film to help them with a project they had in hand. *Torment* did not mark the peak of Sjöberg's career—his screen version of Strindberg's *Miss Julie* won the Palme d'Or at Cannes in 1950—but none of his films seized the feelings

of its time so accurately, with the blackouts by night, the censorship of
the press, and "a war of nerves, . . . of trains rattling through Sweden
by night containing representatives of a regime [the Swedes] hated and
yet could not combat."[12]

The first six months of 1944 may be counted among the most vital in
Bergman's early career. *Torment* was shot in February, March, and May,
but Bergman did not let this deflect him from theatrical activity. During
the spring he staged two one-act plays by Hjalmar Bergman, *The
Playhouse* and *Mr. Sleeman Is Coming,* and revived Else's *Beppo the
Clown* for a short summer season in the People's Park in Stockholm,
with Else as choreographer but not in the lead.

On April 8 there came the announcement that he had been appointed
director of the Helsingborg City Theater, making him the youngest head
of any major theater in northern Europe. The City Theater in this small
coastal town (which lies on the southwest tip of Sweden, facing Hamlet's
Elsinore across the water) was in crisis due to the inauguration in nearby
Malmö of the most spectacularly equipped stage in Europe. The city
fathers of Helsingborg were anxious to revive the glories of their own,
much older establishment and began rehearsals for Brita von Horn's
Mrs. Ascheberg from Witdskövle. Else had fallen ill with tuberculosis
during the summer, and her daughter by Bergman, Lena, was only a
few months old, but she was allowed two days' leave from the sanatorium
to attend the opening in September. During her confinement in the
hospital, Else received various handwritten episodes in Ingmar's con-
tinuing saga of his alter ego, "Punch."

Facilities were modest—twelve spotlights, for example, and just four
sets of horizontal lamps—and the capacity was only three hundred
persons. Bergman's rehearsal time was limited to four weeks per play.
The average age of the company was twenty-three, salaries were small,
and the theater's subsidy was minuscule—in the region of fifty thousand
crowns. "But Ingmar's productions were so good," recalls Erland
Josephson, "that it appeared as though there *were* a lot of facilities. His
use of the stage, the actors, the music, the rhythm, was excellent."

It required courage on Bergman's part to tackle the productions he
did, for Helsingborg was a very conservative community. In his program
notes, Bergman referred to the theater as "the town's unquiet corner."[13]
Lennart Olsson, his personal assistant at Malmö in the fifties, remembers
how as a schoolboy he had gone to Bergman's early productions at
Helsingborg and how he had been struck by the degree to which they
broke with traditions.

In a prodigious two seasons, Bergman produced ten plays. *Macbeth,*
ever his favorite Shakespeare tragedy, opened on November 19, 1944.

Herbert Grevenius, the most influential theater critic in Sweden, traveled from Stockholm to attend the first night and endorsed Bergman's vision of the play as "an anti-Nazi drama, a furious settlement of accounts with a murderer and a war criminal. Ruthlessly, consistently, and psychoanalytically, the all-powerful tyrant is taken to pieces. His crimes, each arising out of its forerunner, proliferate and irresistibly elaborate themselves, until in the end they destroy each other."[14] Another success was Olle Hedberg's *Rabies*, based on a novel by the same author, an expert flayer of bourgeois life. The third memorable production was *Requiem*, marking the dramatic debut of a bright young Swedish writer, Björn-Erik Höijer.

Bergman habitually harangued his audience in the program notes even before the curtain was raised:

> Take a look at this, my friend, and you'll see what you look like. Just because you happen to live here in Helsingborg you aren't any better than anyone else. I hope it upsets you. . . . Because we're going to pull the floor from under your feet, plunge you into lethal torture chambers to take a look at the eyeless monsters that lurk there.

In spite of the anti-Nazi flavor of his *Macbeth*, Bergman remained impervious to political passions. "For the most part I was working like a galley slave to get enough money to support two families," he maintains. "I didn't bother my head about anything except putting on plays and making films."[15] He is frequently associated by critics with the so-called *40-talisterna*, a loose-knit group of friends, writers, and intellectuals who sought a new departure in the arts and in literature in particular. Yet Bergman never really belonged to the movement by either friendship or inclination. The only definite link may be found in an issue of *40-tal* in 1944, where an extract from Bergman's "Punch" novel was printed. "I lost contact with the literary figures of my generation," he admits, "most of whom lived and worked in Stockholm." As will be shown in Chapter 3, his true cultural ancestors belong to a much earlier period. Neither his plays nor his films have ever attempted to reflect the social concern of the moment.

In April 1945 Bergman told Else Fisher that he had fallen in love with a dancer in Helsingborg. Her name was Ellen Lundström, and her physical charms were conspicuous. Bergman, separated from Else by sheer geographical distance, was susceptible to this possessive new woman in his everyday life. Ellen's influence on his work was negligible, although when the relationship grew bitter it did provide Bergman with the spur to write the harrowing matrimonial rows in *Thirst, Prison,* and *To Joy.* As his second wife, Ellen bore him four children, Eva, Jan, and the twins, Anna and Mats. Anna married an Englishman and has appeared on British television; in 1979 she even directed her first film, *The Stewardess,* in Santo Domingo. Mats made his debut as an actor on Swedish television in 1969, while Eva became a program editor at the Royal Dramatic Theater. Their mother has maintained her involvement in theatrical matters, notably at the Atelier Theater in Gothenburg.

On July 4, 1945, Bergman began shooting *Crisis* (*Kris*), his first film as director, which he had adapted the previous month from a play by the Dane Leck Fischer entitled *The Mother Creature.* Carl Anders

Bergman (to right of camera) shooting his first film as a director, Crisis, *in 1945, with cameraman Gösta Roosling and leading actress Marianne Löfgren (Jenny). Photo courtesy Svensk Filmindustri.*

Dymling had visited Bergman in Helsingborg and suggested that he should cut his teeth on a movie that none of the other directors at Svensk Filmindustri was anxious to touch. "I'd have filmed the telephone book if anyone had asked me to at that point," Bergman said later.

Bergman saw at once that Fischer's play was meretricious ("It was an out-and-out bit of whoredom for the public—and no one could have called it anything else"[16]), but for years he had been yearning to direct a film, and the flaws in the material were irrelevant. During the shooting that summer, he responded to the friendly conversation and encouragement of Victor Sjöström, who was still artistic director out at the studios in Råsunda. Lars-Eric Kjellgren was production manager. He and Bergman had become fast friends while working for Stina Bergman in the script office and used to view American films together, marveling at the professional verve of Michael Curtiz in particular.

The film is prosaic in character, a commissioned work into which Bergman tossed his own likes and dislikes—tributes to the French cinema of the thirties, scorn for the bourgeois hypocrisy of Helsingborg, the character of Jack (who emerges from Bergman's own early plays as a ubiquitous devil's advocate), and a fascination with the mirror as a means of reflecting people's inner personalities.

With *Crisis*, Bergman began a custom that has prevailed ever since: Players from his stage productions were given roles on screen. Dagny Lind, for example, a stalwart of the Helsingborg City Theater, played Ingeborg opposite the young Inga Landgré (as Nelly), who during the fifties would appear as the wife of the Knight in *The Seventh Seal*, among her other Bergman parts. Opportunities were not distributed by Bergman out of sentiment, however. Young actors from the Helsingborg ensemble including Birger Malmsten, Åke Fridell, and Erland Josephson did not have roles in *Crisis*.

Crisis begins in a mood of deceptive peace and contentment. A bus brings papers and mail and people with unfamiliar faces. This is a dainty country town, free of the clangor of industry and shipping. In true Brechtian fashion, the offscreen narrator announces that what one is about to witness is "only an ordinary sort of play—almost a comedy." A cheerful maid is seen engaged in her morning housework. The squalor of everyday relations, which imbues the other films of Bergman's early period, is surprisingly absent.

But the plot itself appears far more symptomatic of Bergman's ideas at the time. Nelly is a young girl who lives with her foster mother, Ingeborg. As times are hard, Ingeborg has a lodger, Ulf (Allan Bohlin), who is stolid and worthy and keen on Nelly. The tranquility and tedium of their lives are broken by the arrival of Jenny (Marianne Löfgrer), the real mother of Nelly. Jenny has grown prosperous and blowsy at the head of her own beauty parlor and brings in tow her lover, Jack (Stig Olin).

Jenny wants her daughter back. She sends an expensive dress for her to take to the local ball; Nelly wears it, to the chagrin of Ingeborg, whose own offering is laid aside. Fascinated by Jack's charm, and responding to the allure of the city, Nelly abandons her foster mother and takes a job with Jenny in Stockholm. One evening she is seduced by Jack. Jenny discovers them together, and, after an altercation, Jack shoots himself in the street. His spontaneous decision to take his own life is not adequately explained by Bergman, and the idyllic provincial atmosphere accords uncomfortably with the Zolaesque bleakness of the city sequences. But Bergman's justification for this contrast lies in a remark by Jack, who calls the moonlight a mixture of unreal light and real darkness. *Crisis* is a film of light versus shadow, town versus country, Jenny versus Ingeborg. Appearances are cruelly misleading: the kind, decent Ingeborg learns from her doctor that she is suffering from a mortal disease, and the suave, sophisticated Jenny stares at herself in the mirror and tells Nelly that beneath her made-up face she is in truth as old as the ailing Ingeborg.

By far the most intriguing personality in *Crisis* is Bergman's alter ego, Jack, who is arrogant and maudlin by turns. As he gazes down at the party guests in the town hotel, he sneers, "Look how the marionettes are dancing away!" He sabotages the ball by arranging an impromptu jam session in a neighboring room and relishes the confusion of the pompous little band playing "The Blue Danube" and the efforts of the hesitant contralto to continue uninterrupted by the din next door.

Despite his sadism (a trait latent in all Bergman's scripts, from *Torment* on), Jack's romantic streak redeems him. He is an actor forever out of work (even at this stage, the Bergman artist appears to have no idea of money), yet he sends off Ingeborg at the station with tickets, sleeping berth, candies, and a magazine. "You've given without thinking of anything in return," he tells her wistfully, as though that were an ideal to which he, a mere gigolo, could never aspire. Earlier, he has squired Nelly through the moonlit fields and, sitting with her beside a lake, announced, "One day I shall step out into the dark, my clock will stop ticking, and people will wonder where that young fellow Jack's gone."

His death in the street recalls that of Jean Gabin in Carné's *Quai des brumes*. Two shots ring out. At a nearby theater, people can be heard laughing at some entertainment. Jenny shrieks with grief as the ambulance arrives to bear away Jack's corpse. The street empties of spectators, and Nelly is left to wander disconsolate through the night, just as Michèle Morgan did in the Carné film.

Ingeborg shines as the film's sole spirit of goodness. In spite of her illness, she remains warm and understanding, even when she visits Nelly and her mother and returns profoundly depressed. Her relationship with Nelly is based on music, Ingeborg having taught the piano from an early age. Bergman emphasizes these feelings as being of more enduring quality than the selfish affection extended to the girl by Jack and even by her real mother. In the final shots of *Crisis*, Ingeborg urges the disenchanted Nelly to go on living, through the dark days as well as the light. Ulf and Nelly resume their courtship. A church bell resounds. "We can leave Miss Ingeborg J in the sunshine," says the narrator, "watching two young people."

Crisis opened in February 1946 and flopped, although some of the reviewers saw promise in Bergman's work. Svensk Filmindustri was cautious about giving Bergman the resources to make *Sentimental Journey* (an early version of *Summer Interlude*, shot four years later), and Lorens Marmstedt, an independent producer, took Bergman under his wing. His lively little company, Terrafilm, already supported the work of Hasse Ekman and Hampe Faustman, two of the sharpest talents of the time, and Bergman felt a kindred spirit in Marmstedt, who was much less remote than Carl Anders Dymling and who watched the rushes with his directors every evening. One doubts if Bergman would ever have had the temerity to ring Dymling and say in a flood of tears that he never wanted to make another film (as he did Marmstedt on the day after *It Rains on Our Love* had opened).

Although he continued to write screenplays for SF, Bergman was embarking on a fruitful new phase with Lorens Marmstedt, a phase that would culminate with his most personal film of the forties—*Prison*.

CHAPTER THREE

The Cultural Heritage

INGMAR BERGMAN'S THEMES AND OBSESSIONS ARE HIS ALONE, AND THEY have both enhanced and clouded his international reputation. In the eyes of the world he is gloomy rather than jovial, introspective where other directors paint their passions in bright tones. By extension, audiences regard his somber approach to the world, the flesh, and the Devil as essentially Swedish—or at the very least Nordic—in origin.

Bergman himself accepts that his work is colored by traces of innumerable artists before him. "I'm a radar set," he says. "I pick up one thing or another and reflect it back in mirrored form, all jumbled up with memories, dreams, and ideas."[1] As a creative person, he imagines himself in contact with almost everything that has been created before. "When I hear medieval music, I feel an absolute sense of it somewhere in my body, like a conscience." He mentions one of his favorite composers, Stravinsky, who could turn his hand to madrigals, to an opera in the style of Mozart, or to playing games with Tchaikovsky's melodies. Like him, Bergman enjoys experimenting in certain idioms, certain periods, certain genres; there is nothing, after all, so very peculiar about that.

Bergman is a legatee of the Swedish silent cinema. The early giants were Victor Sjöström and Mauritz Stiller, who between them made some fifty feature films during the period 1914–1920, when a neutral Sweden was cut off from the supply of American and British productions. The sense of continuity in the Swedish studios has always been conspicuous, and Sven Nykvist, who is presently Bergman's cinematographer, learned his craft under the guidance of the great Julius Jaenzon, himself the photographer of many of the most renowned silent movies.

Bergman paid tribute to this inheritance by inviting Sjöström to play the conductor, Sönderby, in *To Joy* (1949) and the aged Isak Borg in *Wild Strawberries* (1957), shortly before the pioneer director died. Their friendship dated back to the early forties when Sjöström was artistic director at Svensk Filmindustri.

Sjöström came from the heart of Sweden. He taught himself the craft of acting, and his teeming enthusiasm for life and art enabled him to respond magnificently to the offer by Charles Magnusson, head of Svenska Bio, to become a movie director. Magnusson, the first great Swedish producer, had already signed up Mauritz Stiller. Both directors matured with a rapidity astonishing for the time (1912–1913); they created a tradition where none had existed before. Sjöström, intrepid as performer, sensitive if also rather stolid as *metteur en scène*, turned to Swedish literature for his inspiration and in particular to the novels of Selma Lagerlöf, set in his own native province of Värmland. He was fascinated by history and by the parallels to his time that could be discovered in the Renaissance and the Swedish nineteenth century. He reveled in location shooting and embarked on the most perilous of stunts for the sake of realism—rowing in choppy seas in *Terje Vigen*, dangling from a cliff by a slender rope in *The Outlaw and His Wife*. As his two major achievements in Hollywood, *He Who Gets Slapped* and *The Wind*, would confirm, Sjöström also liked to smile at life's little ironies, and a comparison with Thomas Hardy, although his medium was literary, is legitimate.

Stiller emerged from a cosmopolitan background and from the start was more sophisticated than Sjöström. He was drawn to the elegant comedy of manners that first De Mille and then Lubitsch were to take to its apogee in America. He even persuaded Sjöström to shine as a comedian in two of his best early works, *Thomas Graal's Best Film* and *Thomas Graal's First Child*. One thinks of Stiller when watching Bergman films such as *A Lesson in Love, Smiles of a Summer Night*, and even *Scenes from a Marriage*; both men look upon sheer style as a brittle defense against the slings and arrows of outrageous fortune.

Four vital themes run through the Swedish film, embodied as much in the work of Sjöström and Stiller as they are in that of Bergman or Alf Sjöberg.

The first concerns the landscape and the elements. Their significance in all Nordic cinema is immense. One finds the shortness and intensity of the summer, for example, emphasized in films like *Summer Interlude* and *Summer with Monika*. The Swedes enjoy a love–hate relationship with nature, rather as the Dutch at once fear and espouse the water. Bergman said in the sixties that each morning during January he would wait anxiously for the tiny thread of light on the wall opposite his window to expand. "This is what sustains me through the black and terrible winter: seeing that line of light growing as we get closer to spring."[2]

The second theme is a moral one: the clash between reproof on the one hand and indulgence on the other (illustrated in Bergman's *The Silence* as the struggle between body and intellect). Allied to this is the idea of expiation through suffering, so vividly expressed in Sjöström's *The Outlaw and His Wife* and in Bergman's *The Naked Night* and *The Virgin Spring*.

The third common factor in Swedish cinema is its appreciation of fantasy and the supernatural, the belief in dreams as representing terror and aspiration. One is confronted by it in silent productions such as Sjöström's *The Phantom Carriage* and Stiller's *Gunnar Hede's Saga* and in Bergman's early and middle periods (for instance, the nightmare at the beginning of *Wild Strawberries* or Liv Ullmann's dream of her own cremation in *Face to Face*).

Finally, a social motif may be found. Not the conventional social commitment of many another country, but an awareness of society's basic dislike of the individual. This is communicated in Sjöström's first outstanding film, *Ingeborg Holm*, when a widow is deprived of her children and confined to a poorhouse where she goes slowly mad. It also permeates Bergman's early films, in which his bohemian protagonists rail against the established order and the smug paternalism of the community.

Much has been written about the artistic mood of the forties, the decade in which Bergman was just striking out on his own as a stage and film director. The notion of man as a Sisyphus, as helpless and disengaged as Kafka's Joseph K, was rife in the literature of Jean-Paul Sartre and Albert Camus. As Jörn Donner has written, "Man was analyzed, not as a product of his class and surroundings, of the concrete circumstances under which he lived. Mankind was transformed into the abstract collective concept."[3] In Sweden itself, as mentioned in Chapter 2, the *40-talisterna* depicted man as a lost entity wandering vaguely on a dark plain with neither purpose nor precedent. As Marianne Höök, an early Swedish biographer of Bergman, has observed, "They differed from earlier generations in their recognition of the war as a relentless blow. Their mode of expression was symbolic and complex. A splintered reality begat a splintered form."[4] The mood of these authors was one of fear and helplessness in the wake of Sweden's complaisant neutrality during World War II. At the close of the forties, Stig Dagerman was to become the greatest writer of the group, but the single most shattering utterance of the decade was Erik Lindegren's sheaf of poems, *the man without a way*, full of discord and jagged rhythms, sonnets composed without the luxurious refuge of traditional form.

When Bergman sought an idiom in which to express his personal problems of identification, he turned readily to the bitter, nihilistic pronouncements of the period. The terror that stalks the pages of his own plays can be found also in Stig Dagerman's writing; the indecision of his antiheroes is echoed in the poetry of Lindegren; and the nagging desire for faith among the sceptics of his early films recalls a central motif in the drama of Pär Lagerkvist. Dagerman wrote: "We must . . . keep fear living in us like a permanently ice-free harbor which helps us to survive the winters, the deep-flowing stream under the winter floods."[5]

The religious streak in Bergman's work may have allied him more closely to Lars Ahlin, a direct contemporary. Born in 1915, Ahlin treats idealists with a blend of sympathy and dismay. *Pious Murders* (1952) is a novel that prompted another Swedish critic to invoke the misguided Knight of *The Seventh Seal*: "Ruled by ideals rather than faith, the pious have replaced God's righteousness with self-righteousness."[6]

But the taproot of Bergman's art drives deeper than that into Scandinavian culture.

The element of magic, which finds its avatar so spectacularly in the cinema, belongs to what Bergman terms "the dark, romantic chord running through Scandinavian literature, art, theater, and music, right up to the present day: Swedenborg, Sibelius, Hamsun, Kierkegaard, and of course Strindberg." Each personality overlaps with the next; each exposes the dimensions of his personal struggle more acutely than the last. Swedenborg (1688–1772) was part seer, part scientist, part mystic. C. J. L. Almqvist (1793–1866), the fantasist and religious radical who died in poverty in Germany, was accused of murdering his chief creditor. August Strindberg (1849–1912) remains the greatest Swedish dramatist of all time. Hjalmar Bergman (1883–1931) was known for his weird imagination, his fascination with the bizarre, and his profession of romantic faith. Hjalmar Söderberg (1869–1941) declared, "I believe in the desires of the flesh and in the incurable loneliness of the soul," a credo that might be Bergman's very own.

Just as film directors tend to stem from either Lumière, the naturalist, or Méliès, the magician, so modern Swedish artists are divided between the heritage of Swedenborg and Strindberg and the sturdy realism that marks the growth of Swedish democratic society. Ivar Johansson, Eyvind Johnson, Vilhelm Moberg, and Harry Martinson are typical of the latter strain, and one quickly recognizes that Bergman's work has little in common with theirs. Paradoxically, however, the pattern of life in Sweden has given rise to both traditions.

"We're such a huge country," said Bergman some years ago. "Yet we are so few, so thinly scattered across it. The people have to spend their lives isolated on their farms—and isolated from one another in their homes. It's terribly difficult for them, even when they come to the cities and live close to other people; it's no help, really. They don't know how to get in touch, to communicate."[7] This physical isolation leads inevitably to an isolation of the spirit. The eye turns inward and speculates upon the soul; there is a preoccupation with self. Artists react to this climate of solitude either with anger at the social inadequacies that perpetuate it or with a fatalism blended with religious fervor that yields its most signal and imaginative surge of genius in the work of Strindberg and Ingmar Bergman himself.

The spirit of C. J. L. Almqvist, present in much of Bergman's work, is most clearly discerned in *The Magician*, Bergman's 1958 film. The figure of the mesmerist and charlatan, Albert Emanuel Vogler (Max von Sydow), recalls many of Almqvist's heterodox personalities. Donner claims that the film recalls *The Book of the Briar Rose* "and the strange fluctuations from mysticism and sensational reporting to realism which we find with Almqvist. His mysticism, like B's, was Nordic, both childishly pious and cunning."[8] Ingrid Thulin's character—Vogler's wife, who masquerades as a male assistant—resembles the androgynous Tintomara in "The Queen's Jewel," a story by Almqvist touching on the assassination of Gustaf III at a masked ball.

Strindberg is an altogether more important progenitor of Bergman's work, even if the two men differ in salient ways. Bergman is free of the fanatical misogyny that disfigures much of Strindberg's literature. He lacks the almost exhibitionistic masochism one is confronted with in Strindberg's autobiographical pieces. There is a vein of mordant humor in Bergman; one can scarcely conceive of Strindberg's writing *Smiles of a Summer Night*. Bergman possesses none of the reformist zeal and political enthusiasm of his predecessor. Both men went into exile from Sweden, but for different reasons: Bergman on account of a trumped-up charge concerning his taxation, Strindberg because he felt repelled by the antagonism of his fellows in the wake of his acrimonious book, *The New Kingdom*.

*August Strindberg. Photo
courtesy Swedish Institute.*

Overwhelmingly, however, the two artists are related.

Born of a shipping agent and a former serving woman, Strindberg
was pursued throughout his life by an inferiority complex writ so large
that there is hardly a nook or cranny of his personality that lies concealed
from the attentive reader. He is eternally the groom in his own *Miss
Julie*, striving to clamber upward to social and spiritual recognition. His
first marriage, to Siri von Essen, lasted fourteen turbulent years; Siri had
left her husband in the belief that Strindberg would lead her to fame as
an actress. His second attempt at getting married collapsed after just
over a year; the Austrian journalist Frida von Uhl divorced him in 1894.
Like many a theoretical misogynist, Strindberg depended on the company of a woman and sought throughout his life the image of his
mother, who had died when he was only thirteen.

A period of profound agony followed the break with Frida, and
Strindberg staved off insanity by plunging into scientific experiments
and alchemy. *Inferno*, written in 1897, when the author was nearing
fifty years of age, is a shattering book of revelations, chronicling the
despair and anguish through which its author had passed. But Strindberg

marshaled his forces and produced a stream of brilliant plays between 1899 and 1901, including *The Dance of Death, To Damascus,* and *A Dream Play.* He also plumped for another disastrous marriage, this time to Harriet Bosse, a Norwegian actress some thirty years his junior. Suicide again tempted him. Somehow he survived his private purgatory and in the final years of his life grew more and more interested in the concept of the *Kammerspiel,* the "intimate theater," which allowed emotions to be registered on stage without being impeded by elaborate scenery and a plethora of performers.

Suspicious of himself and everyone else he encountered, Strindberg doubted the constancy of each new companion. He mixed with the major artists of the day—Edvard Munch he met in Berlin, Gauguin in Paris—and as a painter was more than a mere dilettante. Unlike Bergman, who has coveted his privacy and is not enamored of late nights, Strindberg was an habitué of the smoke-filled tavern and the bohemian coterie. In his comment to Frida von Uhl that "a bad marriage is better than none at all," one finds a harbinger of Bergman's line from *Thirst*: "Hell together is better than hell alone." Strindberg was a professed atheist, and yet he responded to the philosophy of Emanuel Swedenborg, perceiving a divine will in every situation and incident and justifying his pangs of jealousy and mortification.

In his introduction to *Four Screenplays,* Bergman wrote: "My great literary experience was Strindberg. There are works of his which can still make my hair stand on end—*The People of Hemsö,* for example."[9] He knew the opening chapter of *The Red Room* almost by heart. During the thirties and forties he was excited by the great Olof Molander productions of Strindberg at the Royal Dramatic Theater. Most of all, he has responded to Strindberg's alternation between ambitious dream-plays and intimate, pared-down dramas. Strindberg's love of the skerries outside Stockholm may be allied to Bergman's affectionate portrayal of that archipelago in *Summer Interlude* and *Summer with Monika.* The leading character in *The Red Room,* Arvid Falck, is similar to Bergman's early male rebels who find themselves at odds with the hypocrisy of bureaucrats and father-figures.

Strindberg's anguish, sexual fanaticism, and richness of dramatic fantasy make even Ibsen pale by comparison, although the revelation of family secrets and the harrowing domestic quarrel were the stock in trade of both playwrights.

While the one period of Strindberg's life that does not throw light on his work is his childhood, it is worth noting that his view of school-teachers runs parallel to Bergman's. One thinks of the elderly officer in *The Dance of Death* trying desperately to answer the master's question,

"What is two times two?" As Martin Lamm has written, one of Strindberg's "most agonizing nightmares as an adult was to find himself once again in Klara School, threatened with Latin lessons and the cane."

As Bergman's films become more assured, so the affinities with Strindberg grow clearer. *The Seventh Seal* shares common ground with *The Saga of the Folkungs*. The plague rages in both dramas; flagellants scourge themselves and one another; the Kyrie eleison sounds like a last trump. Bergman presents historical characters, as Strindberg did, as rather more than mere figures of heroic myth and legend. *Wild Strawberries* exhibits the same tightly woven texture of dream and reality as *To Damascus* and contains two characters—Alman and his wife (Gunnar Sjöberg and Gunnel Broström), the couple who join Isak Borg (Victor Sjöström) after the road accident—who are the spiritual heirs of the Captain and his Alice in *The Dance of Death*. Forever bickering, they aggravate each other and everyone within range: "But we're welded together and can't get free!" cries Alice. The couple chained together in misery, locked in a combat that only death can resolve, is a theme that runs vividly through the work of both Strindberg and Bergman. Marriage is, at best, "a pact between friendly warriors" (*Creditors*), and as a result the partners gradually begin to resemble each other. In *Creditors*, the notion of the wife's second husband amounts to a blend of the first husband *and* her. In *Hour of the Wolf*, Liv Ullmann as Alma suggests that "a woman who lives for a long time together with a man at last comes to be like that man."

Scenes from a Marriage has had a similar impact on the Swedish public in the seventies as Strindberg's *Married Life* did when it appeared in 1884—even if Bergman was not arraigned like his predecessor. Conversations in the work of both men acquire a danger and tension akin to the duel. Miss Y in *The Stronger* listens in silence to her rival's criticisms and revelations, just as Elisabet Vogler (Liv Ullman) refuses to speak with Nurse Alma (Bibi Andersson) in Bergman's *Persona*. "You've sat there staring at me," says Mrs. X at the end of the Strindberg play, "and winding all these thoughts out of me like raw silk from a cocoon—thoughts, perhaps suspicions."

Martin Lamm, whose lectures Bergman attended, has noted the tautness of Strindberg's *The Father* in terms that apply also to Bergman's later films: "A compact and simple structure, a small cast of characters, an action limited almost entirely to the moment of catastrophe, intensified pathos, and the universal sense of the tragic."[10] Already in the 1880s, Strindberg asserted that a table and a couple of chairs were the only items required for a production of his naturalistic plays, and in a memorandum to the actors of the time he outlined this development as "the chamber music idea carried over into the drama: the intimate procedure, the significant motif, the highly finished treatment."

The same progression may be seen in Bergman's films from the early sixties to date, and Bergman has described many of his own movies as "chamber cinema," a direct tribute to the *Kammerspiel* espoused by Strindberg, as was Woody Allen's *Interiors*.

Bergman and Strindberg agree finally that mankind is condemned to suffering, or, as the recurrent line in *A Dream Play* proclaims, "It's a shame about human beings." Man must journey on into the shadows, like the Stranger in Strindberg's *To Damascus*, in search of "conversion, penitence, and faith." When Victor Sjöström died, Bergman recalled his performance as Isak Borg in *Wild Strawberries*, "forever trying to catch the sound of a reply to his terrified questions and despairing prayers. But the silence is complete."[11] Bergman ended his eulogy with a quotation from Strindberg's *The Great Highway*:

> *Bless me, Thy humanity*
> *That suffers, suffers from Thy gift of life!*
> *Me first, who most have suffered—*
> *Suffered most the pain of not being what I most would be.*

Both these Swedes see their role as dreamers on behalf of men and in their work endow the dream with a significance equal if not superior to the factual event. "My inner being," wrote Strindberg in *Alone*, "is mirrored in my dreams and so I can use them as I use a shaving mirror: to see what I'm doing and to avoid cutting myself." The central characters in *The Pelican*, indeed, imagine they are sleepwalking and shiver at the thought of being awakened. In *Shame*, Eva (Liv Ullmann) complains, "Sometimes everything seems like a long strange dream. It's not my dream, it's someone else's, that I'm forced to take part in. . . . What do you think will happen when the person who has dreamed us wakes up and is ashamed of his dream?" The note of self-criticism sounded here by Bergman recalls Alice's comment about the Captain in *The Dance of Death*: "That's his vampire nature all right, to interfere in the fates of others, to suck interest from their lives, to order and arrange things for them, since his own life is of absolutely no interest to him." Thus emerges the concept of the artist as vampire, a predator whose victims' blood runs inextinguishably in his own veins. Man is a cannibal by nature, devouring the flesh and faith of others in order to sustain himself.

The role of the artist as fantasist is evoked by Strindberg in the preface to *A Dream Play*: "On a slight groundwork of reality, imagination spins and weaves new patterns made up of memories, experiences, unfettered fancies, absurdities, and improvisations. The characters are split, double, and multiply, they evaporate, crystallize, scatter, and converge. But a single consciousness holds sway over them all—that of the dreamer." It's an attitude with which Bergman is profoundly in sympathy. As he told me in 1969: "My films are never meant to be reality. They are mirrors, fragments of reality, almost like dreams."

Hjalmar Bergman, for whose widow, Stina, Ingmar worked at Svensk Filmindustri, turned in his later years to screenwriting. He created "film novels" such as *Love's Crucible* and *A Perfect Gentleman*, and his very first essay in this field, *The Clown*, bears an uncanny likeness to *The Magician*, dealing with hypnotists and "magicians" influenced by Mesmer. Bengt Forslund has suggested that both Bergmans are fascinated by clowns and also by the concept of an evil genius who casts his shadow over young people and stains their lives.[12] Ingmar Bergman's vision of himself as a tightrope walker willed by the audience to plunge to disaster is tantamount to Hjalmar Bergman's clown, Jac, who squeezes his art from his own fear.[13] At the height of his terror, Jac's body contorts into a grotesque pose; this knack dates from the moment when his best friend fell to his death from a trapeze and Jac, numb with terror, listened to the cheers of the crowd. Hjalmar Bergman's characters are often subject to humiliation and manipulation; they move through life at the mercy of an irrational destiny (notably in a play like *Mr. Sleeman Is Coming*). A confirmed traveler, Hjalmar Bergman was intrigued by the Renaissance and spent a considerable time in Florence and Rome. In 1923 to 1924 he stayed in Hollywood with his friend Victor Sjöström, but he was unhappy there and returned to Europe. In spite of ill health, his output was prodigious: his complete works, including novels, short stories, essays, plays, and film scripts, amount to thirty volumes. (Strindberg, even more prolific, rages between the covers of fifty-five.) Like Ingmar, he reveled in the *clair obscur* (compare the images of medieval Italy in *Love's Crucible* with scenes such as the Dance of Death in *The Seventh Seal*).

Yet Hjalmar Bergman remains an author difficult to classify. The idealists in his work seek, clumsily and misguidedly, for the essential truth of existence. He believed in the renewal of love, in the comedy of life; but he was also a pessimist. He shares Ingmar Bergman's gift for comprehending feminine psychology, as may be seen in *Mrs. Ingeborg, Directress*. Johannes Edfelt has compared him with E.T.A. Hoffmann, Alfred de Musset, and Edgar Allan Poe in his violent, bizarre changes of mood.[14] It is perhaps typical of the man that *both* Dickens and

Dostoevsky were among his favorite novelists. Ingmar Bergman has said that *Summer Interlude* owes much to his namesake. Certainly it is a film that emphasizes the sinister undercurrents of family life and that evinces a fatalism akin to Hjalmar Bergman's. The unpredictable death of Henrik (Birger Malmsten) in an accident at the height of the summer is a *coup de théâtre* that might well have occurred in a play by Hjalmar Bergman.

One small and uncanny incident links the two Bergmans. When Ingmar was a boy, he was crushed by the experience of being shut up in a closet by his grandmother. In Hjalmar Bergman's *Granny and Our Lord*, a child is punished in precisely the same way.[15]

Pär Lagerkvist (1891–1974), who won the Nobel Prize for Literature in 1951, is an author whose work Bergman has never staged or filmed. Alf Sjöberg has produced several of the Lagerkvist plays and also directed a film based on *Barabbas*. Nevertheless, Lagerkvist is the only twentieth-century Swedish artist whose religious preoccupations are on a par with Bergman's. As Irene Scobbie has noted, he "continued to express compassion for man who is born with a need for faith and yet has his traditional beliefs swept away."[16] This theme is crucial to Bergman's films of the fifties, and in particular *The Seventh Seal* and *The Virgin Spring*. Lagerkvist, like Bergman, broke his ties with a pious home in his late teens, but his reaction was spurred by modern scientific thought and by an attraction to socialism. Even when, at the age of sixty, he published *Barabbas*, Lagerkvist refused to succumb to a sentimental notion of the Christianity in which his youth had been steeped. Barabbas is unable to achieve release for his soul because of a criminal past and a robust, if also pathetic, worldliness that binds him to the earth.

Like Bergman, Lagerkvist is a questioner rather than a prophet. He calls a series of his one-act plays *The Difficult Hour*—"the moment of death when man is still clinging to life, contemplating the absurdity of living and waiting in the dark for God to answer his prayers."[17] To the extent that both men deny to their characters any decisive answer to their problems and deal with metaphysical dilemmas in an austere, expressionist manner, then Ingmar Bergman and Pär Lagerkvist are akin.

It is difficult for the critics to accept the idea of originality in an artist. Every work, they imply through comparisons, has its forerunner in an earlier artist's vision or style. Why, even Orson Welles, who came to the movies without a shred of experience in the medium, had to spend hours at the Museum of Modern Art, viewing John Ford's *Stagecoach* umpteen times, before embarking on *Citizen Kane*. When an artist's work is as concentrated, as philosophical, and as allusive as Bergman's, it inevitably invites the ascription of all manner of influences. European cinema in particular seems to encourage a critic to look for literary analogies, not only because the movies as an art form are so young but also because European filmmakers direct their appeal to the mind rather than to the viscera.

Apart from the writers mentioned earlier in this chapter, European commentators have invoked numerous other authors. For Béranger, the director has a close affinity to Schopenhauer, who declared that separate, personal life is essentially sinful and must be abandoned.[18] In the opinion of Erik Ulrichsen, Bergman has glimpsed in the egocentric Adrian Leverkuhn, the composer in Thomas Mann's *Dr. Faustus*, a reflection of his own aspirations.[19] Like Jean Anouilh, it has been said, he claims to create his films for everyday purposes and not for eternity.

Smiles of a Summer Night has been widely compared with the work of Marivaux, the eighteenth-century French dramatist. Eugene Archer sees in *Wild Strawberries* the Proustian conception of life as a series of isolated moments given meaning by their temporal relationship to the memories of the man who experiences them.[20] The analytic psychology of C. G. Jung has been discussed by critics analyzing *Persona*.

Occasionally Bergman himself has admitted an influence. In *Hour of the Wolf*, the names of various characters are taken from E. T. A. Hoffmann: Kreisler, the "Kapellmeister"; Heerbrand, the curator; Lindhorst, the archivist. There are even direct parallels with *The Magic Flute*. In *The Serpent's Egg*, the homage to Fritz Lang and his Dr. Mabuse films is thinly disguised.

Some directors never go to the cinema. Others, like Bergman, are genuine film buffs, acquiring prints of their favorite films and keeping up with the new releases. For the most part, Bergman's declared loves have depended on the passion of the hour: in 1960, he extolled *The Lady with a Little Dog*; in 1963, he spoke warmly of films like *Jules and Jim*, *Ugetsu Monogatari*, *Nobi*, *Shadows*, and *Pull My Daisy*;[21] in 1974 he said how much he admired the female personalities of Doris Lessing; in 1980 he was delighted by a Harold Lloyd retrospective on West German television.

Molière remains one of his most cherished playwrights and a god to whom he has remained constant. Many years ago he told Béranger of his respect also for Racine, of whose work no adequate translation existed in Swedish.[22] Although not a methodical reader, Bergman is a persistent researcher when something is close to his heart—*The Magic Flute*,

Louis XIV, the classical period in Vienna, the twenties in Germany, or the Nordic Middle Ages.[23]

So the names are summoned forth, as in some ritual incantation. But they remain mere embellishments to Bergman's art. Dismiss them, and there abides a hard core of originality, composed of painful, honest, tormented responses to each day's fresh experience of life. Idols and mentors may point the way, but the artist himself must step forward into the darkness.

CHAPTER FOUR

Youth in Turmoil

At a meeting of the student film society in the university town of Uppsala on May 13, 1946, Bergman spoke of his admiration for the French director Marcel Carné and the concept of poetic realism. "Film must go outside realism, outside the usual descriptions of reality that surround people," he claimed.

This speech set the tone for Bergman's work in the cinema over the next few years. Not until *Prison* in 1948 would he be able to work from his own screenplay, but the intervening films yield undeniable clues to his own obsessions and craftsman's approach to the medium, much as the obvious style of a Hals or a Rembrandt shines out among a string of portraits of Dutch burghers.

In the summer of 1946 Bergman shot *It Rains on Our Love* (*Det regnar på vår kärlek*). The title suggests the whimsical note that Bergman and his scriptwriter, Herbert Grevenius, wanted to strike. A quaint, amiable film, it was based on a Norwegian play by Oskar Braathen and appealed to the Swedish buffs of the time by virtue of its Gallic charm. As in the films of René Clair and in Prévert–Carné productions such as *Quai des brumes* and *Drôle de drâme*, moments of frivolity are interspersed with scenes of gloom and near tragedy; in one scene, for instance, carols play in the background while a man in a bar drops to the floor in agony.

The use of a ubiquitous narrator—a device that Bergman has never quite abandoned—softens the anguish of a pair of young lovers. Maggi (Barbro Kollberg) and David (Birger Malmsten) meet in the rain at

Birger Malmsten (David Lindell) *and Barbro Kollberg* (Maggi) *in* It Rains on Our Love. *Photo courtesy Swedish Film Institute.*

Stockholm's Central Station. Both are miserable: She (unknown to him) is pregnant, and he has just been released from jail with a mere five crowns in his pocket. They decide to face the future together. David, despite clashes with the police, obtains a job at a flower nursery. But the church refuses to marry them, and Maggi loses her child. They set up house in a tiny cottage, and eventually, after assaulting a persistent eviction officer, the couple are brought to court and acquitted, thanks to the efforts of an attorney—none other than the genial old man with an umbrella (Gösta Cederlund) who has served as Bergman's narrator.

The final courtroom scene was written into the script by Bergman and is a direct forerunner of the "inquisition" in *Wild Strawberries* when Isak Borg (Victor Sjöström) is questioned in front of his acquaintances. All the witnesses in the trial of David and Maggi have appeared earlier in the movie. In *Wild Strawberries* such a coincidence is permitted the status of a dream; here the entire film has a deliberate naiveté that makes the finale quite acceptable in its own right. Benkt-Åke Benktsson, an actor of enormous girth whose stage presence would grace some of Bergman's greatest Malmö productions, plays the prosecuting counsel who rants about the danger to society from such irresponsible behavior as David's and Maggi's. Julia Caesar, another character actress of the period, has some amusing moments as Hanna Ledin, and Maggi's final speech to the court is a kind of apologia to the community. At the close of the film, David and Maggi are seen walking away beneath an umbrella in the rain. Life is a sorry mess, but the best method of dealing with its vicissitudes is to adopt a hedonistic outlook and to shrug off the cares of the world with a defiant laugh.

It Rains on Our Love is the least somber of Bergman's forties' films. True, there are the rebellious, impulsive outbursts of David, lashing wildly at society and all that it represents; and there is the familiar personification of malevolence in Håkansson (Ludde Gentzel), the owner of the cottage where David and Maggi shelter in a storm. Håkansson is maudlin and gazes bitterly at photographs of his wife, children, and grandchildren; his only companions are some bad-tempered cats. Incurably lonely, he talks of his children: "They're grown up in a jiffy," he says, "and they become old and unwelcoming." But his melancholy is offset by the burlesque elements in the story: the fat gardener in his bowler hat who is henpecked by his wife; the narrator's comment on Maggi's loss of her child in labor ("What a stroke of luck!"); and the bailiff (played by Gunnar Björnstrand), who is as clumsy as he is exasperating.

Certain scenes are awkward and obtrusive, but such criticisms are perhaps disarmed by the indulgent nature of the genre itself. Braathen was known as a skillful author of folk plays, and the characters in It Rains on Our Love dwell in a soap bubble of their own fabrication. Different stages in David's and Maggi's life are introduced with charcoal drawings that give the impression of a folk tale. Even the dingy hotel with its brass bedstead where the couple spend their first illicit night together breathes only a stylized seediness.

For Bergman, such films were grist to the mill of experience. "I just grabbed helplessly at any form that might save me, because I hadn't any of my own," he said twenty years later.[1]

In the fall of 1946, Bergman began a long association with the Gothenburg Civic Theater. If the cinema was disreputable in the eyes of academic people in Sweden during the forties, then the theater was regarded with only slightly less disdain. Some critics, like Herbert Grevenius, were sympathetic to Bergman's playing the *enfant terrible* at Helsingborg and now Gothenburg, but the mentor destined to exert a lasting influence on his career was Torsten Hammarén. Bergman remembers him as "a hard, difficult man" but a wonderful teacher.[2] Hammarén instilled into his young colleague the need to be well-

Bergman during his time as director at Gothenburg.

prepared, to take notes, even when one was planning to improvise scenes. He advised Bergman to keep quiet as a director and to let the actors come to him with their suggestions and comments. Hammarén, who stemmed from a wealthy family, had longed to be an army officer. He failed and became instead a benevolent dictator in the theater.

Early on, Bergman's insecurity was reflected in a hard, almost dictatorial attitude to his players. Thanks to Hammarén's advice and his own increasing assurance, he later became susceptible to the actor's own suggestions. By the time of *Persona* in 1965, most scenes were discussed openly—with Liv Ullmann and Bibi Andersson, for example—and his players speak with affection and admiration of Bergman's appeal to their talents.

When he arrived in Gothenburg, Bergman found the actors at the Civic Theater divided into distinct groups: old ex-Nazis, Jews, and anti-Nazis. One of the most brilliant figures was Anders Ek, who worked with Bergman until, literally, the day he fell mortally ill in 1978 while preparing to appear in *The Dance of Death* in Stockholm. "He was a tough and ruthless colleague," recalls Bergman, "at once gentle and ruthless."[3] Ek was a keen proponent of existentialist philosophy, which had reached Sweden from the French literary scene, and embraced the opportunity of playing Camus's *Caligula* under Bergman's direction. "An almost ideal coordination was achieved between [Carl Johan] Ström's carefully controlled setting for the imperial Roman palace and the grotesque, surreal, at times even acrobatic conception of Camus's somewhat cerebral play."[4] Bergman, however, has said that the "inner political and social contexts" of existentialism left him cold.[5]

His second production at Gothenburg was his own play, *The Day Ends Early*, which began with a deranged woman escaping from an asylum and announcing the precise hour of their death to various people she visits. Bitter, elegant even, and up to the minute in sentiment, it painted life as Hell on earth during an otherwise lusty Midsummer's Night. The final parade of the dead owed something in spirit to *Outward Bound*, but while the critics were convinced by Bergman's depiction of a contemporary Sodom and Gomorrah, they doubted his ability to offer any solution to the dilemmas that he posed. Ebbe Lind made the shrewd comment in the magazine *BLM* that "Bergman the director is fatal for Bergman the writer, due to his tendency to bring out every effect without regard for the structure of the drama."

In March 1947 Bergman staged G. K. Chesterton's *Magic*, which in its setting (an aristocratic household) and theme (art versus philistinism) is a harbinger of *The Magician*. Anders Ek again featured in the play, as he had in *Caligula* and *The Day Ends Early*.

Although he was still waiting for the chance to direct one of his own scripts, Bergman found Svensk Filmindustri willing to accept his screenplay *Woman Without a Face*; the company assigned the veteran director Gustaf Molander to direct this searing portrait of a young nymphomaniac and her impact on the man who entered her life. Stig Olin plays the world-weary Bogart figure. "It was the last spring of the war," he says offscreen. "I had a novel behind me, quite a success." Then the film proceeds to describe in flashback a sordid love affair that ends with Martin (Alf Kjellin) trying to slash his wrists in a hotel bathroom while a dance band thunders encouragement below.

It has been said that Rut Köhler (Gunn Wållgren), the cruel and insensitive woman at the heart of this melodramatic script, was based on one of Bergman's earliest loves, prior to his meeting with Else Fisher in 1942. As an act of exorcism and vituperation, *Woman Without a Face* is fiendishly effective, more so under Molander's direction than it would have been under Bergman's own aggressive style of the time. Olin's character is very much the writer's own view of himself—disenchanted, the inevitable cigarette hanging from his lips, a streak of viciousness flickering over his features in moments of stress.

"I remember the spring of 1947," wrote the producer Lorens Marmstedt a few years later.

> We had to discuss and polish a script, and nothing in the world could make me leave the salty waves of the Mediterranean. So it was agreed that Ingmar should fly to Nice. However, at the last moment he changed his mind and only a really hefty steward prevented him from getting off just as the plane was starting. That meeting on the Côte d'Azur was delightful.

The subject of the screenplay was a play by Martin Söderhjelm entitled *A Ship Bound for India* (*Skepp till Indialand,* also known on its release outside Sweden as *Land of Desire and Frustration*), and in the intervals between Marmstedt's excursions to lavish Riviera parties and the neighboring casino, a script was hammered out.

At about this time, *Filmnyheter* printed an article by Bergman in which he referred to the motivation behind his screenwriting: "I want to describe the universal activity of evil, made up of the tiniest and most secret methods of propagating itself, like something independently alive, like a germ or whatever, in a vast chain of cause and effect."[6] In *A Ship Bound for India*, this "evil" is apparent in the character of Captain Blom (Holger Löwenadler), even if he is ultimately a victim of the malevolence that has possessed him. Blom is the most hateful father-figure in Bergman's early period. Blindness encroaches on him like the blackness that threatens the dreams of many Bergman personalities. The film is told, in a single flashback, as Johannes (Birger Malmsten), searching for his beloved Sally (Gertrud Fridh) in the dismal streets of a harbor town, remembers how their affair began. While he has coffee with two women he has not seen for some years, he says that his back is better. "It wasn't your back that was deformed," remarks one of his companions, "but your soul." And in Bergman's films an outward, visible ailment is always the clue to an inner, psychological defect.

Blom has treated his son Johannes with brutality and contempt. Brawling and drinking fiercely, Blom's very behavior constitutes an act of revenge on life. At a fairground in the town he has an argument with a Russian sailor, and later, in a smoky music hall scene that might have been staged by Sternberg or Mamoulian, he enters a blundering, painful fight with the foreigner. Blom is a man whose authority has never been challenged, and when the struggle starts to go against him he slips like a coward under the stage curtain and takes refuge in a dressing room.

But Blom is not altogether unsympathetic. His discovery of his failing eyesight and his cherished room in the town, where he keeps souvenirs from lands he has always longed to visit but has never reached, lend him a human dimension. Blom is a vehicle for Evil rather than its embodiment; his malevolence functions like a magnetic field, affecting everyone with whom he comes in contact. Sally, a chorus girl, is innocence defiled at the hands of this social leper, who takes her back to his salvage vessel like a prize and calmly flaunts her presence before his wife (Anna Lindahl) and son. Sally grasps at any illusion that will grant her liberation from the shabby life of dancing and vaudeville. She is deluded by Blom's extravagant tales and dislikes the cynicism of Johannes when she meets him on the boat.

Bergman sketches in the conflict between father and son swiftly and sharply. The captain is overbearing and mocking; Johannes tortured, rebellious. "You ruin everything for me!" cries Johannes in fury. Blom

Gertrud Fridh (Sally) *and Birger Malmsten* (Johannes) *in* A Ship Bound for India. *Photo courtesy Swedish Film Institute.*

Gertrud Fridh (Sally) *and Birger Malmsten* (Johannes) *in the windmill scene* in A Ship Bound for India. *Photo courtesy Swedish Film Institute.*

taunts him, slaps him derisively. Johannes reaches for his knife but lets it fall listlessly to the ground. Later, in his frustration, he tries to rape Sally. The narrow confines of the vessel, with its slender gangways and tiny cabins, add to the feeling of frustration and captivity. The crew eat together, gathered around a table so small they can barely move.

In their cabin, Blom and his wife reflect on their twenty-five years of marriage. She tells him, in a tone of resignation rather than anger, how her life with him has gradually lost its value. Blom in his turn admits that he is going blind and tells her that he is taking Sally away in a quest for all the things he has ever desired. The moonlight plays on the cabin roof as they share their regrets. A *Ship Bound for India* sets failure against yearning. Blom has aspirations as strong as those that animate his son, but he recognizes that he can no longer achieve them. Like Lear, he is reminded of his failure by physical decay.

Sally becomes aware of Johannes's sympathy with her in the face of the captain's unpredictable moods and the opposition of his wife to her presence on board. One day the pair start a conversation on deck. Johannes catches sight of a ship on the horizon. "Africa, America, India," he muses, and he speaks of his excitement at the prospect of exotic destinations. They sneak ashore and hide in a deserted windmill. Sally tells Johannes that he is the first person to have treated her kindly without demanding something in return. One must have someone to love, or else one might as well be dead, she says. This scene is the emotional peak of the film, and similar moments of unalloyed pleasure may be found in all Bergman's subsequent work. Johannes is a symbol of the fight in Bergman to destroy the worthless illusions on which most human beings build their life. When he returns to the boat, Johannes confronts his father and returns his slap. Sally goes below deck and joins Blom's wife, who confides in her and recalls the dread in which Johannes had grown up under his father's intimidation.

Blom arrives, step by step, at self-awareness. He feels trapped and resorts to desperate remedies. "I've been chained to this boat, to my wife, to Johannes," he tells Sally with bitterness in his voice. When Johannes is underwater, inspecting a sunken ship ready for salvage, Blom cuts the supply of air to his diving suit and heaves his lifeline overboard. Bergman is already adept at seizing the furtive moment: His actors evade one another's gaze; they address a void beyond the camera, as though ruminating in a mirror.

In panic, Blom flees. He hides in his den in the town, unaware that Johannes has been rescued and surrounded by the memorabilia of the voyages he will never make, the illusions that have helped to keep his frustration at bay over the years. Blom vents his fury on these artifacts, wrecking the room and tearing down the fetishes of his obsession in a scene reminiscent of Charles Foster Kane's display of fury after Susan has left him to die at Xanadu in *Citizen Kane*.

Blom sits, half-blind, a pathetic figure awaiting his pursuers, an electric sign outside the window flashing a bar of shadow across his throat. Johannes enters the room and extends his hand in a gesture of reconciliation. "We understand you, you're sick," he tells his father. Blom lurches away between two sailors, but suddenly he breaks free of his escort and flings himself through a high window. Like many an attempt at suicide in Bergman's world, it is a fiasco. Blom is fated to live on, dying at last at some point in the seven years between the end of Johannes's flashback and the opening of the film.

Sally returns to the music hall. Johannes makes love to her for one final time. They lie in each other's arms, lit by a warm, voluptuous light. For Sally, the future is to be feared, for nothing endures. At dawn, Johannes caresses her hair as she lies asleep and steals back to his ship.

Back in the present, Johannes is reunited with Sally, but only after a heated argument. She screams at him that she is worthless and cannot come away with him. "You want to, but you're afraid," replies Johannes. She barricades herself in the bathroom, but there is no window through which she, like Blom, can seek release, and Johannes breaks down the door. Together they go aboard a gleaming new boat, with Johannes in the uniform of mate. Virtually all Bergman's films conclude on this rising note; he is too aware of the dramatic unities to dispense with catharsis.

For all its bizarre decor and glimpses of seafaring life, *A Ship Bound for India* is a chamber work, a string quartet with Blom, his wife, Johannes, and Sally as players. The crudeness of the backdrops and model ships in the very first shots of the film almost help to concentrate one's focus on the human conflicts. The characters prevail over their environment to a remarkable degree. Marmstedt's budget was, as usual, minuscule, and Bergman had to shoot the picture at a dilapidated studio in Djurgården, a park in southern Stockholm.

> The high tension cable taking current up to Skansen [an open-air amusement park and zoo] ran underneath, and if someone carried a mike across it, it said *brrr*; which meant that all the sets had to be built in such a way that the mike-lead didn't have to cross the main Skansen cable.[7]

The film opened in September to good reviews. André Bazin, in *L'Ecran français*, congratulated the young Bergman on "creating a world of blinding cinematic purity." It was one of the first significant notices Bergman received outside Scandinavia.

The autumn months of 1947 were divided between Bergman's production of his new play, *To My Terror*, and the shooting of *Music in Darkness* (*Musik i mörker*, also known as *Night Is My Future*). *To My Terror* was autobiographical in sentiment, with Paul, the budding writer, bringing home a fiancée to his grandmother in Uppsala and announcing that he has recognized God's existence, even though he would never accept it just because people told him so.[8] (That imposing apartment in Uppsala is recreated often in Bergman's plays and films, as though it were a laboratory in which the director might begin his psychological experiments.)

Less than a month later, on November 23, Bergman directed a radio version of Strindberg's *Playing with Fire*; earlier in the year he had broadcast a production of the same author's *Dutchman*. There was already an innate rhythm in Bergman's annual program. Calling on the self-discipline that his parents had drummed into him as a boy, he divided his time methodically between writing, the stage, radio, and the cinema.

There was an intriguing symbiosis between Bergman and his producer of the hour, Lorens Marmstedt. There was no doubt that Marmstedt could take risks when he believed in a talent; in 1941, for instance, he had entrusted *First Division* to an untried director, Hasse Ekman, and the film was a success. With Bergman he had already taken a loss on *It Rains on Our Love* and *A Ship Bound for India*. Now he came to him and, in the director's words, presented him with a friendly ultimatum: "Ingmar, you are a flop. Here's a very sentimental story [*Music in Darkness*] that will appeal to the public. You need a box-office success now." Bergman replied "I'll lick your ass if you like; only let me make a picture."[9]

The screenplay of *Music in Darkness* was written by Dagmar Edqvist, from her novel about a young man whose blindness is exploited by society. The opening sequence shows Bengt (played by the familiar Birger Malmsten) losing his sight in an accident at a rifle range during military service. But although it is vivid and frightening, there is no mistaking the slight confusion in editing that comes from "front office" interference. Bergman claims that Marmstedt "cut that whole sequence to pieces"[10] and that every day he would come to the studio and demand that scenes be reshot. "This is too difficult, incomprehensible. You are crazy! She must be beautiful! You must have more light on her hair! You must have some cats in the film! Perhaps you can find a little dog." But Bergman is too balanced a man to resent Marmstedt's attitude. "He taught me—in a very tough way—much that saved me. I will be grateful to him to my dying day." Nor was there pique on Marmstedt's side. "When we had very bad disagreements," he wrote in 1955, "Ingmar was capable of writing really hateful letters. Often he'd come up himself with the letter, stick it in my hand, and disappear down the stairs. Without a word. But he never harbored a grudge. After a little while, a day at most, all was forgotten."[11]

There are powerful links between *Music in Darkness* and Bergman's preceding film. Both Bengt and Captain Blom are weighed down by physical adversity, the one made blind, the other inexorably losing his sight. This disability stimulates an inferiority complex and a latent masochism. But while Blom is doomed, because he is a member of an older generation despised by Bergman, Bengt has youth on his side. His sole regular companion, a destitute girl named Ingrid (Mai Zetterling), eventually marries him. The film's concern is with the blind man's desire to be treated as an equal, not a pariah. Thus Bengt's greatest humiliation becomes his greatest pleasure, when he is struck a sound blow by Ingrid's jealous and insecure boyfriend (Bengt Eklund). Yet Bergman does not identify altogether with Bengt. There is a flash of his own fractious temperament in the part of the violinist (Gunnar Björnstrand), who vents his loathing of "the boss" at the restaurant where the two young men play for mere peanuts.

Music in Darkness attracted large audiences in Sweden by virtue of its sentimental story (Marmstedt's instinct was right), but by comparison with A *Ship Bound for India* it remains ingenuous in execution and naive in its symbolism. Close-ups are used in an old-fashioned, nudging way to illustrate stress and pain. Only the anguished desperation of its hero, Bengt, marks it out from other commercial films made in Sweden that year. It helps to explain Bergman's remark: "Filmmaking makes me bleed too much. It is always exciting and difficult and fascinating, but it makes one feel hurt, humiliated."[12] But the film also enabled Bergman to express his dread of loneliness. The most touching

Mai Zetterling (Ingrid Olofsdotter) *and Birger Malmsten* (Bengt Vyldeke) *in* Music in Darkness. *Photo courtesy Swedish Film Institute.*

moment in the film occurs at a railroad station, where Bengt waits for a blind colleague's wife to arrive. The couple are so absorbed in their private happiness, though, that they ignore Bengt. He stumbles away in despair, crossing the tracks and only barely escaping serious injury.

However commissioned his films may have been at this point in his career, Bergman was able to put himself and little facets of his character into each new venture. Like Hitchcock, he began appearing for a second or two in his productions (in *A Ship Bound for India* he may be glimpsed in the amusement park near the beginning), and details of his life are evident. In *Music in Darkness* he is a passenger aboard the train when Bengt and Ingrid leave on their honeymoon.

Meanwhile, in London, Peter Ustinov directed a theater version of *Torment*, and Per Gjoersøe produced the same story on the Oslo stage. Bergman put aside film plans in order to concentrate on *Macbeth*, which he was about to present at the Civic Theater in Gothenburg. He had produced the play earlier, but with the meager resources of the Helsingborg theater, and now he was able to give full rein to his fantasy with the help of his designer, Carl Johan Ström, whose magnificent sets enhanced so many Bergman productions in Gothenburg.

During the summer, while Bergman was shooting *Port of Call*, his original screenplay *Eva*, sold to Svensk Filmindustri in February, was being made into a film by Gustaf Molander. It was hoped that the popularity of *Woman Without a Face* might be repeated if Molander and Bergman collaborated again. Built up of flashbacks, *Eva* harks back to Bergman's childhood and his summer holidays in Dalarna when he was so fascinated by his grandfather's trains pulling up the gradient at Gagnef. In his preface to the script, dated January 8, 1948, Bergman says: "I have written this as a protest against myself and the new influences I feel within me." Bo (Birger Malmsten), the leading male character in the film, recounts a tragic event when as a young boy he had driven an engine in secret with a blind girl, Marthe (Anne Karlsson); the locomotive gathered speed, and Bo lost control. In the accident that followed, Marthe died, and Bo was beaten black and blue by his father. The Bergman hero often has to relive such shocking circumstances; the process of unburdening oneself of such a memory becomes an act of atonement.

Bo falls in love with another companion from childhood days, Eva (Eva Stiberg). As they lie together on the beach, the body of a German soldier drifts ashore, reminding them of the war that has so far left Sweden unscathed. Eva's response is to condemn herself for being pregnant, for wanting to bring children into a world so full of anguish and hatred.

Whatever their dramatic failings, these early Bergman scripts and films have a consistency of outlook: Man is governed by the trauma of his birth and the terror attached to his dying; he bears a yoke of guilt that may be discarded only by the most painful confrontation with the past and by an abandonment of his soul to love. In an interlude of pure romance there is redemption, in the psychological rather than the religious sense.

Music in Darkness opened on January 17, 1948, and as soon as the popularity of *Music in Darkness* was assured, Svensk Filmindustri approached Bergman in the hope that he would again join the company. Olle Länsberg had submitted "a manuscript an inch thick, called *The Gold and the Walls*, and [Svensk Filmindustri] asked me if I'd make a film of it."[13] Bergman and Länsberg developed this property into *Port of Call*.

Port of Call was shot on location in Gothenburg, with interiors at the SF studios in Stockholm. The dockland atmosphere is established authoritatively from the outset as Berit (Nine-Christine Jönsson) is seen trying to drown herself in the harbor. Gösta (Bengt Eklund), the seaman who befriends her, is mostly a catalyst for Berit's unhappiness. But he is interesting because he seems solid, pleasant, and relaxed to a degree rare in Bergman's protagonists. Accordingly, when one sees matters through Gösta's eyes they acquire a surprising emotional strength. At such moments Bergman uses his camera incisively, to register the joy and anguish, an intimate technique all the more impressive for being juxtaposed with the naturalistic shots of the dockland.

There are precise reminders in *Port of Call* of Carné's *Quai des brumes* (not least in the brooding chords of Erland von Koch's music, which like his work for *A Ship Bound for India* seems modeled on some of Jaubert's prewar scores); the camera observes the vistas of harbor traffic and wharves in a style that defines "poetic realism." The seamen with whom Gösta lodges in the dingy rooming house are more convincing than the characters in Carné's film; the influence here is Rossellini, with his harnessing of a documentary style to fictional events. "At that time I felt it was tremendously relevant," says Bergman. "Rossellini's films were a revelation—all that extreme simplicity and poverty, that grayness."[14]

The sailors' leader, the "Scanian," sees Gösta reading Martinson's *Journeys Without Aim* (a key text of the forties in Sweden) and comments: "I started drinking: Books only make matters worse." At a later stage he reproaches Gösta for his idealism. "Faith, justice, what do they mean?" he demands. "No, there's only 'self.'" Here is a guide to Bergman's fundamental thought. His characters *know* that such advice is wise, but they cannot tear themselves free of reason.

Berit is linked to Bergman's mature heroines in that she suffers from a profound inferiority complex. She believes, or is led to believe, that she must face a future of torment and misery. The fate of her friend Gertrud (Mimi Nelson), who died after a clumsy abortion, remains a constant reminder of what might happen ·to her; Gertrud was "born to misfortune," as her father says at the inquest. And yet Gertrud has had her joys. At the remand home she was the idol of the other girls because she slept with the gardener's assistant and was thereby able to bring them such luxuries as cigarettes and cosmetics.

The dialog in *Port of Call* already holds some slight promise of the rich commentaries on life that flow from Bergman's more articulate personalities. "What's the use of tormenting each other?" asks Berit during a quarrel. "Loneliness is awful," is another axiomatic remark. "I wish I were dead and you with me!" she shouts at her mother. The tiny apartment, like the cabins in *A Ship Bound for India*, assumes the dimensions of a prison from which only death can bring release.

As happens so frequently in Bergman's films, even the most repellent

Nine-Christine Jönsson (Berit Holm) and Berta Hall (Berit's mother) in Port of Call. *The word* ensam *scrawled on the mirror means "alone." Photo courtesy Svensk Filmindustri.*

characters attract pity. Berit's mother has more illusions than her daughter, for she believes she can live in harmony with her husband, whereas the memories of Berit's youth show a household fraught with altercations and hostility. Life itself is, by definition, to blame for such situations in the majority of Bergman's films. But here, for the first and probably the last time, the director is asking, Is this not the fault of society? Are not these living conditions intolerable? Is Berit not treated as an outcast by her parents and as no more than a chattel in the factory where she works? At the inquiry into Gertrud's death, Berit bursts out with a bitter condemnation of the social system, saying that the poor must survive as best they can, while the well-to-do have access to good doctors.

The determinism in the final words of *Port of Call*—presaging the mood of *To Joy, Summer Interlude,* and *Summer with Monika*—is an implicit answer to such questions.

"We won't give up," says Gösta.

"And soon it will be summer," replies Berit, smiling.

CHAPTER FIVE

Couples

Port of Call WAS EDITED WITHOUT UNDUE PROBLEMS AND OPENED ON October 18. Around the same time, Hollywood producer David O. Selznick approached Lorens Marmstedt with a view to setting up a screen version of Ibsen's *A Doll's House*. Selznick wanted the film to be scripted by Bergman and directed by Sjöberg, but the project was doomed from the start. "Sjöberg had too many ideas, and I had too few," said Bergman, who was nonetheless pleased with the thirty thousand-crown fee that came from Hollywood. Marmstedt enjoyed the sardonic last word: "Ibsen is Ibsen, and West is West." With the Selznick money, Bergman bought himself his first decent 9.5 mm. projector and prints of classics such as *The Cabinet of Dr. Caligari*, *Variety*, *The Niebelungen Saga*, and several Chaplin movies.

Rune Waldekranz, the young and enterprising production manager at Sandrew Film, also sought Bergman's services, suggesting to Marmstedt that Bergman might have a contract with both Terrafilm and Sandrews, with a remake of *Gunnar Hede's Saga* (one of Mauritz Stiller's triumphs in the silent period) in prospect. But nothing transpired.

Everyone acquainted with Bergman in the late forties agrees that he relished controversy and delighted in outraging the audience with his inchoate vision. As he himself told an interviewer, "I don't want to produce a work of art that the public can sit and suck aesthetically. . . . I want to give them a blow in the small of the back, to scorch their indifference, to startle them out of their complacency."[1]

By the middle of 1948, that desire was given full rein.

Prior to the shooting of *Port of Call*, Carl Anders Dymling of Svensk Filmindustri had turned down Bergman's outline for *The Devil's Wanton* (the Swedish title is *Fängelse, Prison*), and it fell to Lorens Marmstedt, ever the gambler, to set up the production. Bergman went up to Dalarna in the autumn and completed the screenplay; within a few weeks he was back in the studios and required a mere eighteen days to shoot the picture. The budget was frugal—150,000 crowns (approximately $25,000). Bergman was allocated just twenty-six thousand feet of negative, composed of short lengths from Agfa, Kodak, Ferrania, and anything else that lay to hand. Only the final rehearsal for each scene could be done with full lighting. "Each time Göran Strindberg [the cinematographer] switched on a photo-flood, an old fellow specially employed for the purpose came up behind him and switched it off again."[2] The actors worked for half their normal fees. Kenne Fant, who played the part of a young actor, remembers how Marmstedt declared that he *knew* the film would be a flop. But everyone was proud to collaborate with Bergman. "I was in the studio only one or two days,"

Bergman at work during the late forties. Photo courtesy Svensk Filmindustri.

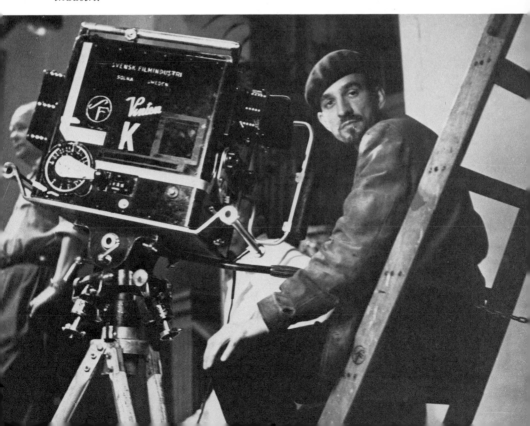

says Fant, "and yet I felt immediately the wonderful atmosphere that he created."

Prison had its origin in a short piece of fiction entitled "True Story," which Bergman had written some time earlier but had never intended for publication. His previous films had each contained lines and sequences that illuminated, for only the tantalizing moment, that dark landscape of his art and mind; but *Prison* is Bergman's first articulate statement about the difficulty of reconciling death and belief in God.

In the program note distributed at the opening of *Prison* in March 1949, Bergman expressed the main proposition of the film:

> Why must a person sooner or later arrive at a point where he for a moment awakes to a painful and unendurable knowledge of himself and his situation, and why is there, in that moment, no help to summon? Is earth Hell, and is there in that case also a God, and where is He, and where are the dead?[3]

The film abounds with symbols and metaphors. It has the texture of a dream, with unrelated incidents and characters impinging on one another in defiance of traditional narrative. Bergman has spoken of the genesis of such films:

> They linger in the twilight, and if I want to get at them, I have to go into this twilight land and seek out the connections, the persons, and the situations. The turned-away faces speak, strange streets, wonderful views become distinguishable through the window pane, an eye gleams in the dusk and is transformed into a glittering gem which breaks with a glassy tinkling. The open square in the autumn twilight is a sea, the old women become dark, twisted trees, and the apples become children playing at building sand castles on the seashore beaten by breakers.[4]

Like many Bergman films of the early period, *Prison* begins with a tribute to the German expressionist cinema. Expressionism is a matter of opposites, the world viewed in solid blacks and whites: love versus hatred; dogma versus anarchy; emotions in conflict with reason; assertion set against hesitancy. The characters in *Prison* wear their emotions like beads around their neck. A beard, a hairstyle, a pair of spectacles, such are the symbols to which the expressionist turns with glee.

An aged figure in a black coat hastens over a stretch of desolate land, heading toward some dark buildings. The shot might come from *Caligari* or *Warning Shadows*, two famous expressionist films. But Bergman delights in unsettling his audience; the old man's destination is in fact a film studio, and viewers are swept at a stroke from the promise of some Teutonic fantasy to the ironical reality of a movie stage. The macabre intruder is a retired math teacher (Anders Henrikson) who tries to persuade one of his former pupils—now a film director—to make a screen version of a curious and beguiling idea that has recently struck him. He suggests a film about Hell—Hell on earth.

"I'd open with the Devil's making a proclamation," he says. (Bergman will in fact start a film—*The Devil's Eye*, twelve years later—with just such a proclamation.) In this opening speech, Bergman's writing is in tune with the preoccupations of the *40-talisterna*, the writers of his own generation—dread of nuclear holocaust, art for art's sake, suicide as an act of logic rather than cowardice. The professor even mentions the bombing of Hiroshima.

Martin (Hasse Ekman), the debonair young director, who is himself shooting a film of unconscionable pretensions, ridicules the professor's proposal. But he mentions it to a friend, Thomas (Birger Malmsten), a journalist who can turn his hand to film scripts. Thomas believes the film could be a success, for he has met the ideal heroine, a prostitute named Birgitta Carolina (Doris Svedlund). He is obviously already involved with her, and his wife Sofi (Eva Henning) is quite predictably irritated by the state of affairs. Birger Malmsten as Thomas and Eva Henning as Sofi (who will play similar roles in *Thirst*, Bergman's next film) epitomize Bergman's view of marriage as nasty, brutish, and long.

After this prologue, a narrator announces that six months have elapsed. Birgitta Carolina is pregnant; she staggers up the stairs to the apartment where she lives with her pimp, Peter (Stig Olin), and her sister. She goes into a labor so intense that she appears to be dying, and though she survives her parturition, Peter and her sister persuade her to relinquish the baby. They drown it in a cellar. Peter is ruthless and utterly cold; the sister, blonde hair cut short, strides about in butch attendance.

When Thomas, having quarreled violently with his wife, meets Birgitta Carolina in the streets one evening, there is a sense of lives crossing in space, of a relationship more abstract and subtle than the pair of them can find words to describe. Thomas and Birgitta Carolina may be seen as direct descendants of Jan-Erik and Berta in *Torment*. By now, however, Bergman's alter ego has grown a beard and lives in the Old Town.

Thomas and Birgitta Carolina induce a landlady to let them sleep in her attic. Here, in a clutter of bric a brac and with the wind sighing through the eaves, the core of the film is concentrated. Thomas speaks of the tenderness he feels toward the girl. One night they run an old movie projector. Thomas cranks it, and for over a minute the couple watch enthralled as a slapstick farce is played out. A man in a nightshirt, who looks like Groucho Marx, is the victim of all kinds of unfortunate misadventures, including the appearance of a skeleton and a hideous executioner. (Fragments of the same film are used in *Persona*.) Because these images are so fleeting and intangible, they become illusion. As the film ends, Thomas comments wistfully, "Things suddenly appearing and vanishing, just like our own lives." Soon afterward, Birgitta Carolina finds a Chinese figure in the form of a music box. It circulates with dainty but mesmeric charm, and she looks at it with longing, as if the simple, mechanistic illusion were an ideal beyond her reach.

This interlude, during which Thomas and Birgitta Carolina make love, is part of Bergman's *schema* in his early period. There is always a point during the film at which the young lovers flee from the perils and claustrophobia of the world oppressing them (Johannes and Sally in the windmill, for instance, in *A Ship Bound for India*). To be aware of the preciousness of the passing moment is a special faculty given to only a very few in Bergman's world; behind and before stands only death and a Stygian night. The couple returns to the squalor of daily reality with a new resolve, a fresh optimism.

But if Birgitta Carolina experiences release and fulfillment in her hiding place with Thomas, she also endures there a nightmare of the kind that Bergman would perfect in the years to come. She wanders through a vast cellar. People stand around her like trees, wisps of mist drift among the shadows, the wind laments. She is offered a sparkling jewel by a statuesque girl clothed in black—an envoy of Death who in reality is the landlady's daughter—and this is later explained as symbolizing her baby. She meets her mother, who tells her to go over to Thomas, seated against an upturned car. But after addressing him for a few seconds she glances up and suddenly realizes that she is talking to a stranger, a man who stares at her with the same minatory, mocking expression as Death's in *The Seventh Seal*.

Unnerved, Birgitta Carolina sees Peter lift a plastic doll from a bath of water. In his hands it changes to a fish, which he twists and rends sadistically before laying it back in the water. This is clearly a metaphor for the murder of Birgitta Carolina's child; the crying of a baby on the soundtrack joins with the sound of the wind (a device that Bergman resorts to once more in *Wild Strawberries*). The end of the nightmare is forceful, as Birgitta Carolina beats at the low ceiling and the camera moves up, like her subconscious, through turbulent waters.

Birgitta Carolina and Thomas are forced apart because the body of the dead infant has been found and Peter wants to confine Birgitta Carolina to his apartment. There a vicious client drives her hysterical; dashing to the cellar, she stabs herself with a knife shown her earlier by a small boy. Bergman's verdict is unequivocal: suicide is the only means of refuge

Doris Svedlund (Birgitta Carolina Söderberg) *before her suicide in* Prison. *Photo courtesy Swedish Film Institute.*

from an intolerable existence. Jack puts a bullet through his head in *Crisis*; Captain Blom hurls himself from a window in A *Ship Bound for India*. Many of his characters harbor a desire for that dreamless sleep they equate with nothingness, a yearning to hide from the world, but in most instances they are, like Hamlet, afraid of the fancies that may lurk beyond the boundaries of existence. The boy who introduces the "bare bodkin" to Birgitta Carolina is also an emblem that will become quite familiar in Bergman films of the future. He is the token of innocence, the talisman of hope—the son who watches his father playing in the orchestra at the close of *To Joy*, the calm, observant Johan of *The Silence*, the angelic girl who sits entranced among the audience in *The Magic Flute*.

In her death throes, Birgitta Carolina imagines Thomas saying, "I feel a great tenderness for you," as he stands separated from her by thick upright bars. She sees the jewel being offered to her once more. And she hears the persistent wailing of the baby. Her last image is of Peter's frantic face as he tries to revive her while she bleeds to death. The fate of Birgitta Carolina has had a profound impact on those around her. Thomas, chastened, returns to his marriage with Sofi. His wild notion of creating the heroine of a film from Birgitta Carolina has misfired. Back in the studio, Martin tells the professor that his film cannot be made because it would end with a question to which there is no response. "There is one if one believes in God. As one no longer believes, there is no point to it at all."

The structure of *Prison* creaks and groans from time to time under the pressures that Bergman's symbolism exerts upon it. There are scenes of pure Grand Guignol that belong more to the stage than the screen, and there are gimmicks and situations that seem inspired by the many German films Bergman was collecting about this time. The film often betrays Bergman's elation at being able to experiment with the medium and escape the confines of the theater: The credits, for example, are spoken offscreen (by a voice sounding suspiciously like the director's).

Nevertheless, *Prison* marks an exciting leap forward in Bergman's career. He uses simple black and white tones to achieve effects that would be impossible in color. When Thomas walks among some barges in the deserted harbor area, his figure hunched up in a somber overcoat, his feet squelching over the duckboards, touching a dead bird with his toecap and tipping it into the oleaginous waters, he looks like Death in *The Seventh Seal*—totally alone, totally cold, totally ignorant. The final shot of *Prison* looks down on the deserted film studio, a piano marooned in a pool of light and shadow, at the mercy of the encroaching darkness.

Bergman to no extent identifies with the film director in *Prison*; Hasse Ekman is allowed to play Grandé in a suave, relaxed, vapid manner. At the time, Ekman and Bergman were uneasy companions in the Marmstedt stable, and Bergman was probably quite content to let his rival perpetuate his fastidious image.[5] Birger Malmsten as Thomas in fact embodies Bergman—he will play Bergman's alter ego in all the films up to *Summer Interlude*, just as Jean-Pierre Léaud is a proxy for Truffaut— but this does not prevent Bergman from viewing him in a cynical light or from dismissing his pretensions as a writer. It is as though for the first time Bergman were able to gaze back coolly and sardonically at the pose he had struck as an angry young man.

When he had completed the film, Bergman wrote a letter to Lorens Marmstedt:

> Thank you, kind Lorens. For letting me do *Prison*. . . . I'm both moved and happy when I look back and think how much you supported me and cheered me the whole time. You ought to know how much you . . . really helped me. Thanks, kind Big Brother, and forgive the sentimental expression of these feelings.

Marmstedt, quoting this letter, said how it revealed the side of Bergman that "some of us have learned to respect: tact, finesse, real feelings."

As soon as *Prison* was in the can, Bergman resumed his shuttling to and fro between Stockholm and Gothenburg, where he was preparing Anouilh's *A Wild Bird* and Tennessee Williams's *A Streetcar Named Desire.* On November 4, 1948, Swedish Radio broadcast his production of Strindberg's *Mother Love,* and the following month his own play, *Draw Blank,* opened in Helsingborg, although Bergman had nothing to do with the production.

His main preoccupation at the turn of the year was *Thirst* (*Törst,* known in the United States as *Three Strange Loves*), a film inspired by a book of short stories by Birgit Tengroth. The screenplay was written by Herbert Grevenius, who used the final story in the collection as the basic plot and turned to one or two others for embellishment. Grevenius is a significant figure in Bergman's early period. He had been the first theater critic to acknowledge the promise of the younger man's productions at Helsingborg. The James Agate or George Jean Nathan of Sweden, he was also a conspicuous dramatist, with what Alrik Gustafsson has termed "a flair for lively, telling dialog and genuine local color together with a born journalist's interest in subjects of current importance." In spite of the success of *Torment,* Bergman still felt hesitant about directing his own screenplays, and he turned to Grevenius for guidance. They worked together on *It Rains on Our Love, Thirst, High Tension, Summer Interlude,* and *Divorced* (directed by Gustaf Molander). One suspects that Grevenius's contribution lies in the professional format of these films, which, however, did not impede Bergman's vision. There was also a practical consideration: Bergman had time to write and prepare only one film per season, yet financial pressures compelled him to take on two, and Grevenius was enlisted to help him with the screenplay of this second film. Grevenius would write during the mornings, and then the two men would meet in a café at the end of the day when Bergman, his rehearsals behind him, could pursue the collaboration. The two men enjoyed talking for hours on end, but after Grevenius became a Catholic convert the relationship dwindled away.

Thirst is filled with bitterness in the face of marriage. Some lines from *The City,* a play Bergman wrote for radio about this time, capture his mood: "We were intoxicated with each other's flesh and so deluded our hearts that this was the great truth. But when our bodies grew tired and sated we could not deceive ourselves, and we accused each

Birger Malmsten (Bertil) *and Eva Henning* (Rut) *in* Thirst. *Photo courtesy Svensk Filmindustri.*

other for a love that was insufficient."[6] Bergman's second marriage had disintegrated, and his stage productions in Gothenburg suffered accordingly.

The feelings, if not the details, of *Thirst* have an autobiographical ring. The obsession with sterility stems from Birgit Tengroth's stories, even if it is the bane of countless couples in Bergman's own cinema. Children, as one sees in somber films like *The Silence* or in brighter excursions such as *The Magic Flute,* stand for hope and fresh life. Without childbirth, the Bergman woman has fulfilled but half her promise. Equally, the destruction of a baby, as in *Prison,* implies the end of life itself. When the married couple in *Scenes from a Marriage* decides simply for expediency's sake to have an abortion, this is the starting point of their breakup.

Part of the friction that exacerbates the male–female relationship in these films derives from the differences in outlook between the sexes: The man suffers from an all-pervasive fear of death, while the woman is concerned with more practical issues. In the early phase of his career, Bergman was blind to the fact that women also demand the meaning

Eva Henning (Rut) *and Mimi Nelson* (Valborg) *in* Thirst. *Bergman's compressed style of composition is already evident. Photo courtesy Swedish Film Institute.*

of life, also endure the emotional and intellectual torment of their male counterparts.

A whirlpool rages in close-up behind the credits of *Thirst*. In the drab neutrality of a hotel room in Basel, Rut (Eva Henning) awakes and glances at a Swiss-German newspaper. Confounded by the unfamiliar language, she tosses it aside and lights a cigarette. The sight of her husband (Birger Malmsten) sunk in sleep exasperates her; one imagines that this is only the latest of countless stale mornings.

Rut paces the room like a caged animal. She cleans her teeth and stares dejectedly at her bleary features in the mirror. A train rumbles past offscreen. Rut starts to fling some clothes into a battered suitcase. It falls off the couch and Bertil, the husband, wakes with a start. The heat in the small room is stifling. Rut draws on her cigarette and, seeking some release, lets her mind stray back to happier days, to an affair with an army officer named Raoul (Bengt Eklund). But like most memories in Bergman's films, the mood assumes a harsher texture. Rut's frustration in the present is given visible and tangible form in the past by one alarming image reminiscent of Buñuel's *Un Chien andalou:*

Raoul drops a snake on top of an anthill, and the creature is instantly covered by thousands of remorseless insects. There follows a confrontation between Rut and the officer's wife; Raoul appears and claims with bravado that he has a right to care for two women if he wishes.

Bertil and Rut are past thirty, at an age when their recollections of youth are at once depressing and poignant. He is interested in archaeology and carries two gold coins depicting Arethusa—tokens not merely of the bright summer days of their holiday in Sicily but also of the inescapable rift between the sexes. "A sea of tears and misunderstandings keep them apart," says Bertil.

Ensconced at last in a compartment on the train from Basel to Scandinavia, Rut nags her partner unmercifully, yet her nagging springs from a recognition of her own shortcomings. The confined space infuriates her. While Bertil is docile, she is forever flitting about, unable to settle down. She tries to solve her problems by drinking. "I hate you so much I want to live just to make hell for you," she says, tipsy. Existentialism attains here its most perverse degree. Rut is possibly the closest to a Strindberg heroine that Bergman has reached. She is jealous even when Bertil manages to fall asleep, and she attempts to arouse him. He for his part dreams that he has struck her with a bottle and is relieved on waking to discover that she is still alive. Thus are juxtaposed his true, subconscious desire and his conscious, practical realization that it is better to have his wife than to be left alone in "hell."

The writing of these scenes between Bertil and Rut is at a much higher level than the rest of the film. Their conversation oscillates sharply between affection and bitter recrimination. All Bergman's vituperation and disillusionment with his private life seem lodged in the dialog. "I said to myself," he recalls, "as a human being I have made an enormous fiasco, therefore I must try to be a very good director."

Thirst is sustained not just by acrimonious repartee. The wretchedness of the couple's lives is counterpointed by shots of the ruined cities of Germany traversed during the train journey. At one station, hungry Germans swarm alongside the train and beg for food. The effect looks clumsy and theatrical, but the meaning is unmistakable. Devastated buildings are glimpsed against the night sky, and some roisterers in the compartment next to Bertil and Rut pull down the blind to shut out the depressing image. Bergman had been in Germany just after the war and was shocked by the desolation.

One wordless encounter is more eloquent than many a verbal argument. Waiting for his wife in the train corridor, Bertil catches sight of his reflection in one of the windows; his features shake, as though he were being jolted in Hell. Rut emerges from the toilet and stares through the window at the alluring night beyond, contemplating suicide. As she does so, Bertil steals up behind her. He stretches out his hand and grasps her shoulder. Rut whirls round and falls into his embrace with a desperation perfectly echoed in the headlong gallop of the train and its long, drawn-out whistle.

The study of Bertil's and Rut's relationship would perhaps be intolerable for a complete film. The screenplay by Grevenius incorporates another major character, Viola (played by none other than Birgit Tengroth, the writer), who as Bertil's former mistress acquires an importance commensurate with Rut's. But the flashbacks and stretches of parallel action mitigate the impact of *Thirst*; the characters remain obstinately unrelated to one another, linked only by the viciousness of the dialog.

Viola is a bumbling personality, easily downcast. Her psychiatrist (Hasse Ekman) recalls with relish her failed marriage, her criminal upbringing, and her unstable affairs. The episode involving Viola and the psychiatrist—who is too obvious a personification of Satan—verges on the banal. She can respond to his goading only by asking what he knows of suffering. "You think you know, but you don't." As the psychiatrist prattles on magniloquently, his phrases almost a parody of consulting room jargon, Bergman examines the two faces in close-up, one seen in profile, the other in full view. The close-up was already a vital weapon in Bergman's armory. ("A close-up is created," he has commented, "by the expression around a person's mouth and by the angle of his eyes and the skin around the eyes."[7])

Viola encounters Valborg (Mimi Nelson), a former ballet school friend of Rut's, almost immediately after Rut in the train has recalled her days of practicing with Valborg, a circumstance that presses coincidence too far. In Valborg's apartment, a sorry ritual is played out. Viola opens the window and gazes forlornly at the preparations for Midsummer's Night festivities in the streets below. Valborg, a lesbian, plies her with wine and tries to dance with her. (Women turn to lesbianism in Bergman's films as a means of eluding on the one hand loneliness and on the other an infernal marriage.) Repelled by her friend's advances, Viola runs downstairs and Bergman cuts back to the train, where two pastors talk in jovial terms about marriage (in ironic contrast to Bertil and Rut, whose bickering reaches a crescendo in the neighboring compartment). Now the tributaries of *Thirst* join in a complex and disturbing montage: As a train (not in fact the one bearing Bertil and Rut) rumbles into Stockholm in the dawn after Midsummer's Night, Viola lurches in despair along a harbor jetty. The camera, aghast, fixes its gaze on a patch of smooth water, while in the distance there is a splash as Viola flings herself from the jetty. Gradually ripples invade the tranquil image and disturb the turbid surface of the harbor. In the train, Bertil and Rut are disturbed by police suddenly coming on board and announcing that a woman has been seen in the water. It is a coincidental irony, of course, for the train is still in Germany, but some qualm strikes the lovers, and they clutch each other in an uneasy truce. The head of Arethusa, the nymph who was transformed into a spring to escape the amorous advances of the river god Alpheus, is superimposed over the end titles, with their shots of shorelines and seascapes.

Thirst is the most narcissistic of Bergman's films. The characters are without exception egocentric and afflicted with self-pity. There are mirrors in all the major scenes. Bertil and Rut, Viola and Valborg, are all fascinated by their own reflections, by the confrontation with their wasting features, their ugliness, their fear, their conscience. Bergman's compositions and sense of pace seem more confident than hitherto; the scenes in the train with Bertil and Rut remain among the finest of his early achievements in the cinema.

François Truffaut has recognized that Bergman's "women are not seen through a masculine prism in his films but are observed in a spirit of total complicity. His female characters are infinitely subtle, while his male characters are conventions."[8] Already in 1949 this principle is established. In the hotel in Basel, for instance, Bertil crouches beneath his duvet while Rut paces, and the best that Raoul can do after Rut (in a flashback) announces her pregnancy is to slap her face and brand her a whore. The men in *Thirst* are sounding boards for the women. They are transparent, pathetic figures who alternately amuse and disgust their partners.

Prison was a commercial failure, but everyone had known it would be, and no one was dismayed. Bergman's energy was tireless. During the first eight months of 1949 he made *Thirst* and *To Joy*, presented two new productions at the Gothenburg Civic Theater, and revived his own play, *Draw Blank*, on Swedish Radio. His staging of *A Streetcar Named Desire* in Gothenburg prompted an enthusiastic response from Elis Andersson in *Göteborgs-Posten*:

> He has coordinated all these thousands of sounds that storm through the house: the street clatter, the shouts of salesmen, music from the local cinema, the squeals and hissing noises from the railway station, thunder, rain, and churchbells—a powerful scenery of sound which, together with neon lights and a rather tatty interior, provides a highly suggestive background to Blanche's fate. In *Desire* the passing of the days and the development of these people's destinies are suggested by means of a symbolic little apple tree, which lives out its life from blossom to harvest.[9]

Bergman wrote the script of *To Joy* during a trip with Birger Malmsten to the French Riviera. They holed up there for a couple of months, and while Malmsten had his own problems with some female companion, Bergman consoled himself by writing. The script was approved by Svensk Filmindustri, and the locations were shot during the summer of 1949 near Helsingborg, a site to which, Gunnar Fischer recalls, the Bergman unit would return for certain scenes in *The Seventh Seal*. The fine weather, and perhaps the tinge of Mediterranean sun in the scenario, rendered *To Joy* the first of those Bergman movies in which the elements play a significant role.

"For me," Bergman has commented, "a Swedish summer is full of deep undertones of sensual pleasure, particularly June, the time around midsummer—May and June. But for me July and August, July especially, when the sun shines day after day, are a dreadful torment."[10]

About this time, a journalist named Gun Grut came down to interview Bergman. There was an instant personal rapport, and the pair spent a long vacation in Paris after the shooting of *To Joy*.

In the film, which takes its name from Beethoven's *An die Freude* and the ode written by Schiller, Bergman begins to break free of the embittered nihilism of his twenties. The end of the decade was at hand, and the film concludes on a note of affirmation. Life is a terrible adversary, but man's spirit is indomitable.

Although some writers have drawn quite close parallels between *To Joy* and Bergman's second marriage—the setting in Helsingborg, the twins born to Martha (Maj-Britt Nilsson) and Stig (Stig Olin), the mentor figure of Torsten Hammarén transfigured into Sönderby (Victor Sjöström), the conductor—there is no doubt that it is an idealistic film by comparison with *Thirst*, in which the marriage to Ellen Lundström was hung, drawn, and quartered.

The opening is brusque. Called away from an orchestra rehearsal, Stig learns that his wife Martha has been burned to death in a fire at their cottage (a melodramatic touch that came about, Bergman admits, because he could not think of a suitable ending). Stig's young son survives, but his life is in ruins. He recalls the idyllic love that began seven years earlier, and the remainder of the film consists almost entirely of a single flashback.

Martha and Stig are members of an orchestra, a symbol of the unifying force of art. A mutual friend, Marcel (Birger Malmsten), is a cellist in the same ensemble. After a party to celebrate Martha's birthday, Stig collapses in a drunken stupor and wakes at dawn. They talk. He is twenty-five and as maudlin and frustrated as any teenager. "Of course one's ridiculous and one sometimes does the wrong thing, but, you

Stig Olin (Stig Eriksson) and Maj-Britt Nilsson (Marta) in the archipelago in To Joy. *Photo courtesy Svensk Filmindustri.*

must admit, the main thing is to be an artist," he claims sententiously.

Martha has been married before. "Everything I've done has been a fake," she admits. Stig moves into her rooms, agreeing to split the rent, and appears to have found the mother-figure he has been seeking (twice during the film he lays his head on her bosom). He is at first appalled by the prospect of a baby's arriving to disturb their bliss: In a crisply written scene, Stig is revealed as the weaker of the two, Martha the wearier and more resigned. They wed with haste at a registry office, with rain pouring down and Sönderby, the aged conductor, as their sole witness. But a light seems to bathe Martha's face as the fateful words of the ceremony are pronounced; and back in the apartment a Mozart quartet is played to summon up serenity.

Stig's ambition as a violinist in *To Joy* doubtless mirrors Bergman's own yearning to achieve success in theater and cinema during the midforties. His striving after harmony and perfection strikes Martha as ugly. She cannot see that Stig wants to order his entire outlook on life. Before Stig's debut as a soloist in the Mendelssohn Violin Concerto, Sönderby tells him, "Music is an aim, not a means."

Stig makes a false start when he joins the orchestra in the concerto, and Martha, pregnant, watches aghast from a room at the side of the hall. His dreams of developing into a famous soloist are in ruins. Like so many early Bergman characters, he hides away from the world. "I'm alone, as I always have been," he declares in a temper. He cannot accept his failure. "It's horrible to hear you talk—it's as though you were dead already," he sneers at Sönderby, when the old conductor claims that there is room in life for mediocrities. As Martha reads the damning review in the local paper next morning, Stig tries—characteristically—to shift the guilt by saying that she and Sönderby will rejoice at his fiasco.

At this point he meets another woman, Nelly (Margit Carlquist), the wife of an actor and a feline seductress breathing the illicit passion that entices the Bergman protagonist in so many films. Succeeding scenes emphasize even further the comparison between a bohemian way of life and an uneventful, perhaps even unintelligent, married existence.

Confronted by his wife's labor pains, Stig behaves in a manner so hapless, so fearful, that he takes to his bed complaining of queasiness. "Shall I make you a cup of tea and a sandwich?" asks Martha ironically, as the sweat runs down her face and she leans over him. Stig escapes from the apartment and joins the orchestra in rehearsing Smetana, only to be told by telephone that he has a son.

The affair with Nelly casts a long shadow. Even three years later, after a glorious summer on the coast with his family, Stig becomes involved with her. He begs Martha to return to Helsingborg to be with him and the orchestra. But when she does not come back, he berates her for not staying out of town. The marriage is finally undermined, and Stig and Martha embark on a protracted argument that sounds somber and acrimonious in contrast to the harmless bombast of the couple's first row before their wedding. Stig beats her face viciously, while sirens wail in the coastal fog beyond the apartment.

When Nelly's actor-husband has a stroke and leaves a dying message accusing her of poisoning him, the event brings home to Stig how much Martha in her turn must have feared and leaned on him. He writes to her after a three-month silence, and in a series of letters they move toward reconciliation. "Never, never, never to be alone," says Martha eagerly, as they are reunited.

Some years later, she and the children go to the country cottage while Stig remains in Helsingborg. Martha takes an oil stove with her.

In the present, having learned of the fatal accident, Stig rejoins the orchestra in a daze. He stares ahead of him in despondency as the bass strings launch into the *An die Freude* theme. Then he takes up his violin and forces a smile as he sees his son enter the room and sit down. The music becomes an assertion of life, a feeling Bergman will evoke again at the close of *Summer Interlude*. The ode is truly a "Daughter of

Elysium" for Stig. It emerges from the death of Martha, from the recollections that have surged through Stig in the few moments since he heard of the tragedy. Sönderby has described the appeal of Beethoven's Ninth to the orchestra: "This is about joy," he says, "a joy so great that it lies beyond pain, beyond despair . . . a joy beyond comprehension."

In many ways the film paints an accurate picture of student life, with its agonized discussions and emotional crises. Stig is rather too predictable a rebel, and his sentimentality becomes overweening (the later Bergman would never have dwelt on the small white bear Stig gives to Martha for her birthday). But Bergman's skill is discernible in the more subtle points of characterization (the long hair Stig grows in spite of Martha's insistence that he have it cut, for example) and in his depiction of summer happiness. Stig and Martha are related, for sure, to the married couples in *Prison* and *Thirst*, but they are less experienced, less sullied by life.

The interlude in the archipelago contains more visual poetry than the sum of Bergman's previous work. Sönderby recalls a day with Stig and Martha outside their summer place and speaks of "the values of a thousand intonations . . . this complicated secret language that two lovers fashion and use as freely as a shield for their most secret and finest perceptions." These lines indicate that Bergman is beginning to formulate what will be recognized later as the overriding philosophy of his middle period: that there are brief instances in life that are of such exquisite beauty that they compensate for all the misery and unhappiness.

Bergman's trip to Paris with Gun Grut in 1949 lasted several weeks; he returned to Sweden only just before Christmas. "I was escaping from everything," he recalled. "It was the first time in my adult life that I did nothing. Absolutely nothing."[11]

That was an exaggeration. He raced round the Paris theaters, and Vilgot Sjöman maintains that Bergman "lit up like a torch" after coming in contact with the French Molière tradition in a performance of *Le Misanthrope* at the Comédie Française. He also paid regular visits to the Cinémathèque in the Avenue de Messine and some years later told Amita Malik, perhaps out of gallantry, that he had enjoyed watching a troupe of dancers from India.[12]

In his quarters in the rue Sainte-Anne, he managed to write a new play, *Joakim Naked*. It was his last fling as a playwright (except for the television drama, *The Lie*), for when he returned to Stockholm and offered *Joakim Naked* and some other plays to Bonniers, the prestigious publishers of his earlier collection, they demurred.

Despite this setback, the fifties opened auspiciously, with Bergman announcing to the *Stockholms Tidning* newspaper on January 19, 1950, that he would start work in August at Lorens Marmstedt's Intima Theater in Odenplan once he had completed work on *Summer Interlude*, which was scheduled to go before the cameras that spring.

Bergman was no longer cultivating quite so outrageous an image. Marmstedt remembered that he "had a savings book in his pocket and a Ford Prefect he'd bought for sixty-two hundred crowns, cash down. Gone is the beard stubble, gone the rumpled hair, gone the dirty finger-nails. But the burning spirit is still there."[13]

Another intimate of the time says that Bergman was inclined to make great pronouncements, a lot of them drivel and some of them occasionally profound. When the composer, Erik Nordgren, first met Bergman to prepare the music for *Thirst*, "I felt that he had some kind of psychic probe, which he thrust into me, looking everywhere at once. Something frightening. After thirty seconds, he knew everything there was to know about me!" Rune Waldekranz heard him deliver a speech about Swedish films and filmmakers: "He called it 'The Empty Gallows,' because he could find no one to hang! He was very nice, almost gentle, about his colleagues."

In February Bergman was back in Gothenburg directing a guest production of *Divine Words*, a black comedy by Ramón María del Valle-Inclán that pulsated with sexual power and superstition. Herbert Grevenius wrote of this Bergman swan song at Gothenburg:

> It is customary to call Ingmar Bergman possessed. That has become the cliche. If by it one is trying to describe his artistic passion, then it must be accepted—provided we do not forget that it is a passion for truth and not an aesthetic passion for beauty. But the time has come to take notice of the control, the method, a search for form that is, for once in a Swedish director . . . more Gallic than Germanic.[14]

CHAPTER SIX

Summer Love

THERE ARE PREMONITIONS OF GREATNESS IN ALL BERGMAN'S FILMS OF THE forties, wisps of thematic material that he would spin and develop into memorable designs later in his career. They are works steeped in the cynicism of youth, and, characteristically for the peaceful—if also ominous—forties in Sweden, their anger stems not so much from political commitment as from emotional frustration. They reflect Bergman's personal deracination, caught between his dreams of achieving artistic independence and his determination to abandon the bourgeois rectitude of his parents.

Like many a young artist, he is obsessed by death in all its manifestations—the crumbling of illusions, the physical decay of the human body, love's dwindling, the congealment of emotions and sympathies. The apparent aimlessness of life's journey perplexes him. Traditional faith has become obsolescent. Justice is suspect. During the fifties, Bergman decides that the individual must solve his own problems. The search for self-knowledge, even if it means reviving the cruellest of memories and sores, is of paramount importance. Love may not endure, but it affords the traveler a charmed interval along his route, bright moments to set against the dark horizon that lies before him. Gradually the everyday world recedes in significance in Bergman's work, for the struggle waged by his characters is psychological and emotional, not social or economic. The quest leads inward rather than outward, to the cellar of the subconscious, where guilt and desire exert their sway.

Bergman was still close friends with Herbert Grevenius, and they collaborated on the screenplay of *Divorced* in 1950. This was intended as a vehicle for the distinguished actress Märta Ekström, who was admired for her work at the Royal Dramatic Theater. But she fell sick (dying a year or so later), and the part in *Divorced* went to her contemporary, Inga Tidblad, who was rather more familiar to Swedish filmgoers.

Although it is always difficult to disentangle the contributions of scriptwriters to a film, there seems little doubt that the melancholy mood of the piece flows from Bergman. "My life ends here," reads an entry in Gertrud Holmgren's diary, as she reflects on her broken marriage. Her son died when very young; her daughter is away studying. Alone in her apartment, on the threshold of middle age, Gertrud considers suicide. Here, as she shuts the window on the sounds of a baby crying in the night, the influence of Bergman is most firmly felt. Her romance with a young neighbor (Alf Kjellin) is more orthodox.

In the early part of 1950, Bergman himself was caught in the throes of a divorce action, signaling the end of his second marriage. He departed from Gothenburg and moved back to Stockholm, where he was able to enjoy a warm and friendly relationship with his mother.

During the spring of 1950, while Bergman was preparing *Summer Interlude*, his friend Lars-Eric Kjellgren was about to direct *While the City Sleeps*. This was scripted from a synopsis Bergman had made of the novel *Hooligans*, by P. A. Fogelström. As such, it cannot be accorded much significance in Bergman's career, although it is invariably mentioned in his filmography.

Each of Bergman's major films constitutes both a distillation of its predecessors and a great step forward into new realms of expression and technique.

Prison was the first of these; *Summer Interlude* the second.

"This was my first film," he has said of *Summer Interlude*, "in which I felt I was functioning independently, with a style of my own, making a film all my own, with a particular appearance of its own, which no one could ape. . . . For sentimental reasons, too, it was also fun making it. Far back in the past there had been a love story, a romantic experience."[1] A girl he had known had contracted polio, and from this tragedy he wrote a short story during the late thirties entitled "Marie." In the film, Bergman replaces the girl's illness with the accidental death of a young boy; in this way he is able to develop the character of Marie more thoroughly and rewardingly. She becomes the portal figure in the drama; the men in *Summer Interlude* are subordinate to her psychological importance. Like all Bergman's films, *Summer Interlude* is not attached

Birger Malmsten (Henrik) *and Maj-Britt Nilsson* (Marie) *in* Summer Interlude. *Photo courtesy Svensk Filmindustri.*

to the precise moment in history at which it is made. Its mood remains nostalgic, as though Bergman were cherishing that first great love, set against the clouds of war at the close of the thirties, and seeking to fix in amber the timeless pleasures of a summer in the archipelago.

Marie (Maj-Britt Nilsson) is a ballerina attached to the Royal Opera in Stockholm. During a summer vacation on her favorite island outside Stockholm, she becomes infatuated with a young man, Henrik (Birger Malmsten). But their happiness is marred by the jealousy of Marie's Uncle Erland (Georg Funkquist), who was once keen on her mother and now lives in bitterness with his wife, Elisabeth (Renée Björling). Henrik's gardienne is also a depressing—if somewhat self-mocking—figure, condemned to die from cancer. (Her name is Calwagen, the same as that of Bergman's maternal grandmother.)

The character of Uncle Erland is brilliantly knitted into the film by Bergman and Grevenius. After their first romantic excursion, Marie and Henrik return to the house, and immediately the shadow of Uncle Erland's melancholy drifts over them. They are in the House of the Dead. Later, Marie recalls how one evening, seated with Henrik outside a wooden hut, she had teased him about being faithful to her forevermore. "If you don't agree," she laughs, "I shall become Uncle Erland's mistress." An owl hoots nearby, and she tries to hide in Henrik's embrace.

Then, just as autumn creeps in and the time comes to return to Stockholm, Henrik is killed while diving. Marie is overwhelmed by grief. More than a dozen years later a journalist, David, tries to comfort her, but Erland's presence dominates Marie during the aftermath of the tragedy. He represents a reality that she still dare not accept. Her emotions contract; she retreats within herself, seemingly following her uncle's advice in "building a wall to shut out evil." Not until Uncle Erland sends her the diary she kept during that idyllic summer can she muster the courage to visit the island again and purge herself of her memories. And in the present, when he meets her in the kitchen of the deserted villa, Erland serves as a reminder of her lost love and also as a warning. His soul is dead. Marie realizes that unless she can brace herself to countenance life again, to shuffle off the bittersweet legacy of her youth, she will be as lonely and cynical a personality as her uncle.

The task is not easy. In her dressing room at the Opera, Marie is confronted by the sinister figure of the ballet master. In his grotesque Coppélius makeup, he is a symbol of death as unsettling as the allegorical figure in *The Seventh Seal*. When he leaves her dressing room after the arrival of David, the journalist, he plants a last deliberate kiss on her lips. It's an action so swift and so unexpected that the spectator is as surprised as Marie. This is no kiss of condemnation, or betrayal, but a sign of reawakening. It marks the end of Marie's bondage to the past. Although she has been—one assumes—mistress of first her uncle and then David, she has never opened her heart to them as blithely as she did to Henrik. With the departure of the ballet master she begins a new life. She asks David to read the diary, and then one sees her the next evening dancing the lead in *Swan Lake*. During an interval she kisses David with sparkling eyes. "The long, grubby years" are over, and she dashes joyfully on stage again, liberated from her self-contempt.

No other film has caught so well the buoyant sensuality of high summer in Scandinavia. The season lasts for such a short time—no more than six weeks or so—that it is both anticipated and regretted with an intensity that must be difficult for people from warmer climes to comprehend. Ironically, the summer of 1950 was spoiled by periods of rain, and Bergman and his crew had to rush out to the island of Smådalarö whenever the sun shone. The film offers a profusion of tranquil images: the stippled waters of an inlet, the wild strawberry patch, the trees in blossom. The serenity of these compositions, enhanced by the photography of Gunnar Fischer and the intelligent

Maj-Britt Nilsson (Marie), *Alf Kjellin* (David), *and Stig Olin* (the ballet master) *in* Summer Interlude. *This is but one example of Bergman's sophisticated use of mirrors. Photo courtesy Svensk Filmindustri.*

music of Erik Nordgren, marks an altogether new phase in Bergman's development as a director. He orchestrates his effects with a confidence that eluded him in the forties.

Two of his most crucial themes, however, persist and are developed more precisely than ever before. The first is the idea that man is governed by some unseen force beyond his ken, a force with neither scruples nor pity that may strike one down in an instant of happiness. "I feel like a painted puppet on a string," says Marie. "If I cry, the paint runs. Let me mourn my youth in peace." The milieu in which Marie works—the Opera with its constant rehearsals and rigid discipline— reminds one again of the notion that humanity flounders through life

Mimi Pollak (Henrik's aunt) *and Maj-Britt Nilsson* (Marie) *in* Summer Interlude. *Photo courtesy Svensk Filmindustri.*

like a marionette obeying its strings. In his later films, Bergman locates this manipulative force in society, in education; but whatever its manifestation, it is never far removed from the concept of destiny as such.

Death and its attendant symbols are used in Bergman's work to stimulate the living into a more vivid appreciation and acceptance of their lot. When Marie returns to the island to relive the past, she discovers elements of foreboding that she ignored during the summer with Henrik. The sights and sounds that accompanied her romance have vanished. Death, and the reminders of Death, are all that have survived the intervening years: the pastor she meets on the boat; the old crone dying of cancer, once Henrik's gardienne, who passes like a black shadow in front of her as she walks across the island; the vast drawing room of the villa, its furniture shrouded for the winter; and Erland, presiding like the Evil One himself.

Bergman's heroes are consumed by spiritual, not physical maladies. Love and self-knowledge are the only two weapons that can resist Death's patient sovereignty. This awareness liberates Marie and emerges as the second motif in the film. Life is neither so gloomy nor so joyful as she has imagined. She learns that even the most rapturous interlude has its fatal streak and that one can recover from the most harrowing ordeal.

Throughout the forties, Bergman had expressed his thoughts and aspirations through male characters, relying in particular on Birger

Ulf Palme (Atkä Natas) *in* High Tension. *Photo courtesy Swedish Film Institute.*

Malmsten. Marie amounts to the first profound female character in Bergman's world. As the son of inhibited parents, he had first met women through his mother and other female relatives such as aunts, and the feminine world held a mysterious fascination for him. Gradually women have become the ideal sex in Bergman's eyes. His men are always the most feckless and pitiful of creatures, even when happy. Henrik in *Summer Interlude* complains, "No one cares about me, except my dog." And he is merely the precursor of such inept males as Harry in *Summer with Monika*, the consul in *Dreams*, and Egerman in *Smiles of a Summer Night*.

Marie was an exacting role for Maj-Britt Nilsson. No Bergman actress had been submitted to such searching scrutiny by the camera. In this film the close-up becomes one of the most striking and effective devices in Bergman's technique. "To examine the face of a human being, that's most fascinating for me," he told Edwin Newman. "The most fascinating thing of all. All the settings and things like that are not very important."[2] Liv Ullmann has written, "When the camera is as close as Ingmar's sometimes gets, it doesn't only show a face but also what kind of life this face has seen."[3]

The ballet master tells Marie in one illuminating sequence that she is meant to be a dancer and nothing but a dancer. The remark held a significance that Bergman did not detect until some years had elapsed. "I was only twenty-eight [*sic*] and I didn't know how true that was. Now I know. My life is to make pictures. I don't think I could ever do anything else."[4]

The interiors for *Summer Interlude* were shot at the studios in Råsunda. "It was easier to build the ballet stage there," recalls Bergman's production manager, Allan Ekelund, "because the studio had all the technical facilities. Besides, the rehearsal rooms at the ballet were in daily use." A double acted for Maj-Britt Nilsson in the dancing sequences, although the deception is hardly noticeable.

Svensk Filmindustri did not release the film immediately, and more than a year elapsed before the premiere in Stockholm, which attracted excellent reviews.

As soon as he had finished making this intense and complex film, Bergman embarked on a "quickie" for Svensk Filmindustri entitled *High Tension* (*Sånt händer inte här*, literally *This Doesn't Happen Here*). "Only once has it happened that I've made something I've known from the beginning would be rubbish," he has said, and there is no doubt that he regrets being involved in what was at best a hollow and contrived thriller about the Cold War. He was physically exhausted and dispirited, and he had no hand in the screenplay, which was written by Herbert Grevenius.

Atkä Natas (Ulf Palme) is an agent trying to sell his secrets to America in exchange for political asylum. In Stockholm he is pursued by his associates when news of his defection leaks out. Bergman treats the charade with a disdain that recalls the Hitchcock of *The Thirty-Nine Steps*. There are moments of amusing incongruity—the meeting of secret agents behind the screen of a movie theater in the city, where a man is humiliated and beaten while a cartoon holds the audience in hysterical laughter. Or the scene in a crowded street when a tire bursts in the villains' car and passers-by turn a blind eye to the forcible abduction of a young girl. Or the insistent droning of hymns on the radio as the young detective recovers from a fight with Natas. Such incidental pleasures aside, however, *High Tension* is worthless. Doubtless the money he earned for directing the film helped Bergman to maintain his family commitments (by now he had five children).

Lorens Marmstedt, who had hired Bergman to direct at his Intima Theater for the fall of 1950, and who had not yet seen either *High Tension* or *Summer Interlude*, wrote in an article in September: "I believe we can expect a development of new, finer strains in his artistry. . . . Now comes the stage in which his rich instrument will give out new tunes, more harmonic chords. But I hope he will never find himself satisfied to the full. That would signify stagnation."[5]

The two men were still on good terms, although Bergman had decided to return to Svensk Filmindustri when Marmstedt became embroiled in a costly coproduction with France, *Singoalla*, directed by Christian-Jaque. The friendship was about to end, though. Bergman's production of *The Threepenny Opera* inaugurated the Intima Theater on October 17 but was greeted coolly by the critics. A double bill of *A Shadow*, by Hjalmar Bergman, and *Medea*, by Anouilh, followed two months later, and the reaction was similar. Bergman disliked the pressure put upon him to produce an evening's entertainment that would fill the theater, and Marmstedt was disenchanted too. Bergman resigned or, as he claimed later, was fired. Hasse Ekman, still his rival for the limelight in Swedish film and stage circles, was appointed in his place.

Bergman now suffered from more than pricked vanity. He was without a regular source of income. Trouble was brewing in the film industry, and no new project was in the cards. He had to be content with occasional guest productions that yielded some twenty-five hundred crowns a time.[6] The one bright note in his life at this point was Gun Grut. So positive was their relationship that in early 1951 Bergman embarked on his third marriage. Gun Grut was a specialist in Serbo-Croatian history and current affairs and a journalist of high caliber. Blond, alert, and endowed with a strong personality, she was the mother of Bergman's third son, named Ingmar. Although their marriage survived only a short while, Bergman and Gun Grut remained friends until her death in a car crash in Yugoslavia in 1971.

The crisis in film production came to a head in 1951, when the studios shut down in protest against the crippling entertainment tax. So high was the proportion of box-office revenue paid back to the government, that a Swedish film needed to attract 800,000 spectators if it was to retrieve its costs. If a domestic feature drew 500,000 spectators (which it often did), the producer lost 120,000 crowns while the state pocketed a tidy 375,000 in taxes. The "strike" was prolonged because the cinemas had kept several new films on ice in anticipation of this stoppage, so the public remained to a large extent unaware of the situation. Finally, in early 1952, the government made some concessions, agreeing to plow back some proportion of the entertainment tax into the industry.

All this prevented Bergman from making a feature film for eighteen months. He grew conscious of the hazardous and uncertain nature of film production. "My finances were in a bad way," he said, "and the child welfare authorities were breathing down my neck."[7]

But Bergman has made a regular practice of turning misfortune to his advantage; he found several new ways to stay afloat. In 1951 he filmed a series of cinema commercials, and his radio play, *The City*, was directed by Olof Molander, one of the gods of his youth. In April he directed his first major production on the small stage of the Royal Dramatic Theater, *Light in the Hovel*, a play by Björn-Erik Höijer about life in northern Sweden, and in November he produced Tennessee Williams's *The Rose Tattoo* at the municipal theater in Norrköping.

The City revived memories of Bergman's childhood. Once again the anguished cry of protest against a claustrophobic environment could be heard: "When Joakim was eight years old, his life was half twilit, fertile and growing but imbued also with a rather merciless and obvious feeling that the world was a world without grace. . . . After his eighth year there began a tumult that continued until he was twenty-three."[8]

By now Bergman thought he could look objectively at his youth. "All these religious questions, all this talk of guilt and punishment—it's beside the point!" cries Joakim's wife as he raves on. Oliver Mortis (signifying Death, of course) is, like all such symbolic figures in Bergman's work, alarming in his ignorance of life's consequences. He knows only that "from your birth to your death runs a curve, logical, beautiful, absolute." Some of the dialog is reminiscent of Strindberg's, with the characters rending each other with verbal savagery and then turning their knives on their own selves with self-pity. Jack returns to his "Granny's house," where the old woman accuses him of adoring his own guilt feelings. "It's your own significance that terrifies you," she says, "not reality with its twisted shadow-play."

The cinema commercials (which until recently have occupied only a footnote in Swedish film histories) were an altogether more original and challenging enterprise. Now, thanks to the zealous research of Hauke Lange-Fuchs and a screening of these one-minute films at the Nordic Film Days in Lübeck, it is possible to do them justice. Bergman was not the only director to stoop to such work; even so committed a film-maker as Hampe Faustman was forced to do so during the stoppage.

Ragnar M. Lindberg, an executive at Unilever in Stockholm, recalls that in 1951 their subsidiaries, Sunlight and Gibbs, were determined to improve the standard of their advertising in Swedish cinemas, and they contacted Bergman. He agreed to tackle the job, providing he was accorded the same technical facilities as he was for a feature film. The product due for treatment was "Bris," the first deodorant soap in Sweden, with a 20 percent share of the home market.

Bergman insisted on using Gunnar Fischer as his cinematographer and on shooting the commercials at the studios in Råsunda. Unilever accepted these terms and allowed Bergman to prepare his own scripts and storyboards (three different versions for each commercial). Bergman thought that the slogan claiming that Bris killed all bacteria was sheer hokum, but he contrived to squeeze it into each of the five advertisements.

Most of these Bris commercials are terse and sardonic. Bergman spent no more than two days on each one and used several of the same actors over and over again, notably the genial John Botvid. In *The Inventor*, a man dreams that he is destined to win the Nobel Prize, and his fantasy is a splendid amalgam of animation and pixillation. In *The Magic Theater*, a gross, sweaty, bulbous figure is engulfed in smoke by a black devil.

Bergman experiments in many of the commercials. He makes use of a television screen as a clever means of expanding and deepening the screen image in *Film Performance*; and in *Movie Making* a girl addresses the camera, and her face is reflected in the lens alongside the man to whom she is talking. The most famous, though not the best, of the nine ads is *The Princess and the Swineherd*—famous because Bibi Andersson made her film debut in it at the age of fifteen, bestowing a hundred kisses on the grubby swineherd in gratitude for a bar of soap!

The competence and verve of these tiny films makes one wonder how

Anita Björk (Rakel) *and Jarl Kulle* (Kaj) *in the first episode of* Secrets of Women. *Photo courtesy Svensk Filmindustri.*

fine a practitioner Bergman might have become of the art of the TV commercial. Such speculation aside, they enabled him to pay his bills and to keep his form.[9]

In the theater, Bergman directed his own "passion play," *The Murder in Barjärna*, at the Malmö Municipal Theater. Its description of evil in a small community was as horrific and ghoulish as the wildest of film fantasies, and Henrik Sjögren thought it the most shocking of all Bergman's stage productions.

When the movie strike was settled, the backlog of projects was considerable. Bergman shot two features, one after another, in 1952: *Secrets of Women* (*Kvinnors väntan*, also known as *Waiting Women*) and *Summer with Monika* (*Sommaren med Monika*, also released as *Monika*). Gun Grut had conceived the nucleus of *Secrets of Women*, with its engaging conceit of three wives recounting an adventure from their marriages while they are all at a summer house awaiting their husbands' return. She even worked with Bergman on the screenplay, and he wanted to give her a credit on the finished film. But Svensk Filmindustri felt that the public needed convincing that Bergman himself could write a smart, witty film. "It was written in a mood of bad

On location in Paris: Bergman shooting Secrets of Women. *Photo courtesy Svensk Filmindustri.*

Bergman (at right) shooting the second episode of Secrets of Women. *Photo courtesy Svensk Filmindustri.*

temper," says Bergman. "Sheer terror, grim necessity." He had to have a project ready for instant shooting the moment the film stoppage was over.

Only the last episode in *Secrets of Women* can really be described as a comedy. There are amusing salvos in the opening and middle flashbacks, but the tone is more grave than gay.

Rakel (Anita Björk) is the first to recount her story, which is a direct reworking of Bergman's early play, *Rakel and the Cinema Doorman*. The theme is infidelity. One afternoon, while her husband Eugen (Karl-Arne Holmsten) is out of the house, Rakel is visited by a lover from her past named Kaj (Jarl Kulle). He is smooth and full of glib seduction. Sex ensues, followed in turn by the inevitable conversation and mood of recrimination. When Eugen returns, an angry scene takes place. Eugen is the archetypal Bergman stuffed shirt, interested only in his beloved antiques (i.e. dead objects) and reluctant to confront the frigidity of his marriage. He takes refuge in a hut in the garden and threatens to shoot himself, but he is dissuaded from doing so by his elder brother, Paul (Håkan Westergen), whose advice, though tossed off lightly, adumbrates a fundamental tenet of Bergman's philosophy: "An unfaithful wife is better than no wife at all. . . . The most terrible thing is not to be deceived but to feel alone."

Rakel, finishing her narrative, tells the other women in the summer house that Eugen is a child she must care for. The concept of the mother-figure in marriage recurs several times in Bergman and again in the third episode of *Secrets of Women*.

Apart from the love scenes between Rakel and Kaj, in which Bergman resorts to reflections and large close-ups to emphasize the narcissistic quality of the affair, this episode is not as adventurous cinematically as the second one, which is set for much of the time in Paris and contains a mere fifty or so lines of dialog. Bergman and his crew traveled to Paris to shoot some street sequences for the story with Maj-Britt Nilsson and Birger Malmsten. It was difficult because the Swedes did not realize that one should report to the head of each Paris police precinct—and pay him for the right to shoot on location. But the results were excellent, and these Parisian scenes evoke a mood of lyricism reminiscent of *Summer Interlude* (especially when Märta walks along the Seine or through the Bois de Boulogne.).

Märta recalls how she fell in love with an artist, had a child by him, and eventually married him. Flashbacks predominate, as they do throughout Bergman's work during the fifties. Learning about the past becomes the only means of comprehending the present.

Märta's memories are given a distorted, romantic tinge by virtue of the labor pains she undergoes in the maternity hospital in Sweden. Thus

Gunnar Björnstrand (Fredrik Lobelius) *and Eva Dahlbeck* (Karin) *trapped in the elevator in the third episode of* Secrets of Women. *Photo courtesy Svensk Filmindustri.*

a nightclub sequence begins in a feverish tone, with the bodies of dancers writhing in a watery dissolve; Märta momentarily regards a shadow flung across a frosted glass door as Death ("It was like a nightmare when you want to scream—and can't"); the sharp ring of a telephone interrupts the serene classical music in her home. These macabre moments are typical of Bergman, but Märta's radiant joy when she has borne her child is surprising at this juncture. A baby begins to symbolize a stable life rather than the end of illicit happiness. Even the act of parturition is given a halo, as Märta summons up images of a fountain, a river, a flowering meadow, a blond child. The rest of society conspires against such felicity. Bergman stresses the callousness of the hospital staff, the hideous screams of other children, and the menacing armory of surgical instruments.

By far the most significant part of *Secrets of Women* remains the final episode, for it furnishes the first evidence of Bergman's gift for the comedy of manners. The premise—a married couple sort out their differences while trapped in an elevator—came from a personal experience of Bergman's. He and his wife had gone on a brief vacation to Copenhagen, where they stayed in the home of some friends who were out of town. But when, "drunk and happy, with everything fully prepared, we put the key in the door—it snapped off! No chance of finding a locksmith. So we spent the night on the stairs."[10]

The sequence posed tricky problems. Technicians built a cramped model of an elevator interior in the studio at Råsunda. Bergman and Hasse Ekman were engaged in a friendly competition to see who could achieve the longest "take" (Hitchcock's *Rope* was still in vogue). Bergman insisted on an extremely long take inside the elevator, and Gunnar Fischer had to heave the hundred-kilo camera hither and thither with his assistants. But in the end Bergman agreed that certain close-ups would have to be intercut with the main dialog. The sequence was shot on slow film, and a great deal of light was required. It was hot and cramped, and tempers were short.

As Karin and Fredrik, the middle-aged pair returning in evening dress from a centenary dinner, Eva Dahlbeck and Gunnar Björnstrand were the perfect foils. Compelled to talk to each other at close quarters for the first time in years, their decorum soon reduced to discomfiture, they arrive at reconciliation. Mirrors inside the elevator are used to suggest the inanity of the repartee.

For Björnstrand, his appearance in *Secrets of Women* signaled the end of a long estrangement from Bergman. He had established himself in comedies at Svensk Filmindustri, and when the call came from Bergman he was able to respond at the peak of his powers. From now on he would be one of the most vital members of Bergman's team. "He had the ability to remain silent," says Björnstrand, looking back on Bergman's approach to that film. "He let the actors develop themselves. We weren't separate, programmed machines—we could work from our own intuition."

Maj, the sister of one of the wives, runs away with her boyfriend in the confusion as the husbands (all brothers, bound together by a pompous complacency) return to the summer house. (She was played by Gerd Andersson, the elder sister of Bibi, who acquired a reputation as a dancer of brilliant skill.) Märta tries to stop the younger girl from leaving, but then she sees in her the adventurous spirit of her own youth, before she was forced to compromise with life. Bergman, using Paul as his mouthpiece once more, says to Märta: "Let them think they are doing something forbidden, let them profit from their summer. The wounds, the wisdom, and other troubles—they'll come soon enough." The couple are glimpsed sailing away across the moonlit waters. This image of hopeful—if indefinite—escape amounts to a particularly Nordic type of optimism.

Secrets of Women was a hit, the first in Bergman's career. Bergman was so delighted that he liked to wait in the foyer of Stockholm's most fashionable cinema, Röda Kvarn, and listen to the audience laughing at the Eva Dahlbeck–Gunnar Björnstrand episode.

One of Allan Ekelund's duties at Svensk Filmindustri was to read new books with an eye to their being purchased for filming. He noted Per Anders Fogelström's novel, *Summer with Monika*, and forwarded it to Bergman along with another collection of short stories by the same author. "We wanted the rights," says Ekelund, "and then later Ingmar was attracted to it, after first thinking it only a simple little story. It was a convenient break for Ingmar, because I don't think he had a script of his own ready at that point."

Bergman's recollection differs on this issue. "It was in the first instance a film treatment. Per Anders Fogelström and I met on Kungsgatan, and he told me the plot in ten words. And I said, we have to make a picture out of this; and then we started to write the script. And subsequently he wrote the novel."[11]

A budget of some 300,000 to 400,000 crowns was established. Carl Anders Dymling had to fight tooth and nail to persuade the board of Svensk Filmindustri to sanction the project. "Some members of his board, I seem to remember, even resigned," says Bergman. "We shouldn't be allowed to make such filth!" Even Dymling was shocked by the inclusion of a nude bathing sequence, but Fogelström argued that it was in the original book, and Dymling acquiesced.

Before *Secrets of Women* even opened, Bergman began work on *Summer with Monika*. Early in August of 1952, the entire crew traveled out to Ornö, a large island in the southern sector of the Stockholm archipelago. By modern standards the group was tiny—a mere dozen or so technicians and actors—and they all lived in the parish clerk's house on Ornö. "For everyone," recalls Gunnar Fischer, "it was our happiest film. Bergman was never secretive and talked eagerly to the crew about what he sought to achieve."

The shooting lasted over two months. One of the reasons for this protracted schedule was Bergman's infatuation with Harriet Andersson, as splendid and uninhibited a relationship as any he has ever had. "I had just seen Harriet in *Defiance*," he recalled later, "and no girl it seemed to me could be more 'Monika-ish.' " Harriet was "eighteen or nineteen, at most, I guess. But she was devastating, and engaged to Per Oscarsson."[12] As she and Lars Ekborg, who played Harry, her lover, were so unknown, Bergman and his project were left in comparative peace.

When after three weeks the first rushes were viewed, a bad scratch on the negative was obvious, so substantial reshooting was necessary. Time and again, Bergman and Harriet returned to the island on some pretext or another—poor sound was a familiar excuse.

Harriet Andersson represents the first great female influence on Bergman's films. She starred in *Monika, The Naked Night, A Lesson in Love, Dreams,* and *Smiles of a Summer Night.* Later she returned to play two memorable roles: Karin in *Through a Glass Darkly,* and Agnes in *Cries and Whispers.* Bergman relished her fierce, wriggling personality, her independence, and her quick intelligence. Born, like Greta Garbo, in the south of Stockholm, she was intent on acting from the start. At age fifteen she paid for her course at a private drama school by delivering newspapers at dawn and then by being an elevator attendant. She danced in a revue theater, and appeared in some small parts on screen before meeting Bergman.

In the movie's early scenes, Monika is no more than a common slattern. Fisherman's socks cling to her ankles, and she snivels at the false sentimentality of a cheap Hollywood film to which Harry, her boyfriend, takes her. But Monika and her gauche, impetuous Harry

Shooting Summer with Monika. *Gunnar Fischer is at the camera.* Photo courtesy Svensk Filmindustri.

Harriet Andersson (Monika) *in* Summer with Monika. *Photo courtesy Svensk Filmindustri.*

steal a boat and flee to an island, and on the archipelago, removed from the Stockholm crowds, her true potency is revealed and fulfilled. Harriet Andersson as Monika is eroticism incarnate; stills from the film have featured in Truffaut's *The 400 Blows* and other movies as symbols of Nordic ecstasy. She wears little makeup, and her allure has a fundamental, carnal quality that thumbs its nose at glamor. The unwashed hair, the mouth perpetually at work on gum, the proud, unboosted bosom: these built a new idiom into movie language.

Their life on the island is wild and idyllic. Monika is caught stealing on private property after they run out of food, and there follows an

Outsiders: Lars Ekborg (Harry) and Harriet Andersson (Monika) in Summer with Monika. *Photo courtesy Svensk Filmindustri.*

amusing scene when she must sit at a bourgeois table; she promptly seizes a joint of meat like a trophy and plunges into the dusk. Bergman's camera fixes her, crouching in the grass, tearing at the meat like an animal in the plains, eyes narrowed and alert for sounds of pursuit— *l'enfant sauvage* at bay. "I remember having to crawl with that hunk of meat through the grass on the backlot at Råsunda Studios!" she laughs now.

As summer ebbs to its close and the wind grows chill, reality envelops the lovers again. There is nothing for it but to return to the city. Monika bears an unwanted baby. The gloomy furnishings of the room where they live with the child drive Monika to frustration. The clumsiness that at first seemed charming in Harry now nauseates her. Monika is an opportunist, not an idealist like Marie in *Summer Interlude*; she has no hesitation, and suffers no remorse, in turning to a new lover. This last passage suggests a return to the bleak, sordid life of the early Bergman films. The greater the selfishness, the greater the disillusionment. Rebellious to the last, Monika gives the camera a long stare—a shot that both Godard and Truffaut have copied.

The essence of *Summer with Monika*, however, lies in the halcyon days of the archipelago in late July and early August. The Swedish summer is at its absolute zenith. Monika and Harry are Adam and Eve in a Garden of Eden. They feel at liberty to shout and scream and dance exactly as they wish. The desire of the flesh is the most perfect means of attaining happiness that Monika knows, and happiness in Bergman's world depends on sexual harmony.

Not a trace of baroque imagery adorns this film. Bergman achieves a purity of exposition that he was unable to recover for years to come. He uses broad, coarse strokes to establish the relationship between Harry and Monika in the early stages, and the film follows a logical progression: a chronicle of the birth and death of love. For all its logic, however, the script suffers from occasional lapses in construction. It strikes one as implausible, for example, that a nasty youth who has already beaten up Harry in Monika's courtyard should suddenly and quite without premeditation happen to be camping on the same remote island as Harry and Monika.

Improvisation in the technical departments was obligatory, given the conditions and miniscule budget of *Summer with Monika*. All the dialog and sound effects had to be dubbed afterward; Gunnar Fischer had only a silent Mitchell camera on Ornö. Oscar Rosander, Bergman's favorite editor, was unavailable, so the director had to buckle down to the editing himself. A visitor to the studios watched Bergman shooting the scene when Monika and Harry hide for the night in a motor boat in Stockholm harbor: A light was directed through a bowl of water atop the hull, to give the illusion of lapping water.

Erik Nordgren, who during the fifties became the regular composer for Bergman's films, says that Bergman actually wrote music into his screenplays. "He knew exactly at what point he wanted music, and of what sort." The sequence when the lovers travel out to the archipelago, beneath successive bridges, is reinforced with *musique concrète*, and that portion of the score was later broadcast on Danish Radio in its own right. "Ingmar performed it himself," says Nordgren. "He stood with the two kettle-drum sticks and hammered on the piano strings."

The summer of 1952 formed one of the hinges in Bergman's life and career. His relationship with Harriet Andersson spurred him to even more intense creative work. His appointment as a director at the already hallowed Municipal Theater in Malmö was the signal for a brilliant period in which films and stage productions seemed to flow without hesitation or interruption from his prodigious imagination. Less than twelve months earlier, he had been on the brink of poverty. But by the time he went down to Malmö, followed by Harriet Andersson, who abandoned her work at the Scala Revue, his energy and his optimism were fully restored.

H. Forsyth Hardy, in his pioneering study of Scandinavian film, wrote in that very same year: "[Bergman] can see and feel in film. What he decides to see and feel will greatly influence the future of the Swedish film."[13]

CHAPTER SEVEN

Triumph and Disaster

MALMÖ IS SWEDEN'S THIRD MAJOR CITY, AFTER STOCKHOLM AND GOTHEN-burg. A port on the coast of Skåne, it lies less than an hour by ferry from Denmark, and a virtuous Swede might say that Malmö was smudged by the license of Copenhagen. Some of the bustle and excite-ment of a border town, a port of entry, has accumulated there, and Malmö's newspapers are among the liveliest in the country.

When Ingmar Bergman arrived in Malmö in the autumn of 1952, the Municipal Theater was less than ten years old but nonetheless revered. Bergman's agreement stipulated that he should act as "full-time director and artistic adviser to the management,"[1] but although the contract was set for an initial three years, neither Bergman nor anyone else could have predicted that he would rule the roost at Malmö for twice that length of time, producing seventeen plays and eight films in what may now be seen as the richest period of his life.

Each year was programmed with rigor. "I devote myself to a kind of crop rotation," Bergman has observed. "I have a piece of land, and sometimes I cultivate rye and sometimes clover."[2] The season at Malmö extended from early September to late May, and Bergman directed one or two new productions each year. The actors were engaged for these eight months or so but for the rest of the year were dependent on film work. This, allied to the vicissitudes of the Swedish climate, helped to dictate the pattern of Bergman's progress.

The Municipal Theater was the brainchild of three architects, Eric Lallerstedt, Sigurd Lewerentz, and David Helldén. Their ideal was to bring the audience in closer contact with the stage and to give an equally good view of the performance to those in the cheap seats and those in the traditionally expensive rows of the auditorium. Promulgated during the thirties by Per Lindberg and others, this concept of "the people's theater" prevailed also in the design of London's National during the late sixties.

The Malmö Municipal Theater was inaugurated on September 23, 1944, with *A Midsummer Night's Dream* as its opening program. In September 1945 Bergman's play, *Rakel and the Cinema Doorman*, received its premiere in Malmö. It was his first taste of the immense proscenium at the Municipal Theater (he called it the "Big Boo"), together with the splendid facilities backstage. The maximum seating capacity is 1,695, but false walls can reduce this number to 1,257, 697, or even 553. A further 100 seats from the front stalls may be removed at will. The false walls glide along rails set into the ceiling, and the theater can be changed in scope in a mere hour.

The huge apron stage, which when fully extended is more than half again as wide as the stage at either Covent Garden or the Paris Opéra, is capable of rising or sinking in four sections and when lowered allows room for a seventy-man orchestra. This gigantic stage must be a director's dream—or nightmare (even though the theater also boasts a sophisticated lighting and scenery-changing system). Almost all Bergman's productions took place on the apron stage, while the back stage was often used for projections (in *Urfaust*, for example). From the front of the apron to the rear of the stage is a vast seventy-nine feet. Many directors have felt it to be a vacuum. How to fill such an area with people and decor?

Lennart Olsson, Bergman's personal assistant and "sorcerer's apprentice" during this period, states, "Ingmar always went to the opposite extreme: he took away things, he simplified matters. He presented Molière's *Misanthrope* with one chair on the big stage, with a painted background and a carpet on the apron stage, and enormous costumes."

"I soon discovered that every stage has its magic center," says Bergman himself. "And the magic center of that huge stage was six meters in that direction and four meters in that direction—a square of twenty-four meters."

The entire building had cost around six million Swedish crowns (approximately one million dollars) to build in 1944, and today its five auditoriums command grants from city and state amounting to more than those given to the Royal Dramatic Theater and the Stockholm Opera combined. But the Malmö Municipal Theater is by no means a white elephant. It can tap a potential audience of around a million people from the most densely populated area of Sweden apart

from Stockholm. During the early fifties, of course, no television dominated the Swedish home. Admission to the theater sometimes cost less
than a cinema ticket, and after a season or two each new Bergman production came to be regarded as a social event. People were ready to
approach and tackle a difficult play when it was presented by Bergman.
In 1954 and 1955, no fewer than ninety thousand attended his version
of the Lehar operetta, *The Merry Widow*, referred to by Malmö
denizens quite simply as "Bergman's *Widow*."

Malmö was also stimulating to Bergman because there were no
limitations on what he could stage. Musicals and operettas were beyond
the range of the much smaller Helsingborg Theater, and in addition
there was at Malmö an "intimate" theater in the same building, as a
complement to the main stage. With only 204 seats and a stage fifty-two
feet wide and thirty feet deep, the Intima could be used for modern and
offbeat drama, ballet, and even opera. Here Bergman staged *Don Juan*,
Kafka's *The Castle*, and Hjalmar Bergman's *Sagan*.

Yet another luxury was the main rehearsal room, which was added to
the complex in 1955 and measures sixty-nine feet wide and thirty-nine
feet deep, with a mirror running along the entire length of one wall. "It
was so wonderful to be at a theater where there is also an orchestra, a
ballet, a chorus, opera singers," says Bergman. "My office was behind
the small stage [Intima], and there was a corridor and at the end of that
corridor was the orchestra's rehearsal room. You went to the rehearsals
of the symphony orchestra, and the ballet, and it was fantastic."

Bergman rehearsed very swiftly at Malmö. The actors were all under
contract and lived in the city, so there was a daily rhythm to the proceedings. "During rehearsals, the atmosphere was very hearty," recalls
Lennart Olsson.

> They were joking like boys and then all of a sudden *very* heavily
> concentrated on what they were doing. Ingmar was so far ahead
> of everyone in his understanding of the play that you never
> questioned him. . . . During the first week of rehearsals he
> would outline to you the basic arrangements he required on the
> stage. Then he left you for two weeks. I had to take over
> rehearsals for that period. Ingmar felt that if he was there all the
> time he would grow tired of hearing the lines over and over. So
> he preferred to come back fresh, with the groundwork already
> established.

At first the actors were startled and confused, but soon they began
to see the wisdom of Bergman's regimen. They respected the fact that
he never changed a classical text. For that matter he never used a written
script of his own; his notebooks were meager, almost empty. Unlike

many directors, he did not abandon a production once it was afloat. Before each performance he went down to the stage and looked things over, talking to the actors. "He hated going on stage after a first night, although once or twice we managed to push him on!" laughs Olsson.

A Bergman production was timed to the point where successive performances all ran to the same length, give or take a minute or so. There was, indeed, only one way in which a Bergman production could be performed by the actors—and yet they never felt restricted. No conflicts occurred between Bergman and his troupe. If he did explode—and he was renowned in Malmö as much for such explosions as for his colossal laugh—it was never for personal reasons but from sheer ambition and the frustration of not being able to attain his goal. Self-esteem was alien to him, even in the face of the international reputation that through his films he was acquiring during the Malmö years. The idea of being an anonymous artist, like the builders of Chartres Cathedral, came to Bergman while he was working in Malmö, as a kind of reaction to the pressure of fame.

His private life was subordinated, if not exactly sublimated, to the demands of work. The Municipal Theater had access to accommodation in the Erikslust area of the city, and Hartvig Torngren, then economic director of the theater, found him a three-room apartment. Harriet Andersson, who was living with Bergman for the first three years of his sojourn in Malmö, remembers that their building housed Eva Stiberg, a rising star of stage and screen, while Åke Fridell, one of Bergman's favorite actors, was installed next door.

"The actors must live in the stables!" joked Bergman to Torngren when he first saw the apartment, a line that would later be spoken by Mrs. Armfeldt in *Smiles of a Summer Night*. By nine every morning he and Harriet would be at the theater, and they did not depart until after ten in the evening. With Bergman's admitted desire for nine hours' sleep, there was not much time for social life. "I think I went to the town center just three or four times a year. I just went from the apartment to the theater," he says. "From the theater to the apartment. Sometimes I had to travel to Stockholm to cut my films, or do some mixing."[3]

One of his few indulgences at the apartment was a model train set, which he tinkered with for relaxation.

Looking back on the Malmö period, Bergman recalls: "I was a little bit hunted by the demons, and there were so many tensions, so many difficulties, so many catastrophes. . . . I was very unsuccessful in my private life, and I tried to compensate in my artistic work."[4] He was still technically married to Gun Grut in Stockholm and was also paying for the upkeep of his children by Else Fisher and Ellen Lundström. A recurrent ulcer, part real, part imagined, laid him low each April, and while in the clinic he would select a draft screenplay from the four or five he was developing at any one time and complete it without delay. Such a script was quite detailed. "When I wrote something like *The Seventh Seal*, there was a frustrated dramatist in me. I wrote stage plays for the screen in those days, because the theater seemed closed to me."[5]

The managing director of the theater was Lars-Levi Laestadius, nine years senior to Bergman and regarded already during the thirties as a promising stage talent. He had made an impact as secretary at the Gothenburg Civic Theater and wrote some contemporary social satires that received good notices. Laestadius had introduced Anouilh's *Eurydice* to Sweden, but at Malmö, where he assumed command in 1950, he lost his touch as a director. Bergman was summoned, and the two men managed to survive each other's presence through the decade.

Laestadius was astute enough to let the *enfant terrible* have his way in the theater. At the outset, a friendly bargain was struck. "You can have Molière, I'll take Shakespeare," said Bergman. Then one day, during his rehearsals of *Romeo and Juliet*, with Folke Sundquist and Gertrud Fridh, Bergman came to Laestadius and declared that he wanted to stage *The Misanthrope*.

"But that's Molière!" protested Laestadius.

"Well, I have one or two ideas about that play," replied Bergman, "and you can keep Shakespeare." So he produced *The Misanthrope* and Laestadius staged *As You Like It!*

Bergman brought several players to Malmö. Once there, they remained—at least as long as he did. Harriet Andersson came direct from the Scala Revue in Stockholm in 1953. Gudrun Brost (the clown's wife in *The Naked Night*) also emerged from a revue in the capital, one year later. Bibi Andersson and Ingrid Thulin arrived in the middle years of Bergman's reign at the Municipal Theater. Others, such as Åke Fridell, had worked with him in the forties. Max von Sydow, Gunnel Lindblom, Allan Edwall, Naima Wifstrand, Gertrud Fridh— the list is impressive. Bergman promoted their careers to a remarkable degree, but their presence stimulated and reassured him too.

"I've felt lonely in the outside world," he has said, "and for that very reason I've taken refuge in a community of feeling, however illusory."[6] He wrote the parts in his films of the fifties with these actors specifically in mind. Those around him found that his methods were similar, but not exactly alike, in both theater and cinema. Max von Sydow mentions the initial read-through that Bergman would have with the entire cast, just as he would on stage. "There was the same discipline," comments Gudrun Brost, "but his instructions were a little more precise."

Often he would break off shooting a movie at 2 P.M., even though the actors were paid to continue until 4 P.M., because he knew that they would perform better after a break.

To maintain the household atmosphere during filmmaking, Bergman organized screening sessions of other movies during the evening. He hired films from all over the world (with the aid of friends at Svensk Filmindustri), and on one or two evenings a week—but always on Thursdays—he gathered the actors and some friends together at the studios in Råsunda outside Stockholm. Hitchcock was a favorite, and Bergman expressed his admiration for Hitch's ability to thrill an audience. Screenings were also mandatory at the apartment in Erikslust whenever Bergman had enough time to spare.

Studio work appealed to him. A studio, after all, resembles the stage, with its confinement and insulation from the outside world. As Lennart Olsson points out, "His films in those days were so intimate in their relationships between people that outdoor shooting was much more difficult for him, what with the weather, the wind, and other distractions. He couldn't *control* the exteriors." Bergman grew nervy as a new production approached, particularly during the two weeks before filming began.

Gunnar Fischer, Bergman's cinematographer during the fifties, also remembers the family mood. For lighting and set-up run-throughs, he had to ask the crew to help him; there were no stand-ins. Bergman himself checked the framing of each shot and used to build up his scenery "through the camera" (in those days an ancient Debrie, wrapped in pillows and blankets to smother its whirring complaints). The contrasts between black and white were so pronounced that *Smiles of a Summer Night*, *The Seventh Seal*, *Wild Strawberries*, and *The Magician* are difficult to reproduce with accuracy on television today.

The wonder remains that the Bergman films made in the Malmö period possessed all the virtues and none of the impediments of a theatrical tradition, while his stage productions drew upon the visual devices of the cinema without sacrificing a jot of dramatic or verbal intensity. Each work was suited impeccably to its medium.

Bergman's first production as resident director in Malmö was *The Crown-Bride*, one of Strindberg's most mystical plays, and yet shot through and through with guilt and fear of humiliation. Kersti, a peasant girl in Dalarna, longs for the purity of a white wedding and drowns her illegitimate baby in order to be accepted as a virgin bride. But although she breaks down at the wedding feast and confesses her crime, fate subsequently leads her to the same death as that of her child—she plunges through the ice of a nearby lake.

Bergman eschewed the temptation to litter the stage with the trappings of Dalarna folklore. Throughout his career he has leaned toward the bare essentials of production design, and when presenting *The Crown-Bride* he even excised parts of Strindberg's text that dealt too fondly with the provincial and picturesque elements of the drama. Instead, he sought to emphasize the universal significance of the play; a critic commented that one felt oneself much closer to the sulphurous waters of Hell than the glittering surface of an idyllic Swedish lake. Adolf Anderberg wrote in *Skånska Dagblabet*: "Ingmar Bergman has achieved one of his finest productions. He can be elusive and sometimes difficult to follow. But, confronted with Strindberg's brilliant poetry, he has found his melody and with humility and firmness has brought forth a creation well worth remembering."[7]

Nordisk Tonefilm suggested to Bergman that he make a film from this triumphant production, but the company took so long to clear the rights from the Strindberg estate that the idea was dropped, and it was only in 1957, when he shot *Brink of Life,* that Bergman fulfilled his obligation to Nordisk.

In the early summer of 1953, Bergman made *The Naked Night* (*Gycklarnas afton,* also released as *Sawdust and Tinsel*), with the location work done at Arild, a small resort on the Baltic Sea.

The film's gestation had been difficult. Rune Waldekranz, then in charge of production at Sandrews, recalls how in 1952 he had met Bergman, who told him that Svensk Filmindustri had rejected the synopsis. Anders Sandrew himself passed Bergman's material around to various friends and colleagues, and all affirmed that it was the worst script they had ever read. So too did Schamyl Bauman, the popular director who was in partnership with Anders Sandrew at the time. But Rune Waldekranz prevailed on the company to tackle the project, pointing out the international acclaim for Sjöberg's film of *Miss Julie* two years before and suggesting that the Swedish cinema could acquire a new lease on life on the European market with a prestige production by Ingmar Bergman.

The Naked Night was a miracle of improvisation in the face of practical hazards. Waldekranz had promised Bergman that he could have his favorite Sandrew cameraman, Göran Strindberg. But Strindberg was suddenly summoned to Hollywood for a course on the techniques involved in the new process of CinemaScope, and Waldekranz had to persuade Bergman to accept the services of a new young cinematographer named Sven Nykvist. Bergman was sceptical, and although an autodidact himself, he insisted on subjecting Nykvist to some rigorous tests. Alf Sjöberg was making *Karin Månsdotter,* and Nykvist was committed to that production by the studio; so the exteriors on *The Naked*

Night had to be shot by Hilding Bladh, which added to Bergman's confusion.

The budget was tight as well. Mago (the professional name of Max Goldstein), who designed the costumes, remembers the panic that broke out when the one and only pair of bejewelled stockings to be worn by Harriet Andersson during a seduction scene could not be located. Lars-Owe Carlberg, who was to become Bergman's regular production manager in the late sixties, had the devil's own task of nursing and supervising a motley collection of chimpanzees, bears, and circus performers.

The unit was on location for a month, living in a small hotel in Arild. Then everyone repaired to Stockholm for the interiors. "By then," says Bergman, "we knew each other like sardines in a tin. We'd eaten and quarreled and got drunk and lived together and had a marvelous time; so the boundary lines between who were the circus artistes and who were the actors and who were film directors or monkeys were by no means clear."[8]

The Naked Night is set in a circus milieu, which for Bergman is a real paradigm of the theater or film studio. Albert (Ake Grönberg), the owner of a scruffy circus troupe that earns a precarious living by touring the south of Sweden, is accompanied by his mistress, Anne (played by Harriet Andersson). During one of the halts in a small Scanian town, their relationship suffers a crisis, for Anne is seduced by one of the local actors, Frans (Hasse Ekman), while Albert visits his estranged wife and son.

In the course of the evening circus performance, Albert and Frans have a fight in the sawdust ring. Albert is defeated, and next morning the troupe moves on, with the circus owner and his mistress again walking beside each other, caught in a vice by their own weakness and vanity. Love is seen by Bergman in this film, as it is by Strindberg in his plays, as a ghastly, totally unsatisfactory function.

Shortly after the film opens, Albert recalls an incident in which Frost (Anders Ek), his clown, was humiliated by his wife, Alma (Gudrun Brost), on the beach. This flashback has become one of the most celebrated of all Bergman sequences, and from a technical and dramatic standpoint it was the most arresting piece of film he had created.

In the original screenplay, the scene takes place in a quarry, where some soldiers are at work beneath a glaring sun. But when Bergman found the perfect location at Sindishamn, he decided to change the scene to the shoreline. Sunlight beats down on the rocks and waves as Alma, dressed in her finery, saunters seductively toward the water and responds to the soldiers' taunts (the film is set at the turn of the century). As she bathes in the nude, Bergman cuts like a surgeon from face to face, while at the same time restricting the sound to an incessant drumming, punctuated with the reverberation of cannon fire.

The opening flashback becomes a germ cell for the film. Frost's humiliation, as he drags his naked wife back to the tents across the stony landscape, will be mirrored in Albert's experience in the circus ring after Anne has betrayed him. Grotesque in his glittering costume and chalky makeup, he resembles some baroque martyr as he staggers ever more pitifully over the sharp rocks. Tears of sweat course down his face. At last he collapses like Christ on the way to Calvary, and Alma is left clinging to him in shame and remorse.

As huge close-ups of mouths, laughing and shouting, fill the screen, one thinks inevitably of Eisenstein and the Odessa Steps sequence of *Battleship Potemkin*, but it is an association alien to Bergman, who regarded Eisenstein with some disdain at the period and had not seen *Potemkin*. There is a more direct link with E. A. Dupont's silent movie

Harriet Andersson (Anne) *and Åke Grönberg* (Albert Johansson) *in* The Naked Night. *Photo courtesy Sandrew Film & Teater.*

Variety, starring Emil Jannings in a similar environment. It was the first film Bergman had bought for his collection, and he has said "It fascinated me so much that I consciously imitated it."[9] But Dupont did not use light in the way Bergman does in this sequence. "My nightmares are always saturated in sunshine. I hate the south, where I'm exposed to incessant sunlight," complains Bergman.[10] Harsh sun is in his eyes a threat, a terrifying phenomenon of the natural world. Evidence of this "heliophobia" may be found in later films such as *Wild Strawberries* and *Hour of the Wolf.* The palpable glare of this sequence was created in the laboratory. A negative was made up from the print, and then a new print from that negative. Yet another negative was struck, until the graininess of the image disappeared entirely, leaving only the stark contrast of black and white.

The characters in *The Naked Night* struggle to move from one type of existence to another but are drawn back inexorably into their original orbit. The masks of the theater disguise meanings as much as they conceal faces. Anne is attracted to this half-real world of masks and players as a moth is to a flame. Conversely Frans, the simpering, mannered actor, is aroused by the earthiness and childlike sensuality of this bareback rider. "You stake your lives, we our vanity," says Sjuberg (Gunnar Björnstrand), the theater director, to Albert. All men, according to Bergman, try to live up to their appearances. The moment of truth is the moment when the mask is torn aside and the real face uncovered. Every Bergman film turns on this process. The mask is shown, examined, and then removed. That is why the close-up forms such a vital part of Bergman's grammar.

The theme of the couple involved in a war of attrition has already been established in earlier Bergman movies, but *The Naked Night* introduces a more complex vision of life. In addition to the sexual skirmishing, a fundamental clash occurs between two kinds of personality. As Max von Sydow has pointed out,

> There is the very sensitive, highly emotional individual who cannot bear his own feelings. He is usually destroyed by the second type of character, the one who is inhibited by his intellect, who has never had any real emotional experience and longs to be almost the victim of an emotional explosion just in order to feel something.[11]

Bergman himself is constantly struggling between these two extremes, and this conflict provides the basic rubato for all his major works of the fifties.

Another motif that enters Bergman's cinema at this point is the notion of the journey as a metaphor for life itself and the discoveries

Harriet Andersson (Anne) *and Åke Grönberg* (Albert Johansson) *after the fight in* The Naked Night. *Photo courtesy Sandrew Film & Teater.*

en route, a journey moreover that unfolds in circular terms: *The Naked Night, The Seventh Seal, Wild Strawberries, The Magician,* and *The Virgin Spring* all take place within a rigorous twenty-four-hour time span, and the characters usually depart as they entered, chastened by experience but treading on the same soil as if in some kind of *perpetuum mobile.*

The relationships in *The Naked Night* impinge on one another, so that the crisis between Albert and Anne cannot be viewed in isolation. In one short scene, Bergman breathes extraordinary feeling into the affinity between Albert and Agda (Annika Tretow), his wife; in another, he creates an erotic tension and collusion between Anne and Frans. But the film is directed from the viewpoint of Albert. When drunk, he can perceive his own predicament. "We're stuck fast in Hell!" he exclaims. "Poor Anne!" he says on another occasion—exactly the same words as Ester addresses to her sister in *The Silence* (in both instances the one who speaks is trapped as hopelessly as the one who is pitied). Albert longs to be in America. It remains an elusive dream.

Anne thinks she can escape from the miserable tyranny of her lover when she sleeps with Frans, only to find that she has been deceived and must return to the circus or face that most deadly of Bergmanian fates—loneliness.

Each is as jealous as the other. When Albert leaves the caravan to see his wife Agda for the first time in three years, Anne cries bitterly. Albert exhibits his anger in more melodramatic and clumsy a fashion.

He challenges Frans to a fistfight in the ring during the evening performance under the Big Top. He is the bull, Frans the matador. He can but charge, while his opponent dances aside with mincing steps, tormenting him with stinging blows to the face and heart. When Albert falls to his knees, Frans kicks sawdust into his bloodied features, obscuring his vision. The parallel with Frost's humiliation on the beach is strengthened by Bergman's use of the same soldiers, gazing on in amusement from the ringside, who watched the incident with Alma seven years earlier.

Like the bull in the *corrida*, Albert cannot distinguish between illusion and reality. He survives physically, but he is destroyed vicariously when he himself staggers out to the cage where Alma keeps her bear and shoots his animal counterpart. By killing the bear, Albert not only purges his own humiliation and cowardice at being unable to turn the gun on himself but also avenges Frost, who was debased in the same manner. This allows him a sense of release, of catharsis. He has eliminated that part of his own being that is fettered in anguish, mortification, and scorn.

Alma weeps over the bear's corpse just as she wept over her husband in the flashback. Bergman himself denies the symbolic significance of the bear, seeing it only as the object of Albert's blind need to inflict cruelty on someone in his own agony; he knows the animal belongs to Alma, and she is somehow the person he wants to hurt most because of her treatment of Frost. (The scenes involving the bear were quite perilous; Gudrun Brost, who played Alma, remembers how nervous she was when the bear embraced her and took sugar from her lips. It blundered out among the extras, who promptly ran off, leaving Gudrun to cope with the bear along with a man equipped with a chain and a revolver. Harriet Andersson was the only one of the group who made friends with the animal.)

Frost remains a parallel to Albert. Even when drunk he urges Albert to dispatch not merely the bear but Alma too. ("That would be merciful," he drools.) And Frost's concluding remarks, as the circus prepares to set out on yet another journey, express in allegorical terms Albert's own secret desires: "Alma said to me, you can sleep in peace in my womb. So I became smaller and smaller until I was only a seed—and then I was gone."

For all its ornamental atmosphere, *The Naked Night* may be seen as a chamber play featuring six characters, Frost and Alma, Frans and Agda, Albert and Anne. Agda is like a mother to Albert. She seems sexually frigid, but she looks after him as she does their son. She offers to sew a new button on his jacket, and as he takes it off his false shirtcuffs dangle ridiculously on his fat arms. Albert, pathetic and self-deprecating in her presence, longs for the competent Agda to allow him to rejoin the nuclear family. "You yearn to be safe and snug," she has told him scornfully. When she remarks that, for her, the quietness of an old-fashioned room represents fulfillment, he replies that it strikes him as "emptiness." Domestic life attracts Albert, but he realizes that he is condemned to the picaresque life of the circus. His restlessness suggests both a basic insecurity and a desire for self-knowledge, traits common to all the major Bergman figures of the fifties and sixties. Rejected by Agda, insulted by the director of the theater, mocked and degraded by Frans, afraid to commit suicide when he has the opportunity, Albert by the end of the film has no room for maneuver. Distressed, defeated, deceived, the Bergman protagonist continues to undertake his forlorn hopes and pursue his shifting loyalties.

Bergman shot the scenes involving Albert in a heavy, almost brutal fashion. The compositions are drained of subtlety, as if to reflect the stupor of Albert's personality. The camera watches Albert lurch toward it until his puffy face, in huge close-up, dominates the screen, excluding all other characters and considerations. But in the sequences at the theater, featuring Anne and Frans, the style is quite different. Anne becomes mesmerized by the weird, outlandish surroundings of the greenroom, with masks and mirrors at every turn, and the malevolent Frans materializing suddenly at her side.

The mirror in Frans's dressing room permits the spectator to spy on Anne and to detect her weakness, her inability to hide her craving for the amulet dangled before her by the actor. Like Mephistopheles, Frans persuades his victim to sell herself for a worthless trinket. Bergman was impressed when he read Thomas Mann's *Doctor Faustus*, and this insidious relationship between body and soul has haunted Swedish art since Strindberg.

Frans, like all "actors" in the Bergman canon, is unable to feel true emotion. The falsity of the stage pursues him into private life. He is the epitome of vanity, as Bergman shows so wittily when Frans stabs himself during rehearsal with a stage knife and proceeds to "die" before an empty house, to the accompaniment of simulated thunder from the wings. "I am but a poor jester in his farce of dark shadows," he has begun, and the rhetoric takes on a horrible logic, just as the blundering antics of the clowns in the ring create a climate of spectacle in which it becomes difficult to disentangle pain from mere pained expression.

Bergman's mastery of cinematic technique requires no qualification. Here is a director in total control of his material, able to select with almost diabolical ease precisely the appropriate sound, light, or camera angle for any given scene. When Albert and Anne arrive at the theater and ask Sjuberg if they may borrow some costumes, they speak *from* the stage, with the footlights exposing their pitiful rig-out and the low camera angles stressing their discomfort. The mirrors in the theater and inside Albert's caravan obviate the need for conventional cross-cutting and add a density to the image, a look of abnormality. Reality is confused with its own reflections, as in the opening scene of the film, when the coaches are glimpsed in the polished surface of a river before the camera swings up to observe the vehicles themselves.

For the music, Bergman approached Karl-Birger Blomdahl, one of Sweden's foremost modern composers. The result was a magnificent and profoundly disturbing score, full of stabbing, grating chords and dissonances, even if the optical soundtrack could scarcely cope with music performed by a forty-piece wind orchestra. The costumes, evocative of the turn-of-the-century setting, were designed by Max Goldstein (known professionally as Mago), who had first met Bergman the day before his wedding to Else Fisher in 1943. They had had a cup of tea together during rehearsals for a production of *Julius Caesar* at Mäster-Olofs-gården, and Bergman had said to him: "One day we'll work together." Ten years later he called Mago to work on *The Naked Night*, and it was the beginning of a long and rich collaboration. Bergman studied in-numerable sketches and drawings before he was satisfied with the costume designs, which were influenced by the German UFA style just as Bergman's own visual approach came from the twenties and the expressionism of Dupont, Lang, and Murnau.

The response to *The Naked Night* when it opened on September 14, 1953, was appalling. The leading critics loathed and detested the film. The fight in the circus ring, although stylized, produced a feeling of revulsion among the Swedes. So too did Bergman's view of life as coarse and sweaty.

The film was greeted fairly by *Dagens Nyheter* and *Svenska Dag-bladet*, but the influential critics—those whose opinion counted among the intelligentsia—were violent in their condemnation, especially Bengt Idestam-Almquist, regarded as the doyen of Swedish movie commenta-tors. Bergman was in Malmö when the film opened and was shattered by the notices. He almost broke down on the phone when Rune Waldekranz called him. In the context of his career, the dismissal of *The Naked Night* was almost as traumatic an incident as the taxation affair of 1976.

The film ran quite respectably in Stockholm but was a complete failure in the provinces. Even in such a big town as Karlstad it was screened only over a single weekend—and then more than a year after its original release, so disliked was the film by exhibitors.

There was some compensation for Bergman in the reception of *The Naked Night* outside Sweden. After a screening during the Cannes

Festival, a South American distributor from Montevideo was so fascinated by it that he flew to Stockholm and purchased several other Swedish films.

And not all the reviews sounded negative.

Mauritz Edström, then just embarking on a career that would make him one of Sweden's most impressive critics, wrote: "Bergman has made a damned good film, better than most that have been done in the country." Carl Björkman felt that it was Bergman's most assured artistic success, and Nils Beyer said that *The Naked Night* was Bergman's best movie to date. Even Idestam-Almquist recanted to some degree when he wrote in *Stockholms-Tidningen* that one's first feelings of repulsion had to be overcome and the importance of the film recognized.

How ironic that a film dealing, in essence, with tolerance—tolerance in all its perplexing disguises—should have been greeted with such want of forebearance!

In the wake of this failure, Bergman was anxious to strike out on a new tack. "I really felt I had to make a commercial success very quickly. Everyone was saying, 'Bergman is finished.' "[12] He and Harriet Andersson spent some days at Arild, and while she sunbathed, Bergman read books in a rented turret room in a nearby villa. From this mood of relaxation, in the euphoria of having finished what he was certain was a good film, and before the storm of rejection that would break in September, he began to develop the idea of *A Lesson in Love*. He sent his screenplay to Sandrews, but the executives were on vacation. So Bergman forwarded a copy to Carl Anders Dymling at Svensk Filmindustri. Dymling was enthusiastic and summoned Bergman to Stockholm. Two weeks later the budget and schedule had been agreed.

The relationship between Bergman and Dymling, if not quite of Pygmalion proportions, was certainly crucial during the fifties. "As a rule," said Dymling, "he and I discuss a picture in detail and at length *before* he starts shooting it. Then we go on talking about it *after* he has finished shooting and editing the picture. Only when the rough cut is ready do we look at it together."[13] Dymling was not in a position to sanction all Bergman's ideas, but he was adept at persuading his board to accept most projects in which he believed. He trusted Bergman when the chips were down and at a time when Bergman was by no means accepted as a national institution.

One tends to agree with Bergman's own description of *A Lesson in Love* as a mere *divertissement*. The figure of Dr. David Erneman's wife is based in part on Gun Grut; her marriage with Bergman had collapsed in the face of his affair with Harriet Andersson, although there remained a friendship between them. Eva Dahlbeck and Gunnar

Björnstrand had demonstrated in the concluding episode of *Secrets of Women* that they were an adroit comedy team, and their sparring has a more satisfying ring to it than the incessant wrangling of Bergman's younger couples from *Prison, Thirst,* and *Summer Interlude.* Idealism has been supplanted by an empirical wisdom. Intelligence, rather than sexual purity, is at a premium in the world of Bergman's sophisticated comedies. There is a maturity about the reasoning of Erneman and Marianne, if not about their behavior. Like their youthful predecessors, they are anxious to flout convention, but they are old enough to recognize that they are bound by the whims of life and that this form of dual survival need be neither as dull nor as harassing as it appears.

Their remarks are tinged with acerbity, not despair. "Life at its best is cooperative," sighs Erneman and then comments on man: "Woman needs him for procreation, otherwise he counts for nothing." His wife, like all the heroines in Bergman's comedies, is down to earth and sarcastic, mocking her partner and mothering him at the same time. Just as Bergman is torn between male idealists and rationalists, so his loyalties are divided between those women who accommodate and tend their partner's inadequacies and those who strike back at the male sex with seasoned blows.

David Erneman is a gynecologist who, having been married for sixteen years, yields to the charms of Susanne (Yvonne Lombard), a patient in his clinic, and embarks on an affair that disrupts his marriage. Marianne, the wife, flounces off to Copenhagen to sleep with her former fiance, Carl-Adam (Åke Grönberg), a rather boorish sculptor. David eventually gives up his relationship with Susanne and recaptures his wife despite the opposition of Carl-Adam during a brawl in a Danish nightclub. Even within the confines of a light comedy, one is faced with the typical Bergman situation of an individual in whom a crisis brings about a fundamental change of attitude to himself and to life.

Erneman is in the throes of the male menopause. "I want your fire to burn away my apathy," he tells his mistress. But a day in the country with his teenage daughter, Nix (Harriet Andersson), shows him that he is out of touch with this girl, his own child. Nix's rebelliousness prompts Erneman to reconsider his philandering as a way of life, and he sets about retrieving the affections of Marianne.

One of the richest sequences in the film takes place in a forest, when Erneman and his wife lie side by side in the summer heat and talk about their dreams. Marianne craves just one more child; David longs for a diver's outfit to explore tropical seas. Another touching moment involves Erneman's aged father (Olof Winnerstrand), who tells his granddaughter that death is but a part of life. "Think how dreary it would be if everything were the same, always, always. Therefore there

Gunnar Björnstrand (Dr. David Erneman) *and Eva Dahlbeck* (Marianne Erneman) *in* A Lesson in Love. *Photo courtesy Svensk Filmindustri.*

is death, so that there may come new life for all eternity. Think only how tiresome it would be for me to wear long underdrawers a hundred thousand years."[14]

The film ends on a note outrageous and impudent in its optimism. A little boy, dressed as Cupid, waddles along the corridor into the room where husband and wife, reunited after a night of roistering in Copenhagen, are sipping champagne. Bergman uses this effect again in *The Devil's Eye*, when Gunnar Björnstrand, the Narrator, manages also to convey in his eyes a look of indulgent salaciousness after "witnessing" the affirmation of love in a bridal chamber.

Bergman enjoyed making *A Lesson in Love* and experimented with narrative structure to such a witty degree that not until midway through the film does it become plain that Erneman and Marianne are married. The rapport between Björnstrand and Dahlbeck, in the manner of Tracy and Hepburn, was so good that when Bergman suggested cutting a particular scene from the screenplay they both chased him off the set and rehearsed it together. Bergman made some phone calls and cashed some checks. "When I got back," he says, "they had rehearsed a wildly funny scene."[15]

During the fifties, Bergman was working seven months out of every twelve in the theater. With two features behind him in 1953, he still managed to produce both Pirandello's *Six Characters in Search of an Author* and Kafka's *The Castle* on the small stage at Malmö as well as prepare a radio version of Strindberg's *The Dutchman*, which was broadcast on October 9.

His productions at Malmö were notable for their invention and dramatic flair. *The Castle*, for example, took place on a bare stage containing a few sticks of furniture and no set decorations whatever. But Bergman fought shy of mutilating the original. "I cannot and will not stage a play contrary to a writer's intentions," he said. "And I never have. . . . I've always seen myself as an interpreter, a reflector."[16] The fact is that Bergman has occasionally cut plays, including *A Dream Play*, but perhaps all for the better.

If there was any hesitancy remaining in Malmö about the worth of Bergman's appointment, then his two major productions of the following year would dispel it. *The Ghost Sonata*, which opened in March 1954, stretched the cunning and resourcefulness of the stage managers to the full. Bergman narrowed the proscenium opening to forty-six feet (from its usual seventy-two), reduced the seating capacity to a mere eleven hundred (from the customary seventeen hundred), and raised the stage, extending it out over the auditorium. In his program notes, he paid tribute to his idol, Olof Molander, whose productions had so impressed him in youth. "This evening's production can perhaps be called a love-child. My Civic Center experiments are the mother, fructified by Molander's *The Ghost Sonata*. And the child—well, of course, the child takes strongly after both parents, without being a slavish copy of either. Rather the contrary, for he has certainly gone his own ways."[17]

The tone of the drama was muted, as Strindberg had specified, and each character was allowed to emerge in clearly defined colors. Benkt-Åke Benktsson, who weighed thirty stone, was a massive Hummel, and Naima Wifstrand (later celebrated for her roles as the old grandmother in both *Wild Strawberries* and *The Magician*) played the Mummy, who finally has her revenge on the old man and sends Hummel to his death in a dark closet.

In the fall came *The Merry Widow*, in honor of the tenth anniversary of the Malmö Municipal Theater. Operetta had been ignored by serious producers in Sweden, but now Bergman, sensing the potential of the huge stage and auditorium, established a relationship with the city's public that made Lehar's effervescent musical comedy the most popular success in the history of the theater. Can-can dancers fanned out over the horseshoe-shaped bridge at the front of the stage, and French perfume was sprayed into the stalls. The performance was as

light and as heady as champagne, and the audience clamored to see it.
Bergman, said Henrik Sjögren, "so far from ironizing over [*The Merry
Widow*'s] fairy-tale world, treated it on the contrary with a kind of
tender respect."[18]

Dreams (*Kvinnodröm*, also known as *Journey into Autumn*) occupied
the summer months of 1954. Once again Sandrews gambled on Bergman
—and lost. The film was too somber to succeed with the general public
and insufficiently exotic to attract foreign interest. The part of the
courtly diplomat, Consul Sönderby, was written with Anders Henrikson
in mind. Henrikson, who had played the count in the film of *Miss Julie*,
was unable to take the role, and Gunnar Björnstrand replaced him.

Susanne (Eva Dahlbeck) owns a fashion photography studio. Her
favorite model, Doris (Harriet Andersson), has just broken off her engagement to a young student. When Susanne has to visit Gothenburg
to take a series of photographs with Doris as model, she makes contact
with her former lover, a married man named Henrik Lobelius (a last
name that crops up repeatedly in Bergman's films, as do Egerman and
Vergérus), played by Ulf Palme. Doris, meanwhile, encounters an
elderly consul, who offers her jewels and expensive clothes merely to
attract her companionship. The consul's daughter, Marianne (Kerstin
Hedeby), arrives on the scene and attacks her father's egotism. Doris,
it transpires, strikingly resembles the consul's wife, now insane.

The two episodes involving Susanne and Doris dovetail cleverly into
each other so that by the end of the film several similarities between
them have become discernible. For the first time, Bergman's interest in
musical form is apparent: The effect of *Dreams* is that of a double fugue.
And again there is the circular, claustrophobic logic of the story line:
the movie begins and closes in the same setting (the fashion salon), a
device that Bergman almost invariably deploys. He does not like his
plots to proceed in a straight line. If they did, they would lose the feeling
of enclosure that generates the drama.

For both Susanne and Doris, the journey to Gothenburg is an excursion into the nether zone, a brush with Death from which they emerge
shaken. Lobelius on the one hand, and the consul on the other, are
painted in livid, cadaverous terms. In the dingy hotel room where
Susanne and Henrik arrange to meet, the atmosphere of futility and
departure dominate the small talk. "I feel tired and hunted," sighs
Henrik, telling her that he's about to be ruined financially. "I've no
desire, and not enough strength, to start all over again." Against his
better judgment, he makes love to her one last time in an effort to elude
his misery. When Susanne asks him if he will regret the interlude, he
answers, "I shall both have regrets and be happy for it at the same time"

Gunnar Björnstrand (Consul Sönderby) and Harriet Andersson (Doris) in Dreams. *Photo courtesy Sandrew Film & Teater.*

—a remark that could easily be spoken by the consul too. Both men see in these women a chance to return to the tender safety of childhood. But the dreams of the unfortunate couple are interrupted by the arrival of Henrik's wife who, like the consul's daughter, pours scorn on their blighted hopes. She accuses Susanne of wanting a child so that Henrik would be tied more securely to her, and adds, "We women have a wonderful gift for romanticizing our reasons for persuasion." She tells her husband that she is no longer jealous and thus poisons his affair with her assurance more effectively than she ever could with tears.

The episode involving Doris and the consul rhymes with the story of Henrik and Susanne. Doris is gazing enviously into a show window when the figure of the consul slides in alongside her. His reflected image, like the costly clothes on display, has an insubstantial and exotic quality; his beard conjures up a momentary Mephistophelian association. This feeling rises again when, having submitted to his flattering offers, Doris comments that he can arrange anything.

"Yes," replies the consul. "I can arrange anything. I'm quite a wizard —as you can see."

Doris is not yet sure of what she must sacrifice in exchange for the magnificent dress, shoes, and jewelry that this affable stranger gives her so freely. Even their excursion to the Liseberg amusement park fails to impress on her the tragic aspect of the whole business. Bergman converts this sequence into a tragi-comic demonstration of the incompatibility of their ages. The consul is exhausted by successive trips on "The Big Dipper," "The Whirlwind," and "The Terror Express." As he emerges from the funfair, he slips to the ground in mid-shot. Bergman cuts to a high angle so that the camera stares dispassionately down on him as he invents a flurry of excuses to delay his getting to his feet.

The consul's villa bears a likeness to a mausoleum. But Doris's host is as relaxed in these surroundings as she was in the bright outdoors. Doris reminds him of his wife who, he tells her, thought that their daughter had the head of a wolf and who has been confined to a mental institution for twenty-three years. When Doris does at last invite him to take advantage of her, he feels too weak and feeble to accept. His daughter bursts in and demands money from him.

"Why do you hate me?" he asks, with that pang of self-contempt so familiar in Bergman's films.

The daughter accuses him of being unbearably parsimonious with money and of withholding her rightful inheritance. When she discovers Doris, cowering in the bedroom, she remarks, "But now the lust has conquered the meanness and the result is rather comical." A clock resounds calmly in the background, and one realizes the inescapable truth of the accusation. This vulpine girl represents reality, the guilty conscience, the destruction of dreams. Although Bergman does not as a rule use amateur players, he gave this part to Kerstin Hedeby, his production designer at Malmö, and she invested it with a cool and threatening authority.

Doris perceives that the price of her Faustian weakness is the annihilation of her romantic illusions. Susanne acknowledges that her affair with Henrik is terminated; when he sends a letter to the studio suggesting a clandestine meeting in Oslo, she tears it up.

"It's only the usual begging letter," she explains to the lecherous fashion director, Magnus.

Bergman's characters in this middle period are forever attempting to break out of their set pattern of existence. They always fail. Doris flings herself into the arms of the fiancé with whom she has had such a tiff in the opening sequence, while Susanne resumes her role as the chic, elegantly coiffured proprietress of her salon. Both women have laid aside their masks for a brief moment, but the security of their daily lives proves more compelling than the temptations of an arid, furtive affair. Seen in a social context, this amounts to an extremely conservative attitude. Bergman seems to be chiding his characters for essaying emotional risks.

Dreams may be viewed as both the last film of Bergman's youth and the first of his middle age. Its production also coincided with the end of his relationship with Harriet Andersson. In the years ahead, Bergman would learn to transmute his reactionary pessimism into more stimulating and inspiring terms.

CHAPTER EIGHT

The Golden Years

BY THE MID-FIFTIES, INGMAR BERGMAN HAD ACQUIRED A STEADINESS OF purpose and pattern of life that enabled him to keep in rein his innermost fears and insecurity. Carl Anders Dymling spoke of his extraordinary will power. "He is a high-strung personality, passionately alive, enormously sensitive, very short-tempered, sometimes quite ruthless in his pursuit of his own goals, suspicious, stubborn, capricious, most unpredictable."[1]

Not a flattering picture.

Yet Bergman aroused an intense loyalty, affection even, among those who worked and lived alongside him in Malmö. Friendship has always been important to him. In his creative work, Bergman needs colleagues he can dominate and colleagues he can protect. His discipline renders him seemingly unemotional, objective, prone to dissect those with whom he comes in contact. "You cannot refuse Ingmar," is a refrain one hears from those who have associated with him through the years. He admits that he is aggressive by nature, "and I often find it hard to repress my aggressiveness."[2]

His routine extended to Stockholm, where he frequently stayed in a small apartment while shooting interiors or editing a new movie. He gathered with friends at the Sturehov Restaurant on Stureplan, famous for its fish specialties. Gunnar Björnstrand, Harriet Andersson, Ulla Jacobsson, Eva Dahlbeck, Mago, and others would sit around the appointed table discussing the film of the day and the isssues of the moment. Tillie Björnstrand, Gunnar's wife, recalls Bergman's "violent sense of humor, which concealed a deep streak of *angst* and melancholy," as well as a pronounced intuition and sensitivity.[3]

These dinners constituted Bergman's main meal of the day. Bibi Andersson describes his invariable lunch as consisting of "some kind of whipped sour milk, very fat, and strawberry jam, very sweet—a strange kind of baby food he eats with cornflakes."[4] As noted in Chapter 7, he spent so much of his waking time at the theater in Malmö that few hours remained for reading or relaxation. Not that Bergman has ever been a bookworm, but he could not survive without a diet of old movies. "I had a longing for contact," he said, apropos of his screening sessions with the crew and the actors. "When we had been in the studio all day, I wanted to maintain the contact. I couldn't stay away from my friends. We gave each other experiences, we taught each other things, we lived together. We were all in a permanent state of curiosity."[5] As Mago says, "With Bergman, you can have a personal contact from morning to night—other directors were always surrounded by assistants."[6]

In fact, Bergman did rely to a marked degree on an assistant. From 1954 until the end of the Malmö period, the "sorcerer's apprentice" was Lennart Olsson. In the early sixties, Lenn Hjortzberg devoted himself to Bergman's business and administrative chores, even to rounding up the livestock to fill the farmyard in *The Virgin Spring*. It was a factotum's role, for Bergman squeezed every ounce of potential from the day, and stage or film set had to be prepared exactly to his prior instructions by the time he made his appearance.

Just as Bergman's precision in daily life masked his doubts and anguish, so his technical mastery of the film medium disguised the frantic turmoil and metaphysical debate that lay at the core of each new movie. Intuition and diligence, a rare combination, joined forces in his art.

During the spring of 1955, Bergman produced three plays at Malmö. *Don Juan* opened on January 4 in the small Intima Theater. Some critics felt that Bergman's desire for shock effects may have diminished his intellectual concept of Molière's play. But on the whole the response was enthusiastic. The appearance of the awesome Statue, who consigns Don Juan to Hell, beside the ghost of Donna Elvira (her face a skull behind a veil), was one of those *echt*-Bergman touches and a scene that he would recreate for the cinema in *The Devil's Eve* (1960).

Another coup was the first entrance of Don Juan, in the words of Henrik Sjögren, "yawning after the night's pleasures, with his bare thigh protruding from the elegant pleating of his nightshirt, itching himself from the fleabites, and on his head a cap with two bright red horns, those attributes of the buck and the devil, adorned with crests and bells."[7]

A month later, on the big stage, Bergman directed John Patrick's study of the clash between East and West, *The Teahouse of the August Moon*, set during the American occupation of Okinawa. This comedy was not entirely to Bergman's taste or perhaps within his grasp. He abandoned the idea of verisimilitude in casting or setting, opting instead for coarse-cut caricature and satire.

Painting on Wood, Bergman's own one-acter, opened in March and formed the basis for *The Seventh Seal*.

Steeped in Molière, and with the triumph of Lehar's *The Merry Widow* still ringing in his ears, Bergman went up to Dalarna, took a room at his favorite hotel on Lake Siljan, and set to work on the screenplay of *Smiles of a Summer Night*. As *A Lesson in Love* had marked a successful return to Svensk Filmindustri, and as Bergman preferred the facilities of that company's studios at Råsunda to the more primitive stages of Sandrews, so *Smiles of a Summer Night* became an SF production.

Bergman claims that the budget was between 350,000 and 400,000 Swedish crowns (around $75,000), although others have put the figure as high as 750,000 ($150,000). There is no doubt that the film was the costliest of the thirty-seven Swedish productions being made in 1955. It was also the most expensive film Bergman had ever shot. The unit and actors were involved for fifty-five days until, Bergman recalls, "We were all on the verge of a nervous breakdown."[8] Exterior photography began on July 21, in Jordeberga castle, three miles south of Malmö. The delightful little theater in which Desirée Armfeldt performs was inspired by the small rococo stage in the town of Ystad.

Smiles of a Summer Night (*Sommarnattens leende*), like many of the world's great comedies, was written and directed during a somber period in its creator's life. The very fact that it was a comedy derived from Bergman's anxiety over his income at the time ("I'd promised Carl Anders Dymling that my next film wouldn't be a tragedy. . . . I needed money, so I thought it wiser to make a comedy"[9]); and the romance with Harriet Andersson had faded.

The summer of 1955 in Sweden grew almost unbearably hot. The gas lamps in the studio "theater" expired for want of oxygen, and tempers ran high. On certain occasions, Bergman would announce that his stomach was giving him hell, and Lennart Olsson was asked to take over and deal with the large crew and cast, most of whom were made up and ready to perform. Bergman told Olsson of his fear that, if the film were a flop, Svensk Filmindustri might sever relations with him altogether. He was also worried because his leading lady, Ulla Jacobsson, was pregnant when shooting began. The secret was restricted to only a very few members of the cast, and Mago had to design costumes that would conceal any changes in the petite actress's figure.

Marianne Höök has said, "In its enormous whiteness, *Smiles of a Summer Night* possesses all the nuances of a color movie and a joy in the rendering of the material which is seldom found in film but often in painting." First and foremost, this visual felicity is a tribute to the genius of Gunnar Fischer, Bergman's cinematographer. But the sumptuous costumes concocted by Mago and the period sets created by P. A. Lundgren also contribute to the evocation of a vanished world of wealth and fastidiousness. When a stage version of the film, *A Little Night Music*, opened on Broadway, there was a similar emphasis on costume design and extravagant settings.

Fredrik Egerman (Gunnar Björnstrand), a prosperous lawyer, has a new young wife, Anne (Ulla Jacobsson). During a visit to the theater, he goes backstage to arrange a rendezvous with his former mistress, Desirée Armfeldt (Eva Dahlbeck). Desirée's lover of the moment is Count Malcolm (Jarl Kulle), who is affronted by the presence of Egerman. Desirée engineers an elaborate house party at her mother's manor in order to bring about a confrontation between Malcolm and Egerman, to whom she is drawn somewhat more profoundly than she will admit.

At the party Egerman's son by an earlier marriage, Henrik (Björn Bjelvenstam), finds himself attracted by the innocent Anne; Petra (Harriet Andersson), Anne's maid, strikes up a lusty relationship with Frid (Åke Fridell), old Mrs. Armfeldt's (Naima Wifstrand) groom; and the lawyer is seduced by the count's wife, Charlotte (Margit Carlqvist), with the result that he has to fight a duel by Russian roulette with his rival. But the gun contains a blank cartridge filled with soot, and Egerman, although humiliated, survives to regain the affections of Desirée.

Bergman is not a humorist by nature, even if he may be by inclination. His comedies amount to a reaction to his icy delvings into the human soul. The joke is often at the expense of the director himself. An amusing line is heard spoken offscreen before the credits of *A Lesson in Love*: "This comedy might have been a tragedy—but the gods were kind." The gods were certainly kind to *Smiles of a Summer Night*.

Egerman is close to being a tragic figure. He suffers the fate of all those Bergman heroes who cannot yield to instinct. He finds himself too circumscribed by pedantic dignity to indulge his fancies. His brief physical escapade with Charlotte is interrupted by Count Malcolm, and even the duel turns out to be a degradation worse than death—which

Jarl Kulle (Count Carl-Magnus Malcolm) *and* Gunnar Björnstrand *in the Russian roulette sequence from* Smiles of a Summer Night. *Photo courtesy Svensk Filmindustri.*

Egerman would surely prefer in the circumstances. Yet this suave, courtly individual remains the most sympathetic person in the film because he recognizes that man must revise his values if he is to endure. He makes one smile with him when he scores off the bristling count in their bout of repartee in Desirée's dressing room. He makes one nod in agreement when he teases Henrik for his hypocrisy.

Desirée is the perfect partner for him because she possesses both a sense of social comportment and an ability to express her appetites in a language that Egerman can accept without being appalled. Her self-pity is organized along strictly practical lines. Aware of her fading youth, Desirée is unwilling to settle for promises of paradise. "No, Fredrik Egerman, I want my reward in *this* world," she demands, biting his finger savagely. Such hedonism also runs in the blood of Fredrik's meek and virgin wife, Anne. But when the opportunity arises, she snatches at it eagerly, without the sardonic calculation that Desirée brings to such affairs. She runs off with Henrik, while Egerman watches aghast in the background. And so Egerman is left to arrive most painfully at his eventual salvation—a relationship with Desirée.

Smiles of a Summer Night makes fun of society's attitudes toward sex. The higher the social class, the more inhibited and attenuated the ritual of love. Anne and Henrik (a theology student, no less) suffer the worst pangs and cherish the greatest illusions. When Henrik accuses his father of joking about everything, Egerman replies tartly, "So will you—the day you learn your folly and the insignificance of your illusions." Charlotte and her Count Malcolm are foils to the hesitancy and discretion of this young couple. Their desires emerge in forceful, confident fashion, but both are in the end bound to the conventions of their upper-class pedigree. Malcolm triumphs over Egerman in the duel but places more importance on the humiliation of his rival than on the retrieval of his mistress.

Charlotte, a feline seductress who despises her husband, suddenly cries to Anne in an unguarded moment: "I hate him! I hate him! Men are beastly! They are silly and vain and have hair all over their bodies. . . . Love is a disgusting business!" The outburst is flung into the camera with such controlled viciousness that one recoils, faintly irritated that one's preconceptions about these elegant characters should be so roughly destroyed.

But sex amounts to the same mechanical principle at whatever level of society it rears its head. Only the form of expression differs. Frid, the groom at the manor, is an uninhibited satyr whose lust for Petra, the maid, is spelled out in two beautifully patterned sequences, the first in the park where Frid pursues his giggling prey between the trees to the accompaniment of equine whinnying, and the second in the hay, where the couple frolic lasciviously and Frid, drawing in a deep breath, exclaims in exultant tones: "There isn't a better life than this!"

Frid is one of those simple beings who relishes love as a form of nourishment divested from idealism. "The love of lovers is denied to us," he says. "We invoke love, call out for it, beg for it, cry for it, try to imitate it, think that we have it, lie about it." Frid's paganism is unconcealed, while in Egerman impulse cannot match comportment.

Throughout the film, everyone pillories the roles of others and yet cannot avoid performing himself. And the more grotesque the mask, the greater the embarrassment of its wearer at the moment of disclosure. Petra and Frid need no disguise; their hedonism is more intense, and more natural, than the cultivated merriment of the party at which they serve. Only Desirée, as she sings *Freut Euch des Lebens* to the assembled guests after dinner, can match their creed. She can never relax as heartily as Frid and Petra, but her commitment to life and its sensations is equally robust.

The inflexible barriers of class maintained in this film are evidence of Bergman's fondness for the refined luxury of a past era (with its attendant vulgarity below stairs, of course). He is not attracted by the sleek, classless outlines of modern Sweden. Lennart Olsson confirms Bergman's complete indifference to politics during the Malmö period. "I cannot remember his ever expressing a political view during those years. He could see the social consequences of some political act, but he was not a political *person*, he was just not interested."[10] This was reflected not only in his films but also in his choice of plays for the Malmö Municipal Theater. None of his productions made any overt comment on the contemporary political or socioeconomic situation in Sweden. Had they done so, they would by now probably have faded into insignificance.

Bergman was by no means confident of the film's success. "I went to it and sat there thinking this is the worst fiasco I've ever known. Not a soul seemed to laugh, nobody was enjoying it, they all sat grim and silent."[11] The critics were divided. Olof Lagercrantz attacked it sharply in *Dagens Nyheter*, saying, with a bitchiness worthy of old Mrs. Armfeldt, that its jokes were suitable for the stable yard. Hanserik Hjertén, later to become critic at the same influential newspaper, also poured scorn on *Smiles* in a film magazine of the period. Word of mouth, however, was good, and Svensk Filmindustri was glad about the release. Once the film had won a major award at the Cannes Festival in 1956, foreign sales began to accelerate.

On a personal level, too, Bergman was happier now. Bibi Andersson had entered his life. She had a promising career at the Royal Dramatic Theater in Stockholm and was attached to SF's pool of actors and actresses. Bergman knew her sister, Gerd, quite well, and when one of the actors at Malmö, during a drive up to Stockholm in Bergman's ancient Volvo, suggested a Midsummer Night's party with Gerd and Bibi, the seeds of romance were sown. Bergman promised Bibi that she could have the part of Anne in *Smiles* should Ulla Jacobsson, then pregnant, wax too fat for the camera. When this failed to happen, Bergman felt embarrassed and offered Bibi a small role instead. So she may be glimpsed, fluttering about on stage in the tiny theater where Desirée Armfeldt reigns supreme.

Bibi meant a great deal to Bergman in these years. Her youth and guileless ardor inspired some of his greatest creations—Mia in *The Seventh Seal*, the Saras in *Wild Strawberries*, Hjördis in *Brink of Life*, and, on the stage, Sagan in Hjalmar Bergman's play. She was fiercely loyal to him and had the ability to stimulate him even in moments of severe depression. Her presence coincided with—or perhaps prompted— Bergman's most idealistic period.

Although they never married, Bergman and Bibi continued to work with each other through the years, their mutual successes reflecting a growing maturity on either side: *Persona, The Passion of Anna, The Touch*, and *Twelfth Night* at the Royal Dramatic Theater. In 1979 Bibi wrote an impassioned defense of Bergman's cinema in *Dagens Nyheter*, responding to those critics who had condemned it for dealing only with the upper classes. "But Bergman's films have been concerned with *feelings*," she insisted, "and we *need* to be concerned with feelings."

Bergman's influence, allied to her own determination and intelligence, succeeded in establishing Bibi as a major international actress, without in any degree subverting that first fine careless rapture of her youth. Beneath her assurance and willfulness in many recent film roles, there lie reserves of humility and gentleness. Throughout that great scene on the hillside in *The Seventh Seal*, when the Knight (Max von Sydow) speaks to her of his unhappiness and spiritual confusion, Bibi's lines are stitched unaffectedly alongside the embroidery of the Knight's eloquence. Yet she is the catalyst, the force that gives the Knight courage to pursue his destiny. So it was with her and Ingmar Bergman for more than three entrancing years.

Just before she leapt to the fore in *The Seventh Seal*, however, Bibi appeared in a leading part in *Last Couple out*, directed by Alf Sjöberg

Bibi Andersson (right) in her first small role in a Bergman film, with Birgitta Valberg in Smiles of a Summer Night. *Photo courtesy Svensk Filmindustri.*

from an idea first put to paper by Bergman around 1950 and then bought in 1952 by Svensk Filmindustri under the title *For the Children's Sake.* "It was an old script," said Sjöberg, "and marked an unhappy stage in our collaboration." The error lay in trying to resuscitate the theme of humiliation and revolt. Maria Bergom Larsson, while dismissing *Last Couple out* as a mediocre film, praises the opening sequence in which a small boy, weeping and trembling, recounts a fantasy of kicking his father's face into a bloody pulp.[12] *Echt*-Bergman.

The genesis of *The Seventh Seal* lies in *Wood Painting*, a one-act play that Bergman wrote especially for the ten students who were in his acting class at Malmö Municipal Theater. The production was by Bergman himself, in March 1955, with Gunnar Björnstrand, Gaby Stenberg, and Toivo Pawlo, in Malmö; the performance that took the critics by storm, however, was on September 16 the same year, when a different cast (this time including Bibi Andersson) played *Wood Painting* at the Royal Dramatic Theater in Stockholm under the direction of Bengt Ekerot—Ekerot, a member of the *40-talisterna*, an accomplished stage director, and the man who would play Death in *The Seventh Seal*.

Wood Painting contains several elements of *The Seventh Seal*: the fear of the plague, the burning of the witch, the Dance of Death. But the concept of the "holy couple," Jof and Mia, is missing, as is the motif of the chess game between Death and the Knight, Antonius Block. Bergman instead lays perhaps too heavy an emphasis on the tomfoolery between the smith and his vagrant wife. Only one character may be found fullblown, and that is Jöns, the Squire, whose dialog in play and film is almost identical, line for line.

To trace the origins of what is Bergman's most celebrated film, one must go back to his childhood. Henrik Sjögren regards the central theme of Bergman's plays as being "Everyman between God and the Devil,"[13] and this Manichaean vision of the world was fostered by his parents. Ever since the Reformation, Sweden had been a Protestant society in which the pastors had occupied a central place. In his scathing book on Sweden, *The New Totalitarians*, Roland Huntford has commented that it remains "one of the rare countries in which men are often antireligious, but rarely anticlerical."[14]

Even during the latter stages of the nineteenth century, when revolution was sweeping through the thought of most European nations, Scandinavia clung to its religious ideals, adumbrated in the works of Kierkegaard and in plays such as Ibsen's *Brand*. The image of God was in terms exclusively of God the Father; Jesus as a creature of flesh and blood is absent, instead He is confined to a secondary role, an anguished figure upon the Cross, set above the altar in innumerable small, bare, well-lighted churches. The asceticism of Luther prevails.

Pastor Erik Bergman acted in private life like a high priest. The odor of sanctity permeated the household. Candles were lit before breakfast on Sundays. Punishment was meted out in ritualistic ways. "One was always in the wrong," says Bergman. Expiation through suffering was the order of the day.

Bergman has of course reacted against this upbringing. But just as certain antidotes contain a degree of the poison they are meant to counteract, so the artist needs to draw on the experiences that he seeks to expunge. Orthodox religion runs in Bergman's blood. He often signs his scripts with the initials *S.D.G.* ("Soli Deo Gloria"—"To God Alone the Glory"), as J. S. Bach did at the end of every composition.[15] He is fond of quoting Eugene O'Neill's dictum that all dramatic art is worthless unless it deals with man's relationship to God.

Bergman has frequently stated that his religious struggle diminished after *Winter Light* (1961). Not so. Although the embellishments and metaphors of religion are missing from his subsequent films, all his work revolves around a conflict between light and darkness, Good and Evil, innocence and guilt, love and humiliation. Or, in Bergman's own words, "The religious problem is an intellectual one to me; the relationship of my mind to my intuition."[16]

Death was the only certainty in Bergman's childhood environment. The meaning of death, both its physical agony and its metaphysical implications, haunted Bergman in the mid-fifties and dominates three major films: *The Seventh Seal, Wild Strawberries,* and *The Magician.* "I was afraid of this enormous emptiness," he said at a press conference in Cannes. "My personal view," he announced in 1973, "is that when we die, we die, and we go from a state of something to a state of absolute nothingness, and I don't believe for a second that there's anything above or beyond, or anything like that, and this makes me enormously secure."[17]

But in 1955, when Bergman was already thirty-seven years of age, the images of the frescoes he had seen in his youth still seared his mind. Albertus Pictor was the finest of all Swedish medieval church painters. In his murals, and in those by other, anonymous artists, the theme of Death is paramount. Bergman announces at the beginning of *Wood Painting* that the story is taken direct from one such fresco, in the vestibule of a church in southern Småland. The ravages of the plague are charted over a twelve-foot span, from the entrance, where "the sun is playing over the quiet green landscape," to "the dark corner where the final incidents occur in the grayish, rain-laden dawn."

The Seventh Seal (Det sjunde inseglet) was difficult for Bergman both to write and to sell. While he was making *Dreams,* he had spoken to Rune Waldekranz at Sandrews about the notion of a screen version of *Wood Painting*, but there was no opportunity at that juncture to persuade Anders Sandrew to finance such a nebulous and potentially expensive project. Even Svensk Filmindustri was dubious, in view of the extravagance of *Smiles of a Summer Night*. (Bergman had apparently insisted on reupholstering all the furniture to create the "whiteish" look of the film.) Besides, two period films on the trot sounded far too much of a gamble. But in the spring of 1956, *Smiles* won the Jury Prize at Cannes, and the Swedish papers were full of Bergman's triumph.

Now was the moment of decision. Bergman approached Carl Anders Dymling once more, urging him to make up his mind. Dymling agreed to support the project, providing it took no more than thirty-five days to make—which it did, exactly. The screenplay, however, was still in gestation. Bergman rewrote it five times, "hidden in a small room in the gatekeeper's cabin in Råsunda."[18] The major development was the replacement of Jöns by the Knight in the main role. Originally, the Knight's character was silent. "The Saracens had cut out his tongue,"[19] comments Bergman with a nice sense of historical verismilitude, although the true reason was that, while one of the director's pupils at Malmö was sufficiently handsome to take the part, he could not deliver dialog.

At Easter, Bergman told Allan Ekelund, his production manager, how intractable the script was proving to be. So many motifs had to be included. Although Bergman is no scholarly researcher, he found himself responding to all manner of rich influences—Carl Orff's *Carmina Burana* song cycle, Picasso's picture of the two acrobats, the two jesters, and the child, Strindberg's *Saga of the Folkungs* and *To Damascus*, the concluding portion of *Outward Bound* (Death's omniscience, coupled with an occasionally disarming disclaimer, recalls the "Examiner," the Reverend Frank Thomson whom Bergman himself had played on stage back in 1938).

How many of these precedents he consciously assimilated into the screenplay is impossible to gauge. There is no doubt, however, about the importance of the church frescoes. Bergman visited Härkeberga Church, north of Stockholm, to look at the paintings and murals; he was accompanied by Allan Ekelund and P. A. Lundgren, his art director, who needed only a nudge from Bergman to devise some brilliant designs. Lundgren seized on the most arresting of the tiny figures depicted in the church murals and enlarged them to grotesque proportions so that they could adorn the side of a caravan or a surrogate stage backdrop.

Somehow Bergman also found time to produce Hugo von Hofmannsthal's *The Old Play of Everyman* for radio transmission in April. Vernon Young, who heard a repeat of this production in 1970, says that it "had the same kind of singleminded, driving purity as had *The Virgin Spring*. . . . Max von Sydow surpassed himself in all his other roles I have heard; his nuances of character and his pious emotional power were compelling."[20]

By June 5 the script of *The Seventh Seal* was ready and dedicated to Bibi Andersson. Preparations for shooting in July began at breakneck pace. Ove Svensson, a student at Uppsala University, was an assistant on the film and remembers his duties as consisting of everything from providing Bergman with his favorite wafer biscuits to selecting extras for the crowd scenes from hundreds of eager applicants.

The budget for the film was set at between 700,000 and 800,000 crowns ($150,000), and comparatively little was shot on location. The opening scene by the seashore and a few other hillside sequences were shot at Hovs Hallar, on the southwest coast of Sweden. Lennart Olsson had spent two weeks searching for the right spot. Hovs Hallar, with its sense of mountains coming literally down into the sea, struck Bergman as being exactly right. He also liked filming in the province of Skåne because the light was so much softer than in the northern parts of the country; colors, landscape, atmosphere, all are smooth and gentle. The

Bergman (seated at right) shooting The Seventh Seal. *Photo courtesy Swedish Film Institute.*

crew stayed in a hotel in Torekov, a short distance along the coast from
Hovs Hallar.

As so often in Swedish cinema, improvisation was the key to success.
Some actors could not work in harmony with Bergman or each other
and had to be replaced during the filming.[21] The unit had barely three
days on location. Everyone was cheerfully press-ganged into carrying the
cameras. Costumes were borrowed from the theater. (The description of
a circus setting up shop in *The Naked Night* is not so far from the
truth where Bergman's productions are concerned!).

The most famous scene in *The Seventh Seal*, the Dance of Death,
was achieved *par hasard*. Early one morning at Hovs Hallar, the unit
was preparing quite another sequence, when suddenly the skies grew
rather dramatic. The light changed. Bergman announced on the spur
of the moment that he would shoot the Dance of Death. But only the
evening before, some of the players had joined a party; Åke Fridell (who
had the role of the smith) had suffered a minor "accident" and could
not walk properly when he arrived at the location. Bergman asked Ove
Svensson to take his place. A costume was found, the scene was shot by
Gunnar Fischer, and Svensson's silhouette joined the immortals of film
history. There was but a single take.

Another stroke of fortune occurred when Bergman was filming the
scene in a forest glade, with Raval, the seminarist, writhing in his death
agony. By chance (or by instinct) Bergman let the camera run on for a
little longer than usual. All at once the sun came out above the lot at
Råsunda, and Raval's corpse was bathed in a ray of beneficent light.

Several of the principal sequences (such as the burning of the witch
and the uproar in the tavern) were shot in or around the studios at
Råsunda. The bonfire lit for the immolation got out of hand. Bergman
claims that the residents of the surrounding suburbs were cleaning oil
off their windows for days afterward.

Bergman preferred the organized precision of studio interiors. "Ingmar
always came into a freshly built set and *sniffed* for the atmosphere,"
recalls Lennart Olsson. "Not checking for minute details, but for the
smell and the mood." His savage sense of humor never deserted him.
Ove Svensson, for example, was made up with a putrid skull to play the
dead monk whom Jöns addresses on the coast near the beginning of the
film; Bergman delighted in dispatching him to the commissary at
Råsunda and seeing how the other diners lost their appetite!

In short, Bergman flourished at that period because his movies were
created in a family environment. Everyone fetched and carried. Else
Fisher, Bergman's first wife, was called on to choreograph the dance
performed by Jof and Mia in the village. Anders Ek, a colleague from

as far back as Gothenburg in the forties, played the monk who harangues the flagellants. The poor folk in the tavern consisted of extras found by Bergman and Olsson in Stockholm's geriatric homes. The scene with the flagellants was shot from 8 A.M. to 7 P.M. in a single day. "It was such a fantastic time," said Bergman later. "We never slept. We only rehearsed and shot."[22]

Colleagues have frequently asserted that Bergman writes a part of his own personality into each of his characters, that he develops a role with a specific actor in mind. That is correct. But to a singular degree, all Bergman's characters are related to one another. In the chaos of life, they are elements of the artist's psyche engaged in a kind of centrifugal dance away from their source. However much at odds two Bergman personalities may be, one may rest assured that beneath the bitter arguments there lie fragments of the same soul.

In *The Seventh Seal*, set during the Middle Ages, when disillusioned Crusaders were returning to Sweden and encountering the ravages of the Black Death, each character has his opposite number. The Knight, Antonius Block (Max von Sydow) is accompanied by his Squire, Jöns (Gunnar Björnstrand), who is captious and sardonic where his master is idealistic and romantic. Jof (Nils Poppe) and Mia (Bibi Andersson), the simple, loving couple who escape Death's (Bengt Ekerot) clutches, are in a way linked to the stupid smith, Plog (Åke Fridell), and his libidinous wife (Inga Gill), who are equally bound to each other. The silent Girl (Gunnel Lindblom), rescued in a deserted village by Jöns, finds her counterpart in the poor young creature who is condemned as a witch (Maud Hansson), they stare into each other's eyes as though into a mirror.

Just as the characters reflect each other, directly or obliquely, so the ideas that dominate the film arise from a tension of opposites: faith versus atheism, death versus life, innocence versus corruption, light versus darkness, comedy versus tragedy, hope versus despair, love versus infidelity, vengeance versus magnanimity, sadism versus suffering.

Some critics, notably Jörn Donner, are suspicious of Bergman's historical films. They feel that the trappings of the past only disguise the questions and assertions of modern man. But Bergman has never denied this. He called *The Seventh Seal* an oratorio in which numerous voices pose the same question: What is the meaning of life?[23] He told Gunnar Björnstrand that the atom bomb corresponded to a twentieth-century plague.

Bergman's metaphysical themes are more easily nurtured and construed in a historical context than in a modern environment. Overt, medieval symbols are more acceptable to the contemporary audience than are the psychological metaphors of today. This explains why *Persona*, which is as rich and complex a film as *The Seventh Seal*, enjoys nothing like the same popularity with the repertory public. Perhaps, too, Bergman considers historical figures less evasive. In his own words: "Medieval actors still represent the sort of theater I love most of all: robust, direct, concrete, substantial, sensual."[24]

That twentieth-century man lives in the shadow of nuclear catastrophe is not fundamental to the film, but it allows one to share the bewilderment of the Knight and his companions. This search for knowledge illuminates all of Bergman's mature films. It imposes a pattern on life, which becomes a voyage through time and space. The transience of human existence does not depress Bergman as much as the pitiful groping of man to comprehend the world about him.

The Seventh Seal opens with a sea eagle hovering in the turbulent sky, while offscreen a choir sings Erik Nordgren's arresting version of the Dies Irae, the jagged rhythm of the chant dying away as a narrator reads from the Book of Revelations: "And when he had opened the seventh seal, there was silence in heaven about the space of half an hour." There is a sense of expectation, corresponding to the text in Revelations. The final seal is broken, the Book of God has been unsealed by the Lamb, the one creature who has endured Death and triumphed over its power, and now the answer to man's eternal questions will be forthcoming.

On a pebbly beach the Knight awakens. The sun peeps over the horizon. The sea looks hostile. The Knight and his Squire appear like discarded wreckage from some vanished ship; they are together on this rocky, inhospitable shore, and yet they are also set apart from each other (the Squire scowls as Block nudges him out of sleep).

Death appears. Suddenly. Soundlessly. Miraculously. Bergman extinguishes all noise, even the lapping of the water, at this precise moment. It constitutes one of the most dramatic "entrances" in all cinema; in the hands of another director, the situation would be ludicrous, but no audience laughs at this point in *The Seventh Seal*.

The Knight sees in Death a challenge and embarks on a chess game with him that will become a recurrent motif in the film. Block is playing for his life, but also for fulfillment; he risks his entire being for the hope of committing one worthy act before the Apocalypse. At this juncture he does not know how or when he will have the opportunity to perform this act.

But the Knight stands in a precarious position. He has returned from the Crusades dejected and defeated, and his profound allegiance to the Church militates against his freedom of action as an individual. He

Gunnar Björnstrand (Squire), *Max von Sydow* (Knight), *and Gunnar Olsson* (painter) *in* The Seventh Seal. *Photo courtesy Svensk Film-industri.*

and Jöns ride inland to a village where they learn of the terror that the Black Death is provoking among the population. In the church, the Knight goes dutifully—but also curiously—to the confessional. Unaware that Death in his black cowl is poised in lieu of the priest behind the grill, Block asks a stream of questions:

> Is it so hard to conceive of God with the senses? How can we have faith in those who believe when we can't have faith in ourselves? What is going to happen to those of us who want to believe but cannot? And what is to become of those who neither want to nor are capable of believing?

Questions to which Death does not respond. Questions that Bergman must have asked of his deepest, inmost self during his adolescence. Bergman, like Descartes, seems to believe that systematic doubt is the most vital step along the path to knowledge.

"The void is a mirror. I see myself and feel fear and loathing," says Block.

"What are you waiting for?" asks Death.

"Knowledge," comes the reply.

The confessional should be a place of liberation; instead, Bergman describes it in terms of incarceration—the cramped stall, the heavy iron bars like those of a prison, with Death as jailer.

The greatness of the Knight's character, however, emerges as soon as he realizes he has been tricked by Death. Nowhere is Block closer to Bergman than when he leans back against the stone wall of the church and flexes his hand with courage unquenched. "This is my hand," he says ardently. "I can move it, feel the blood pulsing through it. The sun is still high in the sky and I, Antonius Block, am playing chess with Death." The action becomes a stirring symbol of the will to live, the source of human love and ideals. Like the Knight, Bergman has reacted with a wry smile to misfortune and deception; like him, too, he is animated by a boundless curiosity.

Jöns, meanwhile, in the chapel porch, engages a painter in conversation. The murals describe the horrors of the pestilence. Jöns, for all his worldliness, is shaken and asks for a quick dram. People do not like to know the truth, and grow scared when they see themselves reflected in art, he tells the painter. Here Bergman identifies with the Squire as much as he does in the parallel scene with the Knight.

Painter, performer, writer—each has a relationship with the public that corresponds closely to the antagonism between the dogmatist and the heretic in the Middle Ages, between those who believe in the doctrines of the Church and those who dispute its authority.

Jof and Mia are performers with their partner, Skat (Erik Strandmark). They are first glimpsed from above, their heads lying close to one another's in a trinity of peace, in sharp contrast to the opening images of the Knight and Squire so widely separated on the beach. Jof is a visionary who glimpses the Virgin walking sedately across a lawn with her child (an incident inspired, Bergman has admitted, by George Bernanos's descriptions in *The Diary of a Country Priest*) and later perceives Death playing chess with the Knight. He also dreams that his baby son Mikael will be a great juggler and perform the one impossible trick—making a ball stand still in the air.

The love that binds Jof and Mia is from the outset stronger than the menace of Death. When, in the morning sunshine, Mia tells Jof to stop juggling and says, smiling, "I love you," the words are so tender and sincere that Death is no more than an empty mask dangling beside the caravan. One has to return to *Summer Interlude* to find such an enchanting picture of human affection; and Jof and Mia are more eternal creatures than Henrik and Marie. Their love remains intact at the end of the film. They are the faultless souls who survive to start a train of hope for humanity again. Bergman has said: "Whenever I am in doubt or uncertain I take refuge in the vision of a simple and pure love. I find this love in those spontaneous women who . . . are the incarnation of purity."[25]

If Mia travels through the drama unscathed, Jof suffers the actor's inevitable humiliation. "People here aren't interested in art," he tells his horse. When he and Mia perform their little farce about a cuckolded husband, the crowd of villagers reacts with scorn and abuse. Skat sidles away behind the caravan to seduce the smith's wife, Lisa (Inga Gill), while Jof and Mia remain on stage. Gaiety turns to dread as a band of flagellants approaches. Throughout *The Seventh Seal*, moments of frivolity are interspersed with moments of terror so that it becomes difficult to disentangle jest from threat.

The flagellants might have sprung from one of the church murals that Jöns has inspected. "Mobs of people who call themselves Slaves of Sin are swarming over the country, flagellating themselves and others, all for the glory of God," the painter has told him. Barbara Tuchman's study of the fourteenth century, *A Distant Mirror*, confirms this image, pointing out that although often sanctioned by the Pope such processions accompanied the plague and helped to spread it. They "marched from city to city, stripped to the waist, scourging themselves with leather whips tipped with iron spikes until they bled." They carried candles and relics, tore at their hair, wore ropes around their necks. The Black Death had eliminated around a third of the population of Sweden during the decade following its arrival in 1349.

As the procession enters the square, Bergman shoots the scene from a series of low camera angles, so as to suggest the terror these wretches inspire in the onlookers. The smoke from the censers, the skulls borne aloft, the cross with its ascetic Christ effigy, the half-naked penitents who lash one another with spasmodic movements—all fuse into an appalling vision, worthy of Hieronymous Bosch.

As they pause, a monk with a twisted face gives vent to his anger and disdain for the crowd: "Do you know, you fools, that you shall die today or tomorrow, or the next day, because all of you have been doomed. Do you hear what I say? Do you hear the word? You are doomed, doomed!"

When the flagellants stumble on their way again, the high camera set-ups reduce them to insignificance. Their wailing diminishes, and by a cunning dissolve Bergman creates the impression that they have vanished into the barren ground, symbolizing the futility of their religious fervor.

Bergman's view of the medieval Church is filled with revulsion and loathing. Death is a surrogate priest; the monk harangues the flagellants with the cynicism of a modern demagogue and a total disrespect for humanity; and now a third cleric, Raval (Bertil Anderberg), comes into the foreground as a blazon of evil. Jöns has found him robbing a dead man and ready to rape a serving girl. Raval—"Doctor Mirabilis, Coelestis et Diabolis," as the Squire calls him sarcastically—had urged the Knight to embark on his Crusade so that he and his accomplices could indulge their thieving instincts at home. He is active, malicious evidence of the unethical advantage the ministers of the Church took of most men's naiveté in the Middle Ages. In the village tavern, he taunts and baits poor Jof like a bear, accusing him of running off with the smith's wife.

"Actor!" he cries with contempt, forcing the clown to dance higher and higher, lunging at him with a flaming torch. Only at the frenetic climax, with beer mugs beating on the table and firebrands licking around the dancer's legs, is Jof saved by the entrance of the Squire—who brands Raval across the face as a reward for his sadism.

How appropriate it is, later in the film, that Raval should fall victim to the very plague that he regards as an instrument of divine disfavor. When he emerges from the forest, he grovels before Jöns and the girl in a last servile plea for water. He, the dispenser of God's word, is the

The flagellants in The Seventh Seal. *Photo courtesy Svensk Film-industri.*

Max von Sydow (Knight) *and Bibi Andersson* (Mia) *in the lyrical scene on the hillside in* The Seventh Seal. *Photo courtesy Svensk Filmindustri.*

most anxious to escape Death, whose clean, withdrawn honesty is preferable to the vicious behavior of this seminarist.

The Knight wanders out of the village, sensing that Death may be waiting for him to continue their game. He meets Mia and her baby son beside their caravan, and when Jof and Jöns join them after the incident at the inn, an interlude of tranquility and reflection begins. Mia prepares a bowl of fresh milk and some strawberries, that recurrent Bergman memento of passing happiness. The Knight relaxes, beginning to perceive that this family must be shielded from the fear of Death. If he can translate his ideals into an effective gesture, he may die without regrets. Wistfully he thinks of his wife, whom he has not seen for ten years, and then describes his doubts with unerring lucidity: "Faith is like loving someone who is out there in the darkness but never appears, however loudly you call."

The pathos and serenity of this scene are most perfectly captured, however, in the Knight's subsequent meditation: "I shall remember this moment, the silence, the twilight, the bowl of strawberries and milk, your faces in the dusk, Mikael sleeping, Jof with his lyre. I'll carry this memory between my hands as if it were a bowl filled with fresh milk.

It will be a sign—and a great consolation." The words have the quality
of an incantation, a blessing. The mood is that of an open-air communion, unimpeded by the constricting walls of the Church. The
Knight's words are spoken gently, with humility, by comparison with the
arrogant, vehement tone of the monk who addresses the flagellants.

The sunlight and charm of this sequence give way to the bleak, chill
atmosphere of the chess game with Death. As the Knight moves away
from the holy family, and finds Death waiting patiently in a corner of
the meadow, he is once again utterly vulnerable, reconciled to his own
fate but still hoping, dimly, to achieve some meaningful goal. When
Death asks him if he means to escort Jof and Mia through the forest,
the knight has an inkling of the family's significance, both to Death and
himself.

The balance in *The Seventh Seal* between the somber and the care-
free, the harsh and the satirical, is one that Bergman has not always
been able to sustain in his other films. Each encounter with Death
gives way to an earthy, humorous episode. Now Jöns strikes up a dialog
with Plog, the smith who is in his cups, wailing about the infidelity of
his wife. Their conversation has a theatrical ring, yet bubbles with
apothegms.

"Love is the blackest of all plagues," remarks Jöns, "and if one could
die of it, there would be some pleasure in love. But you almost always
get over it. . . . If everything is imperfect in this imperfect world, love
is most perfect in its perfect imperfection."

To which the smith replies: "You're lucky, you believe in your own
twaddle." Plog is a caricature of Albert in *The Naked Night* and
thoroughly sick of marriage. "Women's nagging, the shrieking of
children and wet nappies, sharp nails and sharp words, blows and pokes,
and the devil's aunt for a mother-in-law." He is enmeshed in his own
dissatisfaction, but like Albert he fears loneliness more than the way-
ward behavior of his partner.

The burning of those regarded by society as responsible for the Death
forms another image common to many fescoes of the period. Block and
his Squire first see the young girl accused of witchcraft as they enter
the church. She is tied to a stake. Men-at-arms are on duty, legs flung
wide in oppressive stance. A tight-lipped monk mutters orisons over
her. She has been found having "carnal intercourse with the Evil One"
and will be burned in the evening.

On their way through the forest, the Knight and his companions cross
paths with the detachment of men-at-arms bringing the witch to the
stake. The Knight is fascinated by the innocence and calm of the girl.
"I too want to meet the Devil," he tells her. "I want to ask him about

God. He, if anyone, must know." But the girl has been persuaded by the priests that the Devil lurks within her. She does not require, as Block does, oracular proof. She is a victim of the Church, a victim of intolerance, and the despair that lights her eyes as the smoke and flames swirl about her shocks the Knight and Jöns. For if at the moment of death there is no revelation, surely life has no purpose?

The Knight clenches his teeth and cries, "There must be something!"

Jöns comments drily, "Look at her eyes, my Lord. Her poor brain has just made a discovery—emptiness. . . . We see what she sees and her terror is ours."

Although Block shakes his head vigorously at the Squire's assertion, it is obvious that he has become aware emotionally of what earlier he had suspected intellectually—that man must rely on his own resources to counter Death. Block is not quite a zealot, not quite an Ahab, not even an atheist obsessed with God, like the hero of Flannery O'Connor's *Wise Blood*. He longs to believe, to effect a reconciliation between the world's pain and beauty.

Once again Death has assumed a monk's attire. He sits near the pyre, accepted as a member of the Church by all save Block. When the Knight demands to know why the girl's hands have been crushed, Death replies with a trace of irritation, "Will you never stop asking?"

"No," says Block.

"But you get no answer," comes the chilling response.

The dialog between Death and the Knight amounts to a verbal equivalent of their struggle at the chess board; each remark seeks to out-flank and outmaneuver the other.

As the Knight's party resumes its journey, Bergman again reverts to a lighthearted mood. The smith discovers his wife, Lisa, in cahoots with Skat. Both Plog and Skat have the familiar and endearing qualities of the puppet-show villain. Their querulous exchanges and mannered gestures—suave on the one hand, lumbering on the other—become virtually an art in themselves. Their antics offset the remainder of the film the way the porters do in *Macbeth* and the gravediggers do in *Hamlet*. Skat enjoys his fleeting hour of dirty love with the smith's wife, but vanity betrays him. He deludes Plog by pretending to stab himself in the chest, but Death traps *him* in the midst of his self-congratulation, sawing down the tree in which Skat has hidden. This motif, of Death felling a tree with a man in its crown, may be found on a fresco in Täby Church.

In a moonlit glade, the Knight plays his last round with Death. He loses his queen, but at that moment Jof becomes aware of Death's presence. Mia cannot see the Evil One and thinks that her husband is having visions again. But Jof leads her away through the trees, while the Knight, recognizing the importance of the juncture, sweeps his cloak over the chessboard, knocking the pieces awry. Death is distracted, and Jof and Mia escape. Death tells Block that he will be checkmate at the next move. But Block does not care. He has accomplished his task. He is dying, as the memorials always state, so that others may live.

A storm breaks over the land. Nordgren's music whirls and screams. Jof and Mia cling together in the frail caravan that makes their ark. In the dead of night, Antonius Block and his doomed companions reach their destination, the castle where once "the house was full of life." Only the Knight's wife, Karin (Inga Landgré), remains. Like all Bergman's couples, they shift together in uneasy reconciliation. "You too have changed," says Karin. "Somewhere in your eyes, somewhere in your face, is the boy who went away so many years ago."

Block returns her gaze. "It's over now," he sighs, "and I'm a little tired." One can almost feel the melancholy and resignation that steal over him. Death is no longer an adversary; he is a minister of eternal rest. "Home is the sailor, home from sea, and the hunter home from the hill."

This scene in the spartan castle interior is quite simply one of the most moving and concise Bergman has ever directed. Even Karin's listless gesture in tossing a final log on the fire carries a charge of acquiescence in life's round. The smile on her face communicates regret mingled with an intelligent appraisal of the Knight's predicament.

Karin reads to her guests from the Book of Revelations.

"The first angel sounded . . . and the second angel sounded . . . and the third angel sounded." Three mighty knocks resound through the castle. Jöns goes to the door but sees no one. Then, as Karin continues to read, Death stands in the hallway—perfectly erect, motionless, patient, and unyielding, as though he had always been there. The camera dollies back until all six of his victims are in the frame. Each makes an obeisance or supplication to "the Great Lord," as Plog calls him. Jöns, who cannot see Death, urges his master to "feel to the very end the triumph of being alive." "Be silent," Karin tells him. "I will be silent," replies Jöns, "but under protest." His Girl, who has said nothing since the Squire first found her in the deserted village, drops to her knees and gazes up at Death with eager relief.

"It is finished," she whispers passionately, in a faint echo of Christ's words on the Cross.

In the dawn light, Jof sees the Knight and his friends dancing with Death against the skyline while "the rain washes their faces and cleans the salt of the tears from their cheeks" (a direct quotation from chapter 7 of Revelations). Mia smiles indulgently. "You with your visions," she says. Jof turns away in confusion and leads the caravan along the seashore into the morning sun, with Mia and Mikael safe beside him.

And what of Death, the film's most powerful influence?

Bergman's conception of Death is intriguing; he endows him with the sardonic stare of the intellectual, who is both afraid and bereft of emotion. Death glides into the frame from one side or the other, always unexpected. Only few can discern him: Jof, the Knight, the Girl. Even Skat, when he hears him sawing away at the tree trunk below him, treats him like a cheeky woodsman. Bergman has pounced on the fact that in those medieval church paintings Death has a fondness for chess, for the game is emblematic of the logic and lack of imagination that he abhors. Bergman may sympathize with Jöns, but he identifies strongly with the Knight when he sweeps aside the pieces and covers the flight of the holy family. Besides, neither Knight nor Squire relinquish their lives without a struggle; they do not accept the will of God without question.

"Somewhere in your eyes is that boy who went away so many years ago." *Inga Landgré* (Knight's wife) *and Max von Sydow* (Knight) *in* The Seventh Seal. *Photo courtesy Svensk Filmindustri.*

Bergman rehearsing with Inga Landgré (Knight's wife) for the final "Last Supper" scene in The Seventh Seal. *Photo courtesy Svensk Filmindustri.*

Bergman shooting The Seventh Seal, *with Bengt Ekerot (Death) standing by. Photo courtesy Svensk Filmindustri.*

In *The Seventh Seal,* word and image exert equal sovereignty. Berg-man's thoughts and themes are illustrated as well as described. The dialog may at times be theatrical, but the visual strength of so many sequences exceeds the potential of the stage.

Perhaps Bergman even feels a twinge of sympathy with Death himself when, after defeating the Knight, he confesses his ignorance. "I know nothing," he says with a baleful look. Like the humans he overwhelms, Death cannot see beyond the encroaching darkness.

The film opened in Stockholm on February 16, 1957. Reviews were uniformly excellent. But Bergman was lonely. "Nobody, not even the actors, phoned me after the premiere," he told Käbi Laretei some years later. There was consolation in his father's appreciation of the work. He "liked *The Seventh Seal* very much. He knows that I never say what I don't sincerely believe."

Coming on the heels of *Smiles of a Summer Night* in France and Britain, *The Seventh Seal* established Bergman in the top flight of contemporary directors. Critics and audiences alike were stunned not only by the ambitious theme but also by the assurance of the perform-ances and the brilliance of Gunnar Fischer's photography. Swedish craftsmanship was second to none in the world at that point. And in Max von Sydow, who at the age of twenty-seven brought to the role of the Knight a distinction and a gravity worthy of Alec Guinness, Berg-man had found a major new star.

Von Sydow first met Bergman in 1951, although as far back as 1948 he had telephoned the director when he was preparing *Prison* and asked if there was a chance of his obtaining a small part as a policeman. But Bergman cut him short. Not until 1955, when Max von Sydow moved to Malmö, was a rapport established between the two men. For the next few years, Max was a crucial personality in Bergman's films and stage productions.

"He never liked to analyze his own productions," the actor recalls.

> But he managed to stimulate the imagination of his players, by giving everyone a little tidbit of something. Bergman did not give you precise instructions about a scene; instead, he would give you a pace, a rhythm, or a musical score by which to be guided, so to speak. He'd say: "This is a scene where people are indifferent to each other." Or, "Someone is letting out his aggressions at this point."

Max von Sydow enjoys a conspicuous physique by comparison with other actors of his generation. There is the oblong daring of the face, the slightly prognathous lip, the resolution of the gaze. His presence prompts

Max von Sydow and Eva Stiberg in Bergman's Malmö production of Cat on a Hot Tin Roof. *Photo courtesy Malmö Stadsteater.*

hagiolatry and adjectives such as majestic, imperious, exalted, dignified. No modern actor is quite so well equipped to accommodate in word and gesture all those traits men call ideals: religious fervor, belief in the supernatural, loyalty to family, the pursuit of artistic perfection, the pioneer's drive. When Gunnar Björnstrand first saw him at the Royal Dramatic Theater, where Max was a pupil, he thought that this twenty-year-old looked forty!

His second appearance at Malmö Municipal Theater marked his debut with Bergman—*Lea and Rakel,* Vilhelm Moberg's drama based on the Old Testament story of Jacob (whom he played), whose life was torn between a fruitful woman he did not love and a barren one whom he loved with all his heart.

The 1956–1957 season, however, saw the first real triumphs of the Bergman–von Sydow partnership. Playing Brick to Benkt-Åke Benktsson's Big Daddy in Tennessee Williams's *Cat on a Hot Tin Roof,* which opened on October 19, Max demonstrated that he could shine in a modern role too. Henrik Sjögren noted how he contrasted Brick's disgust with life and his nervous tension to a tireless passion for truth.[26] This Williams drama, with its claustrophobic atmosphere of family guilt, the dominance of a dying paterfamilias, and sexual innuendo, was an ideal vehicle for Bergman, whose own plays had never attained such a pitch of intensity, even if they had dealt with similar themes.

Bergman's Christmas production was *Erik XIV*, Strindberg's homage to a medieval king of Sweden who is his time had been considered as mad as Strindberg was by his contemporaries. Toivo Pawlo, an actor who imposed himself as a major force on Bergman's Malmö productions but who rarely played a significant role in the films, created an Erik stretched between cruelty and remorse, laughter and tears, loneliness and the flattery of a huge court. Bibi Andersson was Karin Månsdotter, the peasant girl taken by the king as his mistress and left a widow at the age of twenty-six.

For most of those who lived and worked in Malmö during the fifties, *Peer Gynt*, which opened on March 8, 1957, was Bergman's greatest production. In terms of sheer length, it dwarfed the others. The performance ran for about four hours, with one decent interval after the third act and a shorter one between the fourth and fifth acts.

Ibsen's gigantic play contains some forty scenes and sprang almost entirely from his fantasy. (Peer Gynt was a real person, who lived in Norway in the late eighteenth or early nineteenth century, but few hard facts are known about his life.) Michael Meyer calls the drama the direct ancestor of Strindberg's *A Dream Play*, a "struggle between the divine purpose and our undermining passions and egocentricities, between man's deeper self and his animal, or troll, self."[27]

From the start of rehearsals at the turn of the year, Bergman was very liberal in his attitude to Max, letting him unfold as an actor and develop the role of Peer Gynt. He always applauded when Max achieved something unforeseen during rehearsal: "That's it! That's it! Do it! Let's keep it like that!" One observer was struck by Bergman's habit of working at a high level of tension in rehearsal and then suddenly breaking the mood by telling a funny story, quite irrelevant to the play. He was careful not to take his actors to the absolute peak too early; instead, he brought them to within a few degrees of perfection. Arne Ericsson, a journalist in Malmö during this period, remembers Bergman's precision inside the theater. "He loved silence so much that he had a board erected, with the words *shut up!* written on it in ninety-seven different languages!" He always followed his intuition and might arrive for a crowd scene on stage and announce that the previous day he had been utterly certain of how to handle this scene but that during the night he had dreamed of it in a different form—"And now I'm going to improvise."

The settings for *Peer Gynt* appeared quite conventional (e.g. the Norwegian house) in the early stages of Bergman's production, but in the fourth and fifth acts the style grew more and more impressionistic.

The scene in the Cairo madhouse was unforgettable, with each of the twenty or so inmates a distorted personality in his own right. In the final act, the huge stage was almost bare, with Max von Sydow and Åke Fridell (as the Mountain King) face to face, and then Peer alone with his beloved Solveig. "It all becomes simple and grand," wrote Nils Beyer in *Morgon-Tidningen*. "Just two human beings on an empty stage. And in the background, silent and twisted, the figure of the Button-maker, holding his ladle, with his box on his back."[28]

There were some awkward moments. Naima Wifstrand, playing Mother Aase, was in her late sixties and so fragile that for Max von Sydow to hoist her up on to the roof of the house amounted to a hazardous operation. During rehearsals she cracked a rib but managed to soldier on with the part. Like everybody else, she adored Bergman.

Throughout this busy season, Bergman had been nurturing the idea that would evolve into *Wild Strawberries* (*Smultronstället*). The character of Isak Borg had been conceived the previous year, when Bergman had driven from Dalarna down to Stockholm and paused in Uppsala at dawn. The town was quiet and rather deserted, and the silence had a suggestive quality. Bergman looked up the house in Nedre Slottsgatan where his grandmother had lived, turned the door handle, and thought to himself that when he opened the door he would enter the world of his childhood once again. "Supposing old Lalla (our cook, she was) is standing inside there, in her big apron, making porridge for breakfast, as she did so many times when I was little?"[29]

In the spring of 1957, immediately after directing a television version of Hjalmar Bergman's *Mr. Sleeman Is Coming* (his first contact with the new medium), Bergman settled down to write the screenplay for *Wild Strawberries*. There was no difficulty in setting up the project. The success of *The Seventh Seal* and the foreign sales of Bergman's movies had convinced Svensk Filmindustri that they had an asset on their hands. Carl Anders Dymling, in fact, persuaded the aged and ailing Victor Sjöström to take the part of Isak Borg. Sjöström was seventy-eight years old and sometimes querulous. He was a lonely man whose wife was dead. His health was poor, and during the filming he often forgot his lines, a failing that would only aggravate him the more. Gunnar Fischer says that several scenes had to be shot indoors for Sjöström's sake. "We had to make some very bad back-projection in the car because we never knew if Victor would come back alive the next day." Nevertheless, as long as Victor was home by 5:15 P.M. each day "and had his whiskey punctually, all went well."[30]

An enchanting kinship developed between Sjöström and the young Bibi Andersson. She revived in him the old flair of a ladies' man, and he treated her seriously and with great charm. Bergman, who frequently used his 16 mm. camera to keep a record of his film productions, has a shot of Bibi and Victor flirting quite harmlessly, quite oblivious to the activity of the unit around them. The director also kept a diary during the shooting of *Wild Strawberries* in which he wrote about Sjöström: "I never stop pryingly, shamelessly studying this powerful face. Sometimes it is like a dumb cry of pain, sometimes it is distorted by mistrustful cruelty and senile querulousness, sometimes it dissolves into self-pity and astoundingly sentimental effusions."

And later:

> We have shot our final supplementary scenes of *Wild Strawberries*—the final close-ups of Isak Borg as he is brought to clarity and reconciliation. His face shone with secretive light as if reflected from another reality. His features became suddenly mild, almost effete. His look was open, smiling, tender.
> It was like a miracle.
> Then complete stillness—peace and clarity of soul. Never before or since have I experienced a face so noble and liberated.[31]

One of the phenomena of old age is that childhood memories return with ever-increasing clarity, while great stretches of the prime of life vanish into obscurity.

That is the nub of *Wild Strawberries*.

Isak Borg (Victor Sjöström), the distinguished professor emeritus who lives alone with his housekeeper, can only come to terms with his egocentricity by traveling back in time to his earliest youth, finding there the seeds of his failure as husband, lover, and father.

Bergman disclaims any connection between his own initials and those of Borg. "I chose the name Isak because he seemed icy."[32] Strindberg devotees might note that Borg is the character who proclaims his nihilism at the end of *The Red Room*.

Isak is unusual among Bergman characters in that he does not set out of his own accord on a quest for self-knowledge. At every juncture, he must confront the evidence of his own inadequacy. He reacts with bewilderment rather than complacency. In his opening speech, he admits he's an old pedant and toys for a moment over a chess move after hearing his housekeeper's announcement that dinner is served. There seems nothing vicious or mean about his behavior.

But Bergman's purpose in *Wild Strawberries* is to reach behind the façade that keeps the skeletons concealed in respectable life. As Miss Julie says in Strindberg's play, "Oh, you may run and run, but your memories are in the baggage-car, and with them remorse and repentance." The opening nightmare comes as a shocking reminder of death to Isak. He finds himself in the Old Town of Stockholm, assaulted by a burning sun. He plunges hastily into the few patches of shadow that the street affords. Gateways loom, great areas of black, used by Bergman to suggest a hostile nothingness. Isak is alone, faced by successive portents of disaster: a watch without hands, a human figure that crumbles on the sidewalk, a coffin that contains his own body.

The sequence seems a tribute to Sjöström's own great silent film, *The Phantom Carriage*. Sound effects, as in the opening flashback of *The Naked Night*, leave a deep impression. The silence at one point is so profound that Isak becomes aware of his own massive heartbeat. When the carriage crashes into a lamppost and disgorges its casket, the axle squeals insistently, like a newborn baby, suggesting the proximity of birth and death. Bergman has always been aware of the importance of the soundtrack, seeking the one little extra sound that will give a scene an added dimension.

The set for this sequence was built on the lot at Råsunda, but the shot of the carriage rounding the street corner was taken by Gunnar Fischer in a deserted Old Town at almost 2 A.M. one summer morning. A couple emerging late from a restaurant were startled by the spectacle of a coach without a driver hurtling down the narrow, cobbled lane. The dummy that Borg mistakes for a pedestrian was constructed from a balloon and a silk stocking. All the walls and floors had to be painted a pure white to achieve the glare that Bergman wanted.

Isak Borg is scheduled to appear in the university town of Lund later in the day to receive an honorary doctorate. Disturbed by his dream, he resolves on a whim to drive rather than fly south. His housekeeper, Miss Agda, is irritated. Bergman has been accused of betraying a feudal outlook toward servants; the "faithful old retainer" of Bergman's youth is depicted in some of his plays, and in the character played here by Jullan Kindahl (who performs a similar role in *Smiles of a Summer Night*). But in fact these are just affectionate portraits, tributes to people who had contributed to his childhood happiness; they are not to be confused with major characters integrated in the themes of his work.

In the car, which has the connotations and design of a hearse when viewed in long-shot leaving the city at dawn, Isak talks with his daughter-in-law, Marianne (Ingrid Thulin), who has had a quarrel with her husband in Lund and now intends to rejoin him and have the baby that he rejects. Thanks to the striking personality of Ingrid Thulin, Marianne becomes more than just a foil for Isak. It was Miss Thulin's first part in a Bergman film, although she had featured in some of his Malmö stage productions. Her husband, Harry Schein, had written certain scathing

Bergman checking the breakfast scene in Wild Strawberries. *Photo courtesy Svensk Filmindustri.*

notices of Bergman's films. By inviting Ingrid Thulin to Malmö, Bergman hoped to neutralize one of his most persistent critics. In fact, Schein did abandon film criticism some months later, but Ingrid Thulin became one of Bergman's most brilliant players—and Schein, eventually, one of his closest friends.

Isak, who has been seen in his study puffing away at a cigar in the opening sequence, orders Marianne to extinguish her cigarette in the car. She bridles and opens the case for the prosecution. "You're utterly ruthless and listen to no one but yourself," she says. "You hide behind your old world charm." But Marianne soon reveals an intolerant streak in her own character, when Isak tries to tell her about his nightmare. "I'm not very interested in dreams," she replies, turning away with a bored expression.

The car veers off the main road. Isak has decided to visit the summer villa where he spent his childhood vacations. While Marianne goes down to the lake for a swim, Isak sinks down beside the strawberry patch as though at an altar. Lulled by his recollections and the pleasant morning weather, he dozes off, drifting into the past, his psyche ready at last to accept criticism and to evaluate his life in a radically altered perspective. He sees Sara (Bibi Andersson), his boyhood crush, flirting with his brother. Now giggling, now sniveling or flying into a rage, cousin Sara springs ready-made from the turn of the century, her satins rustling, her ringlets pendulous.

As the gong rings for luncheon, Isak follows the family into the luxurious villa. The ritual of Bergman's summers on Smådalarö is reconstructed with affectionate fidelity. In fact, the house used by the unit was outside the resort of Saltsjöbaden, but the spotless tablecloth, the sparkling appointments, the bickering among the relatives, and the aunt's dominance all evoke the world in which Bergman grew up in the late twenties and early thirties.

Despite the generous terms in which he hears himself described by Sara, Isak already detects the symptoms of malaise that have gradually incarcerated his spirit. "Isak is so refined," she sobs. "He is so enormously refined and moral and sensitive and he wants us to read poetry together and he talks about the afterlife, and wants to play duets on the piano and he likes to kiss in the dark, and he talks about sinfulness."

Anyone who can talk about sin must be suspect in Bergman's book.

Bergman himself is still startled by the speed at which the years pass. He remembers the smallest things—toys, noises, smells, light. "When I look at my brother," he told Liv Ullmann, "it seems it was only yesterday we were running barefoot in the garden, and I feel a fear inside me."[33]

Isak wakes. Beside him is a young girl, a modern reincarnation of Sara, also played by Bibi Andersson. She is traveling south with two boyfriends (Folke Sundquist and Björn Bjelvenstam), who strut and argue like young turkey-cocks to vie for her attention. This contemporary Sara figure arouses all Isak's yearning for his lost youth. Throughout the journey to Lund, her presence reminds him of the past; the two hitchhikers accompanying her evoke the rivalry between his brother Sigfrid (Per Sjöstrand) and himself for the original Sara's love.

Not all Isak's memories are so comforting. The car is involved in a collision with a Volkswagen. Alman and Berit (Gunnar Sjöberg and Gunnel Broström)—husband and wife—tender their apologies for careless driving and travel awhile with the other towards a garage. Their hideous relationship obviously resembles Isak's own marriage. Alman has the same biting sarcasm as Isak (he was based on Bergman's bête noir among Swedish critics, Stig Ahlgren), and Berit (Ahlgren's wife, the novelist Birgit Tengroth) is not dissimilar to Isak's wife as she is revealed in a subsequent sequence in a forest glade.

The sparring between these two pathetic creatures matches some of Strindberg's clashes, where married life is depicted as "a war to the knife." When at last Marianne stops the car and insists that they leave, Alman and Berit are seen together in the empty road, shackled like so many Bergman couples by their own vulnerability and mutual hatred. As Mummy says in *The Ghost Sonata*: "Crime and guilt and secrets bind us together, don't you know? Our ties have snapped so that we have slipped apart innumerable times, but we are always drawn together again."

Isak's reputation in the outside world continues to prosper. When he pauses for gas at a rural filling station, the proprietor and his young wife greet him like a lost soul. Åkerman (Max von Sydow) extols Isak's skill and kindness as a doctor in far-off days. "Maybe I should have stayed here," muses Isak. "Why do you say that?" asks Åkerman. But Isak falls silent. The question hangs in the air, prompting speculation: Was there a scandal, or did Isak succumb to the lure of big city affluence?

In both *The Seventh Seal* and *Wild Strawberries*, Bergman alternates scenes of stress and relaxation. At a tranquil lunch served on a balcony overlooking Lake Vättern, Isak Borg listens to the theological arguments of Viktor and Anders and is spurred to recite one of his favorite poems, a psalm by J. O. Wallin: "Where is the friend I seek everywhere? Dawn is the time of loneliness and care. When twilight comes I am still yearning."

Feeling drawn back once more to his youth, Isak leaves the table with Marianne and motors the few miles to his mother's house. Thunder rumbles overhead as they pause before the huge wooden door of the mother's mansion. In this mausoleum, Isak is confronted with *souvenirs d'enfance*. The old lady shows him a watch she intends to give Sigbritt's eldest son. It has no hands. Recollection of the earlier nightmare simultaneously prepares Isak's subconscious for a second excursion into the imagined past. The decrepit toys and junk in his mother's home have connotations of nostalgia and fear. "I remember when Sigbritt's boy had just been born and lay there in his basket in the lilac arbor at the summer house," sighs the old lady. The image is thus "sewn" into Isak's psyche. His mother's frigid attitudes disturb him, although at this point they unnerve Marianne even more.

Asleep in the car afterward, Isak embarks on his most significant dream. Composed of fantasy, not of memory, it nevertheless contains characters who are familiar. Sara sits facing him in the strawberry patch,

The habitual Bergman "catechism." Gunnar Sjöberg (Alman) *and Victor Sjöström* (Professor Isak Borg) *in* Wild Strawberries. *Photo courtesy Svensk Filmindustri.*

but the sun has vanished and the air is dark and cold. Sara forces him to study himself in the mirror. "You are a worried old man who will die soon, but I have my whole life before me." Bergman's men and women abhor the mirror; it reflects the truth they are unwilling to accept. As Denis Marion has observed, facial expressions and bodily behavior are more suggestive of inner feelings and soul condition than the words pronounced by Bergman's characters.[34]

Isak's character and past are also mirrored in the life around him. Evald his son (Gunnar Björnstrand), Alman, and Isak's mother (Naima Wifstrand) are all thinly disguised reflections of himself. The photographs on his desk at home and in his mother's collection are dead. (Bergman always uses photographs to express mortality, as opposed to drawings, which are much more vibrant. The photographs the waiter shows to Johan in *The Silence* are similarly deathlike). The shadows cast by the windowframe over Evald's portrait in his father's study are recalled at the opening of the scene in the rain between Evald and Marianne, when the camera views Evald from outside the door of the car so that a heavy bar of shadow falls across the upper half of his face. Between the photograph and the individual in the car there exists only a physiological difference: Evald's soul *is* dead.

Sara runs to the lilac arbor and comforts Sigbritt's child. When she has gone, Isak stands for a moment beside the cradle in the twilight. Infancy and old age are fused in a magnificent image for the first time in the film. Isak remains disconcerted, but instead of withdrawing from these painful circumstances he finds himself impelled by some strange masochism toward even greater humiliation. Birds sweep like black dust across the evening sky. Branches loom above Isak like predatory claws. As he pauses beside the summer house, he has to witness an embarrassing tableau in which Sigfrid kisses his beloved Sara while she sits at the piano. He knocks furiously against the darkened French windows, tearing his palm on a nail in the wooden frame. The stigmata —the wounding of the hand—recurs in Bergman's work; one finds it in *The Seventh Seal* (the witch's hands are crushed), *Wild Straw-berries, The Magician,* and *Persona*. The extreme of physical anguish, not surprisingly, is identified in a pastor's son with the suffering of Christ.

The door is opened by none other than Alman. Hostile, brisk, death-like in his assurance, Alman exhibits many of the traits that, one suspects, marked Isak in middle age as a successful doctor. In a previous dream, Isak felt at home in this summer house; now its corridors are harsh and bare, like those of a hospital.

Alman conducts him to an examination room. Sara, Anders, and Viktor are in the "audience," witnesses to Isak's shame and failings. Isak stumbles over every question Alman puts to him. When asked if he wishes to stop the examination, he protests. "No, no, for heaven's sake, no!"

This exclamation is a crucial point in the film, the peripeteia in fact. Isak is already saved because of his willingness to accept the errors of judgment in his life. His fundamentally decent soul has been betrayed by his misconception of the human situation and emotions. Even the scene in the forest glade, when Isak watches his wife having intercourse with another man, is accepted with an air of resignation. He shows interest only in the penalty that he has incurred for his coldness in dealing with others. When Alman tells him that the price is "loneli-ness," Isak asks him, "Is there no grace?"

But Alman, like Death in *The Seventh Seal*, expresses ignorance of the ultimate truth. It is a terrifying moment. Although others attempt to pin down his selfish traits for him, only Isak himself can dispel his in-difference toward others.

Originally the idea was for Borg and Alman to pick their way through a group of writhing snakes, but the terrarium built at the studios proved insecure, and the reptiles escaped before the scene could be set up. Perhaps it was as well, for the presence of snakes, that most distinct psychological symbol of sexual desire, would have "overloaded" what is in the completed film a sequence rich in erotic insinuation.

Bergman with his daughter Lena (twin) and Victor Sjöström *(Professor Isak Borg) during the filming of* Wild Strawberries. *Photo courtesy Svensk Filmindustri.*

Lund is Sweden's second university town, a Yale to Uppsala's Harvard. Strindberg described it as "a mysterious little town, which one can never figure out; secretive, inscrutable; friendly, but not with open arms." Finally arriving in time for the ceremony, Isak discerns "a remarkable logic" in the day's seemingly fortuitous events. Tucked up in bed that night, serenaded from below his window by the three young friends he has driven south, happy in the knowledge that Marianne and his son, Evald, have been reconciled in his presence, he lets his mind slip back to childhood yet again. But only now are these recollections rewarding, free of the distortions wrought by prevarication.

When Sara leads him to the water's edge and his father and mother wave kindly to him from the far shore, Isak has achieved true peace. Aspirations, serenity, and the fields of asphodel are crystallized in this exquisite image. Bergman has said, "We go away from our parents and then back to our parents. Suddenly one understands them, recognizes them as human beings, and in that moment one has grown up." Bergman's father was assailed by doubt where faith and religion were concerned. There is much of Pastor Erik Bergman in the character of Isak Borg.[35]

And Bergman showed his own sympathetic awareness of that past by casting Else Fisher as the mother, glimpsed in long-shot in that final scene, and their daughter, Lena, as one of the fractious twins in the Borg household.

Wild Strawberries, which won the Golden Bear at the Berlin Film Festival in 1958 and was acknowledged around the world as the seal on Bergman's career, has not survived the years as well as *The Seventh Seal*. Its craftsmanship remains impeccable in certain sequences (notably the nightmares) and crude in others (e.g. the conversations in the car and the quarrel in the rain between Evald and Marianne). Gunnar Fischer's cinematography and the haunting, regretful music of Erik Nordgren are beyond reproach. The warmth and gentility of Victor Sjöström's performance render Isak Borg a character so sympathetic that the audience would side with him however damning the accusations.

But there is a fundamental flaw in the notion of the two Saras. Bergman has admitted that he blushes now when he sees *Wild Strawberries* because of his vision of young girls like Sara, the hitchhiker. She appears too ardent, too cheerful, too quaint. Her dialog with Viktor and Anders has a jejune ring to it by comparison with the tautness of the exchanges between other personalities in the film.

The existence of Sara in the present acts as a spark to kindle Isak's memories; she is a symbol of the idealism and simplicity of youth. But the Sara of the past is a much more complex figure; Bergman's attempt to bring her up to date by allowing her to smoke a pipe and wear pants is far too superficial.

Throughout his career, Bergman has been much more at ease in the past than in the present. Characters like the contemporary Sara here, or the homosexual played by Gösta Ekman in *Face to Face*, are contrived to the point of embarrassment. It is no derogation of Bergman to say that he can offer through his evocation of vanished years and faces a more perceptive commentary on human suffering than most directors can through a modish interpretation of the modern world. Nor to say that his dreams are more persuasive than his recording of mere "reality." No director recalls his dreams more clearly or puts them to better use.

"In a dream," asserts Bergman, "you do not register surprise. Everything seems logical. Borg's nightmare [at the start of *Wild Strawberries*] is a dream within a dream."[36]

Some months after the opening of the film, Bergman was up in Dalarna and met a childhood friend, who told him that while he was watching *Wild Strawberries* he "began to think of Aunt Berta, who was sitting all alone in Borlänge. I couldn't get her out of my thoughts, and when my wife and I came home, I said let's invite Aunt Berta over at Easter."[37]

That, says Bergman, is the best review he has ever had.

These films of the Malmö period continue to provoke and deserve close analysis. Bergman has been in the vanguard of world cinema at three significant stages of his career: the late fifties, with *The Seventh Seal* and *Wild Strawberries*; the mid-sixties, with *Persona*; and the mid-seventies, with *Scenes from a Marriage* and *The Magic Flute*. He has always been admired, but in these three decades Bergman took a huge leap forward, ahead of the pack. Directors around the world set off in pursuit. At other times, Bergman has been content to follow himself.

CHAPTER NINE

Behind the Mask

SOONER OR LATER EVERY DIRECTOR LETS SLIP A COMMENT THAT WILL
brand his career. In 1950, Bergman declared that "the theater is like a
loyal wife, film is the great adventure, the costly and demanding mistress
—you worship both, each in its own way."[1]

Twenty years later, he cheerfully recanted. "Forget it—now I'm living
in bigamy!" he said in 1971.

"As a process of working, I actually prefer the stage," he said during
a press conference at Cannes in 1973. Films remain an obsession, while
the theater is a profession, without too much time pressure.

> But when I am shooting a film and I manage to turn in three
> good minutes of film a day, then I'd best be satisfied. . . . . The
> time factor is always threatening, always hanging over you. You
> must always finish quickly. Film is incredibly demanding; it
> requires a permanent mobilizing of all your strength.[2]

During the late fifties, Bergman's life was at an almost miraculous
point of balance. His films were successful, his stage productions
revered, and his relationship with Bibi Andersson a rich and stimulating
fulcrum. Never again would he be quite so absorbed, quite so at ease,
quite so certain of the everyday routine. Max von Sydow has said that
for him personally those five years in Malmö were the most rewarding
of his life. Bergman agrees. "He was so full of the vision of what he
wanted," says Lennart Olsson, "that he could really convince his

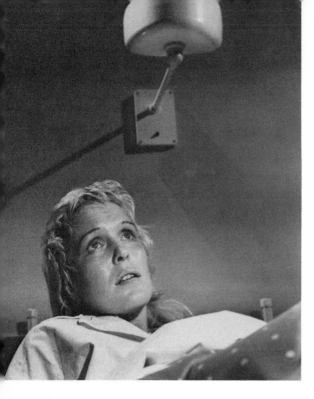

Eva Dahlbeck (Stina Andersson) *in* Brink of Life. *Photo courtesy Nordisk Tonefilm.*

collaborators . . . and they all felt emotionally the way he wanted to go, and they could help him. He never gave orders; he *suggested*. He addressed their fantasies."[3]

In successive screen and stage productions, Bergman registered the conflict between two sides of human existence: the external, with its sordidness; and the internal, with its idealistic dreams. *Brink of Life, Cat on a Hot Tin Roof* (see Chapter 8), and *The Virgin Spring* represent the first; *Sagan, The Magician,* and *Urfaust* the second.

Brink of Life (Nära livet) was shot at the end of 1957, and was based on a short story, entitled "The Aunt of Death," from a new collection by Ulla Isaksson. Bergman had been friends with Ulla Isaksson for some time and had been intrigued by her novel about witchcraft trials. They resolved to collaborate in some way, and when Bergman wanted to settle an old commitment to Nordisk Tonefilm he proposed *Brink of Life.*

There is no doubt that, for all its refined craftsmanship and consummate acting, *Brink of Life* lies in the margin of Bergman's work. In form it resembles a play. One main set: the maternity ward in a Stockholm hospital. An opening crisis: Cecilia arriving after a miscarriage. A dramatic conflict with links to an unseen, outside world: Hjördis's relationship with her lover. And the peripeteia: Stina's unexpected loss of her baby during labor.

Brink of Life is the first of those Bergman movies in which dialog and characterization take precedence over scenery and locations. *The Ritual* and *From the Life of the Marionettes,* two later films, belong to the same category.

In her preface to the screenplay, Ulla Isaksson writes:

> There is a secret with life, with life and death, a secret as to why some are called to live, while others are called to die. We may assail heaven and science with questions—all the answers are only partial. But life goes on, crowning the living with torment and with happiness.

Bergman, who at this period was intent on probing, interrogating the mysteries of life, was drawn to the apparent lack of discrimination between survival and extinction. When Stina (Eva Dahlbeck), the healthiest and most radiant of the three women, wakes up after losing her baby, she listens to the doctor who stands before her both in judgment and ignorance, an impersonal figure with affinities to Death in *The Seventh Seal.* "On the threshold, life failed him," he says without a trace of sentimentality. Beyond a certain point human speculation cannot penetrate. Only nature knows why Stina, possessed of everything in life, suffers such a tragedy. The film demonstrates that Bergman at this juncture was as alarmed by childbirth as he was by death.

Sister Brita (Barbro Hiort af Ornäs), like the doctor, seems powerless to avert tragedy. Appointed by society, as the priest was appointed in past centuries, to minister to the sick and prompt the confession of the patient's innermost fears and woes, she is powerless to solve the horrifying puzzle of life. Toward Hjördis (Bibi Andersson), the sister behaves solicitously, allowing her to telephone her parents from a hospital office.

Hjördis was a role created by Bergman for Bibi Andersson. She does not figure in Ulla Isaksson's original story. With her rebellious spirit in the wake of a stern upbringing, her fragility and femininity at odds with her shield of resolution and carelessness, Hjördis embodies many of Bergman's and Bibi's own traits. She seeks an abortion because her lover refuses to marry her; she even loathes the fact that her pregnancy deprives her cigarette of its taste. Yet beneath this disgust for the business of reproduction, Hjördis continues to be allured by the image of an untroubled domestic life. She fights against childbirth because she does not wish her own unhappy background on another living being; she craves security because she has never enjoyed it herself. Hjördis offers unstinting help to her fellow patients. She talks with Cecilia (Ingrid Thulin), and in one of the film's few concessions to lyricism she brushes Stina's hair and makes her up.

Cecilia and Stina mark the poles of domestic experience. Cecilia's marriage is deteriorating rapidly. Her husband is a remote, disdainful individual, and Cecilia's miscarriage symbolizes the rupture in her relationship with her husband.

Stina, on the other hand, seems blessed with an idyllic marriage. She is full of smiles and energy and longs for her baby to arrive. Her husband appears with flowers from their summer cottage and the pair discuss, with a touching enthusiasm, their plans for rearing the child. This is one of the few happy marriages in Bergman's world because it is founded on simplicity and mutual trust. When Cecilia feels sick after the anesthetic, Stina comforts her. This unbridled affection, of which Stina has such ample reserves, emerges as a new element in Cecilia's life. It epitomizes the true intimacy that makes for contentment.

And that intimacy protects the Bergman character against the isolation that threatens him, even in the crowded setting of a hospital. "True loneliness is a juggling act, and behind it lurks a constant fear," warns Greta Ellius (Inga Landgré), Cecilia's sister, when she visits the ward. The women sense a need to huddle together emotionally. They are stripped of their pretensions and purged of their bitterness by mutual suffering. They behave in some way like babies; they scream and clutch and kick, and they approach the world anew. Bergman offers a magnificent example of this childish impotence. When Stina is back in the ward, after losing her battle in the labor room, she stretches out her hand toward a glass of water on the bedside table. As Hjördis moves to help her, Stina slaps her arm aside violently. She *must* learn to do this herself if she is to survive. She reaches for the glass as a baby reaches persistently for a toy.

Although the hospital may by definition be a place of succor, to Bergman it represents a hostile zone. Throughout the film, he lays stress on inanimate objects, such as surgeon's gloves and electric clocks. The only music comes from a radio in the sister's room. The corridors are deserted and inhospitable, a token of barren emptiness. When Cecilia complains that her baby "flowed from me to serve some scientific experiment," the remark implies Bergman's disapproval of the dehumanizing powers of scientific progress. Had Hjördis, Cecilia, and Stina been attended by midwives in their homes of yesteryear, perhaps their offspring might have flourished. The fact that none of them gives birth is deliberately engineered, so that the prospective mothers themselves may be seen to have profited psychologically from the experience. New attitudes, rather than new babies, are born. "Not only our wombs open here, but our entire being," comments Cecilia.

Brink of Life looks the sort of film that Bergman would have made for television a decade later. It relies on few of the traditional advantages

Gertrud Fridh and Max von Sydow in Bergman's 1957 production of The Misanthrope. *Photo courtesy Malmö Stadsteater.*

of the cinema. No special effects, no exotic characterizations, no "masks," no flashbacks. For the purposes of documentary realism, Bergman shot much of the movie in Karolinska Hospital in Stockholm. Upstairs his sister Margareta was having a daughter, Rose; when Bergman heard about his new niece, he sent up a huge bouquet of roses.

The film itself was greeted with excellent reviews at the Cannes Festival the following May, and news of the special acting award given to all three women in *Brink of Life* cheered Bergman as he lay in bed in Sofia-hemmet and wrote the screenplay of *The Magician*.

On December 6, 1957, Bergman's production of *The Misanthrope* opened in Malmö, featuring Max von Sydow as Alceste, described by the critic Ulf Ekman as "a disoriented Don Quixote who is perpetually shocked to discover that people are not as noble as they are in gothic romances."[4] For Henrik Sjögren, this was the masterpiece of Bergman's entire Malmö era, "the brilliant climax of all Swedish theater in the fifties."[5]

Alceste's violent rebellion against the confines of seventeenth-century society was embellished by Bergman's use of splendid and elaborate costumes. It was not difficult to perceive a connection between Bergman's production of *The Misanthrope* and the "angry young men" of the British stage at that point in the decade. Gertrud Fridh as Célimène, "switching with stunning self-control from ploy to ploy . . . showed what a brilliant comedienne she could be—now soft, evasive, feline; now captivatingly abusive; now murderously swift in riposte." Nils Beyer wrote in *Morgon-Tidningen*:

> One can only hope that the inhabitants of Malmö understand what brilliant theater is being played in their city. For in Stockholm, of course, many people don't. . . . Ingmar Bergman's production of *The Misanthrope* on the big Malmö stage is the finest Molière production we have ever seen in any Swedish theater.[6]

Max von Sydow believes that subtle links existed between Bergman's films and stage productions during the fifties. In *The Misanthrope*—and not just in Max's performance—one can discern the seeds of *The Magician*, where Vogler like Alceste is mocked, exposed, and then—in a flourish of dramatic license—vindicated. In the next play Bergman produced, *The Saga* (*Sagan*), may be found also connections with *The Virgin Spring*, particularly in the notion of the water source and the supernatural properties that lie within it. Hjalmar Bergman, who wrote *The Saga*, was inspired by a spring in which a little girl had drowned herself over a century earlier because her lover had abandoned her. Hjalmar Bergman used to observe the spring in all its moods whenever he stayed with his father-in-law, whose villa was built on a mountainside just above the source. The play was written in 1919–1920 but received its first performance only in 1942; it contains all Hjalmar Bergman's talent for condensing action and deploying a poetic, even ardent imagination. Bibi Andersson played the Saga in Ingmar Bergman's production in Malmö (and again when he revived it in Stockholm). Max von Sydow, Ingrid Thulin, Gunnel Lindblom, Toivo Pawlo, and Naima Wifstrand also starred in what Henrik Sjögren described as "a wry comedy, in romantic costume."

Bergman relied on his ensemble of players to make up the cast of each new film. There was a practical consideration, too; the actors were paid only for part of the year by Malmö Municipal Theater, so it was important for them to work in the summer months.

An annual ritual had been established: Bergman would write his script in the spring, send copies of it to his principal performers and technicians, and often travel up to Dalarna. Several of those involved in the production would gather alongside Bergman at the Hotel Siljansborg, where the details of the script were discussed, as well as Bergman's objectives. Max von Sydow recalls how he was approached by Bergman to play the part of Vogler in *The Magician*: "I'm thinking about a film on a magician who no longer believes in his powers. Would you be interested in that role?" Once Max had accepted, he was sent the complete screenplay.

On April 6, 1958, Jürgen Schildt wrote an open letter to Bergman in the magazine *Veckojournalen*: "Have you a face? What happened to your heart?" he demanded, in exasperation at the aloofness displayed by the director in *Brink of Life*. The letter stung Bergman. The title of his new film—initially called "The Charlatans"—became *The Face* (*Ansiktet*), although the American release title, *The Magician*, may give a clue to another source of inspiration: G. K. Chesterton's play *Magic*, about a conjuror forced to entertain some philistine guests at a duke's house.[7]

But *The Magician* derives most directly from Bergman's role at Malmö, where each new production had to be more daring, more revolutionary, more spectacular, than the last, where the people sat in judgment on his art each evening. Cynicism in an artist is nurtured by either great fame or extreme neglect.

Underlying the gothic intrigue of *The Magician* is Bergman's abiding fear of humiliation.

Albert Emanuel Vogler, the "magician," is caught in the grip of a paradox. He makes his living from beguiling and diverting his spectators and yet stands at the mercy of their ridicule and disdain. Arriving one night at the gates of Stockholm in 1846, he is interrogated and held under house arrest with his troupe by a consul, a Doctor Vergérus (Gunnar Björnstrand), and the local police chief (Toivo Pawlo), who is patently a numbskull. Vogler travels with his wife, Manda (Ingrid Thulin), who is dressed like a young man and pretends to be merely the magician's acolyte. His manager is Tubal (Åke Fridell), a rascally entrepreneur, and his grandmother (Naima Wifstrand) is there to utter spells and frighten the birds. Their laden cart trundles through the wood toward the city, cans and other impedimenta dangling like the baggage one accumulates on life's journey. "Vogler's Magnetic Health Theater" reads the inscription on the side of this frail carriage.

Vogler, like Egerman in *Smiles of a Summer Night,* wears a beard as a mask of protection. Like many masks, it attracts the suspicious gaze instead of evading it. (Bergman made a habit of letting his beard grow until shooting on a film was completed.)

In the ethereal light of the forest, Vogler comes upon a dying actor named Spegel (Bengt Ekerot). "Are you a swindler who must hide his real face?" asks Spegel, recognizing immediately that Vogler is a charlatan. Vogler does not reply, seeing his own failure reflected in this new acquaintance (the word *spegel* in Swedish means "mirror"). The ailing man longs for a knife "with which to lay bare my bowels. To detach my brain, my heart. To free me from my substance. To cut away my tongue and my manhood. A sharp blade that would scrape out all my uncleanliness. Then this so-called spirit would soar out of its meaningless body."

Vogler remembers these words, and when he sets up his confrontation with his opponent, Doctor Vergérus, he leaves Spegel's corpse to be dissected, not his own. This is Vogler's one meaningful act: He permits another's spirit to fly free. When Vogler watches Spegel dying in the coach, "we recognize the look of the Knight in the confessional [in *The*

Max von Sydow (Albert Vogler), *Gunnar Björnstrand* (Dr. Vergérus), *and Ingrid Thulin* (Manda Vogler) *in* The Magician. *Photo courtesy Svensk Filmindustri.*

Bergman talking with Åke Fridell (Tubal) *on the set of* The Magician. *Photo courtesy Svensk Filmindustri.*

Seventh Seal]."[8] Spegel is full of apothegms yet just as ignorant as Death himself.

"One walks step by step into the darkness," he mumbles. "The motion itself is the only truth."

Or again: "Truth is made to order; the most skillful liar creates the most useful truth."

Spegel haunts Vogler throughout the film. He is the ubiquitous Ariel who reminds the artist that he is just as mortal as the pedants he detests and that his hypnotic powers are no more than pathetic tricks.

Bergman scarcely needs such a reminder. He of all artists is amused by the complex interpretations placed upon his work. "So you devote yourself to magic seances?" inquires Vergérus pompously. "We haven't said that," responds Manda. (Vogler refuses to speak, implying that his art speaks for him.) "It's a game, nothing else. We use various kinds of apparatus, mirrors, and projectors. It is very simple and entirely harmless."

From the first instant they clap eyes on each other, Vogler and Vergérus are locked in battle. They accept that they are opponents and that each possesses part of the other. Where Vogler sports wig and Christ-like beard, Vergérus wears pince-nez. Reduced to its simplest state, their duel is that of religion versus rationalism. Bergman is not unsympathetic toward Vergérus, who amounts to an analytical realist as dubious of scientific facts in his heart as Vogler is aware of the flimsiness of the illusion he creates. Indeed, Vergérus believes that Vogler is mysteriously potent, and "is ready to kill Truth in order to possess it in a sterile dissection."[9] He experiences disappointment, however, when he realizes that Vogler has tricked him in the attic with a series of deceptions and mere legerdemain. "Miracles don't happen," he has maintained. "It's always the apparatus and the *Spiel* that have to do the work. The clergy have the same sad experience. God is silent and the people chatter." Even the muscular rigidity induced in the burly coachman, Antonsson (Oscar Ljung), which forms the highlight of Vogler's demonstration in the consul's home, is explicable through the methods of Anton Mesmer (proponent of the theory of animal magnetism, hence "mesmerize").

Bergman delights in deluding his own audience even as he unmasks Albert Emanuel Vogler in the film. He does so, moreover, by resorting to unashamedly theatrical effects. During the attic sequence, in which Vergérus dips his pen into an inkwell containing a human eyeball and is shocked by the appearance of a dismembered hand, the camera movements and editing rhythm are wholly subjective, compelling the spectator to identify with Vergérus. The arrogant victim in *The Magician* is forced to his knees, as Albert is in the circus ring of *The Naked Night*. Plot and mood are manipulated with the same subtle crack of the whip. Vogler, his beard and wig laid aside, begs Vergérus for a safe conduct and some money to leave the city. When Vergérus sneers at him, he replies, "You are ungrateful. Haven't I exerted myself beyond my usual powers to give you an experience?"

But without his disguise Vogler is helpless. "I liked *his* face better than yours," says Vergérus. "I've never seen you before!" cries the consul's wife, Ottilia (Gertrud Fridh), who had been on her knees to him in her boudoir only the night before. But the humiliation is peremptorily dispelled by the arrival of a royal proclamation summoning Vogler to appear before the king on July 14 (Bergman's birthday!).

"Gather the rest of the apparatus and send it to the palace," Vogler tells the footman. "Be careful. They are expensive objects," he adds with the shadow of a smile. Not long before, Bergman had written: "I am either an imposter or, in the case where the audience is willing to be taken in, a conjuror. I perform conjuring tricks with a conjuring apparatus so expensive and so wonderful that any performer in history would have given anything to own or make use of it."[10]

In short, *The Magician* is the most acutely personal of all Bergman's films of the fifties.

One may invoke parallels with the *via dolorosa* of Christ on the road to Golgotha, or with the outrageous conclusion of *The Beggar's Opera*, but the truth is more straightforward than that. "All of a sudden," Bergman recalls, "I was given a grant out of the king's fund, which put my shares up at home with mother and father, anyway." So rain is transmuted into sunshine, and Vogler/Bergman clatters away in his coach in triumph.

Bergman subtitled *The Magician* "a comedy," and the ribald antics in the kitchen bear this out. The love potion administered by Tubal sends Sara (Bibi Andersson) and the coachman Simson into raptures. It contains a mystical element similar to that in the wine distilled from stallions' seed and young mothers' milk in *Smiles of a Summer Night*. In both films, sex requires this stimulant before it embodies any energy. But if—as when the "dead" actor erupts suddenly into the kitchen— there is a laugh behind every shiver, so there is a shiver behind every laugh, behind every melodramatic situation. Without this balance, the weight of melodrama would destroy the film.

Contempt, even cruelty, may be detected in Bergman's attitude to his audience. The women in the film are either lovesick or inane. Sofia Garp, the cook, accepts the libidinous advances of Tubal. "You're a humbug, of course," she says. "Yes, but I've got something, haven't I?" replies Tubal and follows her to her room in triumph. Tubal, like Frid in *Smiles* and Monika in *Summer with Monika*, oozes a natural hedonism: "The future worries me as little as the past. I am a lily of the field, I live for today."

Ottilia, the consul's wife, slips her husband a sleeping draught and greets Vogler as a savior come to redeem her from the loathsome arms of the consul: "You will explain why my child died. What God meant. That's why you have come. To soothe my sorrow and lift the burden from my shoulders." The magician as Christ-substitute. Such a label fits when, the next day, Ottilia "denies" Vogler.

Starbeck's wife, falling gleefully into the most elementary of hypnotic states, denounces her husband before the assembled guests.

Manda is the only sensible presence in this gallery of posturing idiots and hypocrites. Alone with Vogler in their bedroom, each in "a state of nature," *sans* beard, *sans* makeup, *sans* wig, she represents the artist's true friend and companion, who shares his humiliation and his triumph. Vogler pours out his anguish and revulsion as he lies beside her on the bed. "I hate them! I hate their faces, their bodies, their movements, their voices!" Below stairs, the inebriated coachman echoes his words, leveling his fury at Vogler and his troupe: "Charlatans like that, with faces like theirs, they should be flogged." The battle lines are clearly drawn.

In an interview on Swedish television some thirteen years ago, Bergman spoke of his skeptical view of art.

> We who are engaged in art—to express it solemnly—we should be there for *people*. . . . So, in one way or another, we must participate in the world, and I feel that, as artists, we often betray this vision because we fall so easily into some kind of egocentricity, of self-preoccupation—and at that moment, we exist only for own sakes. . . . We become a plague, I feel, sort of parasites existing in the material world without any meaning at all whenever we do not function in relation to other people.[11]

And when the artist is rejected by society, the only remedy to hand for him is to continue his work unstintingly.

The suspicion remains, however, that at the time of making *The Magician*, Bergman felt as disenchanted with his Malmö audience as Woody Allen did with his director-as-superstar status when he made *Stardust Memories*. Only a voracious, insatiable need *for* that audience sustained his growth and development as an artist and entertainer. Furthermore, Bergman places art ahead of all personal considerations. When Gunnar Björnstrand, playing Vergérus, arrived at the studio one morning suffering from migraine, he and Bergman agreed to proceed with a close-up, to register the extra tension and pain in his features. Such are the exigencies of art, and truth becomes illusion as easily as does the reverse.

In style, *The Magician* was far removed from *Brink of Life*. "Because I've always worked in the theater and always had a longing to write stage plays, some of my films have obviously been surreptitious plays," Bergman has noted. The performance given by Vogler and his troupe in the consul's house is a play within a play. The lighting appears theatrical, the acting courtly; the dialog sports the sardonic quality of Molière or Marivaux. The *laterna magica* used by Vogler is a symbol of illusion, the dancing face projected on the curtain an emblem for the intangibility of truth. Even the consul's home and the cobbled street up which Vogler vanishes in jubilation are "false." They were found by Bergman in the Skansen open-air museum in Stockholm, replicas of the past constructed for the inquisitive eyes of tourists.

Kerstin Hedeby earned the least celebration of Bergman's colleagues at Malmö, chiefly because she did not work on his films as much as other members of the Municipal Theater. Her sets and costumes contributed enormously to the impact of Bergman's stage productions, and in *Urfaust*, which opened on October 17, 1958, she surpassed herself.

The costumes were reminiscent of fourteenth-century German paintings, while the basic set consisted of a triptych of gothic arches adorned on either side by a madonna and a gargoyle. Kerstin Hedeby was married to Toivo Pawlo, who played Mephistopheles in this production.

Goethe's first, youthful draft of *Faust*, usually referred to as the *Urfaust*, was divided into twenty scenes by Bergman and made of Faust a philosopher-lover—"a cross between Romeo and Hamlet," wrote the anonymous correspondent of the London *Times*.

The opening of the play was enthralling even by Bergman's standards. The house lights dimmed until the theater, with curtain up over the huge apron stage, was in pitch darkness. Then a single spotlight from high in the auditorium picked out the face of Max von Sydow's Faust, as he entered from stage right. The effect was that of a head floating in space, a cinematic device if ever there was one, and a signal of the brilliant lighting that distinguished the entire production. Minor characters were used as silhouettes against the backdrop; livid greens and reds prevailed among the costumes (with Mephistopheles in a scarlet cloak); and props were sacrificed in favor of pantomime in certain scenes.

When Bergman brought the production to the Princes Theatre, London, in May of the following year, the flashes of Bergmanesque irony pierced through the barriers of the Swedish dialog, and an exultant gallery and upper circle roared back the players for successive curtain calls.

Gunnel Lindblom, "austere and honest and magnificent" (Bergman's words), was Margareta, condemned in the end to die in prison after her illicit child was born—and died.[12] Her erotic presence is wedded to a fine sense of tragedy as she gazes with horror into the face of Mephistopheles, who bends over her with the words, "Judgment has been pronounced," and recognizes in his features those of her beloved Faust. Another outstanding performance was that of Gudrun Brost playing Martha, the love of Mephistopheles.

In theme, there were affinities between *Urfaust* and *The Devil's Eye* (Bergman's 1960 movie in which Don Juan makes a pact with the Devil). In visual texture, however, the stage production was related to *The Magician*, with Max von Sydow's facial makeup almost identical and the lighting equally hard and expressionistic.

The last three months of 1958 were among the busiest in Bergman's career. *Urfaust* premiered on October 17; his revival of Olle Hedberg's play *Rabies* was shown on television on November 7; his final production at the Malmö Municipal Theater—*The People of Värmland*—opened on December 19; and a week later *The Magician* was unveiled in Stockholm.

In November, Bergman and Victor Sjöström were awarded Gold Plaques by the Swedish Film Academy. "Now I've received all the prizes that exist," sighed Bergman. "All that remains is for someone to stuff me and place me in a showcase in a film museum."[13]

The People of Värmland is a folk comedy by F. A. Dahlgren, "a sort of village Romeo and Juliet, padded out with songs and popular anecdotes."[14] As well as Max von Sydow and Bibi Andersson in the leading roles, the presence of the popular star of operetta, Åke Askner, gave the Malmö audience something to cheer. But, as Henrik Sjögren wrote, "The laughter died away and stuck in the audience's throat when, in the end, Askner revealed how tragically and desperately empty is the liar's life-role. It was one of those magical moments one sometimes gets at the theater." By slightly exaggerating the bucolic quality of the entertainment, Bergman set it in perspective, which enabled his satirical—but also affectionate—treatment to be appreciated.

Bergman's contract at Malmö had come to an end, and he decided to return to Stockholm and join the Royal Dramatic Theater. Some of his ensemble accompanied him; for others, it was the close of an era. Bergman's life was changing too. By early 1959 the love affair with Bibi Andersson was over. It had been a singularly rewarding involvement. Bergman was moving on, but he retained, as he does with all the women in his life, a profound symbiosis with Bibi.

"I must be able to exchange souls with my partner," he has said. "The ones I've been together with for the other thing—well, I can count them on the fingers of one hand. And deep down I am faithful—though no one will believe it. My being is actually fidelity: All those whom I have grown fond of in some way, I am faithful to afterward."[15]

At a rehearsal in Malmö, Bergman had met an elegant, accomplished woman named Käbi Laretei. She was already renowned throughout Scandinavia and in Europe and the United States as a pianist of high caliber. She had style and wit and verve. During the spring, Bergman saw her playing on television and asked a friend to arrange an introduction. Käbi's husband was Gunnar Staern, a conductor, and there was a four-year-old daughter. In London in May, Käbi was performing at the Royal Festival Hall on the same evening as Urfaust opened in Peter Daubeny's World Theatre Season. The Swedish press pursued the couple relentlessly, their curiosity heightened by the fact that Käbi was still married.

Bergman's relationship and marriage to Käbi Laretei constituted a significant phase of his life. On the one hand it marked a return to the bourgeois world in which he had been reared; on the other, it awoke in him the need for an altogether new approach to the cinema, an approach at once austere and improvisatory.

For the first time he had found a partner as famous and competent as himself. Intelligent, effusive, assured, Käbi Laretei numbered Stravinsky, Bartók, and Hindemith among her friends. She was born in Estonia, the tiny Baltic state now part of the Soviet Union, and traveled to Sweden during World War II as a political refugee. She later studied in Switzerland with Edwin Fischer, Paul Baumgartner, and Langenhan-Hirzel. In 1946 she made her concert debut in Stockholm and has established a fine reputation in the intervening years, especially for her interpretation of modern piano music. Her performance of Hindemith's *Ludus Tonalis* at Carnegie Hall, shortly before the composer's death, was a high point in her career.

By coincidence, Käbi and Ingmar were born on the same day, July 14. When they met, they discovered little by little that they were "two badly injured people. . . . She had her time as a refugee behind her. And I, I felt myself to be dying."[16]

Käbi still remembered her childhood journeys to Moscow. Her father had been a minister, and she was raised in an aristocratic milieu. When the war broke out, the family had to abandon all its possessions and flee to the neutral sanctuary of Sweden. The experience bred in Käbi a capacity for survival. "No one has the faintest idea of the resources hidden in that girl," said Bergman.[17]

In the early spring of 1959, he and Käbi motored up to Dalarna to enable Bergman to work on the screenplay of *The Virgin Spring* with Ulla Isaksson. Käbi fell immediately in love with the country landscape, which reminded her of southern Estonia. Bergman meanwhile applied himself to writing a first draft for *The Devil's Eye*, a comedy he had agreed to make for Svensk Filmindustri as a form of insurance should *The Virgin Spring*, a potentially downbeat project from a box-office viewpoint, lose money. He and Ulla Isaksson wrote away in separate rooms at the Hotel Siljansborg, while Käbi practiced her piano downstairs. Between such sessions, there were long walks in the neighborhood in temperatures of $-4°$F!

Ulla Isaksson applied her imagination to a medieval ballad, which originated in the Romance languages and assumed the status of a legend in the Nordic lands, about a young virgin, Karin, who is waylaid and killed by three brigands while riding to early mass. In some versions of the legend, three girls are ravished, but in the province of Östergötland there is a recorded incident involving the daughter of a farmer near Linköping, who was kidnapped, overpowered, raped, and killed by a group of vagabonds. The spring said to have welled up beneath the corpse of the ravished girl still exists in the churchyard of Kärna parish and is thought to have healing powers.

Ulla Isaksson was attracted by the purity and rigor of the song, which falls into clearly defined segments and marches relentlessly along its appointed course. The dramatic and visual elements are foremost, and this creates the basis not only for a religious miracle play but also for a Bergman film in which Christian and pagan teachings are in conflict, just as in *The Seventh Seal* the atheism of the Squire is opposed to the yearning belief of the Knight.

Bergman urged Isaksson to preserve the archaic and primitive spirit of the original legend. Sweden had been converted to Christianity long before the ballad emerged, but the Black Mass, a deliberate travesty of Christian ritual, began to percolate Europe in the twelfth century, and weird sacrifices were carried out behind closed doors on the farms of Dalarna and other Swedish provinces. During the fifties, Bergman was drawn compulsively to this metaphysical and religious debate.

> I needed a severe and schematic conception of the world to get away from the formless, the vague and the obscure, in which I was stuck. So I turned to the dogmatic Christianity of the Middle Ages with its clear dividing lines between Good and Evil. Later I felt tied by it, I felt as though I were imprisoned.[18]

Looking back on the film, however, Bergman is almost ashamed. "*The Virgin Spring* must be regarded as an aberration. It's touristic, a lousy imitation of Kurosawa."[19] He believes that by permeating the tale with the notion of therapy and the remission of sin through sacrifice (Töre's building a new church to atone for his negligence toward Karin), he blurred and corrupted the original ballad and its stark outline.

Nevertheless, Bergman was extremely happy during the shooting of the film. His regular cameraman, Gunnar Fischer, had been engaged by the Walt Disney organization to shoot a feature in the far north of Sweden during the bitterly cold winter of 1958–1959 and so could not join Bergman on preparatory work for *The Virgin Spring*. In his place Bergman took Sven Nykvist, who had worked with him on *The Naked Night*. Their understanding was immediate, and with the exception of Bergman's next project, *The Devil's Eye*, Nykvist was to become a major personality in the Bergman team.

Many exteriors were filmed at Styggförsen in Dalarna, not far from Rättvik. The summer was by no means fine, and Bergman recounted his feelings one rain-swept morning when he and the crew were preparing an elaborate tracking shot through the forest. Just twenty-two people were present. The facilities were rather primitive, and complex technical rehearsals were necessary.

Suddenly a break appeared in the clouds, the sun shone, and Bergman elected to shoot. Then a colleague cried out and pointed upwards. Two majestic cranes soared above the pine trees. "We dropped what we were doing and raced up to the crest of a small hill above the stream in order to get a better view of the birds in flight." Eventually the cranes disappeared over the western horizon, and Bergman and his team returned to work, invigorated by the sight.

"I felt a sudden happiness and relief," he said. "I felt secure and at home." In a single incident lies the source of so much that is intimate and resourceful in Nordic cinema.

Problems had to be coped with on a daily basis. According to the script, the buds on the trees should have just been bursting, but the leaves were too far advanced, and Bergman had to keep moving further north to new locations.

In one scene, Max von Sydow, as Töre, uproots a solitary birch tree as the first stage in his solemn cleansing and preparation for the murder of the three robbers. But although Sweden is literally covered with birch trees, no stretch of ground containing just a *single* sapling or tree could be located. So Bergman took his crew and actors to a different area altogether, where in an open field they planted a tree. The sun was going down, and Nykvist waited for the evening light; when he viewed the rushes two days later he realized that everything was in silhouette— too much light had penetrated the film because the focus-puller had forgotten to close the camera! A fortnight later the scene had to be shot again.

On another occasion, two technicians were sent north by Svensk Filmindustri to investigate Bergman's complaints about the poor sound being achieved on the film. At first they could detect nothing wrong with the soundtrack. Finally, they conceded that there were flaws in the recording that were inaudible to normal ears. Bergman has always had a hypersensitive sense of hearing. Erik Nordgren, his composer during this period, recalls an incident in post-production work on *The Seventh Seal*: "There's a place in the score where the double basses—I used five—go down to their lowest tone, a C, and Ingmar was at the recording and reacted immediately and asked what it was. Quite fantastic, because he wasn't a professional musician or composer."

On the other hand, Nordgren regretted that Bergman chose to use two modern flutes for the music of *The Virgin Spring*. The proper instruments for the time would have been recorders.

Bergman does not attempt to pursue the American and Italian style of historical filmmaking, whereby every detail is minutely reconstructed. He relies on a few evocative touches to achieve a startling atmosphere of verisimilitude. Karin (Birgitta Pettersson), for instance, uses the surface of a cask of water as a mirror. Skins are strung for stretching on the walls, and Töre carries his cutlery in a pouch at his belt.

Numerous Freudian motives have been read into *The Virgin Spring* through the years. The structure and texture of the film permit this, for the dialog is sparse. More is disclosed in the silences that elapse between sentences than in the speech itself.

Töre is the dominant figure. His authority on the film and in his family remains unquestioned. He insists that Karin should go to church, accompanied by her foster sister Ingeri (Gunnel Lindblom).

The central battle of the film develops between light and darkness, Good and Evil, Christianity and paganism. Karin represents the unsullied beauty that by its very nature tempts the evil rapists. Töre embodies the Christian ideal of the Middle Ages (he is seen first with his wife, Märeta (Birgitta Valberg), performing daily prayers beneath a wooden crucifix), whereas Ingeri is the stranger, like the toad she ensconces in the bread being prepared for Karin's journey.

Töre's relationship with Karin appears full of affection. She blows and whispers into his ear to gain a favor, while the mother looks on sternly, recognizing her own inferior status in the family hierarchy. Some critics have implied that Töre wants to sleep with his daughter. Bergman offers only a few tantalizing clues to the intimacy of their relationship. One of them is the scene described earlier, when Töre, incensed at the discovery of his daughter's murder, tears a young birch tree out of the ground. As he bears the tree heavily to the ground, he straddles it and lets his breath emerge in a groan of relief and fulfillment. The movement and sound both strike a sexual chord.

Perhaps, though, it may be more plausible to assume that Karin regards her father as the most perfect embodiment of Christian appeal and that when she draws on her magnificent dress she does so less to please God at the church than to appear blithe and gracious in the eyes of her father. A lusty laborer, Simon (Oscar Ljung), greets Karin and Ingeri soon after they leave the farm on horseback. "You've dressed and ornamented yourself like a bride for her groom," he says, reinforcing the sense of Karin's expectancy.

Ingeri's jealousy of Karin belongs in her gesture of placing the toad in the bread, but early in the morning, in "rhyme" with Töre's worship, she has invoked the ancient god, Odin, and cursed her sister in his name. Now, while Karin rides daintily sidesaddle, Ingeri straddles her horse, dark and lowering. But she is appalled by the evil she has unleashed. When they reach the edge of the forest, she refuses to proceed further. While Karin continues, oblivious to danger, Ingeri enters the hut of an old man beside the ford in the stream. Bergman's portrayal of the pagan practitioner is grotesque, even risible. Ingeri reacts to the sound of "three dead men riding north," when the old man says, "You can hear for yourself if you do as I do." His protruding side teeth and croaking voice conjure up the features of the toad that Ingeri has consigned to her sister.

Bergman is at his best when telling the story of the rape and death of Karin; at his worst when seeking to analyze it.

The three goatherds glimpse Karin in a clearing as she pauses to incline her face to the warm sun, and they dash silently along a ridge to intercept her. Bergman uses slow pans in these tense scenes to arouse a sinister mood and to correspond stylistically with the hush in the depths of the forest.

Karin is fascinated by the Jew's harp that the thin herdsman (Axel Düberg) twangs nauseatingly. She is inveigled into sharing her lunch. The tongueless brother (Tor Isedal) leads Karin's horse under a huge fallen tree, into a glade where even more trees are arrayed obliquely. These harsh lines across the frame suggest the sudden change of tone in the journey, and dead branches lie behind the group during the meal.

Max von Sydow (Töre) and Birgitta Pettersson (Karin) in The Virgin Spring. *Photo courtesy Svensk Filmindustri.*

Karin excites the herdsmen by flirting with them as they beguile her with a succession of vulgar compliments. The situation is irresistibly reminiscent of Red Riding Hood and the disguised wolf. Ingeri, having broken free of the old man's lecherous advances, now gazes down at the scene from behind a fallen trunk. She grasps a stone and tries to hurl it at the herdsmen, but her strength fails her, and she lets it roll harmlessly down into the stream—the stream that will eventually yield the virgin spring.

The moment of rape is triggered by the unexpected appearance of the toad, dropping out of the loaf of bread and squatting blackly on a piece of pure white cloth. Karin tries to flee but is caught up in the branches of a nearby tree like a wraith, helpless against the men's strong arms. She finds herself pinned down and violated by both the elder herdsmen; then the little boy (Ove Porath) flings himself on her breasts.

Bergman's treatment of the rape contains no trace of salaciousness. The objectivity of the act, the way it is observed, shocks the spectator, as does the murder of Karin—struck down with a heavy if also merciful thud by the tongueless herdsman as she wanders moaning round the glade.

The Virgin Spring possesses two distinct parts. The first half of the film concludes with the herdsmen robbing Karin of her shift and dashing away, leaving the small boy on guard. Overcome with revulsion, he covers Karin's corpse with a few handfuls of earth and then runs off into the forest as the snow lays silently, like grief, around the dead girl.

> *When this foul deed had they done,*
> *They took the way that she had come.*
>
> *They went along that wooded lane*
> *Until they Vänge village came.*
>
> *They came up to the farm of Töre*
> *And found the farmer at his door.*

Töre allows the herdsmen to enter his farm to shelter for the night. He is suspicious but not alarmed. There is an air of foreboding. Dark shadows fall across the walls of the farm, the three men crouch behind the black bar of the gate, and an owl cries in warning (the same device as in *Summer Interlude*, when Marie returns to the island).

In Bergman's films of this period a seer often emerges, a character whose role is peripheral to the main drama but whose perception and intuition cast light on the crux of the matter. In *The Magician*, Granny fulfills this part. Here, it is the beggar belonging to Töre's household (Allan Edwall). At supper he senses that these unexpected guests are responsible for the continued absence of Karin. "The Queen of the Sun shone so brightly that one forgot all one's dark winter miseries," he intones. "My legs just wanted to dance for joy. I saw the May Queen herself ride out in the sun—but she didn't return."

The next decisive juncture arrives when the little boy retches at table. He has recognized that Töre's grace is identical to the one recited by Karin in the glade. Meanwhile the fire that Ingeri blew into life at the start of the film burns in the left background—a living curse that must be extinguished. The beggar leans over the boy and offers words of solace, telling him that when he is about to be swallowed up in an abyss for murderers and violators, an arm will grasp him and take him beyond the reach of evil.

Yet, as in all ambiguous scenes in *The Virgin Spring*, this mumbo jumbo leaves one dissatisfied and unconvinced. Bergman is on much surer ground when he describes Töre's discovery of the torn and bloodied shift that the herdsmen have foolishly offered for sale. From this moment onward, the film proceeds with classical inevitability. Töre uproots the birch tree, flagellates himself with the branches, and sluices his body with hot water. Ingeri, now home and anxious to assume the guilt for Karin's murder, is merely a tool for fetching Töre's slaughtering knife.

Töre enters the central hall where the herdsmen are sleeping. He examines the contents of their bags, finding there Karin's shoes, the last and most pitiful scraps of evidence available. Then Töre sits like some awesome god in his chair, decorated with portraits of the saints (an interesting contrast to the seat of the old man beside the ford, which is covered with signs and images of pagan gods). Töre drives his knife into the table and awaits the rising of the sun so that his rite of vengeance may begin. Bergman's low camera angle gives Töre the look of a fascist leader. He is bereft of humanity, a medieval Abraham who believes that by cleansing his body he can shed the blood of strangers without compunction.

The eldest brother meets his death. Töre stabs him through the heart and leaves him in a crucified stance at the far end of the hall. The thin brother almost escapes by dodging Töre's first lunge and scrambling up the pole that supports the vent in the roof, using the same grip as Ingeri did when invoking Odin. This association is made even more significant when Töre crushes his victim in the flames of the fire that Ingeri has blown alight.

Finally, the boy is snatched from Märeta's arms, where he has fled for protection. Töre gathers him up in a fireman's lift and flings him against the wall.

Max von Sydow (Töre) *and Birgitta Valberg* (Märeta) *after the slaughter of the robbers in* The Virgin Spring. *Photo courtesy Svensk Filmindustri.*

Silence prevails.

Töre gazes at his bloody hands, and his fury drains from him. As he leads his family and retainers in a precipitous journey through the forest to recover Karin's body, Töre appears stunned, entranced. When Märeta says that she loved her daughter too much, "more than God Himself," her husband replies that she is not alone in her guilt. He had urged Ingeri to go with Karin, and he acknowledges that he had been too proud of the girl, had elevated her to an almost Biblical symbol of goodness and virginity.

While his wife weeps over Karin's corpse, Töre is virtually struck down by some abstract force. He stares skyward in supplication, uttering the words of baffled incomprehension common to such disparate Bergman characters as the Knight in *The Seventh Seal* and the pastor in *Cries and Whispers*: "I don't understand you, God . . . yet I ask for forgiveness, for I know of no other way to live."

He staggers to his feet and, hands raised grandiloquently, vows to build a church of limestone and granite as penance for his sin. The spring that now flows from beneath Karin's head is a direct result of Töre's vow, because when he and Märeta had first lifted her head no water had appeared. As a final act of absolution, Ingeri bathes her face in the fresh stream, thereby exorcising the evil that her summons to a pagan god had invoked.

Bergman cuts to a high-angle shot of the group kneeling in acknowledgment of the miracle. The sound of a choir singing swells over the image, a rare instance of bathos in Bergman's work. In a film where silence and unusual snatches of music have been deployed without extravagance, the introduction of such a cliche is particularly distressing.

Of all Bergman's works, *The Virgin Spring* reminds one of the great silent works of Victor Sjöström. Man is influenced directly by his natural environment. Insensate objects, such as the stone that Ingeri rolls down the embankment, the birch tree uprooted by Töre, and the branches that fence in the scene of the rape, assume an importance in the drama reminiscent of the lashing waves in *Terje Vigen* (1916) and the mountain stream in *The Outlaw and His Wife* (1918).

The ethical aspect of the film also comes from a Swedish tradition. "Our whole existence," Bergman has said, "is based on the fact that there are things we may do and others we may not do, and these are the complications that we uninterruptedly, constantly come into contact with throughout our life." God—more than social and economic conditions—is somehow responsible for all the complexes, vanities, and desires that man is heir to and that reduce him to a posturing idiot, to a Vogler, an Egerman, or even a Töre.

In an interview in 1975, Bergman remarked that Sweden was a Lutheran, Calvinistic country, not consciously perhaps, but "in a subterranean way. Religion talks about two things: law and love. The trouble is, everybody has forgotten love but, inside, everybody remembers the law. That makes for terrible problems."[20]

Bergman's affection for Kurosawa and the Japanese cinema may be felt in the rhythm of *The Virgin Spring*, in the juxtaposition of bouts of violent action and allusive silence, in the tracking shots that accompany Karin and Ingeri, and later Töre and his family, as they hasten through the forest, and in the controlled acting of Max von Sydow and Birgitta Valberg as the parents.

The moral ambivalence of the film recalls *Rashomon*. Bergman, one feels, would like his work to breathe a psychological complexity. But while in *Persona*, or *Wild Strawberries*, or *Hour of the Wolf*, to take but three examples, he succeeds in peering deep into the personalities

Bergman with Bibi Andersson (Britt-Marie) on the set of The Devil's Eye. *Photo courtesy Svensk Filmindustri.*

of his major characters, in *The Virgin Spring* he is prevented by the simple fabric of the legend from presenting any of the dramatis personae in other than emblematic terms. The most durable sequences enact the narrative tension of the original ballad—the ride through the forest, the rape and murder, Töre's vengeance "with unsheathed knife."

On June 28, with *The Virgin Spring* in the can and *The Devil's Eye* in pre-production, Bergman attended the confirmation of his daughter, Lena, in the presence of his parents and of Else Fisher, Lena's mother.

Although he was happy with Käbi Laretei (they were married in Boda Church in Dalarna on September 1), Bergman was passing through a period of readjustment. He had torn up his roots from Malmö and had lost confidence in the theater and in his own abilities.

During the shooting of *The Devil's Eye*, and after toying with the notion of directing the Municipal Theater in Stockholm, he was engaged by the Royal Dramatic Theater. His stomach was troubling him, and he was furious with himself for having agreed to make a comedy for Svensk Filmindustri so soon after the arduous production of *The Virgin Spring*. "I detest the idea," he admitted later, "that some of my films, especially the bad ones, are going to survive."[21]

The Devil's Eye (*Djävulens öga*) was an unhappy experience in every respect. Apart from Bergman's nausea, there was not exactly the burning desire between Jarl Kulle (as Don Juan) and Bibi Andersson (as Britt-Marie, the pastor's daughter) so necessary for the relationship to appear satisfactory. Kulle, as a colleague recalls, "was the type of actor who did not suit Ingmar." *Life* magazine sent a team to do a photographic essay on Bergman. "This was Bibi's first day on the film," he was reported as saying, "and she was terribly nervous. I am never angry with [the actors], for they are such sensitive instruments."[22]

Even more serious from a long-term point of view was Bergman's friction with Gunnar Fischer. On the second day, when the unit sat in the screening room viewing the rushes, he pounced on Fischer in front of everyone for some error of lighting.

Next day, Bergman apologized—as was his wont—but he wounded Fischer by telling him that after working with Sven Nykvist on one film, *The Virgin Spring*, he was spoiled. The relationship had reached its end. Fischer had photographed a dozen of Bergman's films, and his powerful use of monochrome technique had contributed enormously to their reputation around the world. No violent quarrel ever took place, however, and in 1970 Bergman asked Fischer to shoot the credits sequence for *The Touch*—and paid him handsomely.

The Devil's Eye was based on a somewhat elderly Danish radio play, *Don Juan Returns*, written by Oluf Bang. Bergman found it in the archives of Svensk Filmindustri. At first glance, it is difficult to see what attracted him to the subject. In all likelihood, it was his desire to place on film some elements of his enjoyable staging of Molière's *Don Juan* at Malmö in 1955. The fundamental conceit—Don Juan being dispatched from Hell by the Devil, whose stye may be cured only if a women's chastity is breached—is rather engaging. The dialog, too, bubbles with irony and epigrams. During the opening scenes in Hell, a marbled hall where the Devil (none other than the comedian Stig Järrel) struts about in a dark business suit, some of Bergman's finest writing crackles with wit. The only blasphemous words are those that refer to God and the Church (of course), and Satan's noble and respected advisers are Count de Rochefoucauld and the Marquis de Maccopazza, whose "perversions in their time sent voluptuous shudders right up into the archangel's pinions."

Don Juan (Jarl Kulle) receives his briefing about the seduction of Britt-Marie from these counsellors: "Sudden attack is preferable to lengthy siege," and "The Nordic woman is loyal and romantic but ruthless in her emotions." An assistant, Pablo (Sture Lagerwall), is assigned to Don Juan for his assault on the pastor's home. "For three hundred years I've endured the curse of continence," complains Pablo, eager for the chance to seduce the pastor's wife.

Bergman revels in his attack on petty bourgeois pretense. Renata (Gertrud Fridh) thinks it unfair that no one sees her as she really is, without acknowledging that the reason is that her kind attach too much significance to external ceremony. As Don Juan says, in a mocking voice, "Principles are more sacred than life." When Renata asks her husband

Gertrud Fridh (Renata) *and Jarl Kulle* (Don Juan) *in* The Devil's Eye.
Photo courtesy Svensk Filmindustri.

(Nils Poppe) if he could forgive her for being unfaithful, the pastor replies: "I must love you whatever happens." He is not the only prisoner of staid convention in Bergman's world, and like Fredrik Egerman in *Smiles of a Summer Night* and Isak Borg in *Wild Strawberries*, he must undergo the painful experience of watching his wife embrace a lover.

Don Juan remains the most intriguing character in the film. Bergman identifies with him to a certain degree, and his love affair with the young Bibi Andersson earlier in the decade is probably echoed in the tantalizing relationship between Britt-Marie and the great lover. So Bergman scrutinizes his own affections.

Don Juan is mortified at the end because his love lacks feeling and simplicity. He can never ape the simple nuptial bliss of Britt-Marie and her fiance on earth, Jonas (Axel Düberg). Don Juan's self-importance and dandyism conceal his romantic nature; he is entranced by Britt-Marie when she admits to feeling pity for him rather than desire, and not vice versa, as tradition would have it. His final descent into Hell recalls Bergman's stage production, with the immense bearded statue thundering at the door and Don Juan sinking into a mass of flames while the monumental effigy gazes on. The scene has been described by every major writer dealing with the legend of Don Juan, from Tirso de Malina to Lord Byron. In such moments Bergman can, with a snap of his fingers, blend the elements of the theater with those of the cinema and

Kӓbi Laretei and Ingmar Bergman together in Djursholm. Photo courtesy Lennart Nilsson.

create a *frisson* that stays in the mind longer than all the courtly dialog.

But other parts of *The Devil's Eye* betray Bergman's lethargy. The storm around the pastor's house, for example, and the flames in Hell, are crude even by the standards of amateur filmmaking. Certain scenes are too attenuated and lack vibrancy. The entire film sports a misanthropic tone, even if it is redeemed with a final, deadly thrust to the heart of the bourgeois ideal: Britt-Marie tells Jonas on their wedding night that she has never been kissed by another man, thus denying her contact with Don Juan. The lie is sufficiently horrendous to cure Satan's stye!

Bergman had presented Kӓbi Laretei with a harpsichord on condition she select and record some Scarlatti sonatas for *The Devil's Eye*. The film begins and ends with the familiar sonata in E major, and when Don Juan and Pablo emerge on earth there is another burst of Scarlatti, "brilliant and bubbling with the joy of life," says Kӓbi. She received no credit, at her own insistence, and was surprised to read in the newspapers after the premiere that the critics found the music beautifully chosen and played.

Bergman was rather bemused by the attention that his earlier films now attracted outside Sweden. *The Magician* and *Wild Strawberries*, reported *Variety*, would probably earn half a million dollars at the U.S. box office. Bergman was featured in *Time* and *Newsweek*. The *Time* piece resounded with characteristic hyperbole and alliteration: "The Bergman boom fits into the cultural context of the times. His is a voice crying in the midst of prosperity that man cannot live by prosperity alone."[23] It did point out, however, that Bergman's effects were accomplished with antiquated means. Among the more ludicrous proposals put to the Swedish director, it claimed, was Harry Belafonte's offer for him to direct a film on the life of Alexander Pushkin—with Belafonte as the Russian poet.

On the continent, Bergman's achievement was already recognized in Paris, and the first major study and filmography of his career had been published—in Uruguay!

Ingmar and Käbi moved into a capacious villa in the fashionable Djursholm district of Stockholm. He was, in his own words, "embarking on an entirely new way of life."[24] Even more interesting—although scarcely discernible at the time—was his drift toward humanism. The concept of faith no longer obsessed him. His work henceforth would be devoid of the romance that always accompanies the tacit belief in a God.

Some years later, Bergman summed up his feelings on this score: "Now I believe that all the qualities I used to associate with God—love, tenderness, grace, all those beautiful things—are created by human beings themselves, they come from inside us. That, for me, is the big miracle."[25]

CHAPTER TEN

Whose Silence?

*You can't live without feeling how important you
are. And that's the whole truth. You can't bear it if
everything isn't "vitally important" or "significant"
or "meaningful" and I don't know what else.*

Anna to Ester in The Silence

ALTHOUGH SOME FRIENDS CLAIM THAT INGMAR BERGMAN WAS A REBEL
who came home to the arms of the bourgeoisie when he married Käbi
Laretei, the director has never regarded himself as a fugitive from the
bourgeois environment. On the contrary, his films of the early sixties
are more "revolutionary" in texture than any of those he made during
his bohemian days in postwar Stockholm.

During this period, his emphasis switches from man's place in the
universe to the condition and validity of the artist in society, to a closer
examination of man's inner weaknesses and the mysterious labyrinth
of his imagination.

In 1960 Bergman published a mock "interview" with himself, conducted by his alias, Ernest Riffe:

"Where do you stand politically?"
"Nowhere. If there was a party for scared people I would join
it. But, as far as I know, there is no such party."
"Your religious leanings?"
"I don't belong to any faith. I keep my own angels and
demons going."

As a foretaste of the new style he would develop, Bergman directed a television version of Strindberg's chamber play, *Storm Weather*. He also received new impulses from another source—his wife. Käbi Laretei's love and knowledge of music impressed Bergman. He relished concerts and records himself, but through Käbi he met many of the world's great musicians, striking up a nice acquaintance with Stravinsky. "I'd like to make films the way Bartók makes music," he told Käbi after she had played the Hungarian's Third Piano Concerto for him.

Their evenings were calm. Bergman liked Käbi to read aloud to him —Russian literature, including of course the Chekhov short stories, and musical biography were among the favorites. "He would lie back on the sofa with his eyes closed," recalls Käbi. "If I accused him of falling asleep, he would recite back an entire passage parrot-fashion!" She gave him a set of records of the Beethoven Quartets together with the scores, and years later Bergman called from Fårö to say that he was still enjoying them.

The villa in Djursholm dated from 1907. Bergman described it as "a wooden structure surrounded by an overgrown and impenetrable garden as big as Gustaf Adolf's Square. The kitchen is as huge as the one in *Miss Julie*, and the living room is the same size as a full apartment. . . . In all my life I've never seen a house so reminiscent of a colossal circus wagon."[1]

Käbi tried to improve his dress sense. They argued over his fondness for berets and leather coats. The berets disappeared, but Bergman clung to his favorite jacket. "It contained my past," he said.

Bergman was struck by Käbi's difference of attitude toward the press. Käbi remained unconcerned by newspaper articles and reviews. Bergman would wake up early the day after one of her concerts and bring the papers into their bedroom in excitement while Käbi preferred to sleep until the afternoon. Bergman, on the other hand, devoured the Swedish notices after a premiere of one of his films; the foreign ones meant less to him. In the same vein, he would seek an immediate reaction from Käbi to any new screenplay, as soon as Lenn Hjortzberg (his assistant) had finished typing it up from Bergman's handwritten sheets.

In the spring of 1960, the couple went up to Bergman's cherished haunt, the Hotel Siljansborg in Rättvik, in Dalarna. On May 12, Bergman completed the screenplay for *Through a Glass Darkly* (*Såsom i en spegel*) and dedicated it to "Käbi, my wife."

The film is set on a remote island, where a family of four are on summer vacation. At first he thought of shooting on location in the Orkneys, but no suitable site could be found. Then someone mentioned Fårö, the island almost attached to Gotland in the Baltic Sea. "So, on a

Bergman (center) flanked by Lars Passgård (Minus), lending a hand during location shooting for Through a Glass Darkly. *Photo courtesy Svensk Filmindustri.*

nasty, wet day we went over there on the ferry," said Bergman in an interview subsequently. "It was pouring. But I don't know why, it was a kind of instant love. I just felt this was my landscape."[2]

Some years later, he moved permanently to Fårö.

Through a Glass Darkly was shot during the late summer of 1960. Fårö was not always tranquil. In the evening the sheep made a din, and while Bergman was filming the "play within a play" sequence at dusk, the military regiment in Fårösund blew the Last Post, much to the director's chagrin. But the crew and actors were a cheerful group, eating together at night and then often watching movies such as *Mr. Hulot's Holiday* ("It's the fiftieth time I've seen it!" Bergman exclaimed amid laughter).

Through a Glass Darkly should not be regarded in isolation. It forms, with *Winter Light* and *The Silence*, a trilogy. "The theme of these three films," Bergman has declared, "is a 'reduction'—in the metaphysical sense of that word. *Through a Glass Darkly*—certainty achieved. *Winter Light*—certainty unmasked. *The Silence*—God's silence—the negative impression."

All three films are austere in tone and pessimistic in outlook. The quest for the Grail is over. It is as though Bergman were seeking to disencumber himself of the ornamental imagery and high-flown asseverations of films such as *The Seventh Seal, Wild Strawberries,* or *The Magician.* The trilogy is informed with an unerring precision of technique.

It is ironic that the more personal, the more ascetic his films became, the more the wide audience failed to understand him.

Through a Glass Darkly begins with a quotation—containing the title —from Paul's letter to the Corinthians: "For now we see through a glass darkly; but then face to face: now I know in part; but then shall I know even as I am known."

The four characters in the story emerge from the sea. They might be aliens. But soon the air is filled with the ritual chaff of family holidays, recalling Bergman's comment that as a youth he had rebelled against the "atmosphere of hearty wholesomeness" in his home.[3] Each of the four is introverted. Karin (Harriet Andersson), the daughter, suffers from schizophrenia and has only just been discharged from a clinic. David (Gunnar Björnstrand), the father, is a novelist who since the death of his first wife has pursued his career at the expense of the family. Minus (Lars Passgård), the son, has the typical teenager's self-conscious attitude toward sex and resents the teasing of his older sister. And Martin (Max von Sydow), Karin's husband, conceals his longing for freedom beneath a Swedish stoicism and a somewhat patronizing attitude toward those less capable than himself of coping with the anguish of life.

Bergman's exposition of the issues at stake is admirable in its terseness and simplicity during the early part of the film. At an alfresco supper, David comes under scrutiny. He has brought presents for his family that are either unsuitable or mere duplicates of what they already own. And now he announces that he will be leaving them yet again, to conduct some cultural delegation to Yugoslavia. He is finishing another novel, and while on the surface he seems able to place his work ahead of his domestic ties, at root he is shattered with remorse. Bergman shows this in an unexpected, harrowing moment when David goes into the house to fetch some tobacco and sobs in his room, stretching out his arms across the window so that from behind he appears cruciform.

Minus and Karin have conceived a small play with which to welcome their father's return. As he sits in the dusk, watching like Claudius in *Hamlet*, David recognizes that Minus's portrayal of a magniloquent artist is modeled on himself. The artist loses his love because he dare not take the plunge into eternity to join the dead princess (played by

Karin). The sacrifice may be easy, pronounces Minus; what is life to a *real* artist? But love is not worth the sacrifice of a masterpiece.

Just so, David cannot forsake his notions of art for the warmth of family affection.

Troubled though he seems by his daughter's illness, David finds himself observing its progress, charting every aspect of its development, for professional purposes as a writer. Karin, unable to sleep and prying among her father's papers while he is out taking up the nets with Minus, reads these sentiments in his diary. As she learns that her schizophrenia is incurable, she appears shorn of hope. The somber chords of Bach's D Minor Cello Suite underline the depth of her despair.

The environment dictates the mood of *Through a Glass Darkly*. The slender division between night and day affords no rest; only Martin, the most obtuse of the four, can sleep at all. The presence of the quiescent sea, the barren, rock-strewn shore near the house, establishes a sensitivity of sound and image against which the slightest human foible or deviation shows up like a tremor on a seismograph.

Karin's sanctuary is a disused room at the top of the house, where behind the peeling wallpaper she fancies she hears voices summoning her, insisting on the imminent arrival of a God-like figure. In a city setting, the idea would be ludicrous. Here, however, with the reflection of the sunlit waves undulating on the congested floral pattern of the wallpaper, and the forlorn, threatening wail of a foghorn, a plausible impression emerges of some spiritual world with which Karin is in contact. (Bergman uses the same foghorn in *Persona*. It is "as old as the hills, a most ingenious contrivance that regulates itself by means of real Chinese hair. Damp makes the air contract and the thing roars of its own accord!")[4]

Karin is torn between two worlds, like a radio tuned to the scrambled range between two frequencies. The film records her struggle to choose one or the other of these realities. And marching alongside her dilemma are the perplexities of David, wondering if he can subordinate his art to his feelings, and of Minus, emerging painfully from the chrysalis of puberty.

Already at this juncture, Bergman bids farewell to the dogmatic concept of God as part of the Lutheran ethic. Karin yearns for a godhead she can worship, a godhead greater than the emotions and ideals discernible in the everyday world she inhabits. As Bergman says, the film is marked by "the idea of the Christian God as something destructive and fantastically dangerous, something filled with risk for the human being and bringing out in him dark destructive forces instead of the opposite."[5]

Gunnar Björnstrand (David) and Harriet Andersson (Karin) in Through a Glass Darkly. *Photo courtesy Svensk Filmindustri.*

David and Martin leave by boat to do the shopping. Martin proceeds to catechize his father-in-law, accusing him of indifference to Karin's fate. The reproaches sting. Bergman's arguments are the Nordic equivalent of a Catholic's confession—"I, poor miserable sinner . . ."

> "I do my best," protests David.
> "Perhaps," replies Martin unmercifully, "but you fall short."

The worm—as so often in Bergman—turns. David charges Martin with a secret desire to see Karin dead and then, lured into a mood of magnanimity by the confusion he sees in Martin's face, admits to having attempted suicide in Switzerland. The car had stalled with its front wheels over a precipice; the grand gesture had collapsed in fiasco. A love was born within him then, says David, for Karin and Minus—and Martin.

The confession persists as the central motif of *Through a Glass Darkly*. Minus searches for Karin on the island and at last discovers her hiding in the hull of a wrecked boat (Bergman was fascinated by this hulk and included it in his screenplay at the last moment).

There, it is implied, Karin seduces her brother. Both are instantly overwhelmed by remorse. Minus, fetching a blanket and water for Karin, drops to his knees in his father's room. "God!" he exclaims, as though he were talking in church. But of course the "Father" is none other than David. He becomes the surrogate God for both Karin and Minus. When David returns from his expedition to the mainland and sits behind Karin in the hulk, he listens to her admission of sin; in return, he confesses his own selfishness. "We draw a magic circle," he says, "and shut out everything that doesn't agree with our games." His first success as an author had meant more to him than the death of Karin's mother. And so, "The sins of the fathers . . ."

Only through the act of confession and atonement may spiritual peace be achieved in Bergman's world.

Karin's warped yearning for the beneficence of a Christian God is emphasized in the crisis of the film. During a convulsive, orgasmic fit in the upstairs room of the house, she begs Martin to kneel beside her and pray, "Even though you don't believe." The reverberation of the helicopter arriving to collect Karin for hospital causes the door in the wall of the room to swing open.

But the God that emerges, so eagerly attended, is according to Karin no more than a spider, a creature that seeks to penetrate her body. "I have always dreaded spiders," says Harriet Andersson, "and could imagine it trying to consume my personality, consume me like a worm, and crawl over my body, face, and hands."

In the catharsis that follows, Karin is tranquilized and dons a pair of dark glasses, a final metaphor for her rejection of the world about her. There is an ominous knocking at the front door, like the arrival of Death at the castle in *The Seventh Seal*. David talks quietly to the visitors through a half-opened door. No one is seen; the helicopter becomes a *deus ex machina*, provoking Karin's critical trauma and then bearing her aloft to a state of oblivion beyond the reach of family pressures.

The film concludes with a kind of litany in David's room. When he was down in the wrecked ship, Minus tells his father, "Reality burst, and I tumbled out." He looks imploringly at David. "Give me a proof of God," he demands. Once again, Bergman cannot prevent himself from asking the question that has haunted him since youth. And now David recites the lineaments of a new philosophy in Bergman's world: God is love, love in all its forms. "I don't know if love proves God's existence, or if God Himself *is* love," he says. But "suddenly the emptiness turns into wealth, and hopelessness into life. It's like a reprieve from the death penalty."

Alone in the room—in what, with its small, barred window, connotes a church vestry—Minus gazes into the camera. "Papa *spoke* to me!"

Communication has been born of love. In *Through a Glass Darkly*, love remains an awesome virtue, to be revered and spoken of in hushed tones. But in *Winter Light*, a disillusioned Bergman will expose love as a cold, sterile concept and will mock the very words that David utters at the close of this first of the three tragedies. In Strindberg's *The Dance of Death*, Curt describes the Captain in words that might be applied to David in *Through a Glass Darkly*: "He is actually the most conceited person I have ever met. 'I am; therefore, God must be.' " David's definition of love amounts to a thinly veiled existentialism.

Through a Glass Darkly suffers at times from lack of wit; its rhetoric is portentous. The concept of a sex-crazed spider is rather fatuous, and lines like Martin's remark, "Edgar's the only psychiatrist I can rely on," sound a note of self-parody. Such flaws were less obtrusive in 1961, when the film appeared, and one was ready to succumb to the clean, pure line of Bergman's technique.

The editing of *Through a Glass Darkly* occupied more than two months. Ulla Ryghe, who had learned the rudiments of film editing at Europa Film but who was still, by her own admission, inexperienced, cut the movie. She worked late almost every night to correct her mistakes. Bergman arrived at the editing room around 9 A.M. "We started by looking at the reels that I had worked on the previous day," says Ulla, "and then screened some new reels—all this in one of the cinemas. Then we examined the new reels at the editing table, and Bergman told me how he wanted them to be cut. Then he left and I had the rest of the day to do the work."

Bergman could never be accused of being prodigal with his shooting. He would present Ulla Ryghe with about twenty-six thousand feet of finished film, and this had to be reduced to around eight thousand feet. He made his choice between different takes as soon as he saw the daily rushes, and if he kept more than one take for Ulla it meant that he intended to use different segments of each of them.

"I have never worked," she says,

> with any other director who has given me so little material that
> has been at the same time so rich. . . . That does not imply that
> there's less work to do, but there is the advantage of being able
> to come to grips early on with such important factors as the
> general rhythm of the film, the tone, and so on. One of the very
> important things Bergman taught me was first of all to edit a
> movie as it has been planned and shot. If you do that, then you
> have a structure, you have discovered the backbone of the film.

After many years, Bergman at last made his debut on the big stage at the Royal Dramatic Theater in Stockholm. His choice for the occasion was Chekhov's *The Sea Gull*, featuring Eva Dahlbeck, Per Myrberg, Christina Schollin, and Jan Erik Lindqvist. When it opened on January 6, 1961, few critics were in a position to see the links between this production and Bergman's *Through a Glass Darkly*. The staging of the "play within a play" in act one was handled in similar manner to its counterpart in the beginning of the film. The delicacy of nuance, so natural to Chekhov, was harder for Bergman to attain. Ebbe Lind in *Dagens Nyheter* recognized that Bergman's strength lay in the strongly colored scene, the bizarre, the unexpected clutch at the throat. Ivar Harrie in the evening tabloid *Expressen* charged Bergman with exaggerating and even caricaturing the personalities of the play. Chekhov and Bergman are joined, however, by their recognition of the impossibility of love and the self-centeredness of art.

On January 22, Bergman's radio production of a one-act comedy by Strindberg, *Playing with Fire*, was broadcast.

Three months later, Bergman brought off a more striking coup—his staging of Stravinsky's *The Rake's Progress* at the Royal Opera in Stockholm. (During rehearsals, the news came that *The Virgin Spring* had won an Academy Award as Best Foreign Language Picture in Hollywood.) The costumes by Kerstin Hedeby were not the only reminders of such earlier Bergman productions as *Urfaust* and *Peer Gynt*. The journey of Tom Rakewell and his bride-to-be Ann Truelove through the nether regions and eventually to the madhouse was one that took Bergman's fancy. His production was inspired, allowing the singers room in which to turn and maneuver without diminishing the acoustical impact of the music or the arias, and contrasting moments of silence with loud and tumultuous scenes. Curt Berg, reviewing the opera in *Dagens Nyheter*, was delighted that Bergman "has in his direction worked with almost the same chamber music method as Stravinsky. The entire production is *orchestrated* in accordance with the score."

Eighteen months elapsed before Bergman returned to the theater. His film trilogy possessed him in the interval.

In early 1961 a crisis developed at Svensk Filmindustri. Carl Anders Dymling, for twenty years the head of the company, fell mortally ill with cancer. There was confusion. No successor lay obviously to hand. Bergman joined some senior members of the company in a kind of interregnum. The studios, with 135 staff on the payroll, had to be used. So Bergman and Erland Josephson, using the pseudonym Buntel Eriksson, cobbled together a comedy entitled *The Pleasure Garden* (*Lustgården*), revolving around the elegant indiscretions of a schoolmaster—played by Gunnar Björnstrand—in a small Swedish town at the turn of the century. Bergman took an active interest in the processing of the color film (Svensk Filmindustri had not made many productions in color at this point). Alf Kjellin was the director, and the film contained several amusing incidents; the costumes and production design were distinguished. In all other respects, *The Pleasure Garden* remains insignificant.

So, almost in spite of himself, Bergman became involved in matters of state at Svensk Filmindustri. Soon he had recommended the actor, producer, and director Kenne Fant as Dymling's successor and established a cordial relationship with him. Bergman remained, however, a portal figure at SF and an "artistic advisor" in effect, just as Victor Sjöström had been during the forties.

Bergman's room at the studios in Råsunda stood on the ground floor of the main building, its window facing the famous entrance gate. A visitor described it as "furnished with impeccable Swedish good taste. A soft gray rug on the floor, a small divan covered with a moss green and gray blanket, a comfortable cane chair and, alas, three telephones. . . . But on the walls, photos of only two people: Chaplin, in stills from several of his silent films. And a solitary, large photo of his guru, Victor Sjöström."[6]

Käbi Laretei recalls that, before their marriage, Bergman had never taken a vacation in the orthodox sense of the term. They rented a house at the seaside, in a small place called Torö. Bergman loved the barren, stunted shoreline and the denuded landscape, an early harbinger of his devotion to Fårö. Bergman had been struck by the idea for *Winter Light* during the Easter break. He had listened to Stravinsky's *Symphony of Psalms* on the radio and conceived a film somehow concerned with "a solitary church on the plains of Uppland."[7] During the months that ensued, Bergman wrote *Winter Light* in Torö. "It was the first summer I'd had the sea all around me. I wandered about on the shore and went indoors, and went out again." Once a week he drove into the city for meetings at Svensk Filmindustri, working through the pile of letters or keeping an eye on production plans.

Various impulses combined to animate the screenplay. A few weeks after Bergman and his wife had been married in Dalarna, they returned to the church in Boda to see the parson. There they learned that a small girl's father had committed suicide, in spite of the parson's efforts to cheer him. The death of Jonas Persson (Max von Sydow) in *Winter Light* derives from this incident. The principal source of the film, however, stemmed from Bergman's notion of a parson who shuts himself up in his church, "and says to God: I'm going to wait here until you reveal yourself. Take all the time you want. I still won't leave here until you have revealed yourself. So the parson waits, day after day, week after week."[8]

There might also have been a recollection in Bergman's mind from his play, *The Day Ends Early*, in which Pastor Broms finds that his faith is too weak to disperse his fear of death.

And the obsession with eczema, described by Märta (Ingrid Thulin) in the film, sprang from Bergman's second marriage. Ellen Lundström had suffered from allergic eczema.[9]

So, while still writing the script, Bergman drove around the country churches in Uppland, north of Stockholm, accompanied by his father. He wanted to absorb the atmosphere of these small buildings, with their simple, unadorned architecture and their spartan interiors. He inspected the organs, which always appealed to him, in particular the small eighteenth-century models. Bergman studied the organ in youth; he still listens to organ music as a form of relaxation.

By early October, P. A. Lundgren had reconstructed the interior of Torsång Church in the studios at Råsunda. "It was a church in winter," says Sven Nykvist, "and there was no sun at all. There was no light coming in except from the cloudy sky, so we couldn't have any shadows at all. And we tried to make it look exactly like that."[10]

Much of the shooting was done on location in Dalarna. Bergman found it "extremely demanding, and [it] dragged on for fifty-six days. It was one of the longest schedules I've had, and one of the shortest films I've ever made."[11] Gunnar Björnstrand, playing the leading role of Pastor Tomas Ericsson, had to transfer almost without pause from his part in *The Pleasure Garden* to the rigors of shooting *Winter Light*, and his health cracked. Many thought that he might die. Sture Helander, Bergman's physician, prescribed some pills, and these made Gunnar feel even worse, and unusually tired into the bargain. Ironically, this state of health was ideal for the part.

Tension between Bergman and Björnstrand caused problems in the early days of the schedule. Bergman found himself waking at two in the morning with "snakes in [his] stomach."[12] But lighter moments occurred. Late one afternoon, worn out after shooting, Gunnar and Ingrid Thulin traipsed off to a roadside café. They played a record on the jukebox and danced—Björnstrand still in his parson's robe—provoking curious stares from the other customers.

Winter Light (*Nattvardsgästerna*) unfolds between noon and 3 P.M. on a Sunday in winter. Everything about the film is reduced, distilled. Only five worshippers kneel at the altar rail as Pastor Tomas Ericsson dispenses the communion. Bergman makes no concessions to those viewers who might be unfamiliar with Christian ritual. The camera fastens in close-up on the iconography of the church: the chalice, the wafers, the head of Christ on the wooden crucifix, the hand pierced by

Bergman and Sven Nykvist, plus crucifix, while shooting Winter Light. *Photo courtesy Svensk Filmindustri.*

The solitude of the priest: Gunnar Björn-strand (Tomas Ericsson) *in* Winter Light.

the wooden nail. Only the organist, checking his watch to see how much longer the service will drag on, introduces a note of levity to the proceedings.

Tomas is confronted by two unexpected developments: his responsibility for the life of one of his parishioners, Jonas Persson (Max von Sydow); and the arrival of a letter from his former mistress, Märta Lundberg (Ingrid Thulin). The confluence of these pressures compels Tomas to reconsider his life and his faith. As Jörn Donner has written apropos of Bergman, "It is not in the search for meaning that life is decided, but in the choice of action."[13]

Persson, his wife (Gunnel Lindblom) tells Tomas after the service, is apprehensive because he has read about the Chinese being brought up to hate other people. Soon they will possess atomic weapons, and the world will be destroyed. The fisherman is taciturn and bridles at his wife's attempts to make him explain his worries to Tomas.

"We must trust God," says Tomas, with a palpable hint of glibness and condescension. Persson turns for the first time and fixes a terrifying gaze on the parson. Tomas lowers his eyes in confusion. "We must live," he mutters. "Why must we live?" replies Persson, mocking. Tomas cannot answer.

When Persson has left the church, promising to return for a longer talk, Tomas goes to the altar. "God's silence, God's silence," he says to himself in despair. In her letter, Märta tries to comfort him in a worldly fashion. "There *is* no God," she insists. "It's horribly simple, really."

Tomas coughs badly. His sickness is, as always in Bergman, a symbol of an inner, spiritual malady. He glances at photographs of his dead wife. Little by little the dialog of the film reveals that Tomas still harbors an obsessive love for her. Perhaps he even died, in a spiritual sense, when she died.

As a young man, in the Civil War in Spain, he had refused to countenance the terrible reality of war. Now he clings to the husk of his faith like a drowning man to a lifebelt. But Märta's letter sweeps away that last illusion. "Your faith seemed obscure and neurotic," she writes, "and yet I cannot understand your indifference to Jesus Christ." She declares her love for him in spite of everything.

This sequence represents one of the boldest experiments in the film. Ingrid Thulin recites the letter, facing the camera in close-up, for over six minutes, with only one intercut shot of her tearing off her bandages in church, revealing her eczema. The viewer cannot escape the content of the letter; Bergman eschews the customary diversion of descriptive images. In a way, the letter scene epitomizes the austerity of *Winter Light*. As he told one interviewer, "I made this film because I really wanted to, and I made it with no concessions to the public. I know it's a difficult film, but I think that I achieved that much (*holding up two fingers*) of truth concerning the spiritual crisis I've been striving for years to describe."[14]

Jonas Persson returns to the church and, unnerved by Märta's letter, the parson unburdens his own woes to the fisherman. He refers to his wife's death and to his disenchantment as a chaplain in Spain. "He was a spider God, monstrous, whenever I confronted him with my reality," he tells Jonas, evoking Karin's concept of God as a spider in *Through a Glass Darkly*. "Death is just a snuffing out, a disintegration of body and soul," he informs his visitor, thereby offering an unwitting justification for Jonas's suicide plans. "There is no creator, no sustainer," he continues. As Jonas gets up to leave, Tomas seems unaware that he has scarcely asked him about his troubles; instead, Jonas's presence has enabled him to relieve his own burden of anxiety.

"God, why hast Thou forsaken me?" asks Tomas, alone in the vestry, with its barred, cell-like window recalling the window of David's room in *Through a Glass Darkly*, or the confessional in *The Seventh Seal*.

The death of Jonas Persson occurs as a mere formality. When a woman brings the news that he has shot himself down by the river, Tomas packs his case, puts on his overcoat, and drives to the scene of the catastrophe. Switching from close-ups to a series of long shots, Bergman's camera makes plain Tomas's discomfiture as he stares down at the body and helps to lift it so that it may be covered with a cloth before being loaded aboard the ambulance. The dull, fateful roar of the rapids and the spectacle of the frozen roads counterpoint the congealed attitudes, the unassuageable despair, of Tomas and Märta. It is indeed, as Märta has said, a Sunday in the Vale of Tears.

Tomas feels ashamed of his relationship with the schoolteacher. Even when they visit her home at the school itself, he is afraid that Märta's aunt may see them together. "I feel humiliated by all the gossip," he tells her bitterly. Alone with her among the desks and chairs of the classroom, he launches into the most terrifying harangue of the film. He rejects Märta's offer of love. "The real reason is that I don't want you," he informs her with uncompromising bluntness. "When my wife died, I died. She was everything you can never be." The air is full of pain and resentment; Tomas's speech is like black bile, devoid of Christian understanding. "Can't you leave me alone?" he asks. He stalks out of the room, only to pause at the door and suggest that Märta accompany him to vespers at the next church.

In that moment, Tomas decides to change his life. He cannot yet find the words of comfort that security should afford him, when he calls at the Perssons' house to tell the wife about Jonas's death, but he begins to perceive the Church as a profession rather than a vocation.

The cart halts at a level crossing. As the goods train trundles past, its wagons looking like nothing so much as funeral caskets, Tomas recalls his youth: "It was my parents who wanted me to go into the Church," he says. It is a brief sequence, much cut in the making, but one that emerged from Bergman's memories of his grandfather's involvement with the railroads and of childhood days when he would watch the trains go past in Dalarna.

At Frostnäs Church, the sexton and organist are waiting. The sexton, Algot Frövik (Allan Edwall), was inspired by Bergman's admiration for Karl-Arne Bergman, his props man. Frövik is a hunchback but bears his disability with courage and equanimity. He speaks to Tomas about the Garden of Gethsemane, Christ's anguish and disappointment at realizing that for three years the disciples had misunderstood him and were now deserting his side. "Why hast Thou forsaken me?" quotes Frövik, from Christ's words on the Cross, unconsciously echoing Tomas's own plea in Torsång earlier. Perhaps Tomas acknowledges that he too has misunderstood his God for many years.

Märta, alone among the pews, is approached by the organist. He urges her to leave Tomas. He mocks the parson's talk of love, quoting almost to the word David's final homily on love in *Through a Glass Darkly*. Märta says nothing, but her eyes are clear with realization. She waits, as eagerly as any lover, for Tomas to emerge and begin the service.

And so, with a congregation of just one person, Pastor Tomas Ericsson indites the opening words he knows by heart: "Holy, Holy, Holy, is the Lord God Almighty. The earth is full of his glory." At last a line of communication somehow exists.

Communication. Communion. The original Swedish title of the film means "The Communicants."

Severe though *Winter Light* may be, the film is remarkable for Bergman's ability to discuss religion at a time when the religious debate was in decline. "In *Winter Light*," he claimed, "I swept my house clean."[15]

Käbi Laretei's reaction was fair. "Yes, Ingmar, it's a masterpiece; but it's a dreary masterpiece."[16] The critics were respectful, if reluctant to praise the film for anything other than its uncompromising quality. Jürgen Schildt in *Aftonbladet* complained that the film "moves at a snail's pace and barely gets there in the end. It discusses a problem, but from prepared viewpoints. It is simple, but the simplicity is seldom fascinating and almost never evocative."

The religious press, although as individuals affronted by Bergman's description of the parson and his church, sought desperately to locate some hope in the conclusion. Märta Lundberg was regarded as a Christ symbol, although no critic singled out Algot Frövik as the miracle of "living religion" Bergman thought him to be.

Even more than in *Through a Glass Darkly*, the camera in *Winter Light* replaces the mirror at whose reflections earlier Bergman characters had gazed in search of the absolute. From now on, Bergman addresses his audience more directly. There is no escape, either for the characters or the spectator. Music, for example, would have sounded vulgar in the context of *Winter Light*. Yet the very structure of the film is musical. The tick of the vestry clock, like a penitential lash, the boom of the rapids, the noise of tires on a snow-covered road, make up the rhythm of the soundtrack. "Film," Bergman would write in his introduction to the screenplay of *Persona*, "is a language, the sentences of which are literally spoken by one soul to another and which escapes the control of the intellect in an almost sensual fashion."

Bergman began work on the third part of the trilogy, *The Silence* (*Tystnaden*), at Christmas 1961, as soon as he had completed *Winter Light*. He had elected not to return to the theater that season, and his wild idea of making a burlesque fairy tale with Max von Sydow, Allan Edwall, and Martin Ljung, was already evaporating. The editing of *Winter Light* occupied the late winter months. In addition to his own work, Bergman had been responsible for the production of both *The Pleasure Garden* and *The Brig Three Lilies* at Svensk Filmindustri. It had been an arduous year.

The year 1962 began with a meeting with Greta Garbo on January 4. She came to tea in Bergman's room at the studios. "Her voice is so nice and gentle," he told Vilgot Sjöman. "It has a quiet huskiness that makes it interesting. And her eyes! And a quiet sense of humor." Some claim that during this conversation Bergman asked Garbo if she would appear in *The Silence*, but it seems unlikely that he would have done so with any real hope of success.

A month later, press reports circulated to the effect that Bergman intended to turn his back on filmmaking for an entire year, devoting his energies to a study of the life and work of J. S. Bach. "Once in a lifetime," Bergman was quoted as saying, "one must try to realize one's dream and break away from the drudgery of everyday work."[17] Käbi was going to join him in this research.

Nothing came of the dream. But in April Bergman won his second successive Academy Award, for *Through a Glass Darkly* as Best Foreign Language Film.

On June 15, the technicians signed for *The Silence* met Bergman in

Rättvik. In the bridge salon of the Hotel Siljansborg, they discussed the problems the film might pose. "There must not be any of the old, hackneyed dream effects, such as visions in soft focus or dissolves. The film itself must have the character of a dream," Bergman told Sven Nykvist. They decided to use Eastman Double-X negative, which would be developed to a higher gamma than usual.[18]

The threads that mark *The Silence* may be traced back to the forties. In 1946, Bergman spent a few weeks in Hamburg, where tanks still patrolled the streets by night; not long afterward, he stayed at the height of summer in "a nasty little hotel" in Grenôble, in France. The view from the room where Anna makes love with the barman is apparently the same as Bergman's recollection of another hotel in the rue Sainte-Anne in Paris, where he had an assignation with a woman. Some of the material stems from *The City*, Bergman's radio play.

He has also said that *The Silence* grew out of Bartók's Concerto for Orchestra: "the dull continuous note, and then the sudden explosion."[19]

The Silence amounts to a description of Hell on earth. Ester (Ingrid Thulin) and Anna (Gunnel Lindblom) are sisters traveling home to Sweden through an unidentified country in Eastern Europe. Esther, like Pastor Ericsson in *Winter Light*, seems to be already dead, past recovery. She tries without success to retain her hold over her sister. But, as Bergman says, hers is a despotic love. "Love must be open. Otherwise Love is the beginning of Death. That is what I am trying to say."[20]

Bergman likes to introduce characters as they awake, fresh to the world. The opening shot of *The Silence* shows Johan (Jörgen Lindström), the small boy, his head bowed in sleep. Johan is the innocent observer, the one character who has not been stunted and embittered by life. During the course of the film he escapes from his fetal subservience to his mother. He watches, and in sympathy with him the camera becomes a voyeur, peering and prowling, pausing before gliding this way and that.

Johan is fascinated by what he sees from the corridor of the train: a soldier stirring roughly from sleep, the sun rising behind a mountain range, rows of tanks racing past the windows on a parallel track. But Johan is also bored, overwhelmed by the torpor of the climate. The film is coated in this deceptive mood of lethargy.

In the hotel, Anna bathes and lies down on her bed like a contented animal. Anna is sensual; she draws pleasure from fondling and embracing Johan, feeling him scrub her back in the bath. Ester, in stark contrast, moves in a constant state of agitation and anxiety. She smokes incessantly and drinks a local spirit that the waiter brings her. For a while she feels soothed by some romantic string music played on her radio. Then she masturbates. Onanism in Bergman suggests that a person's whole psyche has grown inward, feeding upon itself instead of the nourishment of the outer world. Ester resembles Karin in *Through a Glass Darkly*. From the window she sees an emaciated horse dragging a load of junk through the narrow street. The image counterpoints her own misery and meagerness of soul.

Anna, the body to Ester's spirit, seeks gratification outside the hotel, amid the bustle and noise of the town. At first she is repelled by the spectacle of a couple making love in an adjacent seat at a cabaret (a scene that fired the indignation of censors around the world), made even more grotesque by its being intercut with a display by a troupe of dwarfs on stage, cavorting like dogs to the command of their full-grown trainer. But when Anna returns to the suite, there is no doubt that she has copulated with a waiter (Birger Malmsten) from a nearby bar.

The waiter behaves as a servant to Anna in the same way as the elderly attendant (Håkan Jahnberg) in the hotel ministers to Ester's needs. Each bows reverently to his charge, the hotel waiter presenting Ester with a drink, and the barman bending lasciviously to breathe over

Ingrid Thulin (Ester) *and Gunnel Lindblom* (Anna) *in* The Silence. *Photo courtesy Svensk Filmindustri.*

Anna's calf and knee. The act of giving is achieved without speech, for the language of the strange country sounds impenetrable to the sisters. (Bergman made it up himself, basing it in part on Estonian phrases and words. "Timoka," for example, the name of the city, refers to "The Hangman" in Estonian; Bergman saw it on the wrapper of a book of poetry in Käbi Laretei's shelves.) Communication thus becomes spiritual —Ester drinks the glass of spirits with the reverence of a worshipper accepting the chalice—and corporeal—flesh on flesh, slaking the body's desire.

Music, too, forms a link between civilizations. When Bach's *Goldberg Variations* are played on the radio, both Ester and the waiter know the name of the composer. J. S. Bach is the only comprehensible word in the newspaper Anna scans in the café. (Bach wrote the *Goldberg Variations* for the young Johann Theophilus Goldberg to play at night to his protector, Count Keyserlingk, so as to alleviate the pain and insomnia caused by a serious illness.)

In a second rendezvous with the barman, in a dark claustrophobic room, Anna feels at once protected and trapped by her foreign surroundings. She glances down from the window, watching men in white overalls shifting containers beneath a barred skylight. Looking up, she can see only a patch of sky between the ominous, overhanging buildings on all sides. "How nice that we don't understand each other," she says aloud to herself as she caresses her lover. She touches the scar on his shoulder, feeling his alien presence. "I wish Ester were dead," she breathes, as though in loathing of that part of her which is indeed Ester. The antagonists in Bergman's films are often the opposing poles of a single personality—the Knight and the Squire in *The Seventh Seal*, Vogler and Vergérus in *The Magician*, Alma and Elisabet in *Persona*.

Catechism and humiliation belong as if by divine right to Bergman's world. Ester has interrogated Anna about her movements when she first comes back to the hotel. Now, in a scene stage-managed with diabolical simplicity, Anna takes her revenge. Johan, like an innocent *postillon d'amour*, has led Ester to the door of the room where Anna lies with the barman. The light is snapped on without warning, and Ester is confronted with the tableau of two semi-naked lovers.

Anna bends over the bars of the bedstead, as though she were needling her sister through the bars of a cage. "Everything centers around your self-importance," she says. She reminds Ester that when their father had died she had said she no longer wished to live. "Why are you living still?" she cries to Ester, just as Jonas Persson in *Winter Light* demanded of the parson a reason for living.

The death of that "Father" is the death of God—of faith—of love. Ester emerges, stricken, from the room. The troupe of dwarfs encountered earlier by Johan, and glimpsed performing in the cabaret, now strolls gravely past, with the last in line wearing a death mask.

Ester sinks toward oblivion. In an almost tender soliloquy, with the old waiter seated at the foot of her bed like some wizened, benevolent Charon, she says that we try out attitudes and find them all useless. "You must watch your step among ghosts and memories." With a final brackish laugh she recalls the death of her father and his final words: "Now it's eternity, Ester."

Like that unpredictable spasm of notes at the climax of the Bartók Concerto for Orchestra, a sudden wave of tubercular agony grips Ester. As she clings to the bedstead and opens her mouth in a rictus of pain, sirens boom out over the city. The sound is harsh and dissonant, as imperious as the knocking on the door at the close of *Through a Glass Darkly*.

The sirens die away. Ester draws the sheet over her head, in acceptance of her own extinction. Johan embraces her, but Anna disengages him gently. They leave to catch their train. The camera examines Ester's face and lifeless eyes, staring immobile into a void.

Earlier in the film, Johan has been given by the old waiter some photos of a woman lying dead in an open bier, surrounded by mourners. The boy subconsciously rejects the concept of death, slipping the pictures beneath a carpet in the hotel corridor. He cannot accept that Ester is dead; instead, he responds to the legacy she has bequeathed to him: some words "in the foreign language" scrawled on a crumpled piece of paper. In a ritualistic gesture, Anna opens the window and lets the rain cleanse her face as the train leaves Timoka. Anna has rid her body of its hatred for Ester. But hope for the future lies with Johan. The final image, like the first one, is a close-up of his face, as he mouths the syllables of those words Ester has written down for him.

The Silence displays a fluency of technique altogether new in Bergman's work. The labyrinthine corridors of the hotel, the interior of the suite, the confined space of the cabaret and the café, all are explored by Bergman's camera as though he were familiar with every nook and cranny of these hostile surroundings.

The symbols are tantalizing and undefined: the tank that rolls through the night and stops outside Ester's window; the massive reproduction of Rubens's *Satyr and Nymph*; the dwarfs who dress Johan in women's clothing. So cohesive is the narrative pattern, however, so plausible the situation, that these signs and emblems are not as arbitrary as critics have maintained.

Ingrid Thulin's Ester is the quintessence of bitterness and self-disgust. Gunnel Lindblom's Anna radiates a lazy eroticism, whether drawing a pair of bangles off her arm and laying them with a subtle clink on a bedside table or flicking open a lipstick as though she were freeing a penis from its pouch.

The Silence should not be considered in cultural isolation. Bergman, true, was involved in his *voyage au bout de la nuit*, but his film was modulated to the same pitch as other works by major directors in the early sixties. Antonioni, for example, also detected in the lethargy of the modern world a tendency toward spiritual dissatisfaction. Resnais, in *Last Year at Marienbad*, had chosen as his theater a chateau with corridors as interminable as those in the hotel at Timoka. Robbe-Grillet and Beckett were just two prominent authors who shared Bergman's impression that man was at the most aimless stage of his development (or retardation). The prosperity of the postwar period had led to a boredom and cantankerousness among the bourgeoisie. Material gains had been achieved at the expense of moral equilibrium. Society's goals were obscure; the individual felt himself at the mercy of an overwhelming laxity. Purblind and disconcerted, the ego rejected the outer world and writhed in upon itself, unable to communicate with those around it. *The Silence*, made in a distant Nordic land, recorded with the accuracy of a sonar the echoes of this universal malaise.

Other directors were also in the process of rejecting the literary basis of their material. Dialog was less significant than the mood of a film, than the feelings between the sentences. *Winter Light* is a literary film; *The Silence* is not.

At first, the Swedish censorship bureau intended to make cuts in the cabaret sequence. But a campaign in the liberal press led to an amendment in the rules, whereby a film should not be cut if its artistic quality was beyond reproach. This new statute came into effect just three days before *The Silence* was due to receive its certificate—in July 1963.

The Silence looks tame by comparison with even the soft porn of the seventies. Audiences and authorities of the time, however, were disturbed by the authenticity of its carnal mood. Reaction to the film in Sweden was violent. Certain newspapers ran a permanent column for some weeks, printing arguments for and against the picture. Over six hundred thousand people saw the film during its first seven weeks of release in Sweden, at a mere twenty-seven theaters.

In France, the Censorship Board refused at first to issue a visa to *The Silence*. The minister responsible, Alain Peyrefitte, requested certain cuts in the cabaret sequence and in the lovers' rendezvous in the hotel room. In West Germany, debate over the film reached the Parliament; millions of people flocked to the cinemas, making a temporary fortune for the distributors, Atlas Film. *Soviet Screen* ran a sharp attack on Bergman for the latent fascism and hatred of mankind displayed by *The Silence*. The film was a triumph in Britain and the United States, even though most people were attracted to it for the wrong reasons. On the eve of its release, Bergman quoted a venerable member of the Swedish Academy apropos of *Lady Chatterley's Lover*, who had declared, "This book is going to have a lot of unwanted readers."[21] Bergman added, "And I think this film is going to have a lot of unwanted viewers!" At an earlier stage, when screening the film for Kenne Fant, head of Svensk Filmindustri, he had predicted that no more than a hundred thousand spectators throughout the world would pay to see it. "And I'm not joking, Kenne," he said. "That's the truth."

The anonymous letters were sickening. One contained soiled lavatory paper. Käbi supported her husband loyally but was a little puzzled that Bergman could make such a despondent film while they were so happy in their marriage. Ingmar's reply was that, alongside her, he now felt strong enough to tackle such themes.

Bergman was now a true celebrity in his own country, notorious in certain quarters, but a celebrity nonetheless. His salary for the films at Svensk Filmindustri was not vast—perhaps 200,000 crowns ($35,000)— but from the sale of his *Four Screenplays* in America he earned over $10,000 on the first edition, and Simon and Schuster urged him to let them publish six more. Janus Films, thanks to the enterprise of Cyrus Harvey, was doing well with the distribution of the films. Bergman liked Harvey and respected his business acumen; Harvey was a trifle alarmed by the static nature of Bergman's camera in these productions of the early sixties but remained constant to the leading light of his catalog.

In New York, the film opened at the Rialto (known for its strip-tease movies) and the Trans-Lux East. Bosley Crowther, in the *New York Times*, praised the acting but complained that Bergman had not given the audience sufficient to draw on, to find the underlying meaning or emotional satisfaction in the film. In *Esquire*, Dwight Macdonald criticized the lack of motivation, which made the sisters' actions seem arbitrary and increasingly boring. He regretted Bergman's vision of himself as a philosopher in recent films, when his talent was for the concrete rather than the abstract. And even John Simon, later to become one of Bergman's greatest advocates, wrote in the *New Republic* of his disappointment with *The Silence*. The acting and the photography were excellent, but Simon noted the absence of forward thrust, a want of "human content."

In 1963 Bergman was invited to meet King Gustaf Adolf VI at a court reception. He did not want to attend, but Käbi persuaded him to do so. The other guests made crass remarks, at second hand, about *The Silence*. Then the king led Bergman away into an adjoining room for a chat. Afterward, Bergman told his wife that the king had in fact been rather nice.

But Bergman has remained alert to the brittleness of fame. "Your loyalty is to your work," he told John Reilly. "You can love people, children, women, sofas, houses, everything. You have to have things you can love—things and human beings. You must know that one day you perhaps must go away from things you love because they have imprisoned you."

And he would do so.

"When I was younger, I had illusions about how life should be," he said. "Now I see things as they are. No longer any questions of 'God, why?' or 'Mother, why?' One has to settle for suicide or acceptance. Either destroy oneself (which is romantic) or accept life.

"I choose now to accept it."[22]

CHAPTER ELEVEN

Administrator, Innovator

ON JANUARY 14, 1963, INGMAR BERGMAN WAS APPOINTED HEAD OF THE Royal Dramatic Theater in Stockholm. It was, and remains, the most influential, if not glamorous, stage post in Scandinavia. Founded in 1788 by Gustav III, Dramaten, as it is known in Sweden, has been situated since 1907 in a massive, ornate building overlooking Nybroplan. At its rear lies a small auditorium, Lilla Scenen, where chamber plays and other productions involving small casts and modest settings have been performed since 1947.

Eugene O'Neill was one of the foreign playwrights championed by Dramaten, and as a result the Stockholm theater was entrusted with the world premiere of *Long Day's Journey into Night* in 1956, after O'Neill's death.

The administration of Dramaten was enormously demanding. In 1945, when the building contained just one stage, there were forty-five players attached to it; in 1964, with *three* stages involved, there were still a mere fifty-six under contract. "It's a nasty post, loaded with responsibilities," said Bergman a couple of weeks after the announcement of his appointment. "And amusing at the same time; to tackle and solve problems and complications is my ideal way of life—if I can only stay fit. A hardened film director is, after twenty years in the field, someone who never has time just to think about problems."[1]

He held the stewardship of Dramaten for three years. "I started in the morning at eight o'clock and was there until eleven at night; then I went home and slept. I was at it ten months a year, and there was no place left for demons and dreams."² The job soon began to exasperate him; he wanted more time for his own productions, as well as his films, and he tried to effect radical changes at Dramaten. Some actors and directors were angered and confused by this new policy, but they could not deny that Bergman was fighting like a tiger with the authorities for more recognition of the theater's role. When he joined Dramaten in 1963, its subsidy was something like four million crowns per annum, and when he left in 1966 the figure was more like ten million. One of his revolutionary steps was to mount a series of classical plays for children; Dramaten had always ignored the needs of young people who might be attracted to the theater.

His own office, high up in the building, was characteristically spartan. Outside the door, white plastic letters arranged on a black signboard, spelling simply "Bergman." Inside, a bed for resting, a pot plant, some bottles of mineral water, and glasses on a tray.

Bergman's term of residence began on July 1, when he took over officially from Karl Ragnar Gierow. As usual, he wrung the last drop from the months before assuming the post. The year began inauspiciously, with *Winter Light* dividing the critics. Kenne Fant, head of Svensk Filmindustri, sent Bergman a telegram after the premiere: "Two for, two against, one in between."³ The film did not do well, even if Bergman himself was to remain steadfastly on its side in the years to come.

During the spring he staged Strindberg's *The Ghost Sonata* on Swedish television, and it was rumored that he would make a ballet film in four episodes with Birgit Cullberg, the country's leading choreographer. On May 2 yet another of his productions for television was broadcast: *A Dream Play*, featuring Ingrid Thulin as Indra's Daughter and Uno Henning as the Officer, against ultra-ascetic decor. Two days later, Bergman traveled up to Dalarna with his technical team to prepare for his new film, *All These Women*, in the tranquil opulence of Hotel Siljansborg.

The screenplay credit on *All These Women* (*För att inte tala om alla dessa kvinnor*) also released as *Now About These Women*, is attributed again to Buntel Eriksson. In fact, this is a pen name for Erland Josephson and Ingmar Bergman; Erik was the name of Ingmar's father, and Buntel suited Erland. The two friends collaborated with a fair amount of ease and good humor. Erland was a dab hand at writing dialog, while Ingmar's imagination gave forth a flow of stories and incidents that could be woven into a script. In 1961 their comedy, *The Pleasure Garden*, had appeared to a good-natured reception, and now, in the aftermath of his spiritual trilogy, Bergman felt it an excellent idea to relax and take a swipe at the critics. He is fond of quoting Buñuel's reply to the question, For whom do you make your films? "I make them," said Buñuel, "for my friends and my enemies."

The genesis of *All These Women* stemmed, like so much during these years, from Bergman's relationship with Käbi Laretei. She had told him of various Don Juan types in the musical field and in particular of one of her teachers, who was married to a celebrated German violinist. He would tour the world in that lady's company, staying at castles and manor houses. "He was a little, fat, boss-eyed man who had something remarkably demonic about him, and she had to play traffic cop to all his women."[4] Erland Josephson also contributed several of the plot developments. Once a week he would meet Ingmar and Käbi at the villa, and together they worked on the script. "My idea," says Erland, "and also his idea, was that the important thing in the film should be the women, and the part of the critic was not at all significant. In the event, Jarl Kulle was so dynamic, and Ingmar found him so funny, that it became a film *about* women."

Bergman with the cast of All These Women. *Photo courtesy Svensk Filmindustri.*

Although Bergman regards *All These Women* with hindsight as "an outburst of really bad temper,"[5] and in spite of his tension and weariness in the wake of *The Silence* and on the verge of his new job at Dramaten, he approached the film with painstaking devotion. This was to be his first film in color, and the entire crew was checked for symptoms of color blindness. Svensk Filmindustri paid for a "color film school" for several weeks, with lectures by experts on painting, and so on. Sven Nykvist exposed eighteen thousand feet of Eastmancolor stock before shooting even began, experimenting with tones and effects in color.

All These Women is insufferably ponderous in some parts and egg-shell delicate in others. Cornelius (Jarl Kulle), the fastidious music critic who visits the summer residence of a great cellist named Felix, is Public Enemy Number One in Bergman's eyes. With his monocle and dandi-fied clothes, he is a direct descendant of the line that includes Alman in *Wild Strawberries* and Vergérus in *The Magician*, yet rendered on this occasion in satirical terms.

Cornelius is bent on writing the biography of the late-lamented virtuoso and intends to annotate and analyze every word, gesture, and relationship in Felix's life. As he stands beside the open bier, he asks pompously, "What is genius?" Jillker (Allan Edwall), the dead man's business manager, reminds Cornelius drily that Goethe defined genius as being the ability to make a critic change his mind.

Cornelius stumbles about like Groucho Marx in a fruitless effort to penetrate the defenses of awe and ridicule that surround Felix, who is inscrutable save to his mistresses. As Cornelius leans nonchalantly against a marble statue of the cellist, it collapses beneath his weight: Genius is often too much for the critic to cope with, and the orchestra in the film breaks into a ragtime medley as if to mock his pretensions. Bergman's derision does not cease there. Cornelius is revealed as being somewhat inadequate in bed, tickling Bibi Andersson's "Bumble Bee" character with a red quill feather and not much else.

He swims in the manorial pool, supported by a dummy ring in the shape of a swan. Later he pursues Jillker through the fountains, dressed in Neronic garb with laureled brow; Bergman runs the scene in fast motion, ridiculing the pomp of artistic recognition.

The bulk of *All These Women* consists of a flashback describing Cornelius's hapless attempts to gain admittance to Felix's inner circle. Surrounded by a bevy of women, who act as a human smokescreen for the maestro, Cornelius grows more and more frustrated and com-promised. Eventually he threatens not to write the biography. Bergman and Josephson add a wicked barb of their own, showing that Cornelius is in fact more concerned about the "composition" that he has sent earlier for Felix's consideration. At last, Felix agrees to play the piece—

Mago's costume designs for All These Women. *Photo courtesy Mago.*

Bibi Andersson (Bumble Bee) *and Jarl Kulle* (Cornelius) *in* All These Women. *Photo courtesy Svensk Filmindustri.*

"Fish's Dream, or Abstraction 14"—but expires before he can strike a note *and* just before his enraged wife, Adelaide (Eva Dahlbeck), is about to shoot him. "I betray and deceive you," Felix has written to her, "but remember this: if ever I fail in my art, you are to kill me."

In a final, ironic twist, Cornelius finds himself assuming the role of the dead man, and with the smiling encouragement of the harem he himself becomes enshrined while a down-at-heels young cellist arrives to take *his* place. A room is immediately prepared for him, and Cornelius reaches for his notebook.

"I think the picture was very stiff," commented Sven Nykvist, "because we didn't do anything at all with the lighting—we overlit everything so it would be technically perfect. It was, but it had no atmosphere at all." Such criticism could scarcely be applied to the film's most diverting sequence, when Felix is glimpsed on the balustrade amid a spectacular display of fireworks.

The mood of the twenties is evoked both in the jumpy editing and in the use of ragtime, including a rendering of "Yes, We Have No Bananas," to suggest Cornelius's failure as a Don Juan. At every stage of the film, however, Bergman forces the spectator to keep his distance. One becomes increasingly aware of the theatrical nature of the piece, and the arbitrary switches from lechery to lugubrious disquisition, from boogie to Bach, preclude any emotional involvement. Bergman's own mordant disillusionment dictates the state of play. Even the statues in the garden bleed when struck by a stray bullet. Nothing is quite what it seems; everything is vulnerable. Yet, for Bergman, the critic as such possesses neither feelings nor potency. "How's Stravinsky?" asks Jillker. "I don't know," replies Cornelius. "It was my critical duty to expose him."

There can be no compromise between artist and analyst; Cornelius is denied a glimpse of Felix's face, as is the audience. This is Bergman underlining the artist's claim to privacy.

Somehow, Bergman knew in his bones that the film had not emerged as he had first hoped, and he told Käbi as much. But he had no time to worry about its reception that winter, for the responsibility of the new post at Dramaten preoccupied him. The first production was *Who's Afraid of Virginia Woolf?*, which opened on October 4. Derek Prouse was struck by Bergman's rejection of the seedy realism that had marked other productions of the Albee play. "One enters the theater to find the stage uncurtained, a bare, grey back wall surrounded by black tabs, four pieces of grey furniture, a drinks table and one book. The mood is heightened by changing intensities of light from unrealistic sources."[6] With Karin Kavli as Martha, Georg Rydeberg as George, and Bibi Andersson and Thommy Berggren as the young couple who witness—

and participate in—their sterile war of nerves and words, *Who's Afraid of Virginia Woolf?* impressed the Swedish critics. It was the continent's first production of the drama, and Bergman demonstrated that he had lost none of his power to grip an audience and that he knew how to veer from sordid naturalism to frenzied absurdity.

There followed a revival of Hjalmar Bergman's *The Saga* and then no new Bergman production until June the following year, when Harry Martinson's play, *Three Knives from Wei*, received its premiere. Throughout the winter Bergman had labored on this reconstruction of life in the Tang dynasty of China, with its massive cast and its essential conflict between decorum and reality. He staged it, says Henrik Sjögren, as a poetic tale, "a necklace of lyrical scenes. Kerstin Hedeby's sets and costumes gave the drama a shimmering, pastel quality like that of silk painting, against which only the rig-out of the two concubines, with their strong, saturated colours, stood out." The reviews were united in their praise for Hedeby's designs but less than happy with Bergman's (and Martinson's) grasp of the subtle conflicts that were implied beneath the ritualistic performances. They noted the bland and monotonous style of declamation, and Per Erik Wahlund summed up the prevailing reaction by describing the production as "decorative but artificial, interesting but hollow, original but overstrained."[7]

"I had two fiascos in one week!" recalls Bergman, for *All These Women* opened a few days later and was roundly condemned by the reviewers. One could argue that any other response would have meant failure on Bergman's part, for his vituperation would not have been sufficiently deadly. As usual, however, the critics sidestepped any condemnation of themselves and attacked Bergman for the clumsiness and flatness of the comedy. Swedish audiences were also disappointed. Just as they had assumed that Bergman would follow *The Virgin Spring* with a masterpiece and had found only *The Devil's Eye*, so now they felt cheated by Bergman's tomfoolery in the wake of *The Silence*.

His mood made even more misanthropic by this reception, Bergman embarked on a script entitled *The Cannibals*. It was his longest piece of writing to date, and he intended it to run for four hours and be released in two parts. The idea was that *The Cannibals* be shot the following summer, and although illness intervened and forced Bergman to cancel production, the screenplay was resuscitated in the form of *Hour of the Wolf* in 1966.

Some pride was salvaged in September, when the Swedish Film Institute, announcing a series of annual awards for the first time, gave Bergman a "Gold Bug" for *The Silence*, the equivalent of an Oscar for Best Direction. He was also now "inspector" of the Institute's Film School. Herbert von Karajan invited him to mount a guest production

Mago's design for the main set of Bergman's production of Hedda
Gabler. *Photo courtesy Mago.*

at the Salzburg Festival, but nothing transpired. And in August he had
begun rehearsals for *Hedda Gabler*, destined to become one of his most
brilliant stage productions. Mago was contracted to design the scenery as
well as the costumes and persuaded Bergman that the overall color
should be red. Seven screens were erected to define the acting areas, and
each of the screens was covered with a scarlet material, giving the entire
stage a womb-like impression. Bergman would return to this notion of
enveloping red textures in *Cries and Whispers*.

Mago based his main set on a typical Norwegian interior of the
nineties, with large bookshelves. "Hedda's first costume was a dressing
gown made of dull silk in champagne tints," he recalls. "Its severe lines
were relieved by a touch of lace at the wrists. Another dress was peacock
green." Gertrud Fridh, playing Hedda, had naturally copper-colored
hair, which stood out in striking contrast to the deep red screens.
Bergman himself took care of the lighting. "The morning scenes," says
Mago, "were brilliant and hot, the evening ones dim and cool. The set
contained no windows or any other obvious sources of light."[8]

The stimulus behind *Hedda Gabler*, claims Bergman, was a woman
Ibsen encountered, but the voices in the play are Ibsen's alone. "That's
what I felt a terrible need to release." But in successive revivals of his
production (with Maggie Smith and Christine Buchegger replacing
Gertrud Fridh as Hedda) the feeling has been one of entrapment rather
than release. Even in her most private moments of anguish and in-

decision, Hedda remains in full view of the audience; she is hardly ever offstage, and in scenes that do not involve her she is shielded from the other players by the red screens. As she places the gun to her head in the concluding moments of the play, she stoops to a fetal crouch, suggesting Bergman's familiar vision of death and birth inextricably linked.

Although this production never reached Norway, it was invited to the festival in West Berlin, and four years later Bergman accompanied it to London, with Gertrud Fridh repeating the title role, in the context of Peter Daubeny's World Theatre Season. Ronald Bryden in The Observer hailed Fridh's as "a magnificent performance," and J. W. Lambert in the Sunday Times averred that Bergman's direction "restored the balance of the drama."

Ingmar and Käbi spent Christmas 1964 in Zurich, a few days of peace and relaxation from the pressures of the theater. In January, however, a lung infection took hold of Bergman. It was thought to be an ordinary cold, but a high temperature persisted, and by March, when he became very sick, the doctors were talking of pneumonia (as well as a bizarre ailment of the ear, morbus ménièris). He began to suffer from antibiotic poison.[9]

In April all plans to shoot The Cannibals were shelved. Anders Ek, Bibi Andersson, and Liv Ullmann had been contracted for the film by Svensk Filmindustri. Bergman had announced that this would be his first wide-screen movie and that Sven Nykvist would be filming in black and white. Locations were to have been established on either the Shetland Islands or Hallands Väderö, a small island off the southwest coast of Sweden with somewhat exotic vegetation.

More cancellations were forced on Bergman. He had to relinquish his commitment to stage The Magic Flute in Hamburg, and the illness prevented him from traveling to Utrecht to accept the Erasmus Prize from Prince Bernhard of the Netherlands, an award he shared with Charles Chaplin. Kenne Fant went in his place and read a speech devised by Bergman for maximum impact on the audience. It is one of his most widely quoted declarations.

Speaking of his childhood, he remarked, "I made myself understood in a language that bypassed words, which I lacked; music, which I have never mastered; and painting, which left me unmoved."

Why, he asked, does one continue to practice art?

> The reason is curiosity: a boundless, never satisfied, constantly renewed, unbearable curiosity that urges me on, that never lets me rest, that has entirely replaced the past hunger for fellowship. I feel like a prisoner who has tumbled out into the booming, shrieking, snorting world after a long period of confinement. I

am seized by an irrepressible curiosity. I take note, observe, keep watch, everything is unreal, fantastic, frightening, or foolish. I catch a flying speck of dust, perhaps it is a film. What importance does it have? None whatsoever, but I personally find it interesting; and it becomes a film.

The artist, he said, lives exactly like every other living creature that only exists for its own sake. "This makes a rather numerous brotherhood living together egotistically on the hot, dirty earth under a cold and empty sky."

Bergman has never enjoyed making speeches in person. Harry Schein recalls how, when Bergman came to see him after recovering in a clinic from the shock of his arrest in 1976, he lay on a couch and said that as he was too tired to argue with such a formidable wordsmith as Schein, he had decided to jot down the principal points of conversation—and proceeded to recite them aloud!

The members of Bergman's unit dispersed for the summer holidays, disappointed that *The Cannibals* had been postponed. Three weeks later, however, Mago, who was in Copenhagen for a meeting with Marlene Dietrich, received a telephone call from Bergman's production manager, Lars-Owe Carlberg, asking him to return to Stockholm almost immediately to design a film entitled *Persona*.

People were puzzled. Was *Persona* just a new title for the old script?

Bergman appeared at a press conference, looking sunburned and fit. He said that during his spell in hospital he had started writing to ward off boredom, just to maintain a working routine. And from this activity *Persona*, "a sonata for two instruments," had been born. "In hospital one has a strong sense of corpses floating up through the bedstead. Besides which I had a view of the morgue, people marching in and out with little coffins, in and out."[10] The screenplay was completed on Örnö and bears the date June 17, 1965.

Persona stands as the most mysterious and perplexing of all Bergman's films. In 1964 Bergman had told an interviewer that he saw "more and more clearly that the film as an art form is approaching a discovery of its essential self. It should communicate psychic states, not merely project pictures of external actions."[11] Four years earlier, in the introduction to his *Four Screenplays*, he had confirmed, "A film for me begins with something very vague—a chance remark or a bit of conversation, a hazy but agreeable event unrelated to any particular situation. It can be a few bars of music; a shaft of light across the street."[12]

Bergman's virus infection had been so pernicious that it had affected his sense of balance. For four months, he claimed, he sat staring at a spot on the wall. "If I moved my head, the whole world seemed to turn upside down." (Such an image probably inspired those final clinic scenes in both *The Serpent's Egg* and *From the Life of the Marionettes*.) So he began to contemplate a film involving just two characters, one talking, the other silent. "I was lying there, half-dead, and suddenly I started to think of two faces, two intermingled faces, and that was the beginning, the place where it started."[13] In another interview, Bergman gave Stig Björkman a slightly different account: "One day I suddenly saw in front of me two women sitting next to each other and comparing hands with one another. I thought to myself that one of them is mute and the other speaks."[14]

Bergman at first wanted to call his film just *Cinematography*, but Kenne Fant, loyal though he was to Bergman's whims, "had a fit" and felt that Svensk Filmindustri could not proceed without a better title than that. So Bergman opted for *Persona*, the Greek word for *mask*.

Persona has only four speaking parts, and two of these are minor. So for Bibi Andersson, playing Sister Alma, and Liv Ullmann, as Elisabet Vogler, the film presented an arduous challenge. They had been friends since 1962, when Bibi had been appearing in a Nordic coproduction, *Pan*, and Liv—then only twenty-four—had acted alongside her. When Bibi returned to Stockholm, she told Bergman that she had met a girl of the type he liked and that he might well be able to use her on stage or screen. So when Liv came subsequently to Sweden with her theater group, Bergman met her and found her engaging. The apocryphal story is that Bergman met both women quite by chance on a street corner and was struck by the resemblance between them. The actual idea for *Persona* is far more likely to have sprung from a Polaroid photo of Bibi and Liv together, although Bergman's explanation about the image of two women caressing hands seems more cogent still.

Some months after that first encounter, Bergman contacted Liv Ullmann in Norway and told her that he had a part for her in the screenplay he was writing.

The romance between Ingmar Bergman and Liv Ullmann became as notorious in Scandinavia as Ingrid Bergman's relationship with Roberto Rossellini. Liv, born in Tokyo of Norwegian parents and partly educated in England, would possibly have achieved some fame as an actress without Bergman's influence. Her triumphant progress to international stardom must, however, be largely ascribed to Bergman's influence on her work. In a period when unvarnished sex appeal dictates the status of many female stars, she represents an upright moral stance. She is an exceptionally beautiful woman, but she does not flaunt her attractiveness. For certain men she has become a *Mutter Erde* figure, hers the bosom on which to lay one's head and shed one's woes. A repository of good-ness, she inspires honesty; she is the woman to whom one would least

Bergman with Bibi Andersson (Sister Alma) *and Liv Ullman* (Elisabet Vogler) *during the shooting of* Persona. *Photo courtesy Svensk Filmindustri.*

like to be unfaithful. She unites the freshly scrubbed look of Ellen Burstyn with the mysterious supplication projected by Monica Vitti. Women, too, can admire Liv Ullmann's resolution, her blend of strength and compassion. "One of the things I am most grateful to Ingmar for teaching me," she says, "is that if you keep yourself open to whatever comes out, something will happen. I was very young then [on *Persona*], and I couldn't have verbalized my feelings about the actress."[15] Had Bergman launched into long discussions with her, she might have fallen to pieces. But he never questioned her motives, and she was able to do exactly what she felt was best.

During the first week of shooting in the studios in Stockholm, Liv recalls that Bergman was rather worried, but once the unit moved to Fårö on location, Bergman's mood grew more positive. Liv stayed with Bibi and the makeup artist in a small house near the sea. There was a steadily growing affection between Liv and her director. They would walk together on the way home after the day's shooting, while Bibi Andersson, ever tactful, ran ahead with Sven Nykvist so as to leave the couple in peace.

The circumstances were not easy. Liv had a husband in Oslo. Ingmar was still married to Käbi Laretei.

But Bergman's ability to remain true friends with the women he has abandoned is uncanny. His decision may wound those who are left behind, but at least there is no pus, only bleeding, to quote one of his ex-wives. "The pressures of both our careers built up a kind of tension that made the break-up of our marriage inevitable," says Käbi Laretei. The press pursued her without mercy while she was in New York for a

Bergman and Bibi Andersson during the sixties. Photo courtesy Svensk Filmindustri.

concert, pressing her to comment on the rumors linking Liv and Ingmar.

Bergman decided to move permanently to Fårö and began to build a house there for Liv and himself. It was constructed of local wood and stone, all on one level. "The house was located far away from the sandy beach of summer, the site was all stone and dry earth. No one on the island could understand the man who had bought so much infertile land."[16]

"We walked on the beach," wrote Liv in her autobiography, "which was nothing but rocks, and took pictures of each other." And in another interview: "To me, he was God. I was only twenty-five [*sic*], too young— and he was forty-six. When he spoke, I blushed."[17] Bergman was unstinting in his recognition of her gifts as an actress: "Liv, like the best of all creative artists, has marvelous integrity and enormous faith in her own intuition."

And Liv Ullmann would appear in all his major films of the next twelve years.

Writing in the introduction to his published screenplay of *Persona*, Bergman asserts: "I have not produced a film script in the normal sense. What I have written seems more like the melody line of a piece of music, which I hope with the help of my colleagues to be able to orchestrate during production."

Persona has provoked innumerable interpretations, scholarly, psychological, and aesthetic. A bald summary of the major factors and incidents in the film is important to keep in mind:

Elisabet Vogler (Liv Ullmann) is a famous actress. In the middle of a performance of *Electra*, she falls silent. Even prolonged treatment at a psychiatric clinic fails to restore her speech. The doctor in charge suggests that her nurse, Sister Alma (Bibi Andersson), should spend some time in isolation on the coast with the patient. Faced by the obstinate yet also sympathetic silence of Elisabet, Alma begins to divulge more than she should. Impressed by the physical resemblance between the two of them she even identifies herself, subconsciously, with the actress. But the friendship is disturbed when Alma discovers from an unsealed letter to the doctor that the actress is observing her coolly and condescendingly. Alma now becomes almost hysterical, trying to protect her own feelings of guilt and anguish onto Elisabet, urging her wildly to speak. The actress finally lets slip a single word— "nothing"—and Alma is left to return to the clinic with her patient.

Everything one says about *Persona* may be contradicted; the opposite will also be true.

Persona: *Bergman on location on Fårö with Bibi Andersson (Sister Alma) and Liv Ullmann (Elisabet Vogler). Photo courtesy Svensk Filmindustri.*

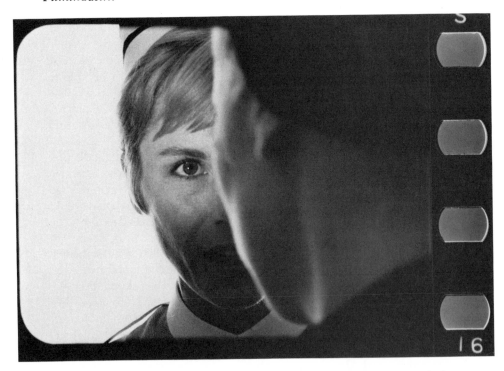

Bibi Andersson (Sister Alma) and Liv Ullmann (Elisabet Vogler) in Persona. *Bergman insisted on including the film sprocket holes in stills from the movie. Photo courtesy Svensk Filmindustri.*

Thus the key to the film is the concept of life and personality as a mirror: the notion that the image staring back at one from a mirror is a double, the other half of one's psyche. Both Alma and Elisabet are divided in two; each is the other's missing half. Carl Jung identified the *persona* (the outer mask one shows to the world) as intellectual, and the *alma* (the inner, soul image) as quite certainly sentimental. The persona develops into a compromise between an individual and the society around him, a visual expression of what a man should appear to be. But the persona may become too mechanical, and then the individual atrophies behind a hard, set mask.

Long before Bergman, Jung realized that liberation becomes an urgent necessity when the individual is caught between the conflicting demands of persona and alma. The fact that Bibi Andersson's character is named Alma is a gesture of acknowledgment by Bergman toward Jung's research in this area. For Jung, the *alma* is that person in dark cloak and shadowed face who crouches in the cellar of the subconscious.

The screen itself is a form of mirror, a glass that both reflects and enables the spectator to pass through into another state of life. Bergman emphasizes the existence of the screen at various points during the film. Film as a medium of communication is under scrutiny in *Persona*, from the pre-credits sequence onward. The film leader runs through the projector with its descending numbers flipping up every twenty-four frames, to the accompaniment of harsh whining noises. Then, a series of images that evoke Bergman's state of mind in the hospital where he wrote the script as well as the motifs of humiliation and death that permeate the film: a hand being nailed to a cross, a lamb being slaughtered, deserted parkland, steps, a pile of sand-like material—all fading away and being succeeded by pictures from a morgue. A dead woman lying in profile, a boy beneath a sheet. And on the soundtrack the inexorable drip of water.

The woman's eyes blink open. The boy stirs and comes to life. He wipes his hand over the screen. But he does so because he is mystified by the image of a woman's face on that screen. As the audience watches the boy, the audience *becomes* the merged image of two women's features. Much later in *Persona*, Elisabet pops up into frame and takes a snapshot of the camera—the spectator—while out on the shore. Bergman thus dissolves the habitual acceptance of a celluloid barrier between the audience and the characters in a film.

The mirror theme governs the idea of the displacement of one personality by another, the merging of two faces, two masks. Alma says after her description of an orgy on the summer shore: "Can you be two different people, both next to each other, at the same time?"[18] And a few seconds later: "I think I could turn myself into you, if I really tried."

The mirror is also the central emotional motif in the movie. Surely it is Elisabet, for example, who is speaking to Alma through Alma's own mouth when one hears of her unwanted child and her behavior during pregnancy? Surely, too, the letter she reads for Elisabet in the clinic at the start of the film is in fact addressed to *her*?

Reflection. Duplication. In a symphony, a theme is frequently recapitulated. Rarely, however, in a film. In *Persona,* when Alma lectures Elisabet about her pregnancy and hatred of her child, Bergman's camera watches the actress's face as she talks. But almost immediately afterward she repeats the speech word for word. This time the camera observes Alma's face.

A more representational mirror image may be found when Alma, shocked and embittered by the revelation that Elisabet has been studying her, stands beside a still lake and is reflected precisely in its surface.

At the very end of the film, Alma is back in uniform, clearing up and closing the cottage for the winter. As she adjusts her hair in a mirror, she suddenly sees the image of Elisabet stroking her in the same manner, a reminder of the other woman's presence within her and of the three-dimensional property of the "mirror."

Persona is not a film based in actuality. Alma enters her patient's room almost, it seems, by the same door through which she had *arrived* to answer the doctor's summons. Then Elisabet, on the island, denies visiting Alma's room by night and stroking her hair, when Bergman has shown the audience such a sequence without giving any clue as to its falsity. Later in the film, Alma appears to sleepwalk when answering the call of the sinister Mr. Vogler.

So there are no readily identifiable border posts between fantasy and reality. Cinema, Bergman may be saying as he shows one the carbons flaring into life, long ago established a unique and tantalizing compound of reality and imagination.

Dreams may encompass both fears and wish fulfillment. They provide the film director with a tempting license. The easiest way of visualizing a dream is also the most spectacular. There are the nightmares, for instance, in such Hitchcock films as *Spellbound* and *Vertigo*. Bergman approaches his material more intuitively. "The reality we experience today," he said on television in 1968, "is in fact as absurd, as horrible, and as obtrusive as our dreams. We are as defenseless before it as we are in our dreams. And one is strongly aware, I think, that there are no boundaries between dream and reality today." The "horrible" reality that Bergman mentions leaks into even such a hermetic film as *Persona*: the newsreel shots of a Buddhist monk immolating himself; or the photo of Jews being rounded up in the Warsaw Ghetto. The more appalled

Alma and Elisabet are by reality, the more they take refuge in a dream state. But, as the doctor says sternly to Elisabet: "Your hiding place isn't tight enough. Life trickles in from outside. And you are forced to react. No one asks whether it's true or false, whether you're genuine or just a sham. Such things are important only in the theater." Bergman addresses himself here; the doctor refers to Elisabet's "constant hunger to be exposed," a line evocative of Bergman's Malmö period, when he bared his feelings nightly on the stage.

Mauritz Edström, reviewing *Persona* in *Dagens Nyheter*, described it as "a confession of fear: fear of your fellow man, fear of failure, fear of being seen through, fear of disappointment, fear of your neighbor's strength and insight—and the wish to see the security of others shattered by a naked fear of death."[19]

Fear and its accomplice, guilt, have remained at the heart of Bergman's work since his youth. Humiliation is both the cause of and the response to such fear. Every remark in *Persona* aims to wound, every question to provoke, every answer to lacerate. As with the sisters in *The Virgin Spring* and *The Silence*, the humiliation suffered by the one is suffered vicariously by the other.

The sexual act itself constitutes for Bergman the supreme form of humiliation—for example, the orgy on the beach recollected by Alma, or the painful episode with Mr. Vogler in the garden by night, when Alma's intercourse with her surrogate "husband" leaves her in shame and mental agony. Communication is possible only through sex or violence of some kind. Words are no longer meaningful.

Persona also comprises a struggle between the artist and his public. Elisabet, the "artist," exerts a voodoo-like hold over her companion—the philistine, or audience—even sucking her blood in a vampiric gesture toward the close of the film. Alma's speech degenerates into incoherency, like a word processor gone berserk. Her exasperation represents the familiar attack mounted by Bergman's antagonists against the artist, for not divulging his secrets. It is amusing that Bergman should give Elisabet Vogler the same last name as he did his other "mute" protagonist—Albert Emanuel Vogler in *The Magician*. He is all too aware of the vampire role the artist plays, devouring his audience in order to glean his material—as Somerset Maugham used to acquire the gist of his Far East stories by listening to the experiences of people he met.

The moment of most willful humiliation occurs midway through *Persona*, when Alma plans her revenge on Elisabet for having written such spiteful comments to the doctor in her letter. She has broken a glass on the terrace outside the cottage and deliberately leaves one jagged fragment on the path in the expectation that Elisabet will emerge

Bibi Andersson (Sister Alma) *watching the broken glass shard in* Persona. *Photo courtesy Svensk Filmindustri.*

from the door and cut her foot. So eloquent is the expression on Alma's face during this wordless scene that one *knows*, long before Elisabet Vogler winces in pain, that Alma has by sheer force of will drawn her toward the shard. Almost immediately afterward, the film burns in the projector, a caesura that suggests that not even the celluloid can withstand the ferocious mental assault of Alma's retaliation, allied to the audience's complicity with her. Ulla Ryghe, Bergman's editor, says that projectionists stopped their machines the first time they ran *Persona*, assuming that the actual film was breaking. Large red labels were pasted on the appropriate reel cans, informing users that the film was neither on fire nor breaking up!

If the majority of Bergman's films describe a journey, then Alma and Elisabet are traveling constantly toward each other, until their personalities blend and blur in a weird osmosis, which Birgitta Steene has called "an ambiguous image of attraction and negation."[20] The discordant halves of a single personality seem to coalesce in the extraordinary picture (achieved in the optical printer) of both Alma and Elisabet staring out at the audience, confusing it as much as *it* does the little boy in the morgue who has been confronted earlier with a similar blended image. "When they saw those two images together on a Movieola," recalls Bergman, "Bibi said, 'What a terrible picture of you, Liv,' and Liv said, 'No, it's not me; it's you.' "[21]

In one of Strindberg's shorter plays, *The Stronger*, two women meet at a park bench. One talks incessantly, the other remains silent. At the end the voluble woman accuses her companion: "Your soul bored itself into mine as a worm into an apple, and it ate and ate, and burrowed and burrowed, till nothing was left but the outside shell and a little black dust." The opposite applies in *Persona*: Alma, the loquacious personality, is consumed by Elisabet, her silent companion—and patient. And yet Elisabet's refusal to speak stems from fear, not voracity.

This vulnerability is best illustrated in the hospital, quite early in *Persona*. In her room, with its bier-like bed and its blank, implacable door, stands a television set. At first one sees only the shimmering reflection of the tube on Elisabet's white robe. Then all at once the transmission invades the screen: A monk is burning himself to death in an Asian street, while an offscreen commentary babbles a stream of news items about the Vietnam War. Elisabet shrinks back in horror, withdrawing like an animal at bay into the furthest corner of the room, her eyes still rooted to the TV screen, one hand lifted to suppress the scream that rises spontaneously to her lips. Thus Elisabet's humanity is laid bare, and never again can one mistrust her silence. Bergman's own anguish and frustration in the face of modern conflict are expressed in this scene, and more and more Elisabet's behavior appears as a logical response to a hostile environment.

When at last Elisabet and Alma succumb to the questing echo of each other's psyche, they are united as victims, not predators.

Although much of the dialog in *Persona* was altered on set, Bergman refused to dilute his material when it proved intractable. Bibi Andersson remembers one scene in the hospital after she had met Elisabet Vogler and was meant to be washing her clothes. Bergman wanted her to improvise the incident, but after a morning of fruitless effort he decided to cut for the day.

Ulla Ryghe found Bergman to be open to suggestions, even if he put up a struggle before accepting ideas. "When we thought that *Persona* was in good shape, we screened it, for the first time, Bergman, Sven Nykvist, and I. When the light was turned on in the cinema I knew that at one point something was wrong with the film. When Bergman asked what I thought, I told him of my feelings, and he got very irritated about my being so vague. After some shouting, we started to go through the movie, sequence by sequence, and then I was able finally to explain what I had felt: The sequence where the two women's faces merge was coming too early in the film. It didn't have enough build-up to it at that juncture. Bergman must have felt similarly, for we took it out, moved it around, tried it in one or two different places and then finally found the right spot for it."

The fact that some parts of *Persona* were in fact created in the editing room made it more challenging and rewarding than Bergman's other films for a technician like Ulla Ryghe.

One of the most evocative and difficult sequences in *Persona* is Alma's recollection of the orgy on the beach. Some people to whom Bergman mentioned this scene thought that he should not include it. Bibi Andersson did, however, providing she could omit various male sex words that the character of Alma, she judged, would not have used. And by 11 A.M. on the first morning of trying the scene, it was in the can. Liv Ullmann had to remain silent throughout Bibi's monologue. "I told Liv how she must gather all her feeling into her lips," says Bergman. "She had to concentrate on placing her sensibility there—it's possible, you know, to place one's feeling into one's little finger, or one's big toe, or into one buttock, or your lips."[22]

Even up to the moment of releasing the film, Bergman strove to maintain the essential artifice of *Persona*. He insisted that stills from the film should be issued to the press with the strip of sprocket-holes seen running down the side to demonstrate the significance of the actual ribbon of film itself. It was a gimmick, and the rule was soon relaxed, but it indicates to what degree Bergman was obsessed at this time with the physical properties of the cinema itself and how much he was speculating on the lengths to which he could go with film as such.

Before beginning work on the editing of *Persona*, Bergman had to take over the direction of *Tiny Alice*, Albee's play about what Hjalmar Söderberg would call "the desire of the flesh and the incurable loneliness of the soul," because Bengt Ekerot had fallen sick during rehearsals. The moment the opening was behind them (December 4), Bergman drove up to Rättvik with Ulla Ryghe and his assistant, Lenn Hjortzberg. In the Hotel Siljansborg, with the temperature outside declining to −15° F., they embarked on the task of reducing *Persona* to a mere eighty-one minutes. In the evenings the talk was of *Auschwitz*, the Peter Weiss play due to be unveiled at Dramaten on February 13.

Bergman's life and career were undergoing yet another sea change. The pressures of administration at Dramaten were colossal, and early in 1966 Bergman resigned, after a mere three years in office (it had been anticipated in 1963 that he would stay for six seasons). His marriage with Käbi Laretei was at an end, and he was starting a new style of existence on Fårö with Liv Ullmann at his side.

Then, less than a month after the opening of *Auschwitz* (which, as an oratorio for the victims—and perpetrators—of the Nazi death camps, received glowing notices), Bergman lost his mother. Liv Ullmann arrived home from Norway the same day. Karin Bergman had suffered her third heart attack. The hospital wanted to call Bergman, according to Liv, but the mother had said, "He's so busy. Leave him alone." She was dead by the time Bergman reached her room.

Erik Bergman, after more than half a century of marriage, was shattered by his wife's death. Ingmar was the only member of the family able to care for him. Margareta, the daughter, was in England; and Dag, Ingmar's brother, was on diplomatic service abroad.

Karin Bergman was seventy-four when she passed away. "My feelings toward her were ambivalent," Ingmar told me. "When I was young I felt that she loved my brother more than me, and I was jealous." He discovered a diary among her possessions. The entries had been maintained scrupulously since 1916. "She wrote in a microscopically small script, with many abbreviations," said Bergman to Charles Thomas Samuels. "But suddenly we discovered an unknown woman—intelligent, impatient, furious, rebellious—who had lived under this disciplined perfect housewife."[23]

The funeral was held at Hedvig Eleonora Church. In a packed congregation, Bergman sat next to his niece, Veronica. The organist at Hedvig Eleonora had nursed an infatuation for Karin, and just before the funeral he suffered a heart attack and died.

Bergman paid a last tribute to his mother's death in the opening scene of *The Touch* (1970), showing Bibi Andersson arriving at a clinic after her mother has died. As a personality, she emerges most clearly in triptych form, in *Cries and Whispers* (1972). She and Ingmar had different artistic tastes, but a sympathy had persisted between them to the last.

Now that his father was lonely and depressed, Bergman behaved toward him with great kindness and affection. Erik moved to smaller quarters in the Grev Turegatan but was eventually compelled to enter the hospital. Bergman visited him every day when he could, and Erik, according to friends and relatives, much appreciated this considerateness. Erik died in 1970.

As a present for his son Daniel's second birthday, Bergman put together a little film, shot on 16 mm., recording some aspects of the boy's infancy. Since Daniel had been born in 1963, Bergman had photographed him on many occasions. Now he sifted through several thousand feet of film and tried to assemble "a testament, something he could have when he grew up."[24] The result was a short documentary, ready for inclusion in Svensk Filmindustri's portmanteau production, *Stimulantia*, which consisted of the work of seven other directors.

"Daniel's face is the finest, most stimulating thing I know," says Bergman offscreen. He shows him gathering mushrooms; reacting to his mother, Käbi Laretei, as she plays children's songs on her piano; playing in the family's villa in Djursholm. In a final, frozen shot, Bergman seizes Daniel's innocence, as he flings up a hand to ward off the gaze of the camera while he lies in a hammock with his grandma.

The intense privacy of this "home movie" gives it the tone of a monody for the life with Käbi Laretei. It had been a rich period in Bergman's middle age, and to Käbi he owed his fascination with ever more ascetic, ever more disciplined, and ever more "musical" cinema.

CHAPTER TWELVE

On the Island

Man is a great concept, like some inconceivable
thought, and in man there's everything from the
highest to the lowest, and man is God's own
image and in God everything exists. And so it
happens, men are created. But also the demons,
and the saints, and the prophets, and artists and
all those who bring destruction. Everything there
is in coexistence, growing into each other in
time. Everything in patterns that keep
changing every second.
But by the same token an infinite and limitless
number of realities, not simply the reality we
always can perceive with our limited senses, but
such myriad realities that stream and flow
over all around, inside us, and outside us.

Eva, in Autumn Sonata

NOW SETTLED ON THE ISLAND OF FÅRÖ, BERGMAN DEVOTED HIMSELF TO
Hour of the Wolf during the summer of 1966. The film grew out of his
screenplay, originally entitled *The Cannibals*, which had been laid
aside at the time of his illness the previous year. He had written it in a
very quiet room. He slept there, too, and after a few weeks felt himself
compelled to cease work on the script. "The demons would come to me
and wake me up, and they would stand there and talk to me."[1]

Before shooting, Bergman cut out certain extremely personal aspects of the screenplay, and all that remains of the framing scenes is Liv Ullmann's monologue at the beginning and end of the film. "I sat in the studio, telling the actors how I'd hit on the idea for the film: about how a woman had handed me a diary—Johan Borg's diary—and how afterward I'd got her to tell me, into a tape recorder, about their life together."[2]

Hour of the Wolf (*Vargtimmen*) is the first of three films featuring Max von Sydow as Bergman's alter ego, the artist as fugitive, retreating into his tiny island world and gradually bending his thoughts in upon himself, until dream and reality merge in terrifying collusion. In *Hour of the Wolf* he is a painter, Johan Borg. In *Shame*, a violinist. In *The Passion of Anna*, he has no pretensions to artistic achievement: "This time his name was Andreas Winkelmann," says Bergman offscreen at the close of the film.

Like an eighteenth-century composer forced to the expedient of varying and embellishing his tunes so as to keep the attention of his audience, Bergman creates a series of variations on the same theme. Each variation seems independent of the others yet, when heard in the context of the whole group, is subtly linked to its surrounding pieces.

> According to the ancient Romans, the Hour of the Wolf means the time between night and dawn, just before the light comes, and people believed it to be the time when demons had a heightened power and vitality, the hour when most people died and most children were born, and when nightmares came to one.[3]

So Bergman introduced the film.

Even on his island fastness, Johan Borg cannot escape his tormentors. Who should come over the brow of the hill one fine day but the Baron von Merkens (Erland Josephson), who claims with an ingratiating smile that he and his wife are two of Borg's "warmest admirers" and invites the painter to dinner. At the Baron's castle, Borg is paraded like a zoological specimen before the assembled guests. Sven Nykvist's wide-angle lens gives the face of each guest an enveloping, predatory quality as each comes forward to greet Borg. The dinner begins with one complete counterclockwise movement around the table; during the meal, the camera whirls about, pausing haphazardly like a bird in flight on each person's shoulder.

Max von Sydow recalls the filming of this sequence.

Bergman wanted to have the whole dinner table conversation . . . all in one take. His idea was to give the actors something near to the kind of continuity in performance that you get in the live theater. Sven Nykvist . . . was seated in front of us, and the table at which we sat was partly surrounding him. . . . I remember Nykvist's total precision in his panning technique— because when you pan from one face to another as fast as he had to do, it's very difficult to stop each pan at a moment when you have an ideal composition on each person.[4]

Bergman has expressed a great fondness for *Dracula*, especially the screen version starring Bela Lugosi. *Hour of the Wolf* has been widely compared with *The Magic Flute* (and, by extension, with the work of E. T. A. Hoffmann), but in technique and visual power it remains a tribute to Bram Stoker's creation. Bird references proliferate throughout the film. The first sign of Johan's illness, for example, comes as he greets Alma outside the cottage after climbing the slope; washed sheets are hanging on a line beside the couple, and the wind causes them to make a noise like the beating of great wings. After dinner at the castle, Lindhorst (Georg Rydeberg), fixes his gaze on Borg, and his face is lit in such a way as to suggest the beaklike nose and cold, ornithic eyes. Much later, Lindhorst appears again, dispatching Johan into the castle vault to search for his beloved mistress, Veronica Vogler (Ingrid Thulin); surrounded by hundreds of small birds, Lindhorst stretches his arms wide like a huge bat in flight. Finally, in the swamp where Borg disappears, Lindhorst's features are transmogrified into those of a vampire bat. The whirring, shrieking music of Lars Johan Werle heightens this association with birds and, of course, with the "bird catcher," Papageno, in *The Magic Flute*.

"I am terribly afraid of birds," admits Bergman. "I become frightened, extremely frightened, when a bird gets into the room if I am sitting there."[5]

In certain ways, *Hour of the Wolf* is a remake of *The Magician*. Once again, Bergman deceives the audience with his slight of hand just as he confuses the characters within his film. Alma is alone outside the cottage when suddenly an old lady materializes on the hillside. Because the sequence is edited so subjectively, one never for an instant suspects Alma's vision. Instead one shares her apprehension. One *believes*. Later in the castle the same ancient woman drops her eyeball into a wine glass and peels off her facial mask with a crackling sound so tangible that for a moment one thinks that flesh is being torn apart. Bergman knows how to disorient the spectator still further by inserting the occasional ludicrous moment: when the sinister von Merkens, for

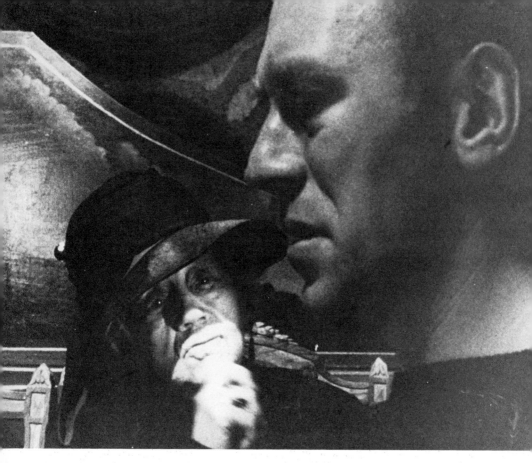

Max von Sydow (Johan Borg) *and Naima Wifstrand* (lady with the hat) *in* Hour of the Wolf. *Photo courtesy Svensk Filmindustri.*

instance, turns and marches *up* the wall and across the ceiling of a room, before the astonished eyes of Johan Borg.

Bergman alights in this film on a cinematic vocabulary commensurate with the dreams and hallucinations he seeks to describe. Sometimes he uses harsh, gleaming light to suffuse the imagery, as in Borg's meeting on the shore with Veronica Vogler, or in the fantasy beside the inlet when Borg is attacked by a young boy (Mikael Rundqvist).

On other occasions, Bergman resorts to heavy penumbras of shadow, inside the castle and its windowless rooms. By contrast, there is the un-mistakable "realism" of Alma's and Johan's return to their cottage after the dinner party: Sunspots are reflected on the lens of Sven Nykvist's slightly shuddering, hand-held camera. In the penultimate sequence, in the swamp, Bergman deploys the optical printer in the laboratory in such a way as to undermine the constituents of the image; faces are glimpsed in huge, grainy close-up, and the background is coarse and obscure.

Borg in the end is consumed by his tormentors. They possess a loathsome strength. Heerbrand (Ulf Johanson), the pathetic "archivist," calmly enters through a door that has just been double-locked. Von Merkens, like Death in *The Seventh Seal*, informs Borg: "Nothing you do will escape me." In a flashback from Johan's "diary," a small, apparently innocuous boy flings himself on Johan while he is fishing and seems endowed with almost superhuman strength. When Johan dashes his head against a rock in desperation, the boy dies with cawing, bird-like cries. Even when Johan has lowered his corpse into the water, the boy's head seeps up to the surface, like violence emerging in the human personality.

This particular sequence not only underlines the vulnerability of Johan Borg at the hands of his predators but also casts light on the struggle being waged between the different elements in his psyche. During a casual conversation with Alma in the cottage, "the boy" is mentioned. Perhaps he is the son of Johan by an earlier marriage. Or an illegitimate child. Certainly there is a degree of shame attached to the matter.

When the boy peers into Johan's boots beside the water, Johan whips up his fishing rod in a frenzy of movement, as though trying to conceal some erotic response. Even the mortal struggle between the two has the rhythm of a violent orgasm. And the ominous reappearance of the body after it has been tipped into the water suggests that the boy's significance cannot be so easily dismissed. It is not too fanciful to deduce from this scene and the earlier conversation about "the boy" at the table that Johan is bisexual and that Alma regards this as a fissure dividing her and Johan. The boy is like a part of himself that Johan dare not acknowledge, and one detects in his attitude, as he lowers the corpse into the pool, the faintest nuance of regret.

The image returns to haunt him in the castle vault after he had been humiliated in public, in the arms of his naked mistress, Veronica Vogler. A huge close-up of Borg's harassed features is supplanted by a repeat shot of the boy's head immersed in the water, linking the ambivalence of Borg's painted and made-up face with his own fear of homosexuality.

In the dark corners of the vault, his enemies chuckle with sadistic relish. "The glass is shattered," gasps Johan, "but what do the splinters reflect?" The question refers not only to his disintegrating personality but also to the structure of the film itself—fragments of truth and fantasy reported by Alma, who appears to be unstable herself.

Johan Borg is neither agreeable nor chaste. His diary reveals his affair with Veronica (quite coincidentally the name of Bergman's niece) and the curious bond with the boy by the shore. When he and Alma visit the castle for dinner, the baron's wife (Gertrud Fridh) draws up her skirt and displays a bruise inflicted, she claims, by Johan during love-making. "Jealous?" she asks of Alma with a mocking smile.

The sole gesture of tenderness Borg extends toward Alma throughout the entire film is in the aftermath of this raucous dinner party, when he lays a shawl around her shoulders. At other times he is oblivious to her presence; he rarely looks directly at her, so preoccupied is he with the presence of the "demons" and by his own urge to locate Veronica. Borg's behavior has but one justification: his abasement at the hands of Lindhorst and his acolytes. Forced back into insecurity, the Bergman artist-figure finds himself assailed by waves of humiliation, guilt, and shame.

> I think it's terribly important that art exposes humiliation, that art shows how human beings humiliate each other, because humiliation is one of the most dreadful companions of humanity, and our whole social system is based to an enormous extent on humiliation . . . the laws, the carrying out of sentences . . . the kind of school education . . . I experienced . . . the religion we officially profess ourselves adherents of.[6]

Others in Bergman's cinema have writhed beneath the probing fingers of guilt, but in *Persona, Hour of the Wolf, Shame,* and *The Passion of Anna,* the humiliation grows more violent in its manifestation.

Johan tells Alma in the cottage about an incident from his childhood based directly on Bergman's own memory of being locked in his nursery closet. He believed that in that closet dwelt a little man who "could gnaw the toes off guilty children." Release was followed by a ritual caning. "Then father said, how many strokes do you deserve? And I said, as many as possible." Thus, for Johan, humiliation is also expiation.

The notion of man as a small, abject creature at the mercy of those who manipulate him is developed in the climax to the dinner party in the castle. Lindhorst presents a toy theater recital from *The Magic Flute,* lighting candles to form a row of footlights. The figure of Tamino slides into the center of the tiny stage. And then, as he begins to sing in a tone of profound despair, one notes that his "puppet" is a real man in miniature, completely in the hands of Lindhorst, who looms over the theater like an evil bird. Tamino, in the hostile courtyard of the Temple of Wisdom, hears the words, "Pamina, Pamina lebt noch!" and Bergman turns his camera on Alma as she sits watching the performance. Johan represents Tamino, Alma stands for Pamina, a symbol of purity beyond the reach of questing man. As Maria Bergom-Larsson has pointed out, Johan's fate is that of Tamino, but in reverse.[7] His journey is a journey not toward the light but down into the darkness.

"Bald oder nie," the chorus has replied when Tamino asks when he will perceive the light. For Johan, the answer is "never."

Yet, in a characteristic Hoffmannesque twist, Johan is beguiled by a "false" Pamina: the figure of Veronica Vogler, stretched out on a slab in the castle vault. Johan is rouged and powdered by Lindhorst before being permitted to see the mistress he seeks. At first he believes Veronica to be dead, but, like Alman's wife in *Wild Strawberries*, she rises up with a cackle of laughter. With the affinities to the Mozart opera already suggested, this scene resembles the incident in *The Magic Flute* when Pamina, her head covered by a kind of sack, is brought before Tamino in the depths of the pyramids. Johan is in the grip of a strange incantation, a magic formula. He can never again find Alma. She calls to him imploringly in the dark swamp, but he is overwhelmed by his demons and vanishes from sight. Alma survives, pregnant; children in Bergman's films are, as previous examples have indicated, emblems of hope for the future. Alma herself is contaminated by Johan's fate.

"Isn't it so," she asks the audience as she addresses the camera in close-up, "that a woman who lives for a long time together with a man in the end begins to resemble him? That they have so much in common that not only their thoughts but also their faces take on the same expression?"

Hour of the Wolf was shot partly on location at Hovs Hallar, the rocky headland in southwest Sweden where Bergman had filmed the opening sequence of *The Seventh Seal*. This landscape, melded with that of Fårö, conjures up the "Frisian island of Baltrum" that Bergman mentions in a note at the start of the film.

Liv Ullmann's personality stamps itself strongly on Bergman's work. He had always felt a keener respect for women than for men in the sexual arena, but in the films he made with Liv this feeling is emphatic. He "thinks women are often stronger than one expects, they have a greater capacity to survive," said Liv Ullmann. "The comfort and safety of a marriage matters more to men, and they want to divorce less than women."[8]

While they were shooting *Hour of the Wolf*, a daughter, Linn, was born to Liv and Ingmar. "I let it happen," said Liv of the pregnancy. "I wasn't afraid. I felt it was very right." Her divorce had not yet become final, and the Lutheran church refused to baptize the baby. "We did not marry," remarked Liv later, "because we were both married when we met and it was never needed. . . . There was no lawyer, no priest in our relationship; it was our friendship, and our love."[9]

Bergman fought for their privacy. He had a high stone wall constructed around the house on Fårö, to keep prying visitors at bay.

Tourists persisted, however, in peering over into the property. It could not have been more remote, for to reach Fårö in the first place one must travel to Gotland, and then take the ferry over Fårö Sound. There follows another fifteen- to twenty-minute ride over rough roads before Bergman's home hoves in sight. Fårö itself is off limits to foreigners because the Swedish army has some top-security radar systems on the island.

The island looks as though it had emerged from the sea of its own volition. Liv Ullmann describes the landscape as covered with "gnarled spruce trees of strange green colors, most of them stunted and bent along the ground. Only the strongest managed to lift themselves upward. . . . The ground was gray and brown—wide fields covered by dry moss."[10] Max von Sydow was struck by the "limestone rock full of fossils, with a lovely gray tone. And there are areas which are absolutely barren, almost like a rock desert. The forests have very low fir trees and juniper bushes, green against the gray."[11] In winter the climate is, if anything, more inhospitable than on the Swedish mainland. The temperature may sink as low as —22° F. when lambing commences in March, and survival is a matter of chance and fitness.

But Bergman finds Fårö congenial.

Once installed there, he could be as lazy as he wished. He could observe the waves advancing and retreating on the barren shore. He could write in peace. He could become acquainted with virtually all the inhabitants of the island (only some seven hundred). "Human understanding and human interaction are authentic there, not artificial as in the big cities," he commented.[12] By the close of the sixties, he had established a pattern of life on Fårö. A man attended to the garden and helped on the property in other ways; two elderly ladies took care of the housework. Soon afterward, a studio was built in the seventeenth-century village of Dämba, in the southeast corner of Fårö, five minutes by car from Bergman's house.

Bergman drove in his favorite Peugeot, catching the 4:45 P.M. ferry to Fårösund to buy the papers. Every morning, soon after 8 A.M., he would take a constitutional along the seashore. He liked to point out to visitors that Fårö was a crossroads for traders and merchants in the eleventh and twelfth centuries. "Russia is only 130 kilometers away, you know," he would remark.[13] In the evening, if television had nothing to offer, he and Liv Ullmann would screen one of the films from his personal collection.

Bergman thrived on this daily round. He is never at home in large cities, for he detests the noise and pressure of urban existence. He has been happiest when living in Dalarna, where he spent those boyhood summers, and on Fårö, with its romantic fulfillment of a life beside the sea.

On October 11, 1966, Bergman made the journey to Holland to collect his Erasmus Prize of a hundred thousand Dutch florins from Prince Bernhard. One week later, *Persona* opened in Stockholm, to enthusiastic notices. Attendances, however, were mediocre: Only 110,725 Swedes saw *Persona*, compared with the 1,459,031 who had bought tickets for *The Silence* three years earlier. This pattern was repeated abroad, where *Persona* became the focus of long articles in the serious film magazines but performed only modestly at the box office.

United Artists had purchased for $1 million a majority of world rights to *Persona* and Bergman's next film. The money went to Svensk Filmindustri, who was producing the pictures, and indeed Bergman's income for the fiscal year 1967 was reported as being 853,180 crowns (about $170,000) before tax—more than others in the Swedish film world, but not excessive by international standards and considering the enormous workload and creativity of Bergman.

Erland Josephson had succeeded Bergman as head of the Royal Dramatic Theater. In the autumn of 1966, he invited Bergman to be guest director on Molière's *The School for Wives*. But the production met with hostile reviews, and Bergman did not return to Dramaten until 1969.

At the turn of the year, Bergman spent some weeks in Oslo preparing for the April 1 opening of his production of *Six Characters in Search of an Author* at the National Theater of Norway. Liv Ullmann played the daughter; Knut Wigert her father. Sven Barthel wrote in the Stockholm daily, *Dagens Nyheter*, that Bergman had presented "a vision of man's vulnerability and impotence, his nakedness." A local critic said that the applause was as resounding as if Norway had defeated Sweden in the Ullevål Stadium.

While in Oslo, Bergman began writing a screenplay about a scientist who conducts experiments. "He shuts up two people in his laboratory, exposes them to various psychic pressures, and observes them."[14] Both Jan and Jacobi in *Shame* originate in this script, but so does Vergérus in *The Serpent's Egg*.

During the spring, his ideas for *Shame* (entitled in draft *The War*, and later *The Dreams of Shame*) became more concrete. Lenn Hjortzberg, his assistant, was sent to Fårö to prepare the buildings and buy furniture for the shooting of *Shame* from September onward. Bergman himself, restless, wrote yet another script in July, a kind of play almost completely dependent on dialog. He placed it to one side, and the following year it developed into *The Ritual*.

Using a crew of forty-five—extremely large by Swedish standards—Bergman spent the final four months of 1967 shooting *Shame*. At his press conference in September, he described the house that had been erected on Fårö:

> We have movable walls, three rooms that are furnished later, and there's a staircase up to an attic. Everything is assembled here so that it can be moved easily. The floor has been specially constructed to enable us to use our camera truck. As Winnie the Pooh says, this is a practical jar to have things in.

Government permission had to be obtained for the grounds to be landscaped. Apart from its military significance, Fårö is also a nature reserve, and no houses may be built without authorization. But when the shooting was finished, Svensk Filmindustri could not understand why Bergman was reluctant for the house to be dismantled. He told them he would make another film there, even though he had no real notion of doing so. "I just didn't want to lose that house. Inside, I had a strange feeling that I had not succeeded in *Shame*, and I wanted to recreate the film in the place where it had failed."[15]

Thus *The Passion of Anna* would come about.

The team spirit so conspicuous in Scandinavian filmmaking prevailed on *Shame*. The script called for the trees to be utterly bare, devastated by fire and bombs. But in the autumn of 1967 the trees still flourished, and Max von Sydow and the others had to climb up ladders and pick off the remaining leaves, one by one.

Bergman continued to experiment with his technique. One of the most affecting scenes in the film, an early supper in the open air involving Liv Ullmann and Max von Sydow, was improvised. Nykvist and his assistant shot the actors with two over-the-shoulder cameras, while Max and Liv continued talking in the mode that Bergman had suggested. The script used indirect speech, rather than orthodox dialog, to point the way in which conversations were meant to proceed.

Shame (*Skammen*) was written over a year before the Soviet Union invaded Czechoslovakia and before the war in Vietnam had assumed catastrophic proportions. "If those two things had already happened," says Bergman, "the film would have worn a different aspect."[16] In a television interview, he traced the genesis of the film:

> There was a newsreel picture from one of these Vietnam films. . . . An old man and woman were walking with a cow—a peasant and his wife walking with a cow. And all of a sudden, a helicopter that had been waiting there on the ground started up and began making a racket and soldiers ran up to it. And the cow tore itself loose, and the old woman dashed away after the cow, and the helicopter rose and rose, and this old man just

stood there, completely nonplussed and utterly confused and desperate. And, somehow, more than all the atrocities I've seen, I experienced that third party's misery, when everything breaks loose over his head. And it was actually that little image that was the entire releasing factor for *Shame*.[17]

In another interview he claims that the film originated "in a panicky question: How would I have behaved during the Nazi period if Sweden had been occupied and if I'd held some position of responsibility or been connected with home institutions?"[18] *Shame*, said Bergman later, is not about bombs falling as much as the gradual infiltration of fear.[19]

One could also maintain that in *Shame* Bergman pays the price for having "eliminated" his faith, in the trilogy that ended with *The Silence*. "From the moment you've no faith," he had admitted, "from that moment you live in a deep inner confusion—from then on you're exposed to what Strindberg calls 'the powers.' "[20]

Jan Rosenberg (Max von Sydow) cannot call on the convenient aid of either fascist or communist convictions. He and his wife/companion, Eva (Liv Ullmann) are musicians who have withdrawn to a remote Baltic island where they eke out a living by growing and selling fruit. The island is invaded. A guerilla movement arises, in-

Liv Ullmann (Eva), Max von Sydow (Jan), and Karl-Axel Forsberg (secretary) in Shame. *Photo courtesy Svensk Filmindustri.*

volving many civilians. Jan's old friend, Jacobi (Gunnar Björnstrand) proves to be a quisling. He arrests Jan and Eva but soon releases them. He comes to their cottage and tries to make some kind of meaningful contact with them. While Jan is asleep, Jacobi and Eva make love together. When Jan discovers this betrayal, he steals Jacobi's savings. The older man is unable to buy himself out of trouble, and Jan becomes his reluctant executioner. Fleeing with their scanty possessions, Jan and Eva purchase a place on board a rowing boat. But food and water run out. The boat is left to drift in the vast sea.

Bergman's approach to Jan's and Eva's situation is cogent in the light of Sweden's historical experience. Not since 1809, when they lost control of Finland to Russia, have Swedes actually been involved in the day-to-day anguish and violence of war. Neutrality has in the postwar period nurtured a condescending attitude toward the superpowers and toward those countries engaged in military squabbles. The Swede sees himself as a keeper of the peace; he has never endured bombardment by day or by night.

To Bergman, who has found it difficult to stray beyond the very personal dilemma, to discuss wider social issues other than in terms of his own familiar characters, the confusion in *Shame* is exemplified in the relationship between Jan and Eva. As in *Hour of the Wolf*, the woman proves more practical than her partner. She sounds as punctilious as Alma about her housekeeping budget. When they awake in the cottage, Eva puts coffee on the stove and washes fearlessly in cold water. Jan can only swallow a tablet, feel an aching tooth, and pick absentmindedly at his toes.

Strange portents disturb their breakfast. Jan notes that the church bells are tolling on a Friday, and the telephone rings incessantly even when Eva lifts the receiver. "It's best to know nothing," says Jan, pronouncing the typical Swede's reaction to crisis. "I'm sick of your escapism," responds Eva.

Jan is inept and insensitive like nearly every husband in Bergman's cinema. He snorts at determinism, only to discover as the situation grows more wretched that his basic reactions are all too predictable. By the end of the film he has become an obtuse psychopath, betraying an old friend of the family and then killing an innocent deserter. Eva tries her best. In that bright supper sequence outside the house, she urges him to take up music again. "Let's play for half an hour every day. We've our instruments, and we must keep our hand in." But their hands are blunted and coarsened by four years of working on the land, and the piano and violin are soon smashed by guerillas. The chance of rehabilitation is swept aside; the artist's privacy is again invaded.

Art, for Bergman, must be a profession or it amounts to nothing. Significantly, therefore, neither Johan Borg in *Hour of the Wolf* nor Jan Rosenberg in *Shame* is seen to be practicing his art. Johan essays a quick sketch of his wife and dabs painfully at a canvas on the pebbly beach before confronting Veronica Vogler. But Jan does little more than caress his violin—and then only in order to mention that Pampini, a contemporary of Beethoven who built the instrument in 1814, had fought with the Russian armies against Napoleon, the implication being that he, the musician of today, is reluctant to accept his obligations in a similar crisis. Jacobi, his friend, speaks in disgusted tones of "the sacred freedom of art, the sacred spinelessness of art."

The disruption threatened by the war makes Jan and Eva aware of the heritage they will lose. Visiting an acquaintance, Lobelius (Hans Alfredson), in the town where they sell their fruit, they admire a delicate Meissen music box. Their eyes roam around Lobelius's antique shop, with its old prints, figureheads, and other memorabilia. At home that evening, they eat fish and drink white wine and talk tenderly to each other; and they make resolutions about their music that will never be honored. At such moments Bergman may be seen to cherish the togetherness that sex and marriage can bring. Harriet Bosse wrote to Strindberg, in the wake of their break-up: "I am very fond of you—whatever may happen—I love you, perhaps because, through such deep and boundless sorrow, you have infused my life with meaning."[21]

The most unconvincing element in *Shame* is the chaotic tendency of war and its impact on the innocent citizen. Jan and Eva can tell no difference between the opposing armies. The fortunes of war seem to shift like currents in a treacherous sea. People like Jacobi are powerful one moment, humiliated the next. Everywhere the "authorities"—so abhorrent to Bergman—are in command. A doctor enters a room full of injured detainees, trips over a corpse, and proceeds to wrench a man's dislocated shoulder into place. As his victim writhes in agony, the doctor says briskly, "Keep off tennis for the next few weeks."

Jan and Eva are not the only people in the film to be overcome by guilt and shame. Jacobi sets his friends free from a group of suspected collaborators and then sits alone, draining a glass of brandy and contemplating a magazine. He *radiates* guilt, as though he had some premonition of his own punishment. When he visits Jan and Eva a short while later, his authority has given way to an insecure self-pity. "I've only known human intimacy a very few times," he says, "always in connection with pain." He entreats Jan and Eva to feel his bare chest, in an attempt to establish some contact, however fleeting, with the two friends who may be able to save his life.

But weakness is all. Eva deceives her husband by sleeping with Jacobi, and Jan deceives Jacobi by refusing to say where his money is hidden. Filip (Sigge Fürst), the local fisherman in charge of a detachment of soldiers, rewards Jan for his treachery by handing him a pistol and forcing him to execute Jacobi. In turn, Filip begins to perceive how the violence and the atrocities search out the bestial responses in all of them, and when, at the end of the film, he is marooned at sea with the other refugees, he commits suicide as a deliberate act of atonement. The boat dwindles to a speck in the indifferent ocean. One thinks of Frost's dream in *The Naked Night*: "I became smaller and smaller until I was only a seed—and then I was gone."

After Filip has slipped over the side, rations are handed round like a Last Supper. (Religious connotations run through even the most naturalistic of Bergman's films. Jan, for instance, denies thrice that he knows the whereabouts of Jacobi's cash.) Eva and Jan are left to die. Their humiliation is complete. They have been tested and found wanting. Their house and their belongings have been reduced to ruins. Their shame is also the shame of Bergman, their creator, and in the most resonant line of the film, Eva says, "It's not my dream. It's someone else's that I'm part of. And what happens when that person wakes up and is ashamed?" War has swept her and Jan off their feet like helpless, tiny animals, but at the last moment Eva has begun to discern a logic in the confusion and turmoil.

Shame was greeted with an unexpected amalgam of scorn and admiration when it opened in Stockholm on September 29, 1968. Bergman's film undermined the complacency of the ordinary Swede; it enraged the politically committed observer, however, by its refusal to take sides. It clung, in short, to the traditional Swedish neutrality at a time when opinion was running strongly against America's participation in the Vietnam War. A week after the premiere Sara Lidman, in the evening paper *Aftonbladet*, condemned Bergman for granting "the contemporary Western intelligentsia total freedom from responsibility for Vietnam by turning this war into a metaphysical issue."[22] In *Dagens Nyheter*, Torsten Bergmark described Bergman's position as coinciding with the sort of intolerable aloofness that the artist attempts to maintain. "It results," he wrote, "in the deepest human degradation and the sort of conduct which is less morally defensible than even that of the quislings."[23]

Bergman's attitude was clear. "I do not know of any party that is for frightened and terrified people who are experiencing the period of dusk and the fact that it has kind of begun and the plane is definitely inclined downwards. I cannot really engage myself in any political activity."[24] He has often reacted against the idea of coercion against the artist and tells the story of Shostakovich being asked to rewrite a symphony on the grounds that it was insufficiently socialistic in thought.

The suspicion remained among several Swedish critics, however, that Bergman's vision of war ascribed blame to no one nation or party but presented the conflict as the work of some nameless Destiny, without roots in any divergent socioeconomic ideologies.

Pauline Kael, writing in the *New Yorker*, spent most of her notice in dismembering Bergman's career, while at the same time dubbing *Shame* a masterpiece, "a flawless work and a masterly vision. Treating the most dreaded of subjects, the film makes one feel elated. The subject is our responses to death, but a work of art is a true sign of life." *Shame* was nominated for an Academy Award but did not win, and it received a pitiful distribution in Britain and the United States.

The ultimate courage of *Shame* is that Bergman thrusts his characters out of the warm, secure, womb-like refuge that constitutes the bourgeois family into an environment as unfriendly and uncaring as a lunar landscape. As he writes in the screenplay, "They're alone, and the world is coming to an end." Perhaps, despite his detractors, he was more shaken than many of his fellow countrymen by the impact of the Vietnam conflict.

The company that Bergman established to produce his films from 1968 onwards was named Cinematograph in affectionate tribute to Louis Lumière's early motion picture machine. Quarters were found at no. 4 Floragatan (the street where Bergman's parents had lived in the early twenties), adjacent to the offices of Sandrew Film & Theater company. At the top of the winding stair stood the ship's figurehead that was seen in both *Persona* and *The Passion of Anna* and that became an emblem for Cinematograph. "Bergman" was inscribed on a brass plate beneath the company plaque, and within the premises a screening room was constructed with sumptuous armchairs in yellow velvet. In the ensuing eight years, Bergman made this his headquarters in Stockholm, and it became a more vital center as Cinematograph branched out into production in the early seventies.

Bergman had written the screenplay for *The Ritual* (*Riten*) the previous summer. Now, during the late spring of 1968, he rehearsed the piece for a month with his four actors, Gunnar Björnstrand, Ingrid Thulin, Anders Ek, and Erik Hell, and then filmed it in a mere nine days in May and June in the studios of Svensk Filmindustri at Råsunda. *The Ritual* was made with Bergman's habitual stringency: "I'd set the footage to a maximum of 15,000 meters [less than 50,000 feet]. We used up 13,500 or something of that order, so I had to know exactly what we were going to include."[25] He and Mago ransacked the studio cellars for all the tables and chairs they could find to save costs on production design.

Shame had drained considerable reserves of energy from Bergman, and, just as he turned to the frivolity of *All These Women* after *The Silence*, so now he sought some relief from the "terrible weight of the filmic process"[26] by making what was in essence a play, free from the pressure of visual invention. Bergman has likened it to one of Godard's cinetracts, but in content it is a distillation of *The Magician*. With the small screen in mind, Bergman uses large close-ups for most of the seventy-four minutes of the film, occasionally whip-panning from person to person during a sharp exchange of words, but more often cutting from face to face. The backgrounds—office walls, hotel rooms, a confessional, a bar, a dressing room—are gray and neutral.

The Ritual consists of nine scenes, during which three cabaret entertainers are investigated by a civil judge. At first they are interviewed together, and then the judge separates them, seeking to impose his will on them as individuals. Meanwhile, the entertainers round on one another, railing at their humiliating profession and their own emotional inadequacies. Eventually they cause the judge's death by heart failure as they perform their "ritual." Although in several Bergman films there are faint prognoses of events or developments in his personal life, the parallel between the content of *The Ritual* and the tax investigations to which Bergman would be submitted in 1976 (see Chapter 15) is uncanny.

The judge, Abrahamson (Erik Hell), is a typical bureaucrat. When he summons the performers to his office, there is small talk about the weather, a pause for a drink, and some dangerous banter about the group's reputed income (lodged in Switzerland, of course). But Abrahamson soon passes to an altogether more serious matter—a speeding offense in Holland when Thea (Ingrid Thulin) apparently removed her clothes and made obscene signs at the police.

As the film progresses, it becomes clear that Abrahamson is not as set apart from his victims as one might assume. Like the women in *Cries and Whispers*, the four characters in *The Ritual* are intimately related to one another. Each seeks his freedom; each discovers that he is inextricably bound to his partners. Sebastian (Anders Ek) and Thea toy vaguely with the idea of murdering the judge. Sebastian speaks of Winkelmann (Gunnar Björnstrand), who is Thea's husband and therefore his sexual adversary, as being "so gentle, so wise, so devilish." Winkelmann himself recoils with loathing from his metier: "I'm tired of our so-called artistry—we're meaningless, disgusting, absurd." His marriage to Thea is on the rocks. As Thea sobs that she would be lost without him, Winkelmann articulates the flaws familiar in so many Bergman relationships: "Our words don't fit. There's an absolute lack of understanding." In the fourth scene, "A Confessional," Abrahamson, like some fugitive from a Graham Greene novel, blurts out his fear of imminent death—to Bergman himself, no less, who plays the priest.

The confession is a central plank in Bergman's cinema. The act of avowal becomes an act of expiation, of liberation, in nearly all the films, whether or not they are tinged with religious overtones. Alma recollects the orgy on the beach in *Persona*. Ester pours out her heart to the old waiter at the end of *The Silence*. Jacobi bares his soul to Jan and Eva in *Shame*.

Although Abrahamson declares himself a nonbeliever, there are significant references to Catholicism in *The Ritual*, not least in the final sequence, when the elevation of the chalice is rendered in grotesque terms.

Each of the four personalities recognizes the artifice that sustains his existence. Thea lives under a false identity; Sebastian is a murderer; Winkelmann is divorced, has a retarded child, and suffers agonies on account of Thea's infidelity; and Abrahamson acknowledges in the last scene his sensual craving for humiliation.

Bergman's characters depend on one another so fundamentally that they can never escape to the "lonely shore" and "protective sea" Sebastian speaks of in *The Ritual*. Every episode takes place indoors; walls constrict the players on all sides. At the end of the first scene, Sebastian stands with Thea by a window, barred like a prison. It is the sole vision of the outside world afforded to any of them. There is only the office. And the confessional, in which the grille appears to incarcerate the judge. And the tiny dressing room in which Winkelmann speaks so despondently of the future. And the minute bar where Sebastian is informed that his financial plight will pin him to the group for years to come.

The film adds up to a personal catechism for Bergman. His characters pronounce lines that he himself has sometimes delivered in interviews. Sebastian, forced on the defensive by the judge's questions, asserts his independence: "I'm my own god. I supply my own angels and demons." Winkelmann admits that he has one great horror—being left alone. Later he says he has learned almost everything about humiliation. "Something about me seems to invite it. . . . The really great artists can't be hurt. I'm not one of them." Like Bergman, Sebastian has to support various children, but "My lawyer knows more about it than I do." Again like Bergman, Abrahamson and the others are obsessed with their physical metabolism. Thea tells the judge that she has suffered from eczema for two years. Sebastian complains of eye-ache and

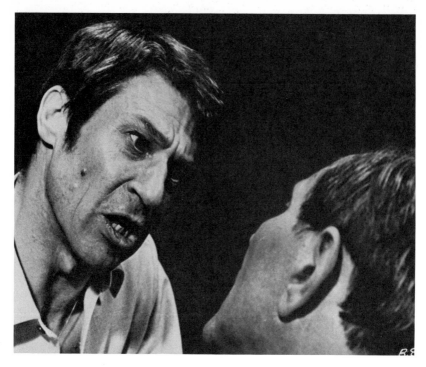

Anders Ek (Fischer) *and Erik Hell* (Judge Abrahamson) *in* The Ritual.
Photo courtesy Darvill Associates.

diarrhea. Abrahamson cannot help himself perspiring freely; "I'm sorry if the smell upsets you," he apologizes to Sebastian. Even a passing reference to cancer carries a cold menace, an implacability that matches Fisher's own attitude to life. Bodily sickness becomes, for the umpteenth time, a sign of spiritual malaise.

Bergman wreaks his revenge not only on Abrahamson but also on the audience, for being witnesses to this disclosure of personality. The two extraordinary illusions in *The Ritual* are the pyre-like blaze that Sebastian starts in the hotel room, as though he were a monk engaging in self-immolation; and the "ritual" itself. In the first instance, the audience is baffled—Sebastian appears hale if unhearty in the next sequence, unharmed by the fire. In the second, it is Abrahamson who is duped—fatally. The elaborate paraphernalia of the ceremony can hardly conceal its ineptness; there is no feat, no sleight of hand. Abrahamson finds himself terrified more by what *might* happen than by what actually *does* (lights out, a spot of mock levitation, wine drinking, and tub thumping). Sebastian holds a knife close to the judge's neck and then symbolically dispatches him with a thrust into a bladder of wine. As the fluid spurts out into a bowl it might as well be blood, the blood of Abrahamson, "the blood of the Host."[27]

"This, briefly, is our number," intones Winkelmann as he finishes drinking, and Abrahamson's "I understand!" is a final gesture of submission. But also an expression of deliverance. One remembers Spegel's words in *The Magician*: "I long for a knife with which to lay bare my bowels . . . to free me from my substance . . . a sharp blade that would scrape out all my uncleanliness. Then the so-called spirit would soar out of this meaningless body."

It is characteristic of Bergman that the judge should be killed not by brute force but almost by proxy, by inducing a degree of empathy in him that makes the ritual, for all its contrivance, a deadly weapon. The Bergman artist exerts a ruthless hold over his adversary, a hold that the philistine (i.e. the spectator) cannot combat because he does not have access to the mechanics of art. *The Ritual*, in the final analysis, embodies Bergman's own hatred of the officialdom—and the critics—that irked him during his years as head of the Royal Dramatic Theater. It was screened on Swedish television on March 25, 1969, and released as a theatrical movie outside Scandinavia.

In the spring of 1968, Bergman spent five weeks on holiday in Rome with Liv Ullmann. It was one of his longest vacations. He visited Saint Peter's practically every day and met Alberto Moravia and other Italian luminaries. There was his first memorable encounter with Federico Fellini. They were brothers within an instant, recalls Liv Ullmann. "They embraced, laughed together as if they had lived the same life. They wandered through the streets in the night, arms around each other, Fellini wearing a dramatic black cape, Ingmar in his little cap and an old winter coat."[28] The admiration was mutual. When *Amarcord* appeared a few years later, Bergman saw it several times. And in an interview in 1966 Fellini had waxed enthusiastic about Bergman's "seductive quality of mesmerizing your attention. Even if you're not in full agreement with what he says, you enjoy the way he says it, his way of seeing the world with such intensity. He is one of the most complete cinematographic creators I have ever seen."

From this meeting grew the concept of a joint film, entitled *Love Duet*, to be shot in Stockholm and Rome. Martin Poll would have been the producer, and shooting was scheduled tentatively for the fall of 1969, after Bergman had completed *The Passion of Anna*. Fellini declared: "It will not be a poker game in which we hide aces up our sleeves. The only person we may hide things from is the producer."

But the dream never materialized. Bergman canceled the contract in 1970, when preparations were at quite an advanced stage (Mago had met Martin Poll at the Grand Hotel in Stockholm to discuss costumes, and Katharine Ross and Viveca Lindfors had been contacted about playing in the movie). Perhaps it was the pressure of approaching *The Touch*, his first English-language film. Besides, in the intervening year or two, Bergman accomplished much more.

Back on Fårö for the summer, he wrote the screenplay for *The Passion of Anna (En passion)*. He was still disillusioned with the Royal Dramatic Theater, and during 1968 he avoided the stage altogether— apart from participating for a week in Peter Daubeny's World Theatre Season in London with his production of *Hedda Gabler*.

Denis Marion has written that Bergman's Fårö films illustrate the dictum, "A landscape is a state of soul."[29] To this extent, *Hour of the Wolf, Shame*, and *The Passion of Anna* comprise a trilogy, linked not just by the presence of Max von Sydow and Liv Ullmann as the protagonists but also by their topography. All three films, however, derive from Bergman's dreams rather than from any particular desire to document the pattern of life on the island. (That would be achieved in 1969, in Bergman's television film about Fårö.) Liv Ullmann recalls Bergman's saying, "I had this dream, I'm confused about it." From then on, she says, they developed it together. "His scripts go directly to the fantasy level, including my own." Bergman describes his screenplay as having been written "straight off the cuff, it was more a catalog of moods than a film script."[30]

The Passion of Anna is divided into four segments, and each of the major actors has an opportunity to speak directly to the camera about his or her role. This still appears to be an error on Bergman's part. The four interludes are stilted and self-conscious. Brecht may have wanted the audience to remain detached from the drama, but these artificial caesuras in *The Passion of Anna* fail to influence one's reaction to the characters in any shape or form.

In other formal respects, however, *The Passion of Anna* bears no trace of the severe difficulties that attended its production. "In some odd way, the film itself infected us; above all, of course, myself," Bergman recalls. He had not disliked making a film so much since *Winter Light*. Max von Sydow was under pressure also, for he was appearing at the Royal Dramatic Theater for two performances each weekend during the forty-five day production schedule and had to commute by boat during the late fall season. Sven Nykvist and Bergman frustrated each other; Bergman felt a recurrence of his old stomach ulcer, and Nykvist suffered giddy spells. In the final stages even the editing proved difficult, and over eleven thousand feet were left on the cutting room floor.

Bibi Andersson was fascinated by Fårö, as she had been during the shooting of *Persona*, and in particular by Bergman's cozy little domain. "It is very strange because when you come in through these walls, you have a feeling that you have neighbors and people around, because it's very warm—all yellow and wood. He has a swimming pool there. You have a feeling you can pick up a telephone and go to a neighbor. And then you go out and there is empty land all over."[31] Conditions for the crew were similar to those on any location. They worked from 7:30 A.M. to 5 P.M. except for Monday, and in their free time they could play ping-pong, bathe in the icy sea, drink wine and eat cheese, and amuse themselves at the holiday campsite of Sudersand, when it was open.

Andreas Winkelmann (Max von Sydow), the principal character in *The Passion of Anna*, has parted from his wife and withdrawn from the world to live in solitude on a Baltic island. But he is without warning confronted with two kinds of violence: physical, in the shape of an unidentified maniac who slaughters sheep; and psychic, in the presence of Anna Fromm (Liv Ullmann), a crippled widow whose husband had also been named Andreas.

The suspense of *The Passion of Anna* originates in this sinister "duplication," the feeling that Andreas is being sucked inexorably along the same path to disaster as his namesake was—deluded, exasperated, and finally driven insane by the passionate idealism of Anna.

The other engrossing theme of the film is more familiar to Bergman devotees: the probing beneath the mask that each person offers to the world. Anna speaks ardently of her striving for spiritual perfection, of the honesty and harmony of her marriage, only to provoke a replica of the terminal clash with her husband. Elis (Erland Josephson), an opulent architect who lives close to Andreas on the island, is painfully aware of his wife Eva's (Bibi Andersson) infidelity despite the sarcastic indifference he affects. Andreas himself, whether he is regarded as a Christ-figure or a criminal on the run, smarts under the well-meaning contempt of his neighbors.

Andreas is caught between the forces of light and darkness. When he visits Elis's studio, he flinches under the bright lights that the photographer uses. Bergman introduces lamps and shade to suggest a penumbra close to the dream state. When Eva, having phoned her husband to say she is quite alone, goes into another room to attend to her toilet, Andreas comments on how dark it is. He lights a candle, but a few seconds later Eva blows it out. And in one of the film's most alarming sequences, when Anna, by now living with Andreas, tightens her embrace around his neck so tightly that in her eyes one glimpses an urge to strangle her partner, the light in the room has been extinguished.

Sleep and the subconscious state beckon Andreas. Eva is found dozing in her car at the roadside. "Sometimes I can't sleep at night," she tells Andreas. "So I fall asleep during the day." Again and again, Bergman shows people half-asleep, discovered in the gray region between waking and dreaming. For there is little doubt that, while one Andreas lives in actuality, the other dwells in a dream zone. When Andreas falls asleep, he enters the world of his dead namesake. (On one occasion, he is even summoned out of a deep slumber by the sound of his name being called—in a dream—by Anna Fromm.) In the original screenplay, Andreas informs Anna that he is afraid of "the sleep, which is always dreams that hunt me here or there, or merely the darkness that rustles with ghosts and memories." Dreams are the repository of guilt for Andreas. He succumbs slowly to the contagion of guilt, the legacy of the dead Andreas, who perished in a car crash while Anna was driving. The ultimate logic of the film is that Andreas should find himself seated beside Anna in a similar situation.

Max von Sydow (Andreas) *and Bibi Andersson* (Eva) *in* The Passion of Anna. *Photo courtesy Swedish Film Institute.*

Earlier, Andreas has fought against the consumption of his spirit by the dead Andreas, staggering through snow-covered woodland shouting, "Andreas! Damned Andreas!" Now, however, he cannot respond. "I came to ask your forgiveness," says Anna ambiguously, and Andreas is left abandoned in a barren stretch of terrain as Anna drives off. He paces this way and that, trapped as it were by the frame of the film image. The camera lens closes in on him as he collapses in a landscape that slowly dissolves before the audience's eyes. The ground becomes a pattern of flickering granules, pulsating cells of light, and Bergman's voice is heard offscreen:

"This time his name was Andreas Winkelmann."

On another occasion he might have been called Jan Rosenberg, or Johan Borg. Or perhaps Barabbas.

For Bergman, violence runs like an essential filament through human life and behavior. And in a film in which ambiguity becomes a virtue, nothing is emphasized by the director as much as the letter that Andreas finds in Anna's pocketbook. The writer speaks of the futility of his relationship with Anna and of "new complications that in their turn will bring on terrible mental disturbances, as well as physical and mental acts of violence." The camera fastens on these words, wheeling over them subjectively in a manner reminiscent of the letter Alma discovers in *Persona*.

The atmosphere engendered by Bergman is sinister and bizarre. The identity of the mysterious psychopath who slaughters the sheep, tortures a dog in the woods, and humiliates Andreas's ailing neighbor, Johan of Skir (Erik Hell), is never disclosed. But the violence growls in the background, like the bass line in a piece of music, and permeates Andreas himself until, in a horrifying outburst, he swings an ax at Anna's head and beats her furiously. Her scarlet scarf lies in the snow like surrogate blood. Bemused and ashamed, Andreas drifts into a light sleep, only to be roused by the noise of fire engines. The island's assailant has poured gasoline over an unfortunate horse, set light to it, locked the door of the stables, and vanished. Nobody is apprehended. *The Passion of Anna* might be described as a detective story without a solution. The reason being that the violence is perennial, both within and without Andreas's world. On television, Anna and Andreas watch a South Vietnamese officer executing a Vietcong prisoner. Moments later, a bird falls with a thump, dead, outside the cottage.

The Passion of Anna, Bergman's first dramatic film to be shot in color, uses both chromatic effects and a jagged editing technique to heighten the audience's apprehension of violence. Blue has been drained from the negative. Gray, brown, green, and above all red predominate, so that the revolving amber light on a police vehicle, the splash of Anna's red scarf on the snow, and the hectic orange of the stable inferno carry an authentic charge of frenzy.

The film is experimental in other respects, too. There are the comments by the actors on their roles, and a convincing dinner table sequence at Elis's house that was wholly improvised. Or rather, "It was a kind of rehearsed improvisation," says Erland Josephson, who played Elis, "because the evening before we had a dinner together where we tried it, but it became a sort of spontaneous improvisation." The camerawork is unusual for Bergman; it forces the spectator to enter the drama—to hasten and lurch through the snow beside a deranged Andreas, to duck and veer away as Andreas attacks Anna outside his cottage, and to pore over the words evoking violence in the "letter."

In Swedish, the title of the film is A Passion. Bergman had a single day in which to think of an acceptable alternative title when United Artists informed him that A Passion could not be used in the United States for copyright reasons. The Passion of Anna was Bergman's choice. In fact, Andreas is far more at the center of the drama than Anna, whose personality remains rather cloudy under Bergman's analysis. Andreas is, like the haunting figure of Johan of Skir (who commits suicide in a kind of martyr's guise), an eternal sufferer. Bergman may have turned his back on orthodox religious debate in his films, but life on Fårö is still viewed in New Testament terms at this point.

As Andreas wanders in fruitless circles in the final shot, like a demented patient in some infernal laboratory experiment, one thinks back also to Erik Lindegren's great suite of poems from the forties, the man without a way, in which the hapless traveler stares in terror at a signpost offering him a cluster of vague and uncertain directions. In The Passion of Anna, Bergman still shares the anguish of those writers of the forties, still bears witness to a collapse of society's frantic attempts to maintain order in the face of war and violence.[32]

CHAPTER THIRTEEN

The International Phase Begins

On January 16, 1969, Ingmar Bergman returned to the Royal Dramatic Theater. He had originally intended to stage Büchner's drama, *Woyzeck*, when he was appointed head of the Theater in 1963. Now he saw an opportunity to present the play in a radical style. The history of the soldier who murders his mistress in a fit of inchoate jealousy would be tackled like one of Bergman's "chamber films." The performance would last about an hour and a half, so Dramaten could offer two sessions each evening. Tickets were on sale at a mere five crowns each (one dollar), and Bergman insisted on some drastic changes in the layout of the theater: The cloakroom area became part of the auditorium, and the audience in effect sat on benches in the stage area. *Woyzeck* was then played out in a concentrated zone between the back of the stage and the stalls—a space 16.5 feet wide and 11.5 feet deep.

The mood of rehearsals was often high spirited. Thommy Berggren was cast as Woyzeck, and Gunnel Lindblom as Marie. Bergman described the start of each scene to his actors and outlined the particular feeling or atmosphere required. His directions were clear, concise, and to the point. As Henrik Sjögren, who followed the entire rehearsal period, has written: "Büchner's laconic, powerful dialog is an ideal skeleton for Ingmar's concrete scenic vision."[1]

Although Bergman had a precise concept of each of the twenty-eight scenes and carried around with him a copy of the play covered with sketches and notes, he was careful to allow his performers a reasonably free rein. "An old actor attacked me when I respectfully gave him some direction. 'Mr. Bergman isn't here to teach us how to perform theater, but simply to see that we don't bash into one another on stage.' I think that was rather well said!"

Another radical aspect of the *Woyzeck* production was Bergman's insistence on open rehearsals. The audience was encouraged to attend, free of charge, on various mornings prior to the opening, and the actors discussed its responses afterward. During one of the last of these open rehearsals, Bergman had a minor altercation with the critic, Bengt Jahnson, in the wings. At one point he shoved him away, quite gently in fact, but Jahnson lost his balance, and immediately there was a sensation. Jahnson, drama critic for the daily *Dagens Nyheter*, took the director to court. Bergman lost the action and was fined five thousand crowns. He paid up gladly, saying that he had defended the good name of his actors and would do so again in similar circumstances.

During the rehearsal period, Bergman attended a concert of Mozart's Mass in C Minor, conducted by Hans Schmidt-Isserstedt. "Music is so exact, it is there in the score," he said. "We must try to work as precisely, with pauses and accents." Bergman's own taste in music remains extremely catholic, ranging from Bach to the Beatles, from Mozart to the Rolling Stones, from organ music to protest ballads. And he likes his music to be as loud as possible.

Woyzeck opened on March 12. Three days later Per Olov Enquist, a distinguished author in his own right, wrote in the evening tabloid *Expressen* that this was "an extraordinarily neat and typical Bergman piece of work, which in its third act also possesses a certain warmth." By then, however, Bergman had already taken the plane to Fårö, and on that same day, March 15, began shooting his documentary on the island and its inhabitants.

The reaction to *Shame* may have stung Bergman into preparing his political statement. More likely, however, his years on Fårö had persuaded him that, if these people were ever to escape the leaden hand of central government, someone would have to brandish a fist in protest. So he approached Sveriges Radio and offered them the idea of a television documentary on Fårö. They accepted. Bergman was excited by the potential of television as a political force. "A single image on TV is a hundred times more eloquent [than theater]," he said.[2]

"My political act," he told me, "is to try to stop this island and its people being crushed. I live there with seven hundred neighbors, and there I am not confronted with the problems of Cuba because I have the problems of my neighbors. Human conscience cannot encompass sorrow for millions of people."

Some foreign observers registered disappointment with *The Fårö Document* (*Fårö-dokument*). They could not accept that Bergman was content to make a simple, unadorned documentary on 16 mm., with grainy photography, a hand-held camera, and a microphone thrust under the noses of interviewees in the tradition of *cinéma-vérité*. There is a handful of color sequences evoking the natural cycle of the island—the slaughter of the sheep, the lambing season, and so on—but the rest is in monochrome.

The film is not inhibited by any formal structure. There are interviews with a taxi driver, a teacher, a churchwarden, a pensioner, a farmer. Bergman records a burial service in sight of the sea as a bell tolls furiously; and a homely communion service as the camera explores the room—the pictures, a clock with revolving mechanism—and a sense of time and death is evoked. The people of Fårö wish to continue in the ways that they have done for centuries; yet they also need better facilities. From this tension between past and future comes the gist of Bergman's interviews. Young folk want to leave the island. Their elders are suspicious of change. Ultimately, however, these people embody Bergman's own attitudes to life. As one farmer says, "It's better to have few friends than too many."

By early May, *The Fårö Document* was complete, and Sveriges Radio telecast it on New Year's Day 1970. More than three million Swedes watched the program.

There was no film to be shot on Fårö in the summer of 1969, and Liv Ullmann was in the United States, on location for Jan Troell's films, *The Emigrants* and *The New Land*. In June Bergman paid a brief visit to London to discuss the possibility of staging *Woyzeck* there. Nothing materialized. Bergman was piqued because the Savoy Grill refused to serve him when he entered without a tie. London has never been a happy haven for him.

The script of *The Lie* (actually titled *The Sanctuary—Reservatet* in Swedish) is dated May 1969, but although he wrote this play for Eurovision, Bergman was quite content to let others direct it in various countries. The Swedish version starred Gunnel Lindblom, Erland Josephson, and Per Myrberg, under the direction of Jan Molander. In Britain, Alan Bridges directed the piece for the BBC, and in the United States CBS Playhouse 90 presented "The Lie" (subtitled "A Tragic Comedy about Banality") in the fall of 1972.

In *The Lie*, Bergman again focuses on the umbilical cord that binds the married couple. Once more, the man is revealed as the more easily undermined of the two sexes, the one who cracks first under the searching, relentless onslaught of his partner during a twenty-four-hour time span. In Swedish, the man and the woman bear the same names as the leading characters in *The Passion of Anna*: Andreas and Anna Fromm. This, perhaps, is the story of Anna and the "first" Andreas, the predecessor in whose tracks Max von Sydow's Andreas found himself treading. Andreas is turning forty, "like having an unmentionable disease," comments his office superior; and Anna is a few years younger. Her brother is a tormented author lying in hospital. "The worst part of it is— I had hopes," he tells her on the verge of a breakdown. Anna has a lover who is weary and suffers from insomnia. The "lie" is the very fact of the marriage. During all these eight years, Anna has never been truly happy with her husband. Their arguments rise in a crescendo until Andreas loses his temper and even threatens Anna with an ax—an explosion of anger identical to the one in *The Passion of Anna*.

Strindberg again seems to be the spiritual inspiration here. The grief and accusations are couched in Strindbergian terms, and there are specific references to his works (*Easter*, for example). Like all Strindberg couples, Anna and Andreas recognize that they are chained to each other for life: "I don't know what it would be without you," says Andreas to himself in the final scene.

Although Bergman is patently the heir to Strindberg as far as uxorious themes are concerned, he has not once attempted to film any of Strindberg's plays, save on television. He believes that, like Ibsen's works, they are so close to the atmosphere of the theater that they resist transformation into another medium. Alf Sjöberg achieved the most satisfying of all Strindberg adaptations to the screen, with *Miss Julie*; his versions of *Erik XIV* (*Karin Månsdotter*) and *The Father* were less successful.

But Bergman has been drawn back to Strindberg in the theater on several occasions. In the winter of 1969–1970, he turned to *A Dream Play*, which examines the human situation from a Buddhist standpoint (Strindberg having been attracted to theosophy in the years before writing the play). Strindberg was fifty-two when he completed it, and always held it in higher esteem and affection than any of his other works. Bergman had directed *A Dream Play* for Swedish television in 1963, and now he prepared an "edited" version for the small auditorium at the rear of Dramaten.

Resisting the temptation to evoke the spectacular production by Olof Molander in 1955, Bergman presented the play in ascetic terms, with spartan decor and the mood of a chamber work. His cuts in the text affect chiefly act three, from which he removed many of Strindberg's digressive reflections on Eastern mysticism. "What was left," says Henrik Sjögren, "was a dream rising from the poet's imagination or, more correctly, the poet's dream, concretely materialized as a stage play precisely calculated to involve each member of the audience in its happenings."[3]

Holger Löwenadler, Malin Ek, and Birgitta Valberg in A Dream Play, *staged by Bergman at the Royal Dramatic Theater in 1970. Photo courtesy Beata Bergström/Kungl. Dramatiska Teatern.*

At the heart of A *Dream Play* stands the elfin, blonde, eponymous figure of Agnes (played by Malin Ek, an actress Bergman admired enormously at this period). Her presence summons up memories and complexes, faded hopes and incidents, rendered either humorous or tragic by age. There is, for example, the fisherman, jolly in a bowler hat, who dreamed of catching the sun in his net when he was still youthful. The action takes place on several time planes. The Crucifixion is enacted, Chopin's Funeral March is heard, and men are crowned with laurels and thorns.

Bergman's production abounded in nuance and invention. Groups of people stood frozen on the stage, as though rooted in time. In the funeral scene, couples dressed entirely in black gazed over black barriers. Later, everyone appeared clad in white costumes. At the end, the cast removed their masks, in a gesture of sacrifice and self-reckoning. Agnes was left alone on the stage. She got to her feet, looked around the low-lit stage disconsolately, and then exited right.

A *Dream Play* opened in March 1970 and was the talk of the town. By November it had celebrated its hundredth performance.

In the midst of the acclaim for A *Dream Play*, Bergman suffered personal grief. His father died on April 26. Solemn, strict, a poet *manqué*, Erik Bergman had grown more and more frail since the passage of his wife four years earlier. In the later stages of his life, he had learned to appreciate Ingmar's accomplishments and self-discipline. Father and son had enjoyed talks together in the room at Sofia-hemmet where Erik lay during the final phase.

About this time, too, Bergman's relationship with Liv Ullmann came to an end. "He was one of two men in my life I have really loved," said Liv some years later, "and I wanted it to last."[4] At first, the couple agreed to a three-month trial separation. Linn, their daughter, accompanied Liv to Oslo. But, although they could talk happily on the telephone, they could not recover the intimacy of earlier years. The strength of the friendship, however, may be measured by the number of films in which Liv Ullmann has starred for Bergman during the seventies and early eighties. Interviewed in 1979, Bergman said that he and Liv were close friends and found even more pleasure in their work nowadays. "As a private person," according to Liv, "Ingmar is very happy and loving and verbal . . . [he] wants to speak to the emotions. He writes out of his own torment and knowledge of people."

In May, Bergman traveled to London to stage *Hedda Gabler*, using the same sets and production notes as he had in the 1964 version at the Royal Dramatic Theater, but featuring English actors, with Maggie Smith as Hedda. The production was staged at the Old Vic, still at that point the home of the National Theatre, and there was friction between Bergman and Sir Laurence Olivier, then in charge of the NT. No animosity sprang up between the two men, but each was a king in his own domain. Bergman was accustomed to being able to switch out a light when he so desired, and Olivier was used to granting permission for such gestures. It was an unhappy, humiliating week. Bergman comforted himself by attending concerts. "I'd have my dinner in the hotel, and then I'd walk over to the South Bank and go to the Queen Elizabeth Hall or Purcell Room."[5]

Instead of returning directly to Stockholm, Bergman flew to Helsinki to supervise the production of *A Dream Play* at the Swedish Theater in the Finnish capital. (He had declined an invitation to present the Strindberg drama at the Comédie Française, on the grounds that he had a poor grasp of French. But the production did go to Belgrade, where it won the Grand Prix at the Theater Festival, and also to Venice and Vienna.)

During the brief sojourn in London, a significant encounter took place. On May 2, Bergman's American agent, Paul Kohner, arranged a dinner in a private room at the Connaught Hotel. Leonard Goldenson, president of ABC Corporation, was present with some of his associates. Martin Baum was head of ABC's new motion picture division, and he and his wife listened as Bergman told them the outline story of the next film he wanted to make, entitled *The Touch*. "We were to give our answer to Mr. Kohner in a few days," said Baum. "But I could see from the faces that [Bergman] had sold everybody in the room. And my *wife*! With her he scored a bull's-eye!"[6]

ABC Pictures Corporation made its commitment for *The Touch* two days later. The American company was willing to pay Bergman a flat sum of one million dollars on delivery of a negative; it would also pay the salary of the English-speaking actor Bergman would choose to play the role of David in the movie (some two hundred thousand dollars, as it happened). ABC would receive from Bergman a screenplay by July 15, 1970, and two months later shooting would begin. Bergman would have control over the final cut. The eventual contract was prolix and elaborate, running to 110 pages.

Bergman had seen Elliott Gould in *Getting Straight* and felt he was ideal for the character he had in mind. He phoned him. Gould for his part was flattered by this approach from one of the world's greatest living directors and immediately agreed to participate in *The Touch*. Bergman then embarked on the screenplay, working steadily from 9:30 A.M. to 3:30 P.M., using pads of yellow lined paper and writing in his laborious, quite large hand. If he made a mistake, according to one observer, he did not cross out and scratch in the new words but copied out the whole page again.[7]

"When I have to sit down to write," Bergman told John Simon, "to start from the beginning and write the script, that is the hateful period— when I have to make up my mind about what I am going to do and actually write it."[8]

On September 5, before shooting began, Bergman held a press conference out at the studios in Råsunda. There was some sorrow at the thought that this represented Bergman's first real production break with Svensk Filmindustri for over fifteen years. But circumstances had changed. Even the studios were soon to be closed, and the State Theater organization (Riksteater) would move into Råsunda. The "film town" still exists today, as does the little room at the back of the commissary where Bergman, Kenne Fant, and his production manager Allan Ekelund used to discuss matters when Fant visited the studios.

While shooting *The Touch*, Bergman spoke of his eventual retirement, citing the physical and mental demands of filmmaking, the burden of administration forced upon the Nordic director, and the shorter shooting schedules dictated by rising costs. "So I have planned to go on, if God is willing and my pants hold, for another couple of years. To make four or five films and then retire." It was the first of several such announcements. Bergman will probably never retire.

Much of the film was photographed in Visby, capital of Gotland, the large Baltic island of which Fårö is geographically a part. Rain pelted down continually, but Bergman maintained his sense of humor beneath a cap and plastic mac. He compared his methods with a boat lying on the Fårö shore and built according to an ancient formula. "So I, in less than thirty years, have built up a 'practical machine,' a method of filmmaking. Why change something that's working so well?"[9]

Max von Sydow and Bibi Andersson were signed to play the husband and wife in *The Touch*, and Sheila Reid, who had appeared in Bergman's production of *Hedda Gabler* in London, was cast as Elliott Gould's sister. Bergman spoke of his enthusiasm for Gould: "the impatience of a soul to find out things about reality and himself, and that is one thing that always makes me touched almost to tears, that impatience of the soul."[10] Gould felt at home in Bergman's team, as though he had always been a member of it.

The story of *The Touch* is as elementary and triangular as a women's picture of the forties. In a Bergman film, however, feeling prevails over both style and content. And the feeling in *The Touch* is painful in its intimacy and warmth. It begins and ends on a note of farewell. Karin (Bibi Andersson) arrives at the hospital where her mother has just died. In the still, private room, she sits beside the dead body. A nurse gives her the wedding bands. Small things are suddenly very tangible, very real. Outside, busses blurt past the window, and bells jostle in a nearby church. The scene is affecting in a subdued way. Bergman may have been thinking of his own mother's death in 1966. He has said that this sequence was inspired by the death of an actor friend some fifteen years earlier, but the more immediate memory was that of his father's corpse in the clinic. "I saw my father fifteen minutes after he died. . . . His head was turned toward the window. The eyes were closed, but not completely. The illusion was that he was looking far away. I found it so extremely strange and beautiful and full of secrets."[11]

The credits come up against a series of shots of the ancient town of Visby (photographed by Gunnar Fischer). The emphasis is on walls, barriers dividing the streets, and, though none is seen, the inhabitants. *The Touch* concerns barriers, some old, built up through fifteen years of marriage, some fresh.

Karin is everyone's image of a prosperous Swedish housewife. Sweden, always in the vanguard of sociological advancement, looked with disdain on the mere *hemmafru* (housewife) long before the women's liberation campaign gathered momentum in other countries. A woman is a failure if she makes her mark on society only in the crudest of terms—child rearing. Bergman does not condemn Karin Vergérus for pottering around in her house, keeping it spick and span, trying out new clothes. But he implies that some spark is missing in her existence.

Andreas (Max von Sydow) is a hospital consultant, and one day he brings home a young archaeologist, David, whom he has been treating for kidney trouble. When David declares his love for her, in almost peremptory fashion, Karin responds to him without hesitation, as though the death of her mother, and now the arrival of this dark, handsome stranger, are auspices of deliverance. "She seeks this wound," says Bergman, speaking of her passion for David. "She seeks it passionately. She immediately takes part and draws the knife toward her own heart with the certainty of a sleepwalker."[12]

David and Karin visit a medieval church at Hammar. They examine a wooden sculpture of the Madonna that has been unearthed in a remote part of the island. The statue wears a calm smile in the light of David's torch. But Karin is not the ideal that her lover assumes her to be. Though unashamed of encroaching middle age, she is embarrassed by the physical aspect of the affair and excuses the imperfections of her body. When they prepare to sleep together, David, beneath amorous childish banter, suddenly violates her with an aggression that startles

Bibi Andersson (Karin Vergérus) *and Elliott Gould* (David Kovac) *in* The Touch. *Photo courtesy ABC Pictures Corporation.*

Karin. A mechanical saw is heard beyond the window of the apartment as David thrusts her away perfunctorily.

There is no ecstasy, nor even quiet gratitude, in this affair. The room where the lovers meet appears dark and forbidding. David's selfish nature molds the pattern of the relationship. When Karin is hungry for sex, for instance, David slaps her and has a fit of temper, smashing furnishings in the room. Then he smarts beneath her forgiving touch.

David announces that he must go away for six months. They send letters to each other. But, in the tradition of the genre, her husband discovers the situation and surprises the lovers in the apartment at Visby. Bitter, he informs Karin that David had not been suffering from kidney disease—he had tried to commit suicide.

Now David tells Karin that the wooden statue of the Madonna in the church is being devoured by insects from within—insects that had lain dormant and inactive for five hundred years and that awoke when the statue was exposed to air and light. They are as beautiful as the image itself, says David of the insects. The parallel with Karin's predicament is obvious. The instincts aroused in her by David are in their way as exquisite and meaningful as her own physical appeal.

Karin visits the empty apartment after David has left Sweden. Her sobs echo in the bare rooms as she clutches the letters and pictures of her he has left behind. Outside, the saw grinds forever.

Reckless and despondent, she flies to London in pursuit of her lover. She finds only another empty apartment with, in one corner, David's sister, Sara. Seated on hard chairs amid the newspapers that cover the floorboards, they sip brandy. Sara's hand is caught in a permanent fist, evidence of a muscular atrophy that runs in the family, clenching emotions as much as fingers.

Anguish prevails. Karin is pregnant and alone. She meets David once more, in the botanical gardens of the small town where she still lives officially with Andreas. When David begs her to join him, she refuses. They talk while the cold wind searches the trees; autumn is in the air, and rain begins to fall. David's old, egotistical self reasserts itself, and he knocks Karin's bag to the ground in pique. "I know you're lying," he says fiercely, and then leaves her for the last time. The dark, mysterious stranger, so familiar a character in the traditional Swedish film, has failed to destroy the even tenor of Karin's bourgeois life.

Gould's characterization resounds long after the film is over. He amounts to a knobbly mixture of clumsiness and culture, aloofness and ardor, charm and solemnity, an exile condemned by his Jewishness to wander restlessly through the world for all time. Bibi Andersson gives one of her finest, most affecting performances as Karin. No other

Swedish actress, save perhaps Maj-Britt Nilsson, could have created such a vivid impression of Karin Vergérus. Bibi was pregnant with her child by Kjell Grede at the time and coped with the English dialog even better than Max von Sydow, whose command of English is equally assured but who in this film (his last for Bergman up to the time of writing) is restricted to the thankless, cardboard role of Andreas.

Bergman concentrated on the editing of *The Touch* throughout the winter, and on May 3, 1971, the representatives of ABC came to view the first print. They liked it very much and met Bergman in the afternoon to express their delight. At the end of the following week, Dick Cavett flew to Stockholm to tape an interview with Bibi Andersson and Elliott Gould about the film. As usual, Bergman by then was already involved with his next production, *Cries and Whispers*. When *The Touch* was released in the United States and Britain, it failed to attract a wide audience. Had it been filmed in Swedish and been presented abroad with subtitles, one cannot help feeling that the film might have established a strong following.

Post-production work on *The Touch* coincided with rehearsals for Bergman's production at Dramaten of *Show*, a play by Lars Forssell based on the life of the entertainer Lenny Bruce. Allan Edwall and Harriet Andersson were featured in the leading parts. Farcical and irreverent, this "show" betrayed as much about Forssell as it did about Bruce. Few modern Swedish playwrights have been so prolific as Lars Forssell. He uses poems and songs to trenchant effect and is a fierce thorn in the side of the Establishment. *Show* opened on March 20, 1971. Bergman then flew to London to prepare his cast and stage personnel for the presentation of *A Dream Play* in the World Theatre Season at the Aldwych. Liv Ullmann brought him the Irving Thalberg Memorial Award, which she had collected on his behalf at the Academy Awards ceremony a few days earlier.

The summer of 1971 was rewarding. Bergman completed the screenplay of *Cries and Whispers* (*Viskningar och rop*) and had fallen in love again. Ingrid Karlebo had met Bergman almost a generation earlier, and now, in 1971, the two realized that they were really remarkably well suited to each other. She was just forty-one years of age, a countess by virtue of her marriage to Count Jan Carl von Rosen. She had four children and lived with her husband in the fashionable area of Djursholm. Bergman's brief affair with Malin Ek lapsed, and Ingrid von Rosen obtained a divorce. The press did not get wind of the relationship until late September, when Ingrid von Rosen was quoted as saying that she and Ingmar would marry between Christmas and New Year's Day.

In fact, they were married in November, and early the next month they flew together to Vienna and on to Sicily. There Bergman was given the Pirandello Award for his achievements as a stage director.

In Ingrid von Rosen, Bergman at last discovered a woman for all seasons. She could help him with his film work, she was elegant and gracious, and she possessed a placid—and highly efficient—disposition that was the perfect complement for Bergman's restless energy. The couple took an apartment in Karlaplan, in the Östermalm district of Stockholm, and on the site of Strindberg's former home. Friends noted that Bergman grew more sociable, more relaxed. This marriage has perhaps brought him more years of continuous happiness than anything else in his life.

"Some years ago," declared Bergman at the press conference he gave after a screening of *Cries and Whispers* in Cannes in 1973, "I had a vision of a large red room, with three women in white whispering together. This picture came back again and again to me." When he was a small boy, his image of the soul was that of a huge red monster; it had no face, and the interior of the creature appeared red and membranous.

The project differed in various ways from Bergman's previous work. Economically, it was established along rather perilous lines. Nobody wanted to invest in *Cries and Whispers* on a big scale. Bergman had to turn to the Swedish Film Institute for some aid and also to his principal colleagues—Liv Ullmann, Harriet Andersson, Ingrid Thulin, and Sven Nykvist—who showed their faith in him by offering to defer their earnings from the production until it was sold.

From a thematic point of view, *Cries and Whispers* represented Bergman's most daring attempt to achieve a dream state on film. "As I turn this project over in my mind," he wrote to his actors and technicians, "it never stands out as a completed whole. What it most resembles is a dark, flowing stream: faces, movements, voices, gestures, exclamations, light and shade, moods, dreams." The script was couched in the language of a story, with more stress on the milieu than the dialog. Once more, Bergman gazed back in time, to a period at the turn of the century when religion still amounted to a significant force in Swedish life and when the social hierarchy was more pronounced. The narrative, or rather the situation, unfolds in a stately mansion set in its own ample parkland. Bergman found this manor in Taxinge-Näsby, outside Mariefred in the Mälar district west of Stockholm. The shooting lasted for forty-two days, and the budget was 1 million crowns (just under $400,000).

In *Cries and Whispers*, certain emotions and sensations coalesce: frustration, solitude, mortification, a yearning for faith and physical companionship. The three sisters in the manor house are named Agnes, Karin, and Maria. Like the sisters in *The Silence*, they seem to be part of a single soul, and Bergman has acknowledged that each evokes an aspect of his mother's personality. As Agnes (Harriet Andersson) sinks toward death, and Karin (Ingrid Thulin) and Maria (Liv Ullmann) reveal their fundamental egoism, two other characters make a mysterious contribution to the proceedings. First the doctor (Erland Josephson), who, in one of the film's most imposing scenes, confronts Maria with her shortcomings—coldness, indifference, indolence, impatience—just as the ballet master tormented Marie in *Summer Interlude*. Then the maid Anna, whose warmth and sincerity bring comfort to Agnes. Anna (played by Kari Sylwan, who had begun her career as a ballerina in the Stockholm Opera) enjoys a simple, unquestioning belief in God, a belief shared by Jof and Mia in *The Seventh Seal*, which immunizes her against the fear of death. The "resurrection" of Agnes suggests that the actual process of death is more hideous than the *meaning* of death, which, as Bergman said at the Cannes press conference, is a logical development of life.

Anna, however, is treated like a pariah by her employers. Her goodness disturbs and provokes them. Karin and Maria have grown into luxury and are hopelessly impractical. Bergman gave Liv Ullmann just one comment regarding her character: "She's the kind of woman who never closes a door behind her." And Ingrid Thulin's Karin regards those who serve her with a hard glaze of indifference. There is even an element of erotic subjugation in the scene when, having been struck in the face for an ill-timed remark, Anna stoops to divest Karin of her clothes.

The most taxing role was unquestionably that of Agnes. Harriet Andersson recalls that Bergman shot her death scene first because the very bright lights used had been hired for only a brief spell. When the film opens, Agnes already lies mortally sick. The camera glides over innumerable ornamental clocks. It is 4 A.M. Agnes wakes with red-rimmed eyes. All at once she is torn by a spasm of pain. She leaves her bed, glances with a smile at the sleeping form of Maria in one of the armchairs, and scribbles an entry in her diary: "It's early Monday morning, and I'm in pain. My sisters are taking turns at sitting up."

The following night, Agnes enters her death agony. Lights are borne in haste through the dusky red rooms. Anna combs her mistress's hair, and Maria reads to her from *Pickwick Papers*. For once, all four women are in communion with one another, free of rancor and suspicion. But

Agnes is afflicted with another terrible tremor of pain. "Can no one help me?" she screams, and Maria turns away, horror stricken and ashamed. Agnes dies.

Karin bathes her face. Maria sobs aloud over the corpse while the others set her limbs straight. Two female undertakers lay her out. Then the priest enters. He performs the official, orthodox prayers and walks around the bed. Now he utters his real thoughts: "Pray for us who are left . . . under a cruel and empty sky." He speaks not of God but "the God." "Ask Him for a meaning to our lives," he implores. The corner of Anders Ek's mouth twists upward, converting a grimace into an involuntary grin. This priest's confession is all the more startling on account of its context. At the most solemn moment of life—death—the steward of God's Church gives vent to his confusion and bitterness. For Bergman, the only authentic priest remains the one who admits his ignorance and impotence: Tomas Ericsson in *Winter Light* and the James Whitmore figure in *The Serpent's Egg* are men like this.

Bergman, however, is not a disbeliever. For him, the difference between the state of death and the state of life corresponds to the distinction between dream and reality. Anna is haunted by the sound of her long dead baby girl crying in the night. She enters the large bedroom and touches both Karin and Maria; neither emerges from what seems like a trance. But when she lays her hand on Agnes, the dead woman stirs. Maria is summoned, only to be drawn down and kissed by Agnes in a rigid embrace. Maria flees, screaming. She and Karin gather their wits and "reject" Agnes. "I have my daughter and husband to think of," says Maria. "She's decomposing already, there are big flecks on her hands," snaps Karin with revulsion.

Only Anna remains at the bed, taking Agnes to her warm bosom while the wind sighs outside the house. The image is composed with care by Bergman to convey the sense of the Pietà—the dead Christ supported by the Virgin Mary.

Karin, the most sophisticated of the sisters, cannot reconcile self-loathing with an almost violent hunger for human contact. In a flash-back, she remembers a *diner à deux* with her disagreeable husband. They eat in silence, and an atmosphere of unbearable tension develops. Karin breaks a wine glass in her exasperation, and as she picks up the fragments she declares, "Everything is a tissue of lies." In her dressing room, she fingers one of the glass shards and repeats the comment, as though it were an incantation.

Then she mutilates her labia. Pain mingles with pleasure as she does so. As her husband enters her bedroom, she anoints her lips with the blood from between her legs. In a film brimming with shocking moments, this is the most visceral in its impact.

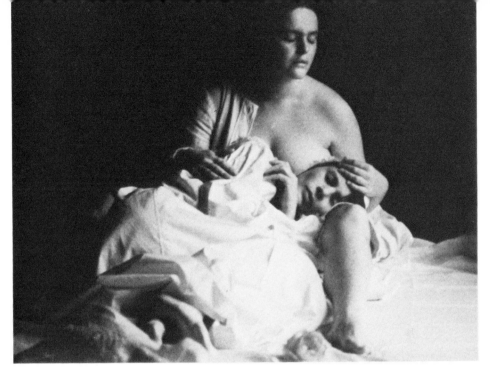

Kari Sylwan (Anna) *and Harriet Andersson* (Agnes) *in* Cries and Whispers: *the Pietà scene. Photo courtesy Svensk Filmindustri.*

The turned-away face. Ingrid Thulin (Karin) *and Liv Ullmann* (Maria) *in* Cries and Whispers. *Photo courtesy Svensk Filmindustri.*

Karin announces her hatred of Maria, who tries to approach her in a spirit of accommodation. "Don't touch me!" she cries, when Maria offers her a kiss. She has contemplated suicide many times, she says. "Nothing escapes me." But, in an almost miraculous moment of redress and release, Karin begs Maria's forgiveness, and the two sisters talk happily and tenderly, caressing each other's cheeks and hands; there is no naturalistic sound, only the serene chords of a Bach cello sonata.

The pent-up anguish dissolves. Like all reconciliations in Bergman's cinema, however, it is short-lived. The parting between Karin and Maria after the funeral is harsh and icy; now Maria takes her turn to be condescending, as she dismisses her sister's pathetic attempt to maintain the contact that has been achieved between them.

Maria emerges as no less egocentric than Karin. When the doctor has finished treating Agnes, he sits at supper with Maria, pecking at his food like a prim bird as she flatters him with soft, endearing words and looks. He fears her seductiveness. Their affair lies, one assumes, in the past. Later the doctor stands behind Maria as she looks into the mirror with complacent pride. One by one, the clues to her true nature are unmasked. The doctor recites the flaws. But Maria, after listening in silence, turns the tables on her former lover: "We resemble each other," she smiles.

In Karin's memory, her marriage drove her to violence; in the flashback involving Maria's relationship with her husband, it is the opposite, for Joakim (Henning Moritzer) plunges a dinner knife clumsily into his stomach and calls for help. Maria merely stands by the door, watching callously. The innate melodrama of the scene suits Bergman's purpose. Both Karin and Maria think in extravagant terms, and every element in their lives is stylized beyond reason.

After the funeral guests have left the manor, along with Maria and Karin, the maid lights a candle and opens Agnes's diary. The dead woman's voice speaks of an interlude of joy and tranquility. The three sisters, dressed in white, stroll through the sunlit park. They sit beside one another in a swing-seat. "I felt the presence of their bodies, the warmth of their hands," says Agnes wistfully. "Come what may, this is happiness. . . . Here, for a moment, I can experience perfection."

The film concludes with a peaceful close-up of Agnes's face. It marks a release from suffering, an expectation of harmony.

The pervasive red of the film lingers on the retina like an after-image. Each sequence fades out to red. The rooms of the mansion are clad in red from ceiling to floor. Bergman's vision of the interior of the soul-monster coincides with the sensation of bloodletting that the film transmits. The glistening white dresses of the women appear all the more striking, even violent, by comparison.

The close-ups in *Cries and Whispers* are captured by Sven Nykvist with a zoom lens that gives the impression of spying on the characters. "Because the camera lenses are more sensitive today," Bergman told an interviewer on the set, "and the raw film is faster and the lighting technique simpler and the personnel handling the camera more capable, we can use more close-ups."[13]

Everyone involved had a good deal of fun on *Cries and Whispers*. For some two months the actors and crew lived in a big country house–type of hotel. On Thursdays there was a party, to which everyone contributed his own food and drink. Harriet Andersson and Ingrid Thulin would make Italian coffee for themselves when not on call. Lars-Olof Löthwall was amused by Harriet's death scene. When she had at last expired and

Bergman with Ingrid Thulin (Karin) *and Sven Nykvist on the set of* Cries and Whispers. *Photo courtesy Lars-Olof Löthwall.*

Bergman said "Cut!", Harriet sat upright with a sharp jerk—and shouted "Booooo!"

The team spirit remained as strong as ever. Bergman said to Harriet: "It's the same old film every time. The same actors. The same scenes. The same problems. The only thing is that we're older."[14]

Cries and Whispers was not screened until more than a year later, when New World distributors purchased the American rights and rushed it into theaters in time to qualify for the Academy Awards of 1972. To Bergman's surprise, the film was a phenomenal success. The critics were ecstatic and lavish with their praises, and the public in New York and other major cities stood in line to see the latest Bergman masterpiece (having overlooked *Shame*, a film of equally uncompromising power, only a few years before).

Perhaps, in spite of the suffering and despair of *Cries and Whispers*, its dream-like vision proved more appealing to audiences than Bergman could have hoped—or dreamed.

CHAPTER FOURTEEN

The Challenge of Television

BERGMAN'S FILMS DO NOT ATTRACT MASS AUDIENCES IN HIS NATIVE Sweden. The public in New York or Paris has often proved more loyal to his particular brand of cinema. By the end of 1971, Bergman was very disturbed by the difficulty of financing his work in Stockholm. He had no desire to seek money from abroad, following the experience of *The Touch,* and he was reluctant to repeat the experiment of *Cries and Whispers,* in which his colleagues had invested their salaries.

Television was the answer.

By early March 1972, Bergman had decided to shoot *Scenes from a Marriage* on 16 mm., using a tiny crew—Sven Nykvist, a focus-puller, a sound man, a production person, and Siv Kanalv, who would double as editor and script-girl. The production was budgeted at $240,000, and Cinematograph sold the television rights to Channel 2 of Swedish Radio & TV for $120,000, a large amount by contemporary standards in Scandinavia.

This was a significant development in Bergman's career. Not since 1972 has he embarked on a film in Sweden without aiming primarily at the television audience. As a result, discernible changes have occurred in both the style and content of his films, even if the emphasis on the pain in human relationships remains immutable.

On March 17, Bergman's production of *The Wild Duck* opened at Dramaten. The prolixity of the dialog was justified by Bergman's sense of the gathering wave of drama in Ibsen's play. Max von Sydow played Gregers, the characteristic Ibsen idealist who disturbs the petit

bourgeoisie and is forever at the mercy of his own inferiority complex, like a huge, ungainly bird. Bergman's most imaginative device was the construction of an area at the front of the stage that acted as Hedvig's loft. In act five, Hedvig (Lena Nyman) could thus be seen in the foreground, gazing at her beloved bird, while Gregers and Ekdal chatted in the "room" behind her; eventually she slumped in dejection and took her own life. This was surely the equivalent of deep focus in the cinema.

Immediately after the premiere, Ingmar and Ingrid traveled to Fårö. Bergman began to write the script of *Scenes from a Marriage* and did not pause for almost three months. "I wrote it," he said later, "in order to tidy up a huge wardrobe of experiences of different kinds. A kind of spring cleaning of the wardrobe. My own and others' experiences have been added to it." He planned the film in six "scenes," each to run 48.5 minutes and thus, with the credits, to constitute a 50-minute TV episode. He started with the third scene; then he wrote the fourth; followed by the second.

The first draft was ready after some four weeks' work. When Erland Josephson and Liv Ullmann came to the island that summer, Bergman rehearsed with them for ten days. Then, in a concentrated shooting schedule of forty-five days, the "scenes" were shot one after the other, each taking about a week to complete. Certain exteriors were filmed in Djursholm, the Stockholm neighborhood frequented by the characters.

Erland Josephson recalls how Bergman soon abandoned the idea of rehearsing each scene.

> We got to know the characters so well that it became a kind of game to make each episode rather quickly. Liv and I would get up at 5 A.M. and prepare our dialog, and Ingmar was surprised that we knew everything when we came on the set! He didn't force us at all, we forced ourselves. The script was very clear, and we did not in fact have lengthy discussions about each sequence, nor did we improvise stretches of conversation. We had to make jokes with each other because we simply couldn't cry all of the time!

Scenes from a Marriage (*Scener ur ett äktenskap*) is interesting above all else for its characters. Liv Ullmann's Marianne is a woman free of Bergman's habitual personality traits. She lives and works in the Stockholm of the seventies and suffers no religious or moral inhibitions. Erland Josephson's Johan is equally modern—as selfish and as vulnerable as the Bergman males of previous dynasties, but brisk and assured in daily life. These were personalities with whom Bergman felt that a television audience could empathize. They drove a Volvo, ate in city

Bergman in 1972. Photo courtesy Bo-Erik Gyberg.

restaurants, and fled like every Swede to the clutter and tranquility of their summer cottage whenever the opportunity arose.

Throughout the six episodes, Johan and Marianne are either leaving or rejoining each other. The time scale covers some years, but by the closing scene these lovers are more tightly bound in divorce than they were at the outset by marriage.

In scene one, Johan and Marianne are being interviewed by an in-gratiating journalist for one of the many women's magazines that flourish in Sweden. Their peremptory, even condescending responses to the interviewer's questions quickly sketch them as the ideal bourgeois couple—well-off, content with their ten-year-old marriage and two children, and involved in different kinds of work (she is a lawyer, he a lecturer at a psychotechnical institute). While Johan espouses a fashion-able cynicism ("The world is going to the devil, and I claim the right to mind my own business"), Marianne believes in fellow-feeling ("If everyone learned to care about each other right from childhood, the world would be a different place, I'm certain of that").

For Johan, marriage is a renewable contract. Marianne appears at this stage to be much more uxorious. She cites Saint Paul's Letter to the Corinthians as containing the perfect definition of love. "The trouble is, his definition squashes us flat. If love is what Paul says it is, then it's so rare that hardly anyone has known it."

Two friends of Johan and Marianne come to dinner. Peter (Jan Malmsjö) and Katarina (Bibi Andersson) leap straight from the pages of Strindberg. Shackled together in primordial misery and prevarication, they needle each other with sardonic remarks. While the men play chess, Katarina and Marianne chat together. Katarina confesses that she has taken a lover. She speaks of her husband's insecurity with women and how he had once threatened to commit suicide by jumping from a ledge eight floors up in their apartment building. Back at the table, Katarina confronts Peter with a savage outburst of emotional anger. It becomes clear that only their common business interests and material wealth are holding them together.

"What is more horrible than a man and woman who hate each other?" says Peter, quoting Strindberg.

The scene leaves a bitter taste, like the marital quarrels in *Thirst* or *Prison*. Johan and Marianne wash the dishes and decide that they are altogether more sensible a couple than their guests. But when Marianne seizes the opportunity of telling Johan that she is pregnant again, the mood alters subtly. A marriage, Bergman is saying, is such a delicate, fragile construction that even the slightest wind may threaten its stability. Johan does not want another baby. With the bewildering, ultra-efficient speed peculiar to Scandinavia, Marianne has an abortion and Johan is visiting the clinic with flowers, assuring his wife that in a few weeks she will have forgotten the whole matter.

Scene one ends at this point. In it, Bergman has distilled a great deal. Marriage as middle-class idyll. Marriage as torture chamber. Abortion as a symbol of annihilation, a rejection of life, of continuity, of the very tie that binds so many couples. From the moment that Johan and Marianne opt for abortion, their relationship is under siege. In a masterly non sequitur, Bergman signposts this threat by cutting from a conversation in which Johan and Marianne seem to accept the idea of a third child, direct to the hospital where Marianne is recovering after the operation.

Marianne, although the more passive of the partners, appears the more bored with the marriage. She dislikes the ritual of each well-programmed day, the visits to relations, the fear of an unfilled square in the pattern of life. Johan remains at ease: "I think that life has the value you give it, neither more nor less. I refuse to live under the eyes of eternity."

In her office, Marianne is confronted with a presentiment of danger when a client, Mrs. Jacobi, explains her reasons for seeking a divorce. She has been married for twenty years, but now she opts for loneliness in preference to living in a relationship devoid of love, "a remote, diffuse thing called love." And while Marianne listens to her client's sad confession, Johan is in his laboratory conducting an experiment in which one must try to touch a brightly shining spot of light in the darkness— a sly metaphor for that elusive form of love of which Mrs. Jacobi speaks. Johan chuckles at his assistant's efforts to fulfill the experiment, as Bergman himself smiles at man's groping for some obscure destiny.

Like most married men, Johan has a need to confide in another woman. His assistant, Eva, has been reading some verses that Johan has been too shy to show to Marianne. She implies that they are mediocre and that Johan has failed to achieve the things that she and his fellow students at university thought that he would. Johan sits slumped in a chair, in an inferior position vis-à-vis the lucid Eva. He cannot evade those words of faint praise so dreaded by the Bergman alter ego.

This scene contains two faint harbingers of Johan's infidelity prior to his blunt announcement of the fact. While Marianne slips into the nursery to waken the children, Johan picks up the phone, but replaces it after a moment's reflection. And when he sits with Marianne in a restaurant after the theater, he remarks that women adopted the best role—that of martyr—from the very first. It is as though he were seeking to find a rationale in advance, to mitigate his desertion of Marianne. When they are preparing for bed at home, Marianne admits that sex with Johan no longer carries the excitement it once did. "Must it always be," muses Johan, "that two people who live together for a long time begin to tire of each other?"

In scene three, Bergman's use of close-ups, with his television audience in mind, assumes an emotional anguish that makes Johan's disclosure of his affair with a woman named Paula one of the cruellest scenes in all his work. The camera concentrates with unrelenting attention on Marianne's face as she learns the facts. She tries to accept them with equanimity.

"You know the truth now, and that's the main thing," says Johan.

"I know nothing. Let's go to bed. It's late. And I suppose you're off early."

The talk continues after they have climbed into bed. Johan says suddenly that he will be away for several months, and Bergman's camera zooms across into Marianne's stricken face, catching the physical impact of this comment in dramatic fashion.

The little ironies of married life persist. Marianne even has to reach across Johan's lazy body to set the alarm clock. "You *are* in a spot," she says wearily, with genuine concern and regret, after Johan has told her more about Paula and of her conviction that the affair will not last. In *Scenes from a Marriage*, Bergman's greatest accomplishment is to apportion one's sympathies between the partners. Just as Johan seems to have made a winning strike, so Marianne will emerge with a line or a monologue that restores the balance.

In the morning, Johan looks as helpless and as egocentric as he did the previous evening. Marianne has to clip a hangnail for him, and his dependence on her for such trifles only irritates Johan the more. She is, like all Bergman wives, conscious of the practical considerations: a plumber's appointment, a forwarding address for Johan's mail, his father's imminent birthday. But when Johan has gone, and the cottage is silent, and she phones a friend only to learn that Johan's affair was common knowledge, Marianne collapses from grief.

At this most painful of junctures, scene three comes to an end.

The second half of *Scenes from a Marriage* takes place long after this rupture. Johan and Marianne have learned to accept life without each other's constant companionship. Bergman ignores the impact of the separation on the children; although featured in the screenplay, they never appear in either the television series or the movie. In a documentary on the break-up of a marriage, this would amount to a major omission. But Bergman has chosen instead to conduct an unremitting scrutiny of the principal relationship, between the man and the woman.

Johan and Marianne enjoy a reunion dinner together. Each is startled and somewhat amused by the other's self-assurance. Johan has been

Erland Josephson (Johan) *and Liv Ullmann* (Marianne) *in* Scenes from a Marriage. *Photo courtesy Svensk Filmindustri.*

offered a lucrative post at a university in America and intends to go there without Paula, whose emotional storms and hysterics have debilitated him. Marianne is poised and gracious, even flirtatious, but she is bent on a formal divorce. "One never knows what may happen," she says. "I may want to remarry. And it would be awfully complicated if you're in America."

And yet again the pendulum swings.

Marianne is soon admitting that she feels tied to Johan. She can cope with the fact only by keeping him at a distance. Over brandy, she reads from a diary she has been writing. Johan nods off to sleep, and one feels sorry for him, as Marianne's monologue is among Bergman's least successful stabs at psychology. Marianne recalls her childhood and her feelings toward her mother and toward Jesus and God.

Johan prepares to stay the night, but just before 1 A.M. he wakes up and leaves. Perhaps he is more conscious than Marianne that a relapse into the armed neutrality of the marriage would be futile. "We must come to terms," he has told her after dinner, "with the fact that our loneliness is absolute. Every so often we fantasize and believe in a state of togetherness, but that's an illusion."

In scene five, Johan and Marianne meet one evening in his office in order to sign the divorce papers and make the final dispositions of goods and chattels. The conversation soon deteriorates into an argument about maintenance for the children. But there is a mature tone to the invective. Each recognizes the weakness and helplessness of the other. Life itself and society's education are now to blame.

"We must have gone wrong somewhere, and there was no one to tell us what we did," says Marianne. To which Johan replies,

> "We're emotional illiterates. And not only you and I—practically everybody, that's the depressing thing. We're taught everything about the body and about agriculture in Madagascar and about the square root of pi, or whatever the hell it's called, but not a word about the soul. We're abysmally ignorant, about both ourselves and others."

When Johan is as sensible as he sounds in such conversations, the audience cannot help but like him, for all his pompous tics. He concedes that he is homesick, and tired of Paula. "I'm beaten," he says, and the camera lingers on Marianne's face, noting the surprise and warmth of response in her features as intimately as it did when Johan announced his departure from Sweden back at the cottage in scene three.

Marianne, however, stands out of reach of the sentimental appeal. She reacts angrily, accusing Johan of self-pity and recounting her dreams (like Rut in *Thirst*) of battering him and stabbing him to death.

And they do fight. Clumsily. On the floor of the office, with no one to witness their shame and confusion. The camera takes Johan's part, remaining with him when Marianne goes to the bathroom to clean up. Johan is sobbing. As Marianne leaves, she turns to him in the doorway. "We should have started fighting long ago," she says. "It would have been much better."

In scene six, Bergman develops his theory of the sins of the fathers. Marianne visits her mother and learns that she too acquiesced in a loveless marriage. "I wonder how it would have been had we confided in each other," ponders the mother. "If we had talked over everything that had occurred to us."

Some years have passed since the divorce between Johan and Marianne. When they meet in scene six, a casual remark about their summer house indicates that Johan has been parted from the family for seven years. But Bergman suggests that they are reconciled, and spend weekends together, and even enjoy sex, in fact, without being jealous of third parties. Johan takes Marianne to a friend's cottage. It is shabby and unkempt, with dirty crockery and a bike lying in the main room. But the bourgeois comforts are no longer mandatory. While Johan prepares the fire, Marianne gazes with affection at his back; his cheerful whistling fills the room.

After supper they discuss themselves and the world. Johan claims that he does battle with futility and reproaches Marianne for being too sententious. In a gray dawn, with a fog horn hooting in the distance, Marianne starts out of a dream and paces the room hysterically like a bewildered animal. When she calms down, she tells Johan: "It grieves me that I've never loved anyone—and that no one's ever loved me." Both have married other people now, but this relationship, born in misunderstanding and forged in anguish, means more to Johan and Marianne than anything else in the world.

Bergman compressed *Scenes from a Marriage* to just under three hours for theatrical release. His cutting had to be drastic—almost 120 minutes of film—and certain scenes disappeared altogether: Marianne's pregnancy and abortion; the meeting in a restaurant between Johan and Marianne; a phone call from Marianne's lover in scene four; a nightwatchman's appearance in scene five, as well as large chunks of dialog from that episode; Marianne's visit to her mother's house; and the conversation between Eva and Johan in scene six. Some omissions are regrettable, such as the chat between Katarina and Marianne in scene one, but each version works satisfactorily, and Bergman is aware of the value of the TV series format, permitting the writer/director to include stretches of uninterrupted dialog that would be unacceptable in a full-length feature film being watched on a single evening.

Scenes from a Marriage was screened over a six-week period from April 11, 1973, to May 16, 1973, on Swedish television and subsequently on foreign stations and networks. The BBC commissioned a dubbed version, as did the American PBS, but these were disastrous, robbing the film of its pinpoint accuracy of inflection. Subsequently the TV series was screened in Britain with subtitles and proved much more popular.

The impact on Scandinavian audiences was startling. In Denmark, police deserted point duty and left traffic congestion to fend for itself while they sat at home watching the latest confrontation between Johan and Marianne. The divorce rate jumped ("That's got to be good," laughed Bergman). Many intellectuals, however, dismissed *Scenes from a Marriage* as mere soap opera. The fact remains, however, that Bergman had discovered a means of reaching millions of people with his art, without in the process compromising with his material.

Economically and aesthetically, *Scenes* was a triumph. In the United States, it joined *Cries and Whispers* as Bergman's most fashionable film in years. With Sven Nykvist winning the Academy Award for Best Cinematography on April 2, 1974, for his work on *Cries and Whispers*, Bergman's rehabilitation in the United States was complete. Cinematograph's income increased by almost embarrassing leaps and bounds. Bergman saw the chance to plow back his earnings into production.

Directors like Kjell Grede and Gunnel Lindblom were encouraged to move forward on projects funded in part by Cinematograph.

On December 1, 1972, Svensk Filmindustri called a press conference to announce that Bergman would make a film of *The Merry Widow*. In Malmö in 1954, Bergman had already written a draft screenplay for such a movie, and the memory of his glittering production at the Municipal Theater there was still vivid. The budget was fixed at some four million dollars, of which Svensk Filmindustri hoped around 80 or 90 percent could be guaranteed by advance sales abroad.

The main revelation, however, was that Barbra Streisand would play the lead in the new movie. During the shooting of *The Touch*, she had visited Elliott Gould and had met Bergman. In principle she agreed to appear in *The Merry Widow*. Shooting was due to begin in the fall of 1974.

But a number of unforeseen difficulties scuttled the project. The oil crisis of 1973 led to a dramatic increase in many cost areas. The budget had to be revised. Dino De Laurentiis offered Svensk Filmindustri a cheque for four million dollars, assuming the film was made entirely in Sweden and providing Svensk Filmindustri took responsibility for any inflation in the budget. Kenne Fant knew immediately that such a proposal was anathema, for Bergman never compromised on a budget once it had been agreed. For example, the screenplay called for around a hundred dancers in certain key sequences. "We studied the budget, and Ingmar said we cannot have eighty. Not sixty. Not even thirty-five. And he said, 'Look, Kenne, let's drop this project.'" Bergman was disappointed, for he had spent eight months preparing for the film.

There was no pause in his productivity, in spite of this setback. During the winter of 1972–1973 he rehearsed a new production of *The Ghost Sonata*. In New York, Stephen Sondheim was embarking on a Broadway musical version of *Smiles of a Summer Night*, to be entitled *A Little Night Music*. "We decided," said Sondheim, "that the songs should bubble and that they should be dry, unsentimental, and un-soulful." Len Cariou played the Gunnar Björnstrand role, and Hermione Gingold, one of the few unqualified successes of that uneven show, was imperious and resplendent as old Mrs. Armfeldt. Bergman planned to visit New York to see the rehearsals and to accept the New York Film Critics' Prize for *Cries and Whispers*. But at the last moment he and his wife canceled the trip. Instead, Bergman traveled to Copenhagen to set up a production of *The Misanthrope* at the Danish Royal Theater. This opened on April 6, 1973, and was telecast in Denmark the following year.

The most exciting event in the Swedish theatrical season that winter

Bergman's production of Strindberg's Ghost Sonata *at the Royal Dramatic Theater in 1973. Photo courtesy Beata Bergström/Kungl. Dramatiska Teatern.*

was the premiere of *The Ghost Sonata* on January 13. From that fevered "dream play," wrought in one of Strindberg's gravest troughs of melancholy, three scenes live in the mind of anyone who saw the Bergman production. There was the astonishing moment when the Milkmaid (Kari Sylwan) without warning surged up through a trap in the floor at the front of the stage, while simultaneously Bergman changed the backprojected image at the rear of the stage from an ordinary building to the stone walls of a prison, dwarfing and surrounding the Milkmaid. Toward the end of the play (running only ninety minutes), the Old Man (Toivo Pawlo) forced the Colonel to his knees. The Colonel (Anders Ek) shed his wig; his uniform was torn back to reveal the quivering breast beneath. Rarely had Bergman conceived on stage such a terrifying image of humiliation.

The death of the Old Man recalled Bergman's own mortal dread of closets. The Mummy ordered the Old Man to hang himself, and he was dragged off and thrust into the closet by his servant. Then came the noise of his neck being broken as his enemy, Bengtsson, gleefully accomplished the murder.

In May 1973 Bergman was persuaded to attend the Cannes Film Festival in connection with a screening of *Cries and Whispers*. Such was the interest aroused by the visit that the authorities had to hold the press conference in the main auditorium of the Festival Palais, an unprecedented honor. Bergman entered like a shy monarch, to be almost engulfed by the photographers. When the hubbub had subsided, he spoke in careful, simple, and affecting English not only of the genesis of *Cries and Whispers* but also of his youthful fear of death, the contrast between working in the theater and making films for the cinema, and the need for directors to learn from one another. "Directors are not sputniks in outer space," he said. "We all learn from, and are inspired by, one another." He defended his intuitive approach to movies. "I've often been termed anti-intellectual. But art is not at all intellectual, and cannot be. Stravinsky was right, when he said: 'One can never understand music, only experience it.' "

Privately Bergman conceded that each new film was draining more of his resources. His health was in fact better than at many periods of his youth, but he was coming to terms with a less hectic schedule: one film a year, and one production at Dramaten, where his old friend Erland Josephson was still head director.

Swedish Radio, which celebrated its golden jubilee in 1975, commissioned Bergman to make a television film of Mozart's *The Magic Flute* for screening on New Year's Day 1975. The search for singers began before the close of 1973. Eric Ericson, conductor of the Swedish Radio Symphony Orchestra, alerted opera companies in Oslo, Helsinki, and Copenhagen, as well as Stockholm, and there were major auditions during the summer at which even well-known soloists like Håkan Hagegård were tested.

Before recording and filming began in earnest, however, Bergman devoted his energies to staging *To Damascus, Parts I and II*, at the Royal Dramatic Theater. The production opened on February 1, 1974. There is a *Part III*, which is not often performed, and together this trilogy deals with Strindberg's frantic struggle with a God beneath whose aegis he had been as strictly reared as ever Bergman was and whose existence he comes finally to accept. It is also motivated by the experience of his marriage to the Austrian, Frida Uhl, and by his guilt at abandoning the children of his earlier union with Siri von Essen.

Just as a sentimentalist may be found lurking behind every cynic, so every advocate of permissiveness conceals a puritan, and Strindberg was trapped between these two extremes when he wrote *To Damascus* from 1898 onward. Henrik Sjögren, an enthusiastic witness of the Bergman production, wrote:

> Swift as a dream, the play shifted virtuosically between the
> moods and projections of the Stranger—i.e. of Strindberg and

everyone else. It was at once defiant, absurd, grandiose, pitiable, fiercely sarcastic and panic-stricken; torn between cruelty and tenderness, between self-assertion on one hand and masochistic self-torment on the other.[1]

The Magic Flute may well take its place among the five or six greatest films that Bergman has directed. Cineastes were wary of its appearance, assuming Bergman had done no more than set up his cameras before the singers; besides, film buffs are conspicuously impatient where opera is concerned. Music lovers, on the contrary, were ready to castigate Bergman for the cuts and emendations he had made to Schikaneder's libretto. But as the film is telecast during the Christmas holidays and at various other times of the year throughout Europe and the United States, so new generations are recognizing the brilliance, warmth, and serendipity of Bergman's homage to Mozart.

In the early forties, while helping out at the Opera in Stockholm, Bergman heard the conductor Issay Dobrowen say, "In about fifteen years I hope I'll be ready to do *The Marriage of Figaro*." Bergman was puzzled by the remark, but in 1974 he confessed that he was glad he himself had waited over twenty years to stage *The Magic Flute*. There is a precision about the way music is laid out and then played by an orchestra or an ensemble that appeals to Bergman. He was determined to involve himself in every aspect of the production, from selecting the singers to checking the color release prints.

The budget was around 3.2 million crowns, but probably nearer 4 million ($950,000) if overheads are taken into account. The other producers at Swedish TV were irritated by *The Magic Flute* project because it drew on the services of almost every department and technician in the organization. There was sustained pressure on all personnel to produce optimum results, and when the venture was complete everyone agreed that the effort had been worthwhile. Måns Reuterswärd, the producer, found *The Magic Flute* a thoroughly enjoyable challenge.

> Bergman is always the first to arrive on the set in the morning, and he's always precise in calling his coffee break at 3 P.M. or 3.15 P.M. or whatever. You can set your watch by him more than by any other director I've worked with. He has a great respect for all the members of the unit, and they feel this, so there is a good team spirit as a result.[2]

The logistical problems, however, were daunting. Bergman wanted to shoot inside the celebrated Drottningholm Palace, in the royal park outside Stockholm, but the scenery proved too delicate to accommodate all the paraphernalia of a TV crew. So Henny Noremark and his colleagues reconstructed the stage of Drottningholm in the studios of the Swedish Film Institute. Rumor has it that Schikaneder spent six thousand florins on costumes and scenery for the original 1791 production at the Theater auf der Wieden in Vienna, and Noremark checked that each prop, curtain, wing, and backdrop, was painted in the same shade and tone as it would have been in the time of Mozart. Bergman claimed that Mozart wrote his score with a specific stage in mind (seven meters wide, if one follows the music when Tamino goes across stage at the Temple of Wisdom).

Even the genial dragon that pursues Tamino upstage in the opening moments proved difficult to build. The Film Institute workshops produced a massive creature activated by six or seven dancers. A film test was made, and Bergman screened it. "He simply roared with laughter," according to Reuterswärd. "I've never seen him laugh so hysterically, and of course I—knowing how to interpret that laugh—realized that we'd have to remake the entire contraption." At last the dragon emerged, a delightful creature of felt and bunting.

The special effects were intricate and hard to arrange in advance. The fire at the end of the film, when Tamino and Pamina pass through apparently endless vistas of smoke and writhing bodies, was meant to be accomplished with gas. But the gas pipes in the Film Institute were too slender, and larger ducts had to be imported from all over Scandinavia.

More than one hundred candidates applied for roles in the film. "The most important factor for me," Bergman maintained, "was that the singers should have natural voices. You can find artificially cultivated voices that sound marvelous, but you can never really believe that a human personality is doing the singing. Records have accustomed us to a kind of absolute perfection, but beauty cannot be perfect without also being vibrant and alive." Ulrik Cold, recently appointed head of the Royal Danish Opera, was given the part of Sarastro; Irma Urrila, the Finnish soprano, was cast as Pamina; Josef Köstlinger, who came to Stockholm from Salzburg in the late sixties, as Tamino; and Håkan Hagegård, one of Sweden's most popular baritones, struck Bergman as an ideal Papageno.[3]

Outside the center of Stockholm lies the huge Circus building, and here Eric Ericson began recording the opera with the Swedish Radio Symphony Orchestra. Bergman presided at every session. He opted for the playback method of filming opera, whereby all the music is prerecorded by the artists and musicians and then replayed in segments in the film studio until the director is satisfied with both lip synchronization and acting performance. Bergman knew also that it would have been prohibitively expensive to keep a full orchestra sitting around in the studios for ten weeks. Tempos, phrasing, and dynamics had to be meticulously controlled for the stereo broadcast, and this was the first occasion on which the Swedes had harnessed a stereo soundtrack to a TV production. Apart from pleasing those listeners with stereo systems, it justified financial participation in the venture by the radio wing of Swedish Radio, to the tune of 15 percent of the budget.

"Bergman was as happy as a sandboy when he came out to the Circus and had a whole orchestra at his disposal for the first time," says Reutersward. "On the first day the first violin was delayed by some plane trouble, so the chair was empty. Eventually Ingmar slipped into it, and he looked *so* happy at being in the very midst of the music making."

Helmut Muhle was the chief sound engineer who, after the first couple of days at the Circus, could tell Eric Ericson exactly how the orchestra should sound. To the very end of the production, however, Bergman was concerned with the quality of the recording. When the film was complete, he accepted the notion of releasing *The Magic Flute* to theaters as well as on television, outside the Nordic area. The film was blown up at 35 mm. at the Filmteknik laboratory and looked superb. But it required skill and patience to convert the soundtrack to optical sound. Bergman rejected several prints before he was satisfied. For the special screening at the Cannes Festival in 1975, a magnetic stereo print was struck. All other release prints had optical sound.

Shooting finished in June 1974, and post-production work occupied the team from September to December. After the last day's filming, Bergman joined the crew for a summer party at a restaurant outside the city. He had a drink in his hand, smoked a cigar for the first time in years, and made a happy little speech thanking his collaborators.

Bergman's is a witty, rumbustious *Flute*, played and sung at fast tempo throughout. The production communicates Bergman's concept of the Mozart opera as "the theater as childish magic and exalted mystery."[4] Like his own better films, *The Magic Flute* embodies a quest. Papageno, with his birdcage and his pipes of Pan, and Tamino, with the simple, wooden flute that wards off evil, arrive in the finale at a celebration of love and fruitfulness.

Hour of the Wolf, with its numerous Mozartean and Hoffmannesque overtones, might lead people to believe Bergman capable of nothing but a sombre, metaphysical *Flute* in which the Queen of the Night and Monostatos would hold sway over the spirits of Tamino and Papageno. In fact, Bergman's judicious cuts in the libretto have eliminated various obscure references to Masonic ritual, and the forces of sweetness and light remain in the ascendant.

Håkan Hagegård's Papageno sets the tone for the rest of the cast. A zestful figure, unencumbered by the elaborate feathers and accoutrements of Schikaneder's traditional bird catcher, he "mm, mm, mm, mm's" deliciously after his mouth is padlocked by the Three Ladies; munches eclairs as Pamina gazes rapturously at the portrait of Tamino; and revels in his encounter with the old hag (Papagena in disguise) in the House of Trials. Ulrik Cold as Sarastro sings in rich, ripe tones that make him a vital as well as beneficent character, the father-figure in whose gift lies the exalted love so eagerly sought by Tamino and Papageno.

Bergman perceives the darkness that lies at the very heart of the opera, in those twelve measures in act two when Tamino exclaims,

Josef Köstlinger (Tamino) *and the* Three Ladies (*Britt-Marie Aruhn, Birgitta Smiding, and Kirsten Vaupel*) *in* The Magic Flute. *Photo courtesy Sveriges Radio/TV2.*

"Oh, eternal night! When will you vanish? When will the light reach my eyes?" and hears the ghostly response of the priests, "Soon, youth, or never." Mozart, Bergman reminds one, was mortally sick when he wrote those words. "He asks his question in darkness and from this darkness he answers himself—or does he get an answer? I have never felt so close to the deepest secret of spiritual intuition as just here, in this moment." But while Bergman refracts Mozart's despair through the prism of his own experience and genius as a screen director, he also mirrors the lightness and exuberance of *The Magic Flute*. The Three Ladies who slay the dragon are pert and jolly; likewise the boys who descend by balloon to pelt Papageno with snowballs just as he is on the brink of hanging himself. Even Monostatos and his minions with their tricorn hats are charmed by the tinkling bells at Papageno's command.

The uses of the cinema allow Bergman to take his audience by the throat at will. As the Queen of the Night, dagger in hand, harangues Pamina in "Der Hölle Rache" in act two, her face is transformed into a mask of fury by waxen makeup and a livid green filter. Later, when Monostatos informs her of his scheme for destroying Tamino, their two faces are seen in close-up, staring slightly away from the camera, like Death and the Knight in *The Seventh Seal*; a greenish-blue light dominates the Queen's features, while a bright one illuminates the ruddy face of Monostatos.

Such moments of trepidation evaporate like mist beneath a morning sun. Tamino is escorted to his Third Trial by two dark men, their flaming helmets and massive beards giving them an unearthly, sinister mien; but all at once they peel off their helmets like skins, to reveal genial faces beneath. And in the depths of the House of Trials itself, the Three Ladies materialize from all sides and rattle gruesome green skulls at Tamino and Papageno; a split second later, however, the mood of fun is recovered as the sisters sing of happy provocation.

Even the climactic journey through "Death's dark night" possesses a comforting theatrical artifice. The brave notes of Tamino's flute seem suspended above a vertiginous gorge, in the depths of which can be heard a ghastly wailing. Nude, shaven couples wrestle and knot, while Tamino and Pamina pass serenely on their way. Monostatos and the Queen of the Night launch a final attack but are overwhelmed by the scarlet forces of Sarastro, while Papageno and Papagena rejoice beneath the greenwood tree with their children.

Bergman's film of *The Magic Flute* emerges as a marvelous tribute by a master of the visual arts to the eighteenth century's greatest artistic spirit. It is as though Bergman's own predilection for chilly metaphysics had been tempered by Mozart's sense of wonder.

In 1962, the late Marianne Höök wrote in her book on Bergman, "He is always primarily the man of the theater who distrusts technical shortcuts, relying solely on the human being and on the spoken word."[5]

The observation makes sense only when Bergman is off form. His best films by some curious process bridge the division between theater and cinema; his worst make one aware of the exits and entrances, the tinny thunder, and the false backdrop. In an interview in a Danish newspaper in 1972, Bergman asserted that there are two kinds of reality, one that is carried within oneself, and mirrored in the face, and then the outer reality. "I work only with that little dot, the human being; that is what I try to dissect and to penetrate more and more deeply, in order to trace his secrets."[6] While the demands of the television medium offer a mundane explanation for Bergman's increasing use of close-ups during the seventies, the yearning to explore and lay bare the lineaments of the soul affords the more basic reason.

Face to Face (*Ansikte mot ansikte*) was shot—like *Scenes from a Marriage*—as a television serial, but in four parts only. The film version was released by Dino De Laurentiis and unveiled at the Cannes Festival of 1976. Bergman finished the screenplay in Fårö in December 1974, and two months later he flew incognito to New York for a series of meetings with De Laurentiis, who had settled in the United States as a major producer.

The flight was rough, and the jumbo jet had to set down in Gander. After two hours the tornado-like winds abated sufficiently to allow the plane to continue to Kennedy Airport. Bergman and Ingrid visited the Max Ernst exhibition at the Guggenheim and also attended a circus show by Ringling Brothers Barnum and Bailey. Bergman was impressed by Liv Ullmann's performance as Nora in *A Doll's House* at the Circle in the Square Theater.

De Laurentiis immediately agreed to finance *Face to Face*. "It's a wonderful, strong story," he said, "and I visualize an ideal relationship with this brilliant filmmaker. I recognize that as a creative artist Ingmar is unexcelled, and I consider myself, above all, as a showman. Both of us saw in *Face to Face* an exciting entertainment that would attract large audiences all over the world."[7] Such hyperbole aside, De Laurentiis was glad to reestablish his connections with Bergman only two years after the collapse of the *Merry Widow* project. And he did not attempt to interfere with the production.

Principal photography on the film began on April 28 and ended in July. Some additional material was filmed in September. During all this period, Bergman's production of *Twelfth Night* attracted huge crowds to the Royal Dramatic Theater. They were delighted by the comfortable Tudor setting, the melodious delivery of the set speeches (Bergman

Erland Josephson (Dr. Tomas Jacobi) *and Liv Ullmann* (Dr. Jenny Isaksson) *in* Face to Face. *Photo courtesy of Dino De Laurentiis.*

regards *Twelfth Night* as among the most musical of Shakespeare's plays), and the piquant performance of Bibi Andersson as Viola—who remained dressed as Caesario, the counterfeit man, throughout the evening.

Two studios were rented at the Swedish Film Institute for *Face to Face.* One of them contained the sickbed of the protagonist, Jenny Isaksson, a psychiatrist. "There is also her office," wrote Liv Ullmann, "and the corridors she runs through when she is in that borderline territory between life and death."[8] In the other studio, Anna Hagegård, the production designer, had constructed Jenny's childhood home in Uppsala. Daniel, Bergman's twelve-year-old son by Käbi Laretei, rushed to the set after school and helped his father as an assiduous clapper-boy.

In his now traditional letter to the cast and crew, Bergman described *Face to Face* as being in two parts, the first "almost pedantically realistic, tangible," and the second as elusive and full of dreams. Dr. Jenny Isaksson is, according to Bergman, "a well-adjusted, capable and disciplined person, a highly qualified professional woman with a career, comfortably married to a gifted colleague and surrounded by what is called 'the good things of life.' It is this admirable character's shockingly quick breakdown and agonizing rebirth that I have tried to describe."[9]

Face to Face was an arduous production for Bergman, but at least the studio facilities enabled him to maintain a regular schedule. He would come on set in his familiar garb of sweater, trousers, and slippers, and sometimes, according to Liv Ullmann, one blue and one yellow sock. At lunch he would take a hard-boiled egg, a slice of toast and jam, and a bowl of sour cream. Crackers, chocolate, and bottles of Ramlösa soda were kept in reserve on a table in the studio.

There is a dearth of fire and venom in *Face to Face*, a deadpan aspect that robs the film of the inner drama Bergman wants so dearly to convey. Bergman is at his most persuasive when describing Jenny's return to the environment of her childhood and least convincing when he tries to grasp the fashionable elements of "modern" drama, such as the party scene in which Dr. Tomas Jacobi (Erland Josephson) is introduced, and the sequence when Jenny (Liv Ullmann) is raped in an empty house.

Even Jenny's suicide attempt is drained of dramatic tension. Recovering, hovering between hallucination and dream, she starts to establish a plausible relationship with Tomas. In these conversations, the inspiration of *Scenes from a Marriage* returns to Bergman. Jenny enters a schizoid limbo in which she acts out the words of both her parents and herself as a child. For his part, Tomas is a twin to Johan in that earlier film, accepting life's beauty in the same instant as he dismisses it as a pile of shit. He longs "to become real . . . to hear a human voice and be sure that it comes from someone who is made just like I am. To touch a pair of lips and in the same thousandth of a second know that this is a pair of lips."

Such soliloquies, like hammocks swinging between the trees of dramatic incident, are much cherished by Bergman.

Face to Face marks Bergman's most decisive and detailed journey back to the world of his childhood since *Wild Strawberries*. The apartment in Uppsala where Jenny's grandparents live is a replica of the one in which Bergman grew up in the early twenties. Gunnar Björnstrand's Grandpa suffers from the same ailment—a paralysis of the legs—that incapacitated Bergman's father. Aino Taube, playing his wife, has the dark dress, drawn-back hair, and serious face of Bergman's Grandma.

Bergman's father had sustained a heart attack when he reached his seventies, and mother and son would sit in the hospital together day after day beside the sick man. Little by little, a reconciliation between them was brought about, a friendship regained. Something of this feeling, this craving for harmony between parent and child, is transmitted in *Face to Face*. Jenny's own failure to impart love to her daughter is echoed in her memories of disputes with her grandparents, of being locked up in a closet, of endless reproaches for being late, using lipstick, wearing the wrong clothes, not eating properly. Such experiences in youth produce what Jenny terms "a vast army of emotional cripples," but by the close of the film she seems in an elegiac, conciliatory mood. As she watches her elderly grandparents together, the man confined to his bed, the woman watching over him, Jenny says offscreen, "For a brief moment I realized that their love embraces everything—even death."

Liv Ullmann's acting matches anything she has done in the cinema. She renders Jenny Isaksson in such ambivalent shades that the character cannot be dismissed as a stereotype. She dreams that she is confronted with her own corpse, laid out on a red bed; then she is shut into a coffin, and the nails are pounded into the wood above her. She herself sets fire to the casket, and her face as she does so contains a guileful smile of satisfaction, which breaks into a wide smile as the cries of "Mummy! Mummy!" from within the coffin grow fainter. The artiste's interpretation of the personality is more profound than it is in the similar, opening nightmare of *Wild Strawberries*, while Bergman's realization of the scene is wanting in suspense and drama.

"He really does have an understanding of what actors are trying to express," says Liv Ullmann. "He always waits until you've done something and then he may say, 'Why not give a little more?' or 'Try not giving so much.' But he never pushes."[10]

Face to Face is a lachrymose, effusive film, and its symbolism (a baleful, blind old lady who represents Death as surely as the haggard aunt does in *Summer Interlude*) sits uneasily with the contemporary nature of its setting—the party with its gays—and the naturalism of the rape scene or the visit to the concert (where Käbi Laretei is glimpsed playing some Mozart). *Face to Face* comprehends both an act of revenge on Bergman's childhood and also an attempt to deal with the legacy of that phase of his life. Tomas comments at one point that the world is full of overgrown children who are crushed to death by a society as cruel as that of the Middle Ages. Perhaps in letting Gunnar Björnstrand's father-figure utter the line, "Old age is hell," Bergman acknowledges that tolerance should be demanded from youth as much as from senior citizens. Childhood, after all, is like old age. A man is helpless when he's old, too.

When Liv Ullmann asked Bergman if audiences would like the film, he answered, "Regard it as a surgeon's scalpel. Not everyone will welcome it." Released just after Bergman's traumatic humiliation at the hands of the tax authorities (see Chapter 15), *Face to Face* failed to impress audiences either on television or in the cinemas.

On September 17, 1975, Bergman was installed as an honorary doctor of philosophy at Stockholm University. "I just wish that my mother and father could have experienced this moment," he said. This, and the appointment of brother Dag as ambassador to Greece in 1972, marked the height of Sweden's official recognition of the Bergman family.

During the fall, Bergman wrote a screenplay entitled *The Petrified Prince* for Warner Brothers. The idea was to create a companion piece for two other erotic fantasies due to be written by Federico Fellini and Mike Nichols. Bergman, the only one of the three to complete his screenplay, devised an aphrodisiac plot involving a prince, his queen mother, and a young whore, set in the Napoleonic era.

On Fårö, Bergman reconstructed an old house. Local farmers and fishermen did the work without the help of an architect. "This is very Swedish," noted Bergman. "People like to plan together, to discuss, to work things out."[11] During that year, which was to be his last in Sweden for a considerable time, he confided to a friend that he was keen to divest himself of the problems of production and distribution. "I only have about ten years in which I can work at full pressure," he conceded.

And yet he could scarcely have predicted the harrowing ordeal that awaited him in January 1976.

CHAPTER FIFTEEN

Exile

*Even if you do not leave anything precious
behind, do not own a stone in your ancestral
home, not a clod in a field; even if you are happy
to have emerged from an environment that was
intolerable, and like the queen bee you carried
everything along so that you have not the slightest
cause to long for home, your
body still feels homesick.*

Strindberg

INGMAR BERGMAN HAD BEEN PLAYING WITH HIS MODEL THEATER AT THE
age of fourteen when the Social Democrats acceded to power in
Sweden. Forty-four years later, in 1976, they were still in the ruling
position in government. During that epoch, the Social Democrats had
made Sweden synonymous with everyone's dream (or nightmare) of the
welfare state.

No regime can bring about equality of mind and spirit; but a resolute
state program may affect equality of earnings, and opportunity, and
standard of living. Since the Middle Ages, the Swedes have regarded
the good of the community as more important than that of the
individual. And over the past fifty years the Swedish state has sought
to accumulate greater and greater funds in order to improve the level
of social and economic security. The Swede is protected against mis-

adventure from birth to death by maternity grants, child benefit, health insurance, and pensions.

But the taxes are lethal.

People earning modest salaries must relinquish up to half, in direct taxation to the government; when they wish to spend what remains to them, they are faced with the MOMS, or purchase tax, which adds more than 20 percent to most bills. If they are successful in life and earn more than the average, they will forfeit up to 80 percent in direct tax. And if they are fortunate or frugal enough to save more than twenty thousand dollars or so, they will be liable to an annual wealth tax.

Bergman, like any good Swede, has never questioned this system. When asked by an interviewer about his political persuasion, he usually professed support for the Social Democrats in the way that a New Yorker might admit to reading the *Times* every day. And still he paid back to the government up to four-fifths of his annual income of $150,000 to $200,000. Fårö, the Baltic island where he chose to settle, suffers in spite of its poverty from one of the highest tax rates in Sweden.

Leaving aside the bitchy comments one hears in Sweden about Bergman's attitude to money—and most of them originate in the pages of the Socialist newspaper *Aftonbladet*—there is no doubt that he is oblivious to the trappings of fortune. He does not drive fast cars, and he eschews the glitter of fine restaurants and nightclubs. His holidays are confined to his beloved island of Fårö. He dresses modestly. He refuses to promote his films as such, even when there is no doubt that his presence at a festival or a premiere would help the box-office fortunes of a new feature. (For example, he declined to come to the United States in 1980, when a distributor was planning to open *From the Life of the Marionettes* during Bergman's visit.)

Not even the claustrophobic drama of *The Ritual*, in which Bergman had studied three artists in the toils of a ruthless judge, could have prepared either him or his acquaintances for the events of 1976.

On Friday, January 30, Bergman was rehearsing Strindberg's play, *The Dance of Death*, at the Royal Dramatic Theater in Stockholm. At around noon, two plainclothes police officers called at the side entrance of the theater in Nybrogatan. They were told that Bergman was in rehearsal and could not be disturbed. Jan Olof Strandberg, then head of Dramaten, wrote subsequently to the newspapers refuting official police accounts of the incident, claiming that it was only the energetic protests of the theater's secretary that prevented the two officers from entering the stage area.

Bergman was summoned to Strandberg's office and confronted by one of the officers, while the other hastened to the stage door, stationing himself there should Bergman try to make a run for it.

Of course he was too startled and confused to contemplate such a move. He was bundled into a car and taken to the local "police tax" office, where he was questioned by Detective-Inspector Bo Stolpe about an alleged tax offense dating back to 1971. (The police later defended their precipitate action on the grounds that a statute of limitations might have placed Bergman beyond their grasp had they not moved swiftly—and Bergman's office had informed them that he would not be free for an interview until after *The Dance of Death* had opened in April). The prosecutor had ruled that Bergman should be brought before a hearing without prior summons.

Meanwhile the matter had been leaked to the press, and forty minutes after Bergman had been driven away from the theater, the first newspaper rang asking for details. Bergman was held for questioning for up to three hours before being allowed to return—under escort—to his apartment in Karlaplan. There his passport was temporarily confiscated, and other personal documents were removed by the police. Bergman's lawyer, Sven Harald Bauer, also had to surrender his passport and had to allow the authorities to search his offices for documents pertaining to the Bergman "affair."

What exactly was Bergman accused of?

In 1967, in order to finance any productions that he might undertake outside Sweden, Bergman was advised to establish a company in Switzerland. But the scheme for a film in tandem with Federico Fellini fell through as described earlier, and the Swiss company, Persona AG of Bern, went into liquidation in 1974. There was nothing illegal about this: Persona AG had been set up with the approval of the Bank of Sweden; Bauer had been scrupulous in attending to such essentials. Bergman only liquidated the company when he withdrew from a tentative arrangement with RAI, the Italian television network, to film a series of programs on the life of Jesus Christ. About six hundred thousand dollars remained in the kitty, and when Bergman transferred this to Sweden he had to pay 10 percent capital gains tax on it immediately.

But an assiduous tax officer, Kent Karlsson, came to the conclusion—after months of investigation—that Bergman should have paid the equivalent of several hundred thousand crowns in personal income tax. In Karlsson's opinion, Bergman had used Persona AG as a front in order to avoid paying taxes in his own country, whereas Bergman maintained that he had wished to accumulate capital for film projects.

The penalty? Either a massive fine or a maximum of two years in jail.

Bergman was not the only individual under threat. An examination of five leading Swedish actors and actresses had been set in motion by the tax authorities who suspected that Bergman's Swiss company had paid some of their fees directly to accounts in Liechtenstein and the Bahamas in order to evade Swedish tax. Bibi Andersson was held for more than twenty-four hours by the police. She protested strongly, saying that her young daughter would be anxious at her whereabouts. But she was treated with contempt, as though she were guilty of tax offenses before even being charged. Her brassiere was confiscated, in case she should "try to harm herself."

Three days after his encounter with the police, Bergman collapsed.

He was not permitted to travel outside the mainland, so refuge in Fårö was out of the question. "I am an artist," he said. " I know nothing about money, and I know nothing about these charges." He became so agitated that his wife and friends took a room for him at the Karolinska Hospital. Officially, his condition was described as a "nervous breakdown."

By now, people in high Swedish places were aware of the situation and very worried about its implications. The Social Democrats were holding a fragile coalition together in Parliament, and the elections that fall were by no means a foregone conclusion. When the world-famous author of children's stories Astrid Lindgren announced to the press that by her calculations she was subject to 102 percent taxation on her earnings, the government realized that the clumsy handling of the Bergman affair might have explosive consequences.

By virtue of Bergman's reputation outside Sweden, the gruesome details of his arrest and hospitalization were already reaching the front pages of the world's newspapers. So it was not surprising that on March 24 Bergman and his lawyer, Harald Bauer, were cleared of all charges and accusations against them. The local public prosecutor, Anders Nordenadler, announced that Bergman was also exonerated as far as his own and his company's tax returns were concerned for the entire period 1972 to 1975. In the public eye, the affair seemed to be over.

But the tax authorities, smarting from their defeat, launched a new round of investigations. They concentrated on the year 1974 and claimed that Bergman was liable to double taxation, to the tune of 100,000 crowns and more, for the money that appeared in the books of both his defunct Swiss company and his Swedish business concern, Cinematograph. According to Bergman, this claim blossomed into a massive demand for the financial year 1975. He was requested to pay tax *twice*—at rates of 85 and 45 percent—on some 2.5 million crowns (well over $500,000).

The reason that so much money was swilling around in the coffers of Cinematograph was simply that *Cries and Whispers* and then *Scenes from a Marriage* had proved lucrative beyond Bergman's wildest dreams. Instead of draining the money to their own advantage, Bergman and his colleagues at Cinematograph plowed it back immediately into production, as part of his policy of providing work for freelance collaborators during the intervals between his own productions. Gunnel Lindblom, the actress from *The Silence* and an excellent stage director, was given the chance to make her first feature, *Paradise Place*; Kjell Grede, whose career was stuttering somewhat, was able to shoot a four-part adaptation of Strindberg's *A Madman's Defense* for television; and a loyal aide, Peder Langenskiöld, began to work on a half-hour short entitled *Per and Yvonne*.

The tax superintendents, confident of eventual victory, now made Bergman an offer they felt he could not refuse. If he agreed to pay the taxes they had claimed originally in January, they would refrain from taxing Cinematograph for 1975 as threatened.

Meanwhile, Bergman's predicament had been the subject of widespread discussion in the press. Detective-Inspector Stolpe, who first questioned the director on January 30, was quoted as saying: "He seems like a very fine person. He kept telling me that 'every newspaper will probably murder me now.' He was very worried about the newspapers, about what people would say about him." Harry Schein, then head of the Swedish Film Institute and a friend and counsellor to Bergman, said, "If there's anything he fears most—the maximum terror—it's humiliation."

Face to Face was finished and ready for broadcasting on Swedish television at the end of April. Bergman was preparing *The Serpent's Egg*, a big-budget film set in the twenties in Germany. There was talk of resuscitating the collaboration with Fellini, with Bergman's half of the project being *The Petrified Prince*. He was also active as a producer on *Paradise Place*.

Nevertheless, even Bergman's friends were stunned when they opened their copy of *Expressen*, Scandinavia's largest evening paper, on April 22, and found a long article by Bergman, headed, "Now I Am Leaving Sweden."

In the piece he attacked some of his tax tormentors by name, declaring with satisfaction that he would not submit to an underhanded deal. If found guilty of tax evasion, he would pay his dues to the last cent. But the tenor of the article left no doubt that Bergman saw exile as the only means of saving his creative sanity and of taking a stand against what he called "a particular kind of bureaucracy, which grows like a galloping cancer. This bureaucracy is in no way qualified for its difficult and delicate task, and society has armed it with powers that are handled by immature individuals."

He had, he wrote, "espoused the ideology of gray compromise. . . . My awakening was a shock, partly because of the almost unbearable humiliation, partly because I realized that anyone in this country, anytime and anyhow, can be attacked and vilified."

There followed a characteristically precise and detailed program of events: Bergman was shutting down his company, Cinematograph (actually it was never closed); the workers at his studios on Fårö were to be laid off, and plans for enlarging the facility were shelved; all personnel were to be compensated. The article concluded with a rapier lunge at *Aftonbladet*, the paper that had branded Bergman as a tax dodger, and with a sentence of Strindberg's: "Watch out, you bastard, we'll meet in my next play!"

The previous day, Bergman and his wife had flown from Stockholm to Paris, resting the first night in a hotel and then staying with friends. They spent a few days there, "just strolling around in the city, sitting and looking at people, doing nothing and feeling free."

On the weekend they took a plane to Los Angeles at the invitation of Dino De Laurentiis and Bergman's agent, Paul Kohner. During a press conference at the Beverly Wilshire Hotel on April 25, at which he looked harassed and unnerved, Bergman explained in English the traumatic developments of the winter.

> The last three months I have been involved in a situation that could have been written by Kafka. . . . I felt I was going to lose my identity. It was terrifying, but I can't blame my country for some clumsy individuals in the administration. . . . I fell into a deep depression, the first real depression in my life, because I couldn't create."

De Laurentiis, who was setting up the production of *The Serpent's Egg*, had suggested that Bergman again give thought to a screen version of *The Merry Widow*. Bergman was enthusiastic, comparing it with *The Magic Flute*: "They are two branches on the same tree, and they are both very green, and the flowers are very beautiful. You have to be very careful with Lehar music—it's pure gold." But he probably knew that such a project was offered as a mere palliative for his present woes.

He put a good face on his circumstances. "What has happened to me has been a tremendously negative experience, but if you can change a negative thing to something positive, it can be very stimulating for your creative work. Today I am extremely grateful to the tax department."

The next few weeks brought home to Bergman the distasteful aspects of exile. Hotel rooms, airport lounges, an inability to settle. He found Paris too noisy and too chaotic for comfort. He and Ingrid visited New York, Berlin, Copenhagen, Oslo, and finally Munich in order to start shooting *The Serpent's Egg* at the Bavaria Film Studios.

> We lived at the Hilton for about six weeks, and I said to Ingrid, "Why not here?" Yes, let's try to find a place. And about the same time, I attended a performance of *Hamlet* at the Residenzteater. It wasn't a very good production, but in a way I liked it very much. I received a cable from the head of the theater, Kurt Meisel, inviting me to go there and meet him. We had a marvelous human contact with each other, and I felt I had to be connected with that theater.

So the Bergmans remained in Munich. They found an apartment in a modern block with a view of the Alps in the distance, furnished it in Scandinavian style, and immersed themselves in the life of the city. Munich, although associated in twentieth-century times with the birth of the Nazi movement and with the florid pronouncements of Franz Josef Strauss, is in many ways the most elegant and civilized of German cities. Its handsome streets and pale yellow buildings lend the central area a look of distinction that not even the encroachment of postwar office blocks can diminish. The Bavarians are friendly to visitors, although Bergman, in company with other foreigners whose orthodox German may be quite passable, found the dialect difficult to grasp.

Culture and its manifestations abound in Munich. The city has two operas, two symphony orchestras, some thirty theaters, and several museums. The weather may be mediocre, but the cultural climate is lively and varied. "What I miss so very much in Stockholm," said Bergman,

> is the fight about culture, the fight between life and death. I don't mind the critics here being very mean—I like it, it's fine; and the audience behaves, and all the time you have the feeling that you are getting reactions from that audience. They may be negative, they may be positive, but you always get reactions. Sometimes in Sweden you have the impression that nobody's there: people applaud politely, and after three curtain calls they disappear. But here they can be very, very mean, and react quite violently.

Swedish newspapers continued to comment on the Bergman exile. Bertil Bokstedt, head of the Swedish Opera, thought it "a disaster for Swedish cultural life," and he could speak with justification, for Bergman's production of *The Rake's Progress*, scheduled for a TV transmission on April 14, had been canceled. The public commissioner (*ombudsman*) considered the Bergman case and vindicated him with few reservations. The Royal Swedish attorney gave a public rebuke to the Stockholm public attorney. Olof Palme, then prime minister, announced that he regretted Bergman's departure and hoped he would return to the country soon. In a cover story in *Time* magazine (June 7, 1976), "Sweden's Surrealistic Socialism," Bergman was quoted as saying: "Security means a lot to us, and here we have made a great mistake. Everything must be in order. Everything must be in its own small box. There is something wrong in our way of handling these things. There is a lack of fantasy, a lack of human experience."

For the Social Democrats, the Bergman affair was catastrophic and could not be swept under the carpet. In the elections that September, they were excluded from office for the first time since 1932. So narrow was the defeat that many observers must be justified in believing that the scandal aroused by Bergman's persecution (and, to some extent, by Astrid Lindgren's attack on the taxation system) persuaded moderate Swedes that the welfare state had progressed beyond desirable limits and that the time had come for a change.

This sorry episode drew at last to a close on November 28, 1979, when Bergman's lawyer announced that the dispute with the government was over. The Supreme Administrative Court upheld a lower court ruling that Cinematograph need pay only 150,000 crowns in back taxes, or some 7 percent of the original demand. The Swedish government was called upon to cover the vast court costs that the case had entailed, amounting to almost 2 million crowns, or half a million dollars.

Long before that date, Bergman had returned to Sweden in all but name, spending summers on Fårö and meeting friends and associates in Stockholm. But the wounds inflicted on him by his arrest that winter morning in 1976 are visible in his work to this day.

As a welcome guest in West Germany, Bergman was at pains from the start to emphasize that *The Serpent's Egg* would not be a condemnation of the German people as such. "What happened to Germany during the war could have happened anywhere," he said. "It could have been the French or the Italians or the Swedes." And the more the project progressed, the more obvious it became that Bergman was denouncing the atmosphere of persecution and psychological sadism that was engendered by the authorities in Sweden and that had led to his self-imposed exile.

Disharmony reigns in all Bergman's films, but in *The Serpent's Egg* (*Das Schlangenei*) the pessimism is almost cosmic. It is no longer restricted to one family, or one couple. "Man is an abyss," wrote Georg Büchner, "and I turn giddy when I look down into it." Bergman sets this quotation at the head of his screenplay for *The Serpent's Egg*.

The film unfolds during a single week, November 3–11, 1923, an eight-day spell during which the value of the German mark dwindled virtually to nought, the Bavarian government seemed about to use armed force to eradicate communist elements in the south of the country, other provincial governments were preparing to resist possible fascist coups, and everywhere the Jews were being branded as both Marxists and the manipulators of international finance. Adolf Hitler, at the head of a tiny but vociferous National Socialist German Workers' Party, was laying plans for a *Putsch*. *The Serpent's Egg* concludes with the news of the failure of that attempt to seize power. "Herr Hitler and his gang underrated the strength of German democracy," says Inspector Bauer in the final line of the movie. Gustav Stresemann was to assume control of Germany in the months that followed, and the mark was restored to its former strength. But, as Ivo Jarosy has written, "like the structure of a house that has only survived an earthquake, the fabric of democratic society had been fatally weakened."

The city of Berlin has always fascinated Bergman. "Berlin exerted an almost demonic suggestiveness over me, due to an early collection of short stories about Berlin by Siegfried Siwertz. So Berlin wasn't the real Berlin at all, but a city of black destruction."[1] He was inspired by the awesome anonymity of the place to draft a screenplay in the fifties about a pair of acrobats who had lost their third partner and were trapped in a German city during the last phase of the war. "As the end approaches, their relationship gradually falls to pieces." But in a process of sea change, that screenplay developed into *The Silence*.

The sense of deracination is identical in both *The Silence* and *The Serpent's Egg*. The city appears as an alien moonscape; its huddled masses are cowed and shapeless, relating to the film's major personalities only on an elementary level. In *The Serpent's Egg*, Bergman exerted a tremendous effort to broaden the scope and depth of his drama. As a result, Abel and Manuela, the protagonists, are subservient to the social chaos surrounding them. In the end they are less sharply defined than the brutality and paranoia of the city as such.

The strain on Bergman must have been immense. In the wake of his departure from Sweden, he had to cope with the logistical problems attached to an international production, budgeted by Dino De Laurentiis

and Rialto Film of West Berlin at $3,266,000. It was the first time he
had shot a film outside his native country. Max von Sydow had been
mentioned as a probable star for the role of Abel, but Bergman had to
look elsewhere. Dustin Hoffman, Al Pacino, and George Segal were
all reputedly considered before Bergman decided on Richard Harris. But
Harris fell sick, and the part went finally to David Carradine, whose work
in *Bound for Glory* Bergman had much admired. Then there were some
three thousand extras to be supervised; a gigantic set by Rolf Zehetbauer,
recreating an entire block from the Berlin of the twenties; and a
shooting schedule of fifteen weeks. Apart from Sven Nykvist as
cinematographer and Liv Ullmann as Manuela, Bergman had to rely on
a new team of actors and technicians. And all the while he was
keeping in touch with his associates in Stockholm, giving advice and
instructions to Gunnel Lindblom, whose *Paradise Place* he was producing under the Cinematograph banner.

Zehetbauer's set lay at the heart of the production and absorbed a
large segment of the budget. Bergman and his colleagues had made
several trips to Berlin, searching for suitable streets in which to begin
filming. Then, quite by chance, Bergman was flicking through the pages
of an old issue of *Berliner Illustrierte* and found a picture of a curved,
bustling street. So Zehetbauer, who had won an Academy Award in
1972 for his production design on *Cabaret*, set to work.

A visitor to the Bavaria Studios in Munich spoke of the gas lamps at
the intersections of the cobbled street, the peeling posters, the no. 11
streetcar en route to the Oranienburg Gate, and the double-decker
Halensee bus. "Horse-drawn cabs and drays, Fords and aged Adlers
rumbled across the cobbles; along the sidewalks the people of old
Berlin—men in derbies and long coats, women in fox furs and seamed
stockings—shuffled earnestly past my archway toward destinations I
could not see."[2]

Another set on which Bergman lavished considerable attention was
the cabaret where Manuela sings. "It was a very interesting set to build,
from an architectural point of view," he said, "because one had to create
a feeling of desolation, misery, and mediocrity." Each new cabaret turn
describes the level to which love has been debased and contorted.[3]

Liv Ullmann visited various tatty nightclubs in West Berlin to give her
the mood of the cabaret sequences. She and the other actors were shown
documentaries from the twenties, as well as films like Phil Jutzi's *Mutter
Krausens Fahrt ins Gluck* (1929). Bergman himself pays homage to
Fritz Lang both covertly and overtly. At one point Inspector Bauer calls
up a colleague named Lohmann—the name of the police officer in *The
Testament of Dr. Mabuse*—and says that he is involved in a similarly

Rolf Zehetbauer's gigantic set for The Serpent's Egg. Photo courtesy Enterprise Pictures Ltd.

One of the cabaret scenes in The Serpent's Egg. Photo courtesy Enterprise Pictures Ltd.

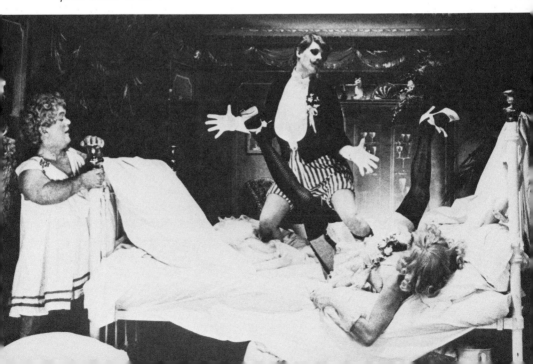

insane case. (Bauer himself bears the same name as Bergman's tax lawyer in Stockholm.)

Nevertheless, this elaborate iconography does not imply that Bergman was seeking to make a documentary on the Berlin of 1923. "I've simply tried to grasp the spirit of that period and the threatening atmosphere that prevailed."[4] The snow and rain, for example, that fell ceaselessly during that cold November week were reproduced not for the sake of verisimilitude but rather to accentuate the desolation of the characters' predicament.

The credit sequence affords the definitive clue to *The Serpent's Egg*. A crowd of people trudge in slow motion toward the camera, their gray faces jostling with one another's in the foreshortened perspective of Nykvist's telephoto lens; on the soundtrack there is an ominous silence, punctuated only by the syncopation of ragtime music as each credit card appears. Anguish and sensationalism, then, are the primary factors of the film to come.

Each stage of *The Serpent's Egg* traces the impact on Abel Rosenberg (David Carradine) of the all-pervasive despair that seems to rise from the very pavements and streets of the city. In the brilliant opening, Abel returns slightly drunk to his shabby boarding house, blunders by mistake into a lavatory, where a stout woman screams with indignation, and glimpses in another room a group of well-dressed men around a table singing lustily. He plods up to his quarters, opens the door, and is confronted by the corpse of his brother, Max.

Bergman uses a medium shot—almost a long shot—to register the shock of the dead man's shattered face; most other directors would have chosen a gruesome close-up. Offscreen, there is just the vague sound of the men singing downstairs. Bergman's technique was similarly dispassionate in *Winter Light*, when he viewed the fishermen's corpse from a distance. "It's good sometimes to jump back with the camera," he told Vilgot Sjöman, "and just stand far away and register."[5]

Abel is stunned. Like Borg after the initial nightmare in *Wild Strawberries*, or Albert after his recollection of Frost's debacle at the start of *The Naked Night*, he is reduced to a state of submission, a prey to the forces enveloping him. As his name intimates, Abel is "related" to the craven Jan Rosenberg of *Shame*, who also crumbles under pressure.

Once he has reported the suicide to the police, Abel finds himself sucked into a vortex of fear and intrigue from which there is no escape. Penniless, he is treated to a dinner by the circus promoter, Hollinger (Georg Hartmann), who reveals himself as a near-demented fascist. Tracking down Manuela (Liv Ullmann), Max's estranged wife, in the cabaret where she performs, Abel discusses the curious letter that the

dead man has left at his bedside: "There's poisoning going on here."
Strolling back through the dark streets, he witnesses the humiliation of
an innocent man at the hands of Neues Vaterland thugs. After a sleep-
less night in Manuela's apartment, he sees through the window a line of
people in the snow, waiting for a bakery to open at dawn. "It's like
waking up and finding that the reality is worse than the nightmare," he
says. The remark springs from Bergman's heart. The reality of his
interrogation at the hands of the tax authorities in 1976 exceeded his
nightmares.

Soon Abel is again in the hands of the police commissioner (Gert
Froebe), who drags him down to an infernal mortuary, where the
victims of a mysterious killer are laid out on slabs. Abel is not suspected
of being responsible for these murders, any more than Andreas is accused
of the bizarre outrages committed on the island in *The Passion of Anna,*
but their disclosure accelerates his giddy descent toward madness.
"Nothing works properly anymore," comments the commissioner,
"except fear."

Abel runs amok, is restrained and, after an interval, released. But he
has been contaminated by the terror and nihilism surrounding him. Like
Jacobi in *Shame,* he betrays his friend by stealing her money. Knowing that Manuela has earned it from prostitution salves his conscience.
But Abel's panic is petty and inchoate. He hurls a brick through a
shop window for no apparent reason other than the sight of his name
above the premises, and when a woman rushes out to protest, he seizes
her in a violent embrace, kissing her on the mouth until she almost
expires.

"Film as a medium is well suited to destructive acts, acts of violence,"
Bergman has remarked. "It's one of the cinema's perfectly legitimate
functions: to ritualize violence."[6] Bergman has bombarded Abel—and
the audience—with a succession of appalling incidents.

A protest march, shuffling forward to the dry sound of drumbeats.

Huge piles of garbage, infested with rats.

A raid by brownshirts on the cabaret where Manuela works, ending
with the Jewish manager having his face smashed almost to pulp.

The sight of horsemeat, warm and quivering, being offered for sale
(and Bergman, in one of the most devastating cuts of his career, follows
it with a shot of a frenzied crowd in a scarlet dance hall).

"The people in my films," he has admitted, "are exactly like myself—
creatures of instinct, of rather poor intellectual capacity, who at best
only think when they're talking. Mostly they're body, with a little hollow
for the soul."[7]

Eighteen years earlier, in *The Magician,* Bergman's alter ego engaged
in a titanic struggle with a Dr. Vergérus—and won, with his wagon

swinging away jauntily through the sunlit streets to the Royal Palace. It is a measure of Bergman's dejection in 1976 that Abel is seen not in a moment of triumph but in a prison infirmary, moving like a zombie. This time the victory belongs to Vergérus (Heinz Bennett). In *The Serpent's Egg* he is, like his predecessor in *The Magician*, suave and cynical behind his spectacles. He carries out his fiendish experiments on human beings in the bowels of the Saint Anne's Clinic, where he offers work to Abel and Manuela, trapping them effectively within its confines.

Vergérus is the only character in the film who fights against the overwhelming despair. This mad scientist both abhors and perpetrates the deviancy of Nazi ideology. Devoid of human sympathies, he yet has the prescience to describe the Nazi world to come. "Man is a misconstruction," he announces. "A perversity of nature. That is where our experiment comes in. . . . We deal with the basic construction and reshape it. . . . We exterminate what is inferior and increase what is useful." He confesses that the bodies discovered by Bauer and his men are those of victims of his laboratory. The future, he proclaims, is easy to see for anyone concerned to make the slightest effort.

"It's like a serpent's egg. Through the thin membranes you can clearly discern the already perfect reptile."

As the police thunder at the door, Vergérus bites on a cyanide pill. By this brilliant conceit, Bergman enables those two signal elements of fascism—theory and force—to collide in a kind of deranged dialectic.

The Serpent's Egg makes a visceral impact greater than any other Bergman film of the seventies. But there are flaws in the production that debilitate many sequences. The dubbing into English is far from perfect and deflects one's attention at crucial moments. The dialog sounds not so much false as unsubtle. The scene in the church, where Manuela goes to visit an American priest in a vain search for reassurance, smacks of Bergman's earlier spiritual debates and seems incongruous in the Berlin of 1923—and even more so in the seventies that Bergman is trying, however obliquely, to reflect. The cabaret sequences lack the bite and insolence required, and the brothel interlude, where a black customer fails to perform with two prostitutes, amounts to a rather frantic attempt to encapsulate the impotence of America.

Perhaps *The Serpent's Egg* could have been a great film had it been made prior to Bergman's departure from Sweden. Its crushing despair might have been couched in less garish and hysterical terms. Those conversant with the director's appalling personal situation can accept the *cri de coeur* that springs from *The Serpent's Egg*, but to spectators without that knowledge the film seems overheated, melodramatic, and occasionally turgid. Although it attracted a respectable number of people in West Germany, *The Serpent's Egg* was a resounding failure in the United States, France, Britain, and even Sweden. It soon became clear that the best the producers could hope for was an art-house success, which could never recoup the high budget of the film.

Fortunately, before *The Serpent's Egg* opened simultaneously in Stockholm, Paris, and New York, on October 28, 1977, Bergman had already shot his next film, *Autumn Sonata*, which was financed for the most part by an advance sale of rights to Lord Lew Grade and his American production colleague, Martin Starger. So the familiar caveat, "You're only as good as your last film," did not apply to Bergman as it would after *From the Life of the Marionettes*.

On Tuesday, September 20, 1977, at 10 A.M. precisely, Bergman began shooting *Autumn Sonata* (*Herbstsonat*) in the studios of Norsk Film in Oslo. He had formed his own company in Munich, Personafilm, and *Autumn Sonata* was presold throughout the world before a meter of film was in the can. The shooting occupied only forty days, but prior to that Bergman had been rehearsing for two weeks at the Swedish Film Institute—without too much publicity, as this was the first time since his exile that he had returned openly to mainland Sweden—with Ingrid Bergman and Liv Ullmann, whose parts as mother and daughter respectively bestride the film. The first script, according to Ingrid Bergman, would have run for four and a half hours had Bergman not removed large chunks of dialog during the rehearsal period.

The press played up the fact that the two Bergmans, *monstres sacrés* of the Swedish cinema, were working in tandem for the first time. For several years, Ingmar and Ingrid had promised each other that they would make a film together, and at Cannes in 1973, when she was president of the Jury, and Ingmar a rare guest on account of *Cries and Whispers*, she reminded him of his promise to write a story to feature her on screen.

Two years later he called her and suggested the idea of *Autumn Sonata*, with Ingrid to play the mother of Liv Ullmann. His advisers urged him to shoot the picture in English to ensure access to the widest international market. Ingrid demurred. "Your friends are completely wrong," she said. "I want to do it in Swedish."[8]

Ingrid Bergman was vindicated, for *Autumn Sonata* was welcomed almost with relief by Bergman's devotees as a return to his best chamber cinema, redolent of the Nordic *angst* that had seemed diffused on the vast canvas of *The Serpent's Egg*.

"Of course his reputation is formidable," said Ingrid Bergman.

I heard he was a beast, very temperamental, always yelling and
screaming, but he never raised his voice once to me. He was a
lamb. . . . And he listens to his actors; he's big enough to listen
to your ideas and if he likes them he'll use them. He's very
flexible and open, allowing his actors to feel they are creating
too, and are not just marionettes in his hands.[9]

She did not relish the long takes and the large close-ups but accepted
when Bergman explained their necessity. No one liked *Autumn Sonata*
more than Ingrid when it was finally edited.

For Bergman it was a pleasure to film again in Swedish (even if the
tax problems had led him to use the studios in Oslo). In Munich he
had read as many Swedish books as possible. "I love my national
language," he told an interviewer, "and, living so far from my native
country, I don't want to lose contact with things Swedish."

Only fifteen people were involved in the day-to-day shooting of
Autumn Sonata, in complete contrast to the huge crew Bergman had
orchestrated for *The Serpent's Egg* at Bavaria Studios. Two-thirds of
them were women; Bergman told Ingrid that he found them much more
efficient and less hysterical than men.

Autumn Sonata placed a particular burden on Ingrid Bergman
because she was being asked to play both herself *and* against her habitual
screen image. The figure of Charlotte, a world-renowned pianist, may
on the surface appear to be a replica of Käbi Laretei. But, in fact,
Charlotte's separation from her daughters must have reminded Ingrid
of her own difficulties in seeing Pia after she had left Petter Lindström
for Roberto Rossellini. Moreover, the essential problems of dealing with
celebrity and trying to maintain domestic relationships were familiar
to Ingrid Bergman.

On a technical level, she was surprised by the number of close-ups
Bergman demanded. "I'd been so long in the theater where you have to
play out to people up in the third balcony that I'd always been very big
in my gestures and my voice."[10] Close-ups have become more and more
predominant in Bergman's work in the past decade. Under this kind of
scrutiny, even the most carefully composed mask lets the true persona
leak out for an instant. "I would like once in my life to make a
120-minute picture with just one close-up," he told William Wolf. "I
think it's impossible, but I would love to do it once. To have the right
actor and to have the talent to accomplish this."

Autumn Sonata is held in a miraculous balance by the revelation of
these close-ups and by the stream of incisive, searching dialog. No action
whatsoever occurs, in the accepted sense of the word. Bergman is
audacious in his use of theatrical devices: for instance, he allows both

Viktor (Eva's husband, played by Halvar Björk) and Charlotte to address the camera with no other character within earshot, as though they were talking to a close friend, or even an interviewer. The camera remains static, "a stranger who has blundered at the worst posssible moment into the privacy of someone's life," as Vernon Young has written apropos of Bergman's style. "Fearful of attracting attention, it either tiptoes away to a discreet position, or simply freezes while the person intruded upon, all unknowing, exposes the torment or the absurdity he had hoped to conceal."[11]

Charlotte arrives at the parsonage where Eva lives with her husband, Viktor, and her catatonic sister, Helena (Lena Nyman). Mother and daughters have not seen one another for seven years. At first the mood is one of rejoicing, but Charlotte is no sooner settled in her guest room than she unburdens herself of the lingering agony of seeing her lover, Leonardo, die in hospital. Leonardo had accepted death with a grave nobility that almost exasperates Charlotte, pained though she is by his loss. Then, her grief flung aside like a coat, she shows off her new clothes to Eva.

The visit, however, is irrevocably clouded when Eva discloses that the handicapped Helena is living with her and Viktor in the parsonage. Charlotte's guilt and memories surge up like unwelcome guests. The imperfection of Helena would have marred the studied perfection of

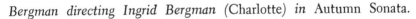

Bergman directing Ingrid Bergman (Charlotte) *in* Autumn Sonata.

Charlotte's career image, and so the child was discreetly installed in an institution. Eva was already something of an embarrassment, having exhibited intellectual tendencies, lived with a doctor for some years after graduating from university, and then married a minister.

The heart of the film, taken from this point on, consists of a running duel between Eva and her mother. The atmosphere is claustrophobic. Bergman applies his close-ups without mercy; occasionally the faces of Eva and Charlotte are crammed into the composition together, unable to evade each other's accusations; more often, one head alone fills the frame, betraying emotion, strain, and bitterness.

Autumn Sonata, and its central quarrel, are built on a series of revelations. Eva is startled by Charlotte's feelings at Leonardo's death. Charlotte reacts with shock to the news that Helena is under the same roof. The audience learns that Charlotte is easily seduced by money (she talks to herself about Leonardo's legacy in a Swiss bank, and when her agent calls after dinner she accepts an inconvenient engagement purely on account of the size of fee involved).

The richest surprises of all are contained in the sequence when mother and daughter play the Chopin A Minor Prelude. As Charlotte listens to Eva essaying the piece with worthy, conventional technique

Bergman rehearsing the "Chopin" sequence in Autumn Sonata, *with Ingrid Bergman* (Charlotte) *and Liv Ullmann* (Eva). *Photo courtesy Personafilm.*

but also a kind of stunted emotional intensity, she shrinks back with alarm and suspicion. She recognizes, perhaps, that had she spent time with Eva as a child she might have ironed out the flaws in her playing and allowed that emotion to flower in a more rewarding and fulfilling interpretation of life. By contrast, when Eva watches Charlotte embark on the prelude, she is amazed at her mother's capacity for feeling and recognizes that she has poured that feeling exclusively into her career and her music. *That* is where she was during Eva's lonely youth.

Charlotte's declaration about the meaning of the prelude, just before she plays it, houses words of great perspicacity and understanding, but Ingrid Bergman speaks the piece with just the right hint of condescension. She addresses Eva as a pupil rather than as a relative. She (and through her of course Bergman) remarks on Chopin's suppressed anguish, of how the music contains pain neither heightened nor diminished. "It must never become ingratiating. It *should* sound wrong. You have to battle your way through it, and emerge triumphant."

This is a singularly moving scene, one of the great anthology pieces of Bergman's cinema, if only because it shows with such aching accuracy the gulf between art and life. Charlotte comprehends the music to the last drop of feeling, yet she fails to read her daughter.

Gradually it becomes apparent that Eva is as retarded emotionally as her sister is physically. She may wax eloquent about the role of man, the significance of the adagio in Beethoven's Hammerklavier Sonata, and the fact that one lives in a world without limitations; but she has grown numb over the years. When they married, Viktor tells his mother-in-law, Eva conceded that she was incapable of loving him. She was happy only while expecting her first child, Erik. And then, in a cruel stroke of fate, he was drowned on his fourth birthday. Eva's very guise is a mask for her repressed pain: the old-fashioned spectacles, the plaited hair reminiscent of stern childhood routine, the downcast eyes, the disgruntled mouth. She wallows in her self-pity, while Charlotte thrusts such feelings aside whenever they threaten to invade her.

In the depths of the night, after Charlotte has been awakened by a nightmare, imagining that someone (Helena?) is stroking and embracing her in the darkness, the two women have their most incisive encounter. The eternal fissure between parent and daughter becomes an abyss of shame and despair. Yet, lacerating though the argument becomes, there is in Bergman himself a compassion for both characters. He told John Simon:

> I want very much to tell, to talk about, the wholeness inside every human being. It's a strange thing that every human being has a sort of dignity or wholeness in him, and out of that

develops relationships to other human beings, tensions, misunderstandings, tenderness, coming in contact, touching and
being touched, the cutting off of contact and what happens
then.[12]

Of course he must always lend his sympathy in the last resort to the
child rather than to the parent, because of his personal experience. "A
contact-seeking child," he wrote many years ago, "beset by fantasies, I
was quickly transformed into a hurt, cunning, and suspicious day-
dreamer."

Eva levels one accusation after another at her mother who, like David
in *Through a Glass Darkly*, finds that her role as a parent inhibits her
from fighting back. There is the specter of an affair, with a man named
Martin; Charlotte had left the family for some months to live with him
(the love of Bergman's own mother for someone outside her marriage
must have made an impact on the director in his formative years).
Charlotte was always too preoccupied with her music to talk to Eva.
Bergman illustrates this neatly in a flashback, ending with the small girl
drawing two massive, somber doors together as she leaves her mother in
peace. Charlotte "had taken charge of the words in our house. . . . Your
words didn't match the expression in your eyes." Only her father
continued to be kind and gentle to Eva, like the Viktor she chose to be
her husband in adult life.

Charlotte admits some of the guilt and recalls how an aged conductor
friend had told her she was leaving herself a target for so much
humiliation in neglecting her children. But Eva, flushed from the wine
she has been gulping, grows more and more hysterical in her castigation.
She was denied self-expression, she maintains, and in a paroxysm of
tears she accuses her mother of forcing her to have an abortion when she
became pregnant while still unmarried.

"You're a menace, you should be locked away so you can't do harm to
others," she exclaims.

Then, in a moment of calm after the storm, she reflects: "Is the
daughter's tragedy the mother's triumph? Is my grief . . . your secret
pleasure?"

And so Charlotte is permitted at last to deliver an apologia. She
confesses that she too has had to resort to something—music—outside
her family in order to express her emotions. She admits her own inability
to fix her mother's image, or that of Eva, or Helena. All she recalls of
the deliveries is that "they hurt." A sense of reality is just a matter of
talent, and most people do not have it, her lover Leonardo had told
her.

But Bergman allows her only a temporary respite. Helena has awoken and crawls from her room, calling for her mother in strangled, desperate tones. Eva blames her mother for the deterioration in Helena's condition and remembers how Leonardo, visiting Norway, had aroused in Helena a genuine love and admiration; but Charlotte, feeling threatened, had made Leonardo leave aburptly. "There can be no forgiveness," says Eva sternly, recalling the tone of Alman in *Wild Strawberries* as he passes judgment on Isak Borg in the forest glade. At this moment of climax, Bergman elides the anguish of Charlotte and Helena. Lurching toward the stairhead, Helena cries, "Mama—come!" just as Charlotte implores Eva with the words, "Help me!" Both phrases are uttered twice, like an incantation in some harrowing oratorio.

After her mother's departure, Eva recoils with misgiving. She strolls through the lakeside churchyard where her son, Erik, is buried. "I can't die now. I'm afraid to commit suicide, and one day maybe God will want to use me. And then he'll set me free of my prison." Her comfort is that Erik remains with her forever, stroking her cheek, and whispering in her ear.

Meanwhile, on the train bearing her southward, back to the protective custody of her career, Charlotte sits with her avuncular agent and one real friend, Paul, whom she looks to for justification. "The critics always say I'm a generous musician. No one plays Schumann's concerto with a warmer tone nor the big Brahms sonata. I'm not stingy with myself, or am I?" Soon she confesses to him that she does not really know what the concept of home means to her, and that she could not do without him. She turns away, with a sudden sense of foreboding, and stares into the dark void of the carriage window as it passes through a tunnel.

Eva writes one final letter to her mother, begging forgiveness for her outburst. First Viktor reads it to the camera and then Eva finishes it, speaking the sentences on a delicate note of hope and affirmation. Bergman intercuts this shot with a close-up of Charlotte, in an arbitrary declaration, as it were, of appeasement.

But what is said is said. Bergman's religious upbringing still urges him to effect a reconciliation between his warring characters, however deeply they wound each other, and even though no dialog on earth could ever convincingly eliminate their differences.

Far more important than this artificial degree of harmony is the sense of release experienced by Eva. At the very beginning of the film, her husband has quoted from one of her books: "My biggest obstacle is to know myself." And *Autumn Sonata* follows Eva's quest for identity. As she goes upstairs to answer the cry of Helena, her surrogate child, she has arrived at the maturity Viktor has mentioned in conversation earlier: "Being grown-up means being able to handle your dreams and hopes."

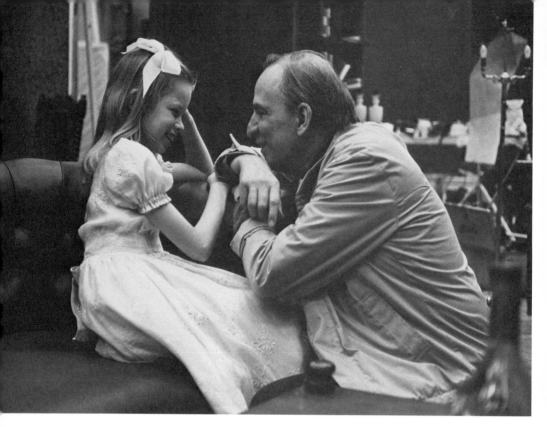

Bergman with his daughter by Liv Ullmann, Linn (playing Eva as a child), on the set of Autumn Sonata.

Perhaps the film would have been even cleaner in form had Bergman not included the character of Helena, who appears on most occasions as a mere living symbol of Eva's own incoherency and emotional paralysis. Perhaps Liv Ullmann's performance is too emphatic, too strident. But *Autumn Sonata* will endure as one of Bergman's most intimate, painful, and illuminating films, and Ingrid Bergman endows the role of Charlotte with a blend of hauteur and vulnerability that encourages the audience to forgive her the sins of which she is accused by Eva.

Käbi Laretei supervised the playing of the two actresses during the scene at the piano. "I stepped straight into the special atmosphere of intimacy and solidarity that is typical when Ingmar Bergman is shooting a film," she said. "There is joking and laughter and teasing and, all of a sudden, silence. There is tension and excitement in the air, and tremendous concentration emanating from each one of the team." Käbi played the Prelude twice, first as it would be performed "by a naive amateur with a stereotyped conception of Chopin," and then as a professional pianist would do it.

Behind the camera stood Sven Nykvist. To the left of it sat Ingmar giving the odd word of direction, almost inaudibly, to Liv. I crouched on the other side of the camera, telling Ingrid just as quietly when, for instance, both hands were to be still during a pause, when the left hand only was to play or when her eyes were to follow the movements of her hands on the keyboard.[13]

Bergman has always associated film with music among the arts. "Both affect our emotions directly, not via the intellect. And film is mainly rhythm; it is inhalation and exhalation in continuous sequence."[14]

At the Residenzteater in Munich, Bergman could relax and produce work of which he might be proud, even if the critics were sometimes hostile in their reaction to it. Kurt Meisel was the perfect foil and administrative boss for Bergman; an excellent actor himself, he radiated a calmness and sanity that touched everyone in the theater.

There were difficulties concerning the language, for Bergman found himself unable to communicate the nuances of his thought in German.

Suddenly you're in the rehearsal room in front of an actor from Austria or Germany, and although he may understand *A Dream Play* emotionally—you can't understand it any other way—you want to translate thoughts you have, and you realize you don't have the words at your command. You speak German fluently, but you cannot explain to these people what the meaning of *your idea* about the play actually is.[15]

A Dream Play, Bergman's first production in Munich, opened on May 19, 1977. It was the third time he had staged the Strindberg play, but, according to his own custom, he ignored his notes on previous approaches to it and started from scratch. "That's the most fascinating way to deal with a play," he said.

Just over a year later, on June 22, 1978, his production of Chekhov's *The Three Sisters* had its premiere at the Residenzteater. He had rehearsed the players for fifteen weeks. Less than a month later he flew back to Fårö to celebrate his sixtieth birthday. It was a massive reunion. All eight of Bergman's children assembled on the island; some were meeting each other for the first time in their lives. Then there were the four children of his present wife, Ingrid, by her former marriage. Bibi Andersson was also there.

At summer's end, Bergman returned to Stockholm to begin work on a production of Strindberg's *The Dance of Death*—that very production so harshly interrupted by the tax authorities two years earlier. But again it seemed doomed, for Anders Ek, Bergman's colleague from the forties on, collapsed with a fatal illness, and died not long afterwards. The enterprise was abandoned.

For the first time in the seventies, Bergman had seen a year elapse without his shooting a film. He spent the fall of 1978 preparing *Tartuffe* for its opening at the Residenzteater on January 13, 1979. The production, he told some American visitors, was consciously designed to emphasize the "ironic charm" of the play rather than its "blackness." He was concerned "not with the religious impostor who hoodwinks those around him, but rather with the nature of the absurd society— epitomized by Orgon's upside-down household—which allows such a creature as Tartuffe to flourish."[16]

Bergman weathered the fairly savage reviews that *Tartuffe* provoked and revived his production of *Hedda Gabler*, this time with Christine Buchegger in the name part. Mago's marvelous blood-red set again dominated the evening, and if the character of Hedda herself had changed at all, it was toward a greater composure and detachment from her fate. "Her husband," wrote Lise-Lone and Frederick J. Marker, "was an affable, middle-aged fool whom she treated with bored, impatient politeness and whose ceaseless pursuit of data from a dead and meaningless historical past epitomized the futility of her own situation."[17]

In Stockholm in July, Bergman's charming version of *Twelfth Night* was brought back to Dramaten, with Bibi Andersson once more the boyish Viola.

The crowds were huge and fervent. Ingmar Bergman was welcome in his own country again.

CHAPTER SIXTEEN

The Way Home

*I want to stop now. I want to go to the island. I want to stay
there and read the books I haven't written. To listen to music
and talk to my neighbors. To live together with my wife a very
calm, secure, very lazy life. It's a temptation to say: Now it's
enough, it's done, I want to stop, to go away, to retire.*[1]

IN THE DARK DAYS OF HIS EXILE, IN 1976, BERGMAN COULD CONTEMPLATE
abandoning Sweden: never Fårö. He closed down his studios on the
island but retained the house he had built a decade earlier. Not long
afterward, he resolved to make a new documentary about Fårö and its
people, and for two years, beginning in the fall of 1977, cameraman
Arne Carlsson and a sound engineer were put to work, recording everything within sight: "Work, salmon fishing, funerals, weddings, auctions,
christenings, home-guard maneuvers, shooting competitions, autumn
sowing, flounder fishing, the tourist invasion, the eternal caravan of
cars. . . . What we have filmed," said Bergman, "lasts for 28 hours but
will finally become a film of 1 hour 58 minutes."[2]

The island yields a certain type of human being; and the inhabitants
of Fårö dwell in a remarkable, inexplicable symbiosis with their environment. It is hard to imagine the place without the people. The rhythm
of life there appeals to Bergman. Above all, its simplicity. "When one
has had all the success, all the money, everything one has ever wanted,
ever striven for—power—the lot—then one discovers . . . its nothingness."
According to Bergman, "The only things that matter are the human

limitations one must try to overcome and one's relationships with other people."[3]

Bergman's 1979 tribute to Fårö is at once less ascetic and more optimistic than its predecessor. Some of the 673 people who live and work on the island have left since 1969, but the young no longer deny their birthplace. Bergman traces a calendar year as it elapses on Fårö: the lambing, the shearing, the thatching, the slaughter of sheep and pigs, a funeral, and eternally the fishing smacks plying their trade in the waters of the Baltic. A fatalism imbues these frugal people, a quality exemplified to haunting effect in Walter, the solitary, self-sufficient farmer who cooks a meal for himself with all the solemn ritual of a priest preparing the communion.

The Swedish critics welcomed the unpretentious message of the film. "Bergman probably agrees—between cries and whispers—with the poet Kleist," wrote Jürgen Schildt in *Aftonbladet*, "that the most fundamental need in our existence is quite simply 'to till the land, plant a tree, father a child.'" For Marianne Zetterström, in the woman's weekly *Veckojournalen*, the documentary breathed "a tender, passionate love over land and sea, on forest and stone, and not least on the people who live there, all-the-year-round people, for he looks a little askance at the tourists."

Bergman told William Wolf that in some degree the film "was a medicine, a remedy, coming back here."[4]

Perhaps the most mysterious properties of Fårö emerge more forcefully from Bergman's feature films than from this admirable, if all too earthbound, documentary. The rock formations that rose from the Silurian Sea over three hundred million years ago seem to watch over the characters in *Through a Glass Darkly*, *Persona*, and *Shame*. "When the sea is silent, it is very strange," claims Bergman. "But it is never frightening." To a visitor, however, he admitted that he knew fear just once, in the mid-seventies. "One night when there was a strange light to the sky, I had this horrible feeling that something was going to happen. And the next morning they found two fishermen had drowned just here."

Bergman spent the entire summer and early fall of 1979 on Fårö, following a hallowed routine, doing the same things at the same time each day—being, by his own admission, just lazy. Bergman is living proof of the axiom that only a truly efficient person can be truly lazy.

The screenplay for *Fanny and Alexander* was written during that summer.

Just as *Persona* emerged from the abortive screenplay known as *The Cannibals*, so *From the Life of the Marionettes* (*Aus dem Leben der*

Marionetten), which Bergman began shooting in October 1979, developed from the remains of a massive script (*Love without Lovers*) in which the characters of Peter and Katarina from *Scenes from a Marriage* figured prominently: "The film foundered," says Bergman in his introduction to *From the Life of the Marionettes*, "but the two refused to go to the bottom with the rest of the wreckage. They kept stubbornly recurring in my plans."[5]

The film hinges on a particularly violent, squalid incident. A Munich businessman, Peter Egermann (Robert Atzorn), murders and then rapes a prostitute. The victim is known simply as Ka (Rita Russek), short for Katarina—which also happens to be the name of Egermann's wife (Christine Buchegger). In his dreams, Peter Egermann has imagined himself killing his wife, and now, in a brief, horrible moment, the savagery of the dream invades his conscious state. The opening sequence, describing the murder, assaults the audience with its garish colors and flashing, pulsating lights in the prostitute's boudoir. Then, as the scene ends, Bergman reverts to black-and-white cinematography—to the austerity in which his characters have so often been immured and against which they struggle to assert their true desires. "I have a strange feeling," Bergman had remarked a decade earlier, "that the black-and-white silent picture will come back—because it forces the audience to use its imagination, and I am a fervent believer in the human imagination. We have become lazy because color, stereophonic sound, wide screen, leave nothing to our imagination."[6]

Only in the concluding sequence does the color return, showing Peter in an asylum cell, playing with a chess computer and then, in a listless gesture reminiscent of Abel at the end of *The Serpent's Egg*, reaching his hand up to the barred window. The Bergman alter ego finds himself thus totally emasculated, deprived of resistance. As another character has commented earlier, Peter Egermann is dying emotionally, as some people die of hunger and thirst.

Although *Marionettes* contains thematic links with *Scenes from a Marriage*, the new film does not permit its audience the reassurance of watching an everyday reality. *Marionettes* bores deep into the infernal regions of the subconscious. The structure appears rigid, for the film is recounted with the even temper of an autopsy; but overshadowing every sequence lies the threat of what Strindberg termed *Makten* (the Powers). Even the investigating psychiatrist, Professor Mogens Jensen (Martin Benrath), reveals himself in as vulnerable a light as the Judge in *The Ritual*. Each character is at the mercy of another.

Jensen seeks to peel away the various layers of fear and dissimulation that mask the motives for Peter's crime. Like a perverse nest of Chinese boxes, however, the crime refuses to divulge its secret heart. One learns

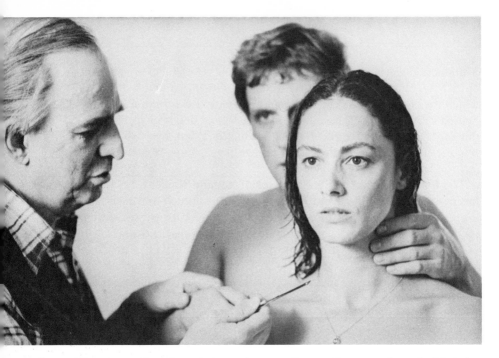

Bergman directing Robert Atzorn (Peter Egermann) *and Christine Buchegger* (Katarina Egermann) *in* From the Life of the Marionettes. *Photo courtesy ITC International.*

that Ka is a surrogate victim in place of Katarina Egermann; that in childhood Peter developed as a sensitive plant (his mother describes it in words that summon up Bergman's own early years); and that Peter has been more and more troubled by nightmares. In the final analysis, though, "all roads are closed." The psychiatrist's closing summary of the case is too glib, like his counterpart's at the end of Hitchcock's *Psycho.* Bergman almost invites us to reject his "preliminary report." The human being remains too complex, too elusive a creature to be classified by the medical profession. No one can share his dreams—his phantoms. Just as Alma discloses her own personality rather than un- covering that of her patient in *Persona,* so Jensen bares more of him- self than his analysis does of Peter Egermann.

Humiliation governs this film, touching each character in turn. There is no doubt that, for Bergman, *Marionettes* approximates to an act of revenge against the tormentors who provoked his exile from Sweden. Conversations are couched in the manner of an interrogation. Bergman notes that human beings are constantly manipulated, as much by forces outside their control as by their fellow creatures. Education and society are just two such forces.

Katarina, ostensibly the most assured and balanced of the characters, admits to being bound up with her husband's fate. "Neither of us wants to grow up," she says. "That's why we fight and quarrel and cry our eyes out. Neither of us wants to be wise and mature. But we have the same circulation, our nerve centers have grown together in some awful way." And yet they appear divided, unable to "see" each other in spite of their proximity. Katarina runs a fashion salon in the city (Bergman shows the mannequins parading in slow motion, as if to emphasize their malleability), but fear of the future dominates her attitude.

> There is something *menacing* going on which we don't speak about because we have no words. . . . Why don't we stop hoping for all kinds of political wonders, although we hear the roar getting louder and know that the catastrophe is approaching? Why don't we shatter a society that is so dead, so inhuman, so crazy, so humiliating, so poisoned?

She turns to drink and cigarettes, but nothing can banish her inner loneliness. "I speak, answer, think, get dressed, sleep, and eat—it's a daily compulsion, a hard, peculiar surface," she tells her mother-in-law. "But underneath that surface I'm crying all the time."

Peter's mother resembles the old lady in *Wild Strawberries*. As Katarina arrives, an ancient retainer opens the forbidding gates. The house breathes the air of a mausoleum. The mother speaks to Katarina of her solitude, her guilt and shame for what Peter has committed. She looks like a senior version of Katarina, a projection of Katarina in thirty years' time—self-centered, much wounded by life, wary, drained of warmth and hope. Through her, Bergman exorcises some of the debt he owes to the past, acknowledging his rejection of both his parents and their type of relationship.

The most sympathetic figure in the film is Tim (Walter Schmidinger), a Jewish homosexual whose inferiority complexes allied to a refined intelligence and articulacy produce one of the finest soliloquies in Bergman's work. Entertaining Katarina in his elaborate, fastidious apartment, he gazes into the mirror and traces the lines of incipient age in his face, kneading and squeezing the flesh as though it were a mask that might somehow be detached.

> I shut my eyes and feel like a ten-year-old—I mean my body too. Then I open them and look in the mirror and there stands a little old man. . . .
>
> I bend forward to the mirror and gaze into my face, which is more or less familiar to me, and see that right inside that combination of blood and flesh and nerves and bone are two incompatibles. . . . The dream of nearness, tenderness, fellow-

ship, self-forgetfulness—everything that is alive. And on the
other side—violence, filthiness, horror, the threat of death.

Tim, shocking in his vulnerability, sympathetic in his self-loathing, expresses an ardor beyond the range of the other characters. He confesses
to the investigator that he introduced Egermann to the prostitute
as a means of detaching him from his wife and bringing him within
reach of his own craving. "I saw the awful lovelessness of his marriage and was obsessed by the thought that he would turn to me, that
at last he would discover me, that he would realize I loved him
deeply."

Once again, then, Bergman has the courage to confront and discuss
his own deepest feelings of sexual ambivalence. Not for nothing does
he admire Fassbinder for using the cinema to flirt with his own pro-
clivities. In every artist there exists to some degree that exquisite sensitivity habitually associated with the homosexual temperament. The need
for nearness to another human being; conversely, the need also for
infidelity.

And Peter Egermann himself, at the epicenter of this convulsive
drama? What of him?

"I'm tired." These are his first words, addressed to the prostitute, who
tells him he needs to sleep and takes him into her room, brightly lit
and furnished in appalling taste. As he murders her and has anal
intercourse with his victim, Peter may be viewed as nothing more than a
particularly ruthless psychopath. The rest of the film adds up to a testi-
mony on his behalf, not justifying his outrage but explaining how the
violence that inhabited his dreams—that inhabits everyone's dreams—
breaks like an avalanche over his waking experience. Peter admits to his
psychiatrist, Professor Jensen, that for two years he has harbored a desire
to kill his wife; he even describes in detail how he imagines himself
slitting her throat with a razor.

The professor, however, betrays Peter. He invites his patient's wife,
Katarina, to his consulting rooms immediately after the meeting with
Peter and proposes first that she accompany him on vacation and then
that they have sex right there in his office. Meanwhile, Peter lurks, a
watcher in the shadows, having hidden behind the door in order to
spy on the proceedings.

So, like Isak Borg in *Wild Strawberries*, Peter Egermann observes his
wife's dalliance with another man. The humiliation is palpable, if also
theatrical. But Peter should be reassured, for Katarina rejects the psychiatrist's advances. Her love for Peter, insufferable though he may be,
is too strong, even after ten years of marriage. Doubtless Katarina's
"loyalty" to Peter corresponds to a mother's devotion to her son; and

Peter's petulance resembles a child's revolt against the authority of his parents.

Yet the screenplay fails to penetrate the innermost recesses of Peter's mind, as it does the old professor's in *Wild Strawberries*. One sees him prowling through the apartment at dead of night, sharing a drink with Katarina who awakes at the same time; one hears him reacting with fairly justified annoyance to Katarina's procrastination when the couple is due for a luncheon appointment; one listens to him dictating an interminable business memorandum to his secretary. One watches as he outlines a dream in which he lies side by side with Katarina in a white, enclosed space, the implication being that in his dreams he is alive and in the conscious world he is—dead. One sympathizes with Peter in the long argument he has with his wife in front of their friend Arthur, following Peter's pathetic threat of committing suicide. But does one actually share these moods and actions?

If *Marionettes*, for all its intensity of feeling (and it cost Bergman "blood, sweat, and tears"[7]), fails to touch the sentiments and imagination of a wide audience, the character of Peter may be to blame. Robert Atzorn, an excellent stage actor, appears too wooden, too limited in his expressiveness. His performance is somnolent, lethargic, drained of passion. Only in his brief conversation with the prostitute does he sound natural, as though he were aware of his destiny and reconciled to it. Touched by Ka's humanity, he makes one final effort to evade his nightmare; but the doors to the nightclub are locked. "All roads are closed": He must strangle Ka/Katarina.

For the first time in many years, Bergman has used fantasy sequences to illustrate the phantoms that consume his characters. Bleached bodies seen from a distant height, his facing up, hers down, as though each were a half of the same person; a razor applied to a snow-white throat, the blood spilled in words but not in pictures. Such images are all the more disturbing for occurring in the midst of a dour, unemotional inquiry, as in *Ritual*, with its gray, neutral backgrounds and its low-key acting.

Bergman finished shooting *From the Life of the Marionettes* just before Christmas and, after a brief rest over the holidays, began the editing process. The Austrian actress Christine Buchegger (Katarina) played the lead in various Bergman stage productions in Munich, including *Hedda Gabler*, and the other parts were assigned to members of the Residenzteater company. "Most of the actors had never seen a camera," said Bergman, "and it was very stimulating to teach them the fascination of film acting." The crew was small, about the same size as Bergman had been accustomed to working with in Sweden.

In March 1980, Bergman began rehearsals at the Residenzteater for *Yvonne, Princess of Burgundy,* by the Polish author Witold Gombrowicz.

Bergman's appointment as president of the Jury at Cannes had been announced with characteristically premature zeal by the authorities of the French film festival. "I had the feeling," said Bergman in February, "that perhaps after the disaster of last year, when Françoise Sagan was president [and had subsequently complained about venal pressures on the Jury], and the scandals after the awards, I had the feeling that with some small changes in the regulations, and with a very tough president, the honor and absolute integrity of the Cannes Jury could be restored. My experience is that the prizes in Cannes can be very important for certain films."[8] Accommodations were set aside for Bergman at the luxurious resort of Cap d'Antibes, but in April he resigned. The festival had doubtless refused to amend the rules as he had suggested. Kirk Douglas assumed the presidency. So Cannes proceeded in its serene, purblind fashion.

Marionettes did not reap the box-office rewards that Lord Grade and his production arm, ITC, had anticipated. Even in Paris, some respectable opening figures were unable to conceal the failure. In the United States, the picture met with somewhat dismissive notices and flopped. In Sweden, the average attendance at each theater on the film's first run was a mere sixty-four persons. In Malmö, only twelve tickets were sold at one performance.[9] *Winter Light* and *Shame* had met a similar fate. Like them, *Marionettes* makes no compromise toward the public demand for action and entertainment, in spite of the gruesome murder at the beginning.

Bergman has always refused to promote his own films outside Sweden. Interviews are rarely given, and Bergman reacts with anger and disappointment when a distributor seeks to exploit his presence for the purposes of promoting one of his productions. He had agreed, for example, to lead a delegation of Scandinavian film personalities to the United States in the fall of 1980, coinciding with a special week at the Museum of Modern Art and further tributes (to the contemporary Nordic cinema in general as much as to Bergman himself) at the Chicago Festival and in Los Angeles.

At the very last moment, Bergman cabled his regrets at being unable to attend the various functions that had been arranged. Word had reached him that *Marionettes* would open a few days after his scheduled arrival and that AFD had chosen such a release pattern in order to capitalize on the interviews and publicity accruing from Bergman's appearance. "I was not informed," Bergman announced, "that there was this tie-in of my film and my presence in the United States. It has long been my policy not to participate, directly or indirectly, in the promotion of my films."[10]

Nevertheless, Bergman's profound shyness at facing the press and the public probably influenced his decision. The number of invitations he has at first, from courtesy, accepted, and then canceled, is legion. The humiliation, the manipulation of the artist, has developed into an ordeal that goes well beyond the borders of Bergman's own films.

Even before his contract with the Residenzteater expired in 1982, Bergman had begun spending more and more time in Sweden, less and less in Munich. Fårö has become once again a solid base for him and his wife. There are signs that the torrent of his activity is starting to abate. *Fanny and Alexander* went into production in September 1981, almost two years after *Marionettes* began shooting in West Germany. On the stage, the 1980–1981 season was marked by just one startling achievement, the staging of a triptych: Ibsen's *A Doll House*, Strindberg's *Miss Julie*, and a theatrical version of Bergman's own *Scenes from a Marriage*. The Ibsen and Strindberg followed each other with barely a half-hour's interval in Munich's Residenzteater, while *Scenes from a Marriage* was performed in the little annex, Theater im Marstall. Spectators in this small auditorium were surprised to find that the interviewer who addresses Johan and Marianne at the beginning of *Scenes* did so from among the audience itself. Much abbreviated from its original length of some hours, Bergman's vision of the sex war had a lightness lacking in its Swedish original, thanks in part to the effervescent performance of Gaby Dohm as Marianne. Åke Janzon in *Svenska Dagbladet* spoke of the almost spectral opening of *A Doll's House*, with Nora seated on a gigantic neo-rococo sofa, "an image of comfortable yet unconscious imprisonment." Robert Atzorn, thought Janzon, was the most natural Helmer he had ever seen; Rita Russek, the prostitute in *From the Life of the Marionettes*, played Nora. Bergman treated the famous closing scene of the play with astonishing audacity. Nora "rises up like a phoenix from the marital bed. Torvald awakens and sees to his amazement his wife dressed for travel."[11]

Miss Julie, featuring a classical Swedish set by Gunilla Palmstierna, was the most realistically staged of the three plays, and Janzon saw Michael Degen's Jean, the groom, as a marionette at the mercy of women and of life in general.

The effort required to mount three such productions all at once must have been enormous and explains why Bergman had done little else in the preceding months.

———

Fanny and Alexander amounts to a kind of climax in the career of Ingmar Bergman—a fairy tale that has cost $6 million and contains some sixty speaking parts, plus around 1,200 extras.

A fairy tale that proved more difficult to finance than any previous Bergman film. Disenchanted with *From the Life of the Marionettes,* and appalled by Bergman's insistence on a TV version of some 5 hours and a theatrical version running to 2 hours 45 minutes, Lew Grade and his financiers withdrew their initial interest in the project. Jörn Donner, at that time managing director of the Swedish Film Institute, read the screenplay, liked it, and told Bergman that if he proceeded with his plans to make the film in Sweden, in Swedish, then the cash would somehow be raised.

And it was. The bulk of the budget was covered by the Swedish Film Institute, Gaumont in Paris, and West German television (ZDF in Mainz).

"It has been suggested," said Bergman at a press conference in November 1980,

> that *Fanny and Alexander* is autobiographical, that it portrays my childhood, and that twelve-year-old Alexander is my alter ego.
>
> But this is not quite true. *Fanny and Alexander* is a story, the chronicle of a middle-class, perhaps upper middle-class family, sticking closely together and set in a medium-sized Swedish town in 1910. The materfamilias is the paternal grandmother with three married sons who in their turn have children. The film shows a little over a year of their lives.
>
> It is, as I see it, a huge tapestry filled with masses of color and people, houses and forests, mysterious haunts of caves and grottoes, secrets and night skies.

Fanny and Alexander mingles elements of comedy, tragedy, farce, and horror. "It's not so much a chronicle," says Bergman on reflection towards the close of the shooting, "as a Gobelin in tapestry, from which you can pick the images and the incidents and the characters that fascinate you." The film was conceived as Bergman pondered a comment from his friend Kjell Grede, the director of *Hugo and Josephine.* Why, asked Grede, when Bergman so obviously loved life and found parts of it so amusing, did he consistently produce gloomy and depressing movies?

Fanny and Alexander encompasses both business and the arts. Oscar Ekdahl was sufficiently wealthy at the end of the nineteenth century to purchase the theater in the university town (patently Uppsala) where he lived with his actress wife, Helena Mandelbaum (Gunn Wållgren). But on his death Helena confides the management of the theater to her

Bergman with Bertil Guve (Alexander) *on the set of* Fanny and Alexander. *Photo courtesy Svensk Filmindustri.*

eldest son, Oscar (Allan Edwall), and his wife Emilie—she too an actress. This key role is played by Ewa Fröling, regarded by many as the most gifted young actress in Sweden today. Oscar suffers a stroke during a rehearsal of *Hamlet* (in which he has been playing, grudgingly and appropriately, the ghost), and Emilie falls victim in her widowhood to the charms of the local bishop (Jan Malmsjö). The life of the family undergoes a dramatic change; the Bishop's ways are harsh, and his house is damp and inhospitable. Eventually, with the help of a merchant friend, Isak Jacobi (Erland Josephson), Emilie's children—Fanny (Pernilla Allwin) and Alexander (Bertil Guve)—are delivered from this virtual prison, while Emilie herself turns a blind eye to the Bishop's "accidental" immolation in a pile of blazing bedclothes.

"There's a lot of me in the bishop, rather than in Alexander," concedes Bergman cheerfully. "He's haunted by his own devils." Fanny may be modelled on Bergman's younger sister, Margareta, who shared his incipient love of puppet theatre and silent movies.

Though weary by the end of six months' shooting, Bergman relished *Fanny and Alexander.* He was once again able to direct in his native tongue, and he was ogled and applauded like royalty whenever he appeared on location in Uppsala, where several major sequences were shot. Bertil Guve, his choice to play Alexander, was just eleven years of age, but proved a resilient and natural performer. The film's vast list of credits contained various Bergmans—Anna, Ingmar's daughter, as the ingenue Hanna Schwartz; Mats, his son, as Aron; Käbi Laretei, his fourth wife, as Aunt Anna; Daniel, their son, as grip; and his present wife, Ingrid, as an invaluable solvent of production problems.

There was but one frustration: in January, 1982, Bergman caught influenza, and for several days was confined to his quarters. Peter Schildt, the assistant director, had to film a massive funeral cortege through Uppsala—and by all accounts acquitted himself with agility and resourcefulness. For Bergman the interruption was exasperating, for he attends to the tiniest detail of production. Even the temperature in the sound stages of the Swedish Film Institute were kept at the level Bergman regards as ideal—64° Fahrenheit—for technicians and players alike to work in. Sven Nykvist remarks that in Hollywood, such scenes as a procession of flagellants (one of the fantasies imagined by Alexander as he listens to old Isak Jacobi) would require up to fifteen takes. "With Ingmar, two or three, and it's in the can."

Bergman claims that *Fanny and Alexander* will be his last Swedish film. He may be tempted to embark on some TV plays, and perhaps on the screen version of a great opera. "But now I prefer to leave film-making to younger people," he muses. "I need too much energy. Besides," he adds with a laugh, "it can never be more fun than it is right now!"

From his earliest days as a director, Bergman grasped the essentials of film technology. He felt as much at home in the laboratory as he did on the set. He loves the editing process, and nothing more than the moment when, in creating a dissolve between shots, *both* pictures lie double *in each other* for thirty frames.[12] "Film is above all else concerned with rhythm. The primary factor is the image; the secondary factor the dialog; and the tension between these two creates the third dimension."[13]

On the set, Bergman tries if possible to shoot his scenes in chrono-logical order. "I always reshoot the first day's work," he says.[14] In the broadest sense of the term, improvisation plays a major role in his strategy. Actors are not allowed to ramble on, Cassavetes-fashion, until the camera runs out of film, but nothing is specified too rigidly in advance. A study of Bergman's published screenplays shows that incidents and movements within a scene are subject to change as frequently as lines of dialog. Some scripts (for example, *The Touch* and *Cries and Whispers*) are more evocative than precise. Close-ups are never indicated, even though they constitute one of the director's favorite means of expression. Bergman prepares each scene well in advance. Often he makes a sketch of it, asking himself where the camera should be placed. "He allows technical rehearsals," says Liv Ullmann, "but then he likes to take on the first emotional reading, because sometimes that is the best take."[15]

"He is courageous enough to follow his own intuition," according to Käbi Laretei, "and nothing can change his mind. He's one of those rare people who really *believes* in his intuition."[16] Bergman himself told an interviewer ten years ago: "My impulse has nothing to do with intellect or symbolism; it has only to do with dreams and longing, with hope and desire, with passion."[17]

Bergman has his detractors.

His rigid, some would say inflexible, view of the world leads to a certain repetition of themes, doubts, and aspirations. The unremitting obsession with death and betrayal, belief and disillusionment, produced in the fifties and sixties a style ripe for parody, as the American directors, Davis and Coe, achieved so beautifully in their short film, *The Dove* (showing Death playing badminton and an old man speculating on life while emerging from an outdoor privy). Bergman cannot be accused of religious sentimentality, but many of his characters suffer from a self-pity that becomes tiresome and overweening. The men in his films are rarely lit by any kind of enduring virtue. Sterile more often than not, they appear damned by the director from the outset. Abortion in Bergman's world still carries a sense of sin, turpitude even. The contradiction, as Denis Marion has pointed out, is that if human beings are led inexorably to unhappiness in this life, and if no hereafter exists, why give birth to future unfortunate creatures?[18]

Humor, in spite of the epigrammatic dialog in films such as *A Lesson in Love* and *Smiles of a Summer Night*, does not burst easily through the brooding pessimism of Bergman's cinema. At certain moments, the spectator may be forgiven for sighing with intolerance at the dismal, stolid attitudes of many characters in the Bergman *oeuvre*. When Bergman does try to present a scene free of psychological tensions, the result can be disastrous—for instance, the meeting on the ferry between Jan, Eva, and the Major and his wife at the beginning of *Shame*. Smiles, lines, and gestures: All are theatrical and unconvincing.

Dilys Powell, long a candid critic of Bergman's films, picked with some persuasion on the comment that he made about wanting to be like one of the unknown builders of Chartres Cathedral. "He has often deplored the passing of an age," she wrote, "when artists were anonymous. One might, then, have looked for self-effacement in his work."[19]

Bo Widerberg, who was just starting a career that would include *Raven's End* and *Elvira Madigan*, attacked Bergman in a polemical booklet in 1962, condemning him for a "vertical," metaphysical vision of human problems, dealing merely with man's relationship to God. And it is undeniable that Bergman is rarely engaged by political problems of his time. If the society he evokes in his postwar films is maladjusted, it is maladjusted in a spiritual rather than any socioeconomic sense. Yet *Shame* may outlast many a noisome war movie, and *Scenes from a Marriage* may have influenced more couples than any number of pious TV documentaries on divorce. The particular truth, in Bergman's work, becomes by some magic formula the universal truth.

Bergman has been accused of a certain detachment. His films radiate compassion, however, because they pity human beings. Man has the instincts and the body of an animal, yet he still cherishes the unconquerable hope. He is embittered by the gift of reason that fate has somehow forced upon him. Bergman's characters seek always to extend their range of experience, as if eager to cram as much into life as possible. In the absence of the Christian God, they are confronted with a loss of identity. For Bergman, the lapsed Christian who cannot quite dispense with Christian idiom, the difficulty lies in finding some compensation for the apparent lack of purpose in life. Against the encroaching darkness, love forms a fragile shield. Art no longer serves as either protection or justification. In the fifties, Bergman described the artist as a martyr to the cause of lost faith. Since then, his "artists" have been discredited, even cowardly, figures, reluctant to assume responsibility for the affairs of the world.

The concern with the human soul, the puritanism and sense of sin that colors even Bergman's most lissome work, belongs to the Nordic temperament. Given the historical and religious background from which Bergman has sprung, one can scarcely blame him for dwelling on matters of guilt and expiation, any more than one can take Fellini to task for his Latin insistence on the lewd and the grotesque, or reproach Renoir for the casual, even frivolous, Gallic grace of his films.

Bergman's most abiding virtue is the personal quality of his filmmaking. It is this that strikes a chord of identification in audiences the world over; people recognize in Bergman's straitened characters some replica of themselves. No film director with the exception of Rainer Werner Fassbinder has been at once so prolific and spurred by the need to bare his sores on screen. Bergman has never pretended to possess an answer to the problems of human existence. He neither denies nor affirms the Christian tradition in which he was so sternly educated.

Instead he probes, he interrogates.

Hearing the weeping of the wind during the fade-outs in *Cries and Whispers*, one senses the terrible loneliness that lurks at the heart of

Bergman's labyrinth. His protagonists stumble through the night, their path lit by the occasional charmed space:

The romance on the island in *Summer Interlude*.

The milk and strawberries on the hillside in *The Seventh Seal*.

The sorting of the mushrooms in *Persona*.

The meal outside the cottage in *Shame*.

The sisters' stroll through the park in *Cries and Whispers*.

Jenny's final meeting with her grandparents in *Face to Face*.

The dream that Peter Egermann describes in his letter to the psychiatrist in *From the Life of the Marionettes*.

And yet just as the journey matters more than the arrival, so the yearning for such moments means more than their possession. For the yearning provokes spiritual pain, and in that pain the cinema of Ingmar Bergman is somehow forged, tempered, and shaped with neither compromise nor regret.

Notes

Uncredited quotations from Ingmar Bergman are taken from interviews between him and the author conducted at various times between 1969 and 1982.

CHAPTER 1

1. Margareta Bergman, *Karin vid havet* (Stockholm: Raben & Sjögren, 1980). English translation by Paul Britten Austin.
2. Ingmar Bergman, *Bergman on Bergman*, ed. Stig Björkman, Torsten Manns, and Jonas Sima, trans. Paul Britten Austin (New York: Simon & Schuster, 1973).
3. Ingmar Bergman, *Four Screenplays of Ingmar Bergman*, trans. Lars Malmström and David Kushner (New York: Simon & Schuster, 1960).
4. Ingmar Bergman, "Self-Analysis of a Film-Maker," *Films and Filming* (London) (September 1956).
5. Jörn Donner, *Three Scenes with Ingmar Bergman* (Documentary film, 1975).
6. Bergman, "Self-Analysis of a Film-Maker."
7. Donner, *Three Scenes with Ingmar Bergman.*
8. Ingmar Bergman, "The Snakeskin," *Sight and Sound* (London) (Autumn 1965).
9. *Bergman on Bergman.*
10. Ibid.
11. Donner, *Three Scenes with Ingmar Bergman.*
12. Birgitta Steene, "Words and Whisperings: An Interview with Ingmar Bergman," in *Focus on the Seventh Seal* (Englewood Cliffs, N.J.: Prentice-Hall, 1972).
13. Henrik Sjögren, *Ingmar Bergman på teatern* (Stockholm: Almqvist och Wiksell, 1968).
14. *Bergman on Bergman.*

CHAPTER 2

1. Carl Anders Dymling, "A Preface by Ingmar Bergman's Producer, Carl Anders Dymling," in *Four Screenplays*.
2. Quoted in *Theater* (New Haven) 11, no. 1 (Fall 1979).
3. Quoted in *Nutid* (Stockholm) no. 16 (1955).
4. Author's interview with Erland Josephson in Stockholm, November 1979.
5. Author's interview with Gunnar Fischer in Stockholm, November 1979.
6. *Bergman on Bergman*.
7. Birgitta Steene, *Ingmar Bergman* (New York: Twayne, 1968).
8. Quoted in *Theater* (New Haven) 11, no. 1 (Fall 1979).
9. Henrik Sjögren, *Stage and Society in Sweden* (Stockholm: Swedish Institute, 1979).
10. Bengt Forslund, *Victor Sjöström: Hans liv och verk* (Stockholm: Bonniers, 1980).
11. Maria Bergom-Larsson, *Ingmar Bergman and Society* (Stockholm: Norstedts, 1978).
12. Irene Scobbie, *Sweden: Nation of the Modern World* (London: Benn, 1972).
13. Quoted in *Theater* (New Haven) 11, no. 1 (Fall 1979).
14. Sjögren, *Stage and Society in Sweden*.
15. *Bergman on Bergman*.
16. Ibid.

CHAPTER 3

1. *Bergman on Bergman*.
2. Interview in *Playboy* (June 1964).
3. Jörn Donner, *The Personal Vision of Ingmar Bergman*, trans. Holger Lundbergh (Bloomington: Indiana University Press, 1964).
4. Marianne Höök, *Ingmar Bergman* (Stockholm: Wahlström och Widstrand, 1962).
5. Alrik Gustafson, *A History of Swedish Literature* (Minneapolis: University of Minnesota Press, 1961).
6. Torborg Lundell, *Lars Ahlin* (Boston: Twayne, 1977).
7. *Playboy* interview.
8. Donner, *The Personal Vision of Ingmar Bergman*.
9. *Bergman on Bergman*.
10. Martin Lamm, *August Strindberg*, trans. and ed. Harry G. Carlsson (New York: B. Blom, 1971.).
11. "Bergman on Victor Sjöström," *Sight and Sound* (London) (Spring 1960).
12. Bengt Forslund, "Bergman och Bergman," *Göteborgs Handels & Sjöfarts Tidning* (Göteborg), September 23, 1959.
13. Bergom-Larsson, *Ingmar Bergman and Society*.

14. Johannes Edfelt, "Introduction," *L'Avant-Scène théâtre* (Paris), no. 199 (1959).
15. Vilgot Sjöman, *L. 136. Diary with Ingmar Bergman*, trans. Alan Blair (Ann Arbor, Mich.: Karoma, 1978).
16. Scobbie, *Sweden.*
17. Steene, *Ingmar Bergman.*
18. Jean Béranger, *Ingmar Bergman et ses films* (Paris: Le Terrain Vague, 1959).
19. Erik Ulrichsen, "Ingmar Bergman and the Devil," *Sight and Sound* (London) (Summer 1958).
20. Eugene Archer, "The Rack of Life," *Film Quarterly* (Berkeley) (Summer 1959).
21. Interview with Bengt Forslund, "En oavbruten rörelse," *Chaplin* (Stockholm) (January 1963).
22. Jean Béranger, "Rencontre avec Ingmar Bergman," *Cahiers du cinéma* (Paris) (October 1958).
23. Interview with Matts Rying, *Röster i Radio TV* (Stockholm), February 3–9, 1963.

CHAPTER 4

1. *Bergman on Bergman.*
2. *Playboy* interview.
3. *Bergman on Bergman.*
4. Quoted in *Theater* (New Haven) 11, no. 1 (Fall 1979).
5. *Bergman on Bergman.*
6. Bergman in *Filmnyheter* (Svensk Filmindustri), ed. Torkel Bragée, no. 11 (1947).
7. *Bergman on Bergman.*
8. Bengt Forslund, "Prästsonen Ingmar Bergman," *Ord & Bild* (Stockholm) (1957).
9. Charles Thomas Samuels, *Encountering Directors* (New York: Putnam's, 1972).
10. Ibid.
11. *Nutid* (Stockholm) no. 16 (1955).
12. Ann Morrissett, "The Swedish Paradox," *Sight and Sound* (London) (Autumn 1961).
13. *Bergman on Bergman.*
14. Ibid.

CHAPTER 5

1. Bergman interviewed in *Vänd* (Stockholm) [1960].
2. *Bergman on Bergman.*
3. Donner, *The Personal Vision of Ingmar Bergman.*
4. "Self-Analysis of a Film-Maker."

5. The character of Grandé may be found in an unperformed play by Bergman, *The Puzzle Makes Eros* (dated October 9, 1946), as well as in *Woman Without a Face*.
6. Höök, *Ingmar Bergman*.
7. *Focus on The Seventh Seal*.
8. François Truffaut, *The Films in My Life* (New York: Simon & Schuster, 1978).
9. Sjögren, *Stage and Society in Sweden*.
10. *Bergman on Bergman*.
11. Interview with Cynthia Grenier in *Oui*, no. 3 (1974).
12. Amita Malik, in *Sunday Statesman* (New Delhi), December 12, 1965.
13. Lorens Marmstedt, "Ruda eller Gamba?" *Obs* (Stockholm), no. 18 (September 13, 1950).
14. *Theater* (New Haven) 11, no. 1 (Fall 1979).

CHAPTER 6

1. *Bergman on Bergman*.
2. Interview with Edwin Newman, in the WNBC-TV "Open Mind" series, reprinted in *Film Comment* (New York) 4, nos. 2, 3 (1967).
3. Liv Ullmann, *Changing* (New York: Knopf, 1976).
4. Interview with Eugene Archer in *New York Times*, April 2, 1967.
5. Marmstedt, "Ruda eller Gamba?"
6. Hauke Lange-Fuchs, *Wie Reklame zu Kultur wurde* (Lübeck: 1979).
7. *Bergman on Bergman*.
8. Höök, *Ingmar Bergman*.
9. Hauke Lange-Fuchs has pioneered research into these cinema commercials.
10. *Bergman on Bergman*.
11. Interview with the author in Munich, February 1980.
12. *Bergman on Bergman*.
13. H. Forsyth Hardy, *Scandinavian Film* (London: Falcon Press, 1952).

CHAPTER 7

1. Sjögren, *Stage and Society in Sweden*.
2. Interview in *Expressen* (Stockholm) March 15, 1980.
3. Interview with the author in Munich, February 1980.
4. Ibid.
5. *Focus on the Seventh Seal*.
6. *Bergman on Bergman*.
7. Sjögren, *Ingmar Bergman på teatern*.
8. *Bergman on Bergman*.
9. Samuels, *Encountering Directors*.
10. *Bergman on Bergman*.
11. Author's interview with Max von Sydow in London, November 1979.

12. Interview with the author in Stockholm, January 1969.
13. Dymling, "Preface."
14. Donner, *The Personal Vision of Ingmar Bergman.*
15. *Bergman on Bergman.*
16. Sjögren, *Ingmar Bergman på teatern.*
17. Ibid.
18. Sjögren, *Stage and Society in Sweden.*

CHAPTER 8

1. Dymling, "Preface."
2. *Bergman on Bergman.*
3. Tillie Björnstrand, *Inte bara applåder* (Stockholm: Tidens Förlag. 1975).
4. Richard Meryman, "I Live at the Edge of a Very Strange Country," *Life* (1971).
5. Interview with the author in Munich, February 1980.
6. Author's interview with Mago in Stockholm, November 1979.
7. Sjögren, *Ingmar Bergman på teatern.*
8. *Bergman on Bergman.*
9. Ibid.
10. Author's interview with Lennart Olsson in Malmö, November 1979.
11. Sjöman, L. 136. *Diary with Ingmar Bergman.*
12. Bergom-Larsson, *Ingmar Bergman and Society.*
13. Sjögren, *Stage and Society in Sweden.*
14. Roland Huntford, *The New Totalitarians* (London: Allen Lane, Penguin Press, 1971).
15. Sjöman, L. 136. *Diary with Ingmar Bergman.*
16. Dymling, "Preface."
17. Interview with Nils Petter Sundgren on Swedish TV, 1973.
18. Lars-Olof Löthwall, "Ingmar Bergman och Diger döden," *Stockholms-Tidningen,* July 5, 1956.
19. *Bergman on Bergman.*
20. Vernon Young, *Cinema Borealis* (New York: David Lewis, 1971).
21. Samuels, *Encountering Directors.*
22. Ibid.
23. Höök, *Ingmar Bergman.*
24. *Bergman on Bergman.*
25. Jos Burvenich, *Thèmes d'inspiration d'Ingmar Bergman* (Brussels: Club du Livre de Cinéma, 1960).
26. Sjögren, *Ingmar Bergman på teatern.*
27. Michael Meyer, *Ibsen: A Biography* (Garden City, N.Y.: Doubleday, 1971).
28. Sjögren, *Stage and Society in Sweden.*
29. *Bergman on Bergman.*
30. Ibid.

31. "Bergman on Victor Sjöström."
32. *Bergman on Bergman.*
33. Ullmann, *Changing.*
34. Denis Marion, *Ingmar Bergman* (Paris: Gallimard, 1979).
35. Hollis Alpert, "Bergman as Writer" and "Style Is the Director," both in *Saturday Review*, August 27, 1960, and December 23, 1961.
36. Interview with the author in Stockholm, February 1971.
37. Interview in *Året runt* (Stockholm), no. 17 (1964).

CHAPTER 9

1. Quoted in *Filmnytt* (Stockholm), no. 6 (1950).
2. Edith Sorel, "Ingmar Bergman: I Confect Dreams and Anguish," *New York Times*, January 22, 1978.
3. Olsson interview.
4. *Theater* (New Haven), 11, no. 1 (Fall 1979).
5. Sjögren, *Stage and Society in Sweden.*
6. Ibid.
7. Young, *Cinema Borealis.*
8. Jacques Siclier, *Ingmar Bergman* (Paris: Editions Universitaires, 1960).
9. Burvenich, *Thèmes d'inspiration d'Ingmar Bergman.*
10. "Self-Analysis of a Film-Maker."
11. Interview with Nils Petter Sundgren on "Forum," Swedish TV, September 29, 1968.
12. *Bergman on Bergman.*
13. Gunnar Oldin, "Ingmar Bergman," *American-Scandinavian Review* (Fall 1959).
14. Sjögren, *Stage and Society in Sweden.*
15. Sjöman, L. 136. *Diary with Ingmar Bergman.*
16. Ibid.
17. Ibid.
18. Ulrichsen, "Ingmar Bergman and the Devil."
19. *Bergman on Bergman.*
20. A. Alvarez, "A Visit with Ingmar Bergman," *New York Times Magazine*, December 7, 1975.
21. Sorel, "Ingmar Bergman: I Confect Dreams and Anguish."
22. Bergman quoted in *Life* (International), February 15, 1960.
23. *Time*, March 14, 1960.
24. *Bergman on Bergman.*
25. Alvarez, "A Visit with Ingmar Bergman."

CHAPTER 10

1. Arne Sellermark, "Den okände Ingmar Bergman," *Hemmets Journal* (Stockholm), (1959).
2. Donner, *Three Scenes with Ingmar Bergman.*

3. Dymling, "Preface."
4. Oscar Hedlund, "Ingmar Bergman: The Listener," *Saturday Review*, February 29, 1964.
5. *Bergman on Bergman.*
6. Malik, in *Sunday Statesman* (New Delhi), December 12, 1965.
7. *Bergman on Bergman.*
8. Sjöman, L. 126. *Diary with Ingmar Bergman.*
9. *Bergman on Bergman.*
10. Sven Nykvist, "Photographing the Films of Ingmar Bergman," *American Cinematographer* (Los Angeles), 43, no. 10 (October 1962).
11. *Bergman on Bergman.*
12. Sjöman, L. 136. *Diary with Ingmar Bergman.*
13. Donner, *The Personal Vision of Ingmar Bergman.*
14. Derek Prouse, "Ingmar Bergman: A Problem Genius," *Washington Post*, April 5, 1964.
15. *Bergman on Bergman.*
16. Ibid.
17. Quoted in *Times* (London), Februray 11, 1962.
18. Nykvist, "Photographing the Films of Ingmar Bergman."
19. *Bergman on Bergman.*
20. Prouse, "A Problem Genius."
21. Author's interview with Nils Petter Sundgren in Stockholm, November 1979.
22. Prouse, "A Problem Genius."

CHAPTER 11

1. Interview with Rying.
2. John Simon, *Ingmar Bergman Directs* (New York: Harcourt, Brace, Jovanovich, 1972).
3. Sjöman, L. 136. *Diary with Ingmar Bergman.*
4. *Bergman on Bergman.*
5. Ibid.
6. Prouse, "A Problem Genius."
7. Sjögren, *Ingmar Bergman på teatern.*
8. Randolph Goodman, *From Script to Stage: Eight Modern Plays* (New York: Brooklyn College, City University of New York, Rinehart Press, 1971).
9. Simon, *Ingmar Bergman Directs.*
10. *Bergman on Bergman.*
11. Hedlund, "Ingmar Bergman: The Listener."
12. Dymling, "Preface."
13. Simon, *Ingmar Bergman Directs.*
14. In Stig Björkman's documentary film, *Ingmar Bergman* (1971).
15. Quoted in *Newsweek*, March 17, 1975.
16. Ullmann, *Changing.*

17. Quoted in *Time*, December 4, 1972.
18. Interview with Sundgren (1968).
19. Quoted in *Film in Sweden* (Stockholm), no. 3 (1966–67).
20. Steene, *Ingmar Bergman.*
21. Simon, *Ingmar Bergman Directs.*
22. *Bergman on Bergman.*
23. Samuels, *Encountering Directors.*
24. *Bergman on Bergman.*

CHAPTER 12

1. Meryman, "I Live at the Edge of a Very Strange Country."
2. *Bergman on Bergman.*
3. Interview with Nils Petter Sundgren on Swedish TV, February 21, 1968.
4. Interview with Gordon Gow, *Films and Filming,* (London) (July 1976).
5. Interview with Sundgren (1968).
6. Ibid.
7. Bergom-Larsson, *Ingmar Bergman and Society.*
8. Interview with Liv Ullmann in *Radio Times* (London), January 30, 1975.
9. Quoted in Richard Kaplan, *A Look at Liv* (Documentary screened on BBC-TV on October 3, 1979).
10. Ullmann, *Changing.*
11. Interview with Gow.
12. Sorel, "Ingmar Bergman: I Confect Dreams and Anguish."
13. Interview with Grenier.
14. *Bergman on Bergman.*
15. Samuels, *Encountering Directors.*
16. *Bergman on Bergman.*
17. Quoted in interview with Nils Petter Sundgren on Swedish TV, September 29, 1968.
18. *Bergman on Bergman.*
19. Samuels, *Encountering Directors.*
20. *Bergman on Bergman.*
21. August Strindberg, *From an Occult Diary: Marriage with Harriet Bosse,* trans. Mary Sandbach (London: Secker and Warburg, 1965).
22. Bergom-Larsson, *Ingmar Bergman and Society.*
23. Ibid.
24. Interview with Sundgren (February 1968).
25. *Bergman on Bergman.*
26. Interview with the author, Stockholm, January 1969.
27. Peter Cowie, *"The Rite," Focus on Film* (London), no. 5 (1970).
28. Ullmann, *Changing.*
29. Marion, *Ingmar Bergman.*

30. *Bergman on Bergman.*
31. Meryman, "I Live at the Edge of a Very Strange Country."
32. Gustafson, *A History of Swedish Literature.*

CHAPTER 13

1. Henrik Sjögren, *Regi: Ingmar Bergman* (Stockholm: Aldus Books, 1970).
2. Sjögren, *Ingmar Bergman på teatern.*
3. Sjögren, *Stage and Society in Sweden.*
4. Quoted in *Newsweek,* March 17, 1975.
5. Interview with the author in Stockholm, March 1972.
6. Meryman, "I Live at the Edge of a Very Strange Country."
7. Ibid.
8. Simon, *Ingmar Bergman Directs.*
9. Quoted in Björkman's documentary, *Ingmar Bergman.*
10. Meryman, "I Live at the Edge of a Very Strange Country."
11. Ibid.
12. Björkman documentary, *Ingmar Bergman.*
13. *Focus on the Seventh Seal.*
14. Quoted in *Film in Sweden* (Stockholm) (1972).

CHAPTER 14

1. Sjögren, *Stage and Society in Sweden.*
2. Author's interview with Måns Reuterswärd in Stockholm, November 1979.
3. Peter Cowie, "Bergman's *Magic Flute,*" *High Fidelity* (Great Barrington, Mass.), 25, no. 6 (June 1975).
4. Quoted in libretto supplied with Sveriges Radio's boxed set of discs of *The Magic Flue.*
5. Höök, *Ingmar Bergman.*
6. *Theater* (New Haven) 11, no. 1 (Fall 1979).
7. Quoted in brochure issued by CIC at Cannes for *Face to Face.*
8. Ullmann, *Changing.*
9. CIC Brochure.
10. Guy Flatley, "Liv and Ingmar Bergman Remain . . . Such Good Friends," *New York Times,* April 9, 1972.
11. Alvarez, "A Visit with Ingmar Bergman."

CHAPTER 15

1. *Bergman on Bergman.*
2. Jan Morris, "When an Artist Feels Anxiety," *Horizon* (New York) (November 1977).
3. James Jacobs, "Ingmar Bergman au travail," *Positif* (Paris), no. 204 (March 1978).

4. Ibid.
5. Sjöman, L. 136. *Diary with Ingmar Bergman.*
6. *Bergman on Bergman.*
7. Ibid.
8. Ingrid Bergman, with Alan Burgess, *My Story* (New York: Delacorte Press, 1980).
9. Emma Andrews, "The Bergman Principle," *Film Illustrated* (London) (February 1978).
10. *My Story.*
11. Young, *Cinema Borealis.*
12. Simon, *Ingmar Bergman Directs.*
13. Sleeve notes to *Närbilder: Käbi Laretei spelar musiken till Ingmar Bergmans filmer*, PROP 7809 (Stockholm: Proprius Förlag, 1980).
14. *Four Screenplays.*
15. Interview with the author in Munich, February 1980.
16. *Theater* (New Haven) 11, no. 1 (Fall 1979).
17. Ibid.

CHAPTER 16

1. Bergman, in an interview with the author in Munich, February 1980.
2. Quoted in *News*, October (Swedish Film Institute, Stockholm) 1, no. 19 (1979).
3. *Bergman on Bergman.*
4. William Wolf, Interview with Bergman in *New York Magazine*, October 27, 1980.
5. Ingmar Bergman, *From the Life of the Marionettes*, trans. Alan Blair (New York: Pantheon Books, 1980).
6. Interview with the author in Stockholm, January 1969.
7. In a letter to the author, November 1980.
8. Interview with the author in Munich, February 1980.
9. Reported in *Film og Kino* (Oslo), no. 1 (1981).
10. Quoted in *Variety*, October 29, 1980.
11. Åke Janzon, "Tre utsökta uppvisningar av tvåsamhetens diabolik," *Svenska Dagbladet* (Stockholm), early May 1981.
12. Sjöman, L. 136. *Diary with Ingmar Bergman.*
13. Interview with the author in Stockholm, January 1969.
14. Samuels, *Encountering Directors.*
15. Interview with the author in Stockholm, January 1975.
16. Interview with the author in Stockholm, November 1979.
17. Samuels, *Encountering Directors.*
18. Marion, *Ingmar Bergman.*
19. Dilys Powell, in *Sunday Times Magazine* (London), May 8, 1977.

Bibliography

BOOKS, SCRIPTS, AND ARTICLES BY BERGMAN

Autumn Sonata. Translated by Alan Blair. New York: Pantheon Books, 1979.
Bergman on Bergman. Edited by Stig Björkman, Torsten Manns, and Jonas Sima. Translated by Paul Britten Austin. New York: Simon & Schuster, 1973.
"Bergman on Victor Sjöström." *Sight and Sound* (London), Spring 1960.
"Chacun de mes films est le dernier." *Cahiers du Cinéma* (Paris), no. 100, 1959.
"Dreams and Shadows." *Films and Filming* (London), October 1956.
"Each Film Is My Last." *Films and Filming* (London), July 1959. Reprinted in *Tulane Drama Review*, 1966.
Face to Face. Translated by Alan Blair. New York: Pantheon Books, 1976.
A Film Trilogy. Translated by Paul Britten Austin. New York: Orion Press, 1967. Screenplays of *Through a Glass Darkly*, *Winter Light*, and *The Silence.*
Four Screenplays of Ingmar Bergman. Translated by Lars Malmström and David Kushner. New York: Simon & Schuster, 1960.
Four Stories by Ingmar Bergman. Translated by Alan Blair. New York: Doubleday/Anchor Press, 1977. Includes *The Touch, Cries and Whispers, Hour of the Wolf.*
From the Life of the Marionettes. Translated by Alan Blair. New York: Pantheon Books, 1980.
"Ingmar Bergman: The Serpent's Skin." *Cahiers du Cinéma in English* (New York), no. 11, September 1967.
Oeuvres. Translated into French by G. C. Bjurström and Maurice Fons. Paris: Robert Laffont, 1962. Screenplays of *Summer Interlude, The Naked Night, Smiles of a Summer Night, The Seventh Seal, Wild Strawberries,* and *The Magician.*
"A Page from My Diary." *Cinéma 60* (Paris), November–December 1960.
Persona and Shame. Translated by Keith Bradfield. New York: Grossman, 1972.

Scenes from a Marriage. Translated by Alan Blair. New York: Pantheon Books, 1974.
"Schizophrenic Interview with a Nervous Film Director." By Ernest Riffe (pseudonym for Bergman). *Film in Sweden* (Stockholm), no. 3, 1968. Reprinted in *Take One* (Toronto), January–February 1969.
"Self-Analysis of a Film-maker." *Films and Filming* (London), September 1956.
The Serpent's Egg. Translated by Alan Blair. New York: Pantheon Books, 1978.
"The Snakeskin." *Sight and Sound* (London), August 1965.
Staden, Hörspel. Presented by Claes Hoogland. Sveriges Radio, Stockholm, 1951.
The Virgin Spring. Translated by Lars Malmström and David Kushner. New York: Ballantine Books, 1960. Note: screenplay by Ulla Isaksson.
Wood Painting: A Morality Play. Translated by Randolph Goodman and Leif Sjöberg. *Tulane Drama Review,* 1961.

BOOKS ABOUT BERGMAN

Béranger, Jean. *Ingmar Bergman et ses films.* Paris: Le Terrain Vague, 1959.
Bergom-Larsson, Maria. *Ingmar Bergman and Society.* San Diego: A. S. Barnes, 1978.
Billquist, Fritiof. *Ingmar Bergman: teatermannen och filmskaparen.* Stockholm: Natur och Kultur, 1960.
Burvenich, Jos. *Thèmes d'inspiration d'Ingmar Bergman.* Brussels: Club du Livre de Cinéma, 1960.
Chiaretti, Tommaso. *Ingmar Bergman* Rome: Canesi, 1964.
Donner, Jörn. *The Personal Vision of Ingmar Bergman.* Translated by Holger Lundbergh. Bloomington: Indiana University Press, 1964.
Gibson, Arthur. *The Silence of God: Creative Response to the Films of Ingmar Bergman.* New York: Harper & Row, 1969.
Guyon, François D., and Béranger, Jean. *Ingmar Bergman.* Lyon: Premier Plan, SERDOC, 1964.
Höök, Marianne. *Ingmar Bergman.* Stockholm: Wahlström och Widstrand, 1962.
Kaminsky, Stuart, ed. *Ingmar Bergman: Essays in Criticism.* New York: Oxford University Press, 1975.
Manvell, Roger. *Ingmar Bergman: An Appreciation.* New York: Arno Press, 1980.
Marion, Denis. *Ingmar Bergman.* Paris: Gallimard, 1979.
Marker, Lise-Lone, and Marker, Frederick J. *Ingmar Bergman: Four Decades in the Theatre.* Cambridge: Cambridge University Press, 1982.
Mosley, Philip. *Ingmar Bergman: The Cinema as Mistress.* Boston: Marion Boyars, 1981.
Nelson, David R. *Ingmar Bergman: The Search for God.* Boston: Communication Arts Division, Boston University, 1964.

Oldrini, Guido. *La Solitudine di Ingmar Bergman*. Parma: Guanda Editore, 1965.
Petrić, Vlada, ed. *Film and Dreams: An Approach to Bergman*. South Salem, N.Y.: Redgrave, 1981.
Ranieri, Tino. *Ingmar Bergman*. Florence: La Nuova Italia, 1974.
Siclier, Jacques. *Ingmar Bergman*. Paris: Editions Universitaires, 1960.
Simon, John. *Ingmar Bergman Directs*. New York: Harcourt, Brace, Jovanovich, 1972.
Sjögren, Henrik. *Ingmar Bergman på teatern*. Stockholm: Almqvist och Wiksell, 1968.
————. *Regi: Ingmar Bergman*. Stockholm: Aldus Books, 1970.
Sjöman, Vilgot. *L. 136. Diary with Ingmar Bergman*. Translated by Alan Blair. Ann Arbor, Mich.: Karoma, 1978.
Steene, Birgitta. *Focus on the Seventh Seal*. Englewood Cliffs, N.J.: Prentice-Hall, 1972.
————. *A Reference Guide to Ingmar Bergman*. Boston: G. K. Hall, 1982.
————. *Ingmar Bergman*. New York: Twayne, 1968.
Törnqvist, Egil. *Bergman och Strindberg*. Stockholm: Prisma, 1973.
Wood, Robin. *Ingmar Bergman*. New York: Praeger, 1969.
Young, Vernon. *Cinema Borealis: Ingmar Bergman and the Swedish Ethos*. New York: David Lewis, 1971; reprinted New York: Avon, 1972.

RELATED ARTICLES, INTERVIEWS, AND BOOKS

Aghed, Jan. "Conversations avec Ingmar Bergman." *Positif* (Paris), no. 121, November 1970.
Alpert, Hollis. "Bergman as Writer." *Saturday Review*, August 27, 1960.
————. "Style Is the Director." *Saturday Review*, December 23, 1961.
Alvarez, A. "A Visit with Ingmar Bergman." *New York Times Magazine*, December 7, 1975.
Archer, Eugene. "The Rack of Life." *Film Quarterly* (Berkeley), Summer 1959.
Austin, Paul Britten. "Ingmar Bergman, Magician of Swedish Cinema." *Anglo-Swedish Review* (London), April 1959.
Béranger, Jean. "Rencontre avec Ingmar Bergman." *Cahiers du cinéma* (Paris), October 1958.
Bergman, Ingmar. "Interview." *Playboy*, June 1964.
————. Transcription of his press conference on *Shame*. *Continental Film Review* (London), December 1967.
Bergman, Ingrid, with Burgess, Alan. *My Story*. New York: Delacorte Press, 1980.
Björnstrand, Tillie. *Inte bara applåder*. Stockholm: Tidens Förlag, 1975.
Brightman, Carol. "The Word, the Image, and *The Silence*." *Film Quarterly* (Berkeley), Summer 1964.
Cowie, Peter. "Bergman's *Magic Flute*." *High Fidelity* (Great Barrington, Mass.) 25, no. 6, June 1975.

————. "Ingmar Bergman: 'The Struggle with the Beyond.'" *New York Times*, October 26, 1980.

Fleisher, Frederic. "Ants in a Snakeskin." *Sight and Sound* (London), Autumn 1965.

Forslund, Bengt. "Prästsonen Ingmar Bergman." *Ord & Bild* (Stockholm), 1957.

————. *Victor Sjöström. Hans liv och verk.* Stockholm: Bonniers, 1980.

Fovez, Elie; Ayfre, Amedée; and D'Yvoire, Jean. "Le Septième Sceau." *Télé-ciné* (Paris), August–September 1958.

Gauteur, Claude. "Ingmar Bergman." *Cinéma 58* (Paris), July–August 1958.

Godard, Jean-Luc. "Bergmanorama." *Cahiers du cinéma* (Paris), July 1958.

Grafe, Frieda. "Der Spiegel ist verschlagen." *Filmkritik* (Frankfurt), November 1968.

Gravier, Maurice. "Ingmar Bergman et le théâtre suédois." In *Textes sur théâtre et cinéma.* Edited by Henri Agel and Georges-Albert Astre. Paris: Lettres Modernes, 1960.

Grenier, Cynthia. Interview with Bergman. *Oui,* no 3, 1974.

Hedlund, Oscar. "Ingmar Bergman: The Listener." *Saturday Review,* February 29, 1964.

Hervé, Alain. "L'Univers d'Ingmar Bergman." *Réalitiés,* (Paris), February 1964.

Holba, Herbert. "Triebhaus der Neurosen. Der frühe Bergman." *Action* (Vienna), October 1968.

Johns, Marilyn E. "Strindberg's 'Folkungasagan' and Bergman's 'Det sjunde inseglet': Medieval Epic and Psychological Drama." *Scandinavica* (London), 18, no. 1, May 1979.

Kawin, Bruce F. *Mindscreen: Bergman, Godard and the First-Person Film* Princeton: Princeton University Press, 1978.

Kinder, Marsha. "*From the Life of the Marionettes* to *The Devil's Wanton,*" *Film Quarterly* (Berkeley), Spring 1981.

Lange-Fuchs, Hauke. *Der frühe Ingmar Bergman.* Lübeck: Nordische Filmtage, 1978.

Lefèvre, Raymond. "Ingmar Bergman." *Image et son* (Paris), March 1969.

Löthwall, Lars-Olof. "Moment of Agony: Interview with Ingmar Bergman." *Films and Filming* (London), February 1969.

Lundell, Torborg, and Mulac, Anthony. "Husbands and Wives in Bergman Films: A Close Analysis Based on Empirical Data." *Journal of the University Film Association,* (Houston), 33, no. 1, 1981.

Lundvik, Ulf (Justitieombudsmannen). "Affären Ingmar Bergman." Stockholm: Swedish Government, February 28, 1978.

Maisetti, Massimo. *La Crisi spirituali dell'uomo moderno nei film di Ingmar Bergman.* Varese: Busto Arsizio, Centro Communitario di Rescaldina, 1964.

McCann, Eleanor. "The Rhetoric of *Wild Strawberries.*" *Sight and Sound* (London), Autumn 1961.

Morris, Jan. "When an Artist Feels Anxiety." *Horizon,* November 1977.

Nykvist, Sven. "Photographing the Films of Ingmar Bergman." *American Cinematographer* (Los Angeles), 43, no. 10, October 1962.

Oldin, Gunnar. "Ingmar Bergman." *American-Scandinavian Review*, Fall 1959.

Persson, Göran. "Bergmans trilogi." *Chaplin* (Stockholm), no. 40, 1964.

Prouse, Derek. "Ingmar Bergman: A Problem Genius." *Washington Post*, April 5, 1964. Reprinted from the *Sunday Times* (London), March 15, 1964.

Renaud, Pierre. "Les Visages de la Passion dans l'univers de Bergman." In *La Passion du Christ comme thème cinématographique*. Edited by Michel Estève. Paris: Lettres Modernes, 1961.

Sammern-Frankenegg, Fritz R. "Learning 'A Few Words in the Foreign Language': Ingmar Bergman's 'Secret Message' in the Imagery of Hand and Face." *Scandinavian Studies* 49, no. 3, Summer 1977.

Samuels, Charles Thomas. *Encountering Directors*. New York: Putnam's, 1972.

Sarris, Andrew. "*The Seventh Seal*." *Film Culture* (New York), no. 19, 1959.

Schein, Harry. "En ny Bergman?" *BLM* (Stockholm), November 1951.

Seton, Marie. "Ingmar Bergman: The Director Seeking Self-Knowledge." *The Painter and Sculptor* (London), Spring 1960.

Sjögren, Henrik. *Stage and Society in Sweden*. Stockholm: The Swedish Institute, 1979.

Sontag, Susan. Review of *Persona*. *Sight and Sound* (London), Autumn 1967.

Sorel, Edith. "Ingmar Bergman: I Confect Dreams and Anguish." *New York Times*, January 22, 1978.

Tabbia, Alberto, and Cozarinsky, Edgardo. *Flashback 1: Ingmar Bergman*. Buenos Aires: Vaccaro, 1958.

Theunissen, Gert H. *Das Schweigen und sein Publikum*. Köln: M. Du Mont Schauberg, 1964.

Ullmann, Liv. *Changing*. New York: Knopf, 1976.

Ulrichsen, Erik. "Ingmar Bergman and the Devil." *Sight and Sound* (London), Summer 1958.

Waldekranz, Rune. *Modern Swedish Film*. Stockholm: Swedish Institute, 1961.

———. *Swedish Cinema*. Stockholm: Swedish Institute, 1959.

Widerberg, Bo. *Visionen i svensk film*. Stockholm: Bonniers, 1962.

Wolf, William. Interview with Bergman. *New York Magazine*, October 27, 1980.

Filmography

A Passion (U.K.) (En passion). 1969.
The Passion of Anna (U.S.) (En passion). 1969.
Persona (Persona). 1966.
Port of Call (Hamnstad). 1948.
Prison (Fängelse). 1949.
The Rite (U.K.) (Riten). 1969.
The Ritual (U.S.) (Riten). 1969.
Sawdust and Tinsel (U.K.) (Gycklarnas afton). 1953.
Scenes from a Marriage (Scener ur ett äktenskap). 1973.
Secrets of Women (U.S.) (Kvinnors väntan). 1952.
The Serpent's Egg (Das Schlangenei). 1977.
The Seventh Seal (Det sjunde inseglet). 1957.
Shame (U.S.) (Skammen). 1968.
The Shame (U.K.) (Skammen). 1968.
A Ship Bound for India (U.K.) (Skepp till Indialand). 1947.
The Silence (Tystnaden). 1963.
Smiles of a Summer Night (Sommarnattens leende). 1955.
So Close to Life (U.K.) (Nära livet). 1958.
Stimulantia (Stimulantia). 1967.
Summer Interlude (U.K.) (Sommarlek). 1951.
Summer with Monika (U.K.) (Sommaren med Monika). 1953.
Thirst (U.K.) (Törst). 1949.
This Doesn't Happen Here (Sånt händer inte här). 1950.
Three Strange Loves (U.S.) (Törst). 1949.
Through a Glass Darkly (Såsom i en spegel). 1961.
To Joy (Till glädje). 1950.
The Touch (Beröringen). 1971.
The Virgin Spring (Jungfrukällan). 1960.
Waiting Women (U.K.) (Kvinnors väntan). 1952.
Wild Strawberries (Smultronstället). 1957.
Winter Light (Nattvardsgästerna). 1963.

FILMS SCRIPTED BY BERGMAN

Divorced (Frånskild). Director: Gustaf Molander. 1951.
Eva. Director: Gustaf Molander. (Bergman co-wrote the screenplay with Molander.) 1948.
Last Couple Out (Sista paret ut). Director: Alf Sjöberg. 1956.
The Pleasure Garden (Lustgården). Director: Alf Kjellin. (Bergman co-wrote the screenplay with Erland Josephson, under the pseudonym "Buntel Eriksson.") 1961.
Torment (U.S.) or *Frenzy* (U.K.) (Hets). Director: Alf Sjöberg. 1944.
While the City Sleeps (Medan staden sover). Director: Lars-Eric Kjellgren. (Bergman wrote only the synopsis; the screenplay is by Lars-Eric Kjellgren and Per Anders Fogelström.) 1950.

Woman Without a Face (*Kvinna utan ansikte*). Director: Gustaf Molander. 1947.

FILMS DIRECTED BY BERGMAN

1946
KRIS
(*Crisis*)

Screenplay: IB, from the play, *Moderhjertet/Moderdyret*, by Leck Fischer. Photography: Gösta Roosling (assistant: Jarl Nylander). Stills: Louis Huch. Sound: Lennart Svensson. Music: Erland von Koch. Art Direction: Arne Åkermark. Editing: Oscar Rosander. Artistic Adviser: Victor Sjöström. Production Manager: Harald Molander. Assistant Director: Lars-Eric Kjellgren. Unit Managers: Harry Malmstedt, Ragnar Carlberg. Scriptgirl: Seivie Ewerstein. Production Company: Svensk Filmindustri. 2,540 meters. 93 minutes. Swedish premiere: February 25, 1946.

Cast: Dagny Lind (*Ingeborg Johnson*), Inga Landgré (*Nelly*), Marianne Löfgren (*Jenny*), Stig Olin (*Jack*), Alla Bohlin (*Ulf*), Ernst Eklund (*Ingeborg's Uncle Edvard*), Signe Wirff (*Ingeborg's Aunt Jessie*), Svea Holst (*Malin*), Arne Lindblad (*mayor*), Julia Caesar (*mayor's wife*), Dagmar Olsson (*singer at ball*), Siv Thulin (*assistant in beauty salon*), Anna-Lisa Baude, M. Carelick (*customers in beauty salon*), Karl Erik Flens (*Nelly's friend at ball*), Erik Forslund (*gentleman at party*), Wiktor Andersson, Gus Dahlström, John Melin, Holger Höglund, Sture Ericson, Ulf Johansson (*musicians*), Margit Andelius (*treasurer's wife*), Monica Schildt (*a lady*), K. Koykull (*man in street*), John Björling, Per Hugo Jacobsson (*men*), Singoalla Lundbäck (*Gypsy*), Carin Cederström, Mona Geijer-Falkner (*two ladies in sleeping car*), Nils Hultgren (*man in street*).

1946
DET REGNAR PÅ VÅR KÄRLEK
(*It Rains on Our Love* or *The Man with an Umbrella*)

Screenplay: IB and Herbert Grevenius, from the play, *Bra mennesker*, by Oskar Braaten. Photography: Göran Strindberg, Hilding Bladh. Sound: Lars Nordberg. Music: Erland von Koch, with extracts from Richard Wagner and Bernhard Flies. Art Direction: P. A. Lundgren. Editing: Tage Holmberg. Scriptgirl: Gun Holmgren. Producer: Lorens Marmstedt. Production Company: Sveriges Folkbiografer, distributed through Nordisk Tonefilm. 2,605 meters. 95 minutes. Swedish premiere: November 9, 1946.

Cast: Barbro Kollberg (*Maggi*), Birger Malmsten (*David Lindell*), Gösta Cederlund (*man with the umbrella*), Ludde Gentzel (*Håkansson*), Douglas Håge (*Andersson*), Hjördis Pettersson (*Mrs. Andersson*), Julia Caesar (*Hanna Ledin*), Sture Ericsson, Ulf Johansson (*peddlers*), Gunnar Björnstrand (*Mr. Purman*), Åke Fridell (*assistant vicar*), Torsten Hillberg (*vicar*), Benkt-Åke Benktsson (*prosecutor*), Erik Rosén (*judge*), Magnus Kesster (*Folke Törnberg, bicycle repairman*), Sif Ruud (*Gerti, his wife*), Edvard Danielsson (*hotel porter*), Bertil Anderberg, Gösta Prüzelius (*police constables*), Gösta Qvist, Karl Jonsson, Nils Alm (*guests in café*), Wiktor Andersson (*bum in station*), Carl Harald (*man on duty in station*), Erland Josephson (*clerk in vicar's office*).

1947
SKEPP TILL INDIALAND
(A *Ship Bound for India* or *The Land of Desire*)

Screenplay: IB, from the play, *Skepp till Indialand*, by Martin Söderhjelm. Photography: Göran Strindberg. Sound: Lars Nordberg, Sven Josephson. Music: Erland von Koch. Art Direction: P. A. Lundgren. Editing: Tage Holmberg. Title Design: Alva Lundin. Production Manager: Allan Ekelund. Scriptgirl: Gerda Osten. Producer: Lorens Marmstedt. Production Company: Sveriges Folkbiografer, distributed through Nordisk Tonefilm. 2,690 meters. 102 minutes. Swedish premiere: September 22, 1947.

Cast: Holger Löwenadler (*Alexander Blom*), Anna Lindahl (*Alice, his wife*), Birger Malmsten (*Johannes*), Gertrud Fridh (*Sally*), Lasse Krantz (*Hans*), Jan Molander (*Bertil*), Erik Hell (*Pekka*), Naemi Briese (*Selma*), Hjördis Pettersson (*Sofie*), Åke Fridell (*director of variety theater*), Peter Lindgren (*foreign sailor*), Gustaf Hiort af Ornäs, Torsten Bergström (*Blom's companions*), Ingrid Borthen (*girl in street*), Amy Aaröe (*young girl*), Gunnar Nielsen, Torgny Anderberg (*men*), Svea Holst (*woman*), Kiki (*the dwarf*).

1948
MUSIK I MÖRKER
(*Music in Darkness* or *Night Is My Future*)

Screenplay: Dagmar Edqvist, from her novel by the same name. Photography: Göran Strindberg. Sound: Olle Jakobsson. Music: Erland von Koch, with extracts from Chopin, Beethoven, Badarczewska-Baranowska, Schumann, Handel, Wagner, and Tom Andy (pseudonym for Thomas Andersen). Art Direction: P. A. Lundgren. Editing: Lennart Wallén. Production Manager: Allan Ekelund. Scriptgirl: Ulla Kihlberg. Producer: Lorens Marmstedt. Production Company: Terraproduktion, distributed through Terrafilm. 2,400 meters. 85 minutes. Swedish premiere: January 17, 1948.

Cast: Mai Zetterling (*Ingrid Olofsdotter*), Birger Malmsten (*Bengt Vyldeke*), Bibi Skoglund (*Agneta Vyldeke, his sister*), Olof Winnerstrand (*Kerrman, the vicar*), Naima Wifstrand (*Beatrice Schröder*), Åke Claesson (*Augustin Schröder*), Hilda Borgström (*Lovis*), Douglas Håge (*Kruge, restaurant owner*), Gunnar Björnstrand (*Klasson, violinist*), Bengt Eklund (*Ebbe Larsson*), Segol Mann (*Anton Nord*), Bengt Logardt (*Einar Born*), Marianne Gyllenhammar (*Blanche*), John Elfström (*Otto Klemens, blind worker*), Rune Andreasson (*Evert*), Barbro Flodquist (*Hjördis, his mother*), Ulla Andreasson (*Sylvia*), Sven Lindberg (*Hedström, music director*), Svea Holst (*post office lady*), Georg Skarstedt (*Jönsson, a waiter*), Reinhold Svensson (*half-drunk man*), Mona Geijer-Falkner (*woman with garbage bin*), Arne Lindblad (*chef*), Stig Johansson (*man*), Britta Brunius (*woman*).

1948
HAMNSTAD
(Port of Call)

Screenplay: Olle Länsberg, IB. Photography: Gunnar Fischer (assistant: Bengt Järnmark). Stills: Louis Huch. Sound: Sven Hansen (assistant: Aaby Wedin). Music: Erland von Koch, Adolphe Adam, Sven Sjöholm. Art Direction: Nils Svenwall. Editing: Oscar Rosander. Production Manager: Harald Molander. Assistant Directors: Lars-Eric Kjellgren, Stig Ossian Ericson. Unit Manager: Gösta Ström. Scriptgirl: Ingegerd Ericson. Production Company: Svensk Filmindustri. 2,722 meters. 99 minutes. Swedish premiere: October 11, 1948.

Cast: Nine-Christine Jönsson (*Berit Holm*), Bengt Eklund (*Gösta Andersson*), Erik Hell (*Berit's father*), Berta Hall (*Berit's mother*), Mimi Nelson (*Gertrud*), Sture Ericson (*her father*), Birgitta Valberg (*Agnes Vilander, social worker*), Hans Strååt (*Vilander*), Harry Ahlin (*man from Skåne*), Nils Hallberg (*Gustav*), Sven-Eric Gamble (*"the Oak"*) Sif Ruud (*Mrs. Krona*), Kolbjörn Knudsen (*seaman*), Yngve Nordwall (*factory foreman*), Torsten Lilliecrona, Hans Sundberg (*his friends*), Bengt Blomgren (*Gunnar*), Helge Karlsson (*his father*), Hanny Schedin (*his mother*), Stig Olin (*Thomas*), Else-Merete Heiberg, Erna Groth (*girls in reformatory*), Britta Billsten (*street girl*), Nils Dahlgren (*police commissioner*), Bill Houston (*Joe*), Herman Greid (*German captain*), Kate Elffors (*Berit Holm as a child*), Gunnar Nielsen, Georg Skarstedt (*two men*), Britta Nordin (*salvationist*), Vanja Rudefeldt (*girl on dance floor*), Greta Blom (*policewoman*), Estrid Hesse (*salvationist*), Carl Deurell (*priest*), Edvard Danielsson (*parish clerk*), John Björling (*stevedore*), Rune Andreasson (*Squirt*), Siv Thulin (*girl*).

1949
FÄNGELSE
(Prison or The Devil's Wanton)

Screenplay: IB. Photography: Göran Strindberg. Sound: Olle Jakobsson. Music: Erland von Koch, Alice Tegnér, Oscar Ahnfelt. Art Direction: P. A. Lundgren. Editing: Lennart Wallén. Production Manager: Allan Ekelund. Scriptgirl: Chris Poijes. Producer: Lorens Marmstedt. Production Company: Terraproduktion, distributed through Terrafilm. 2,150 meters. 78 minutes. Swedish premiere: March 19, 1949.

Cast: Doris Svedlund (*Birgitta Carolina Söderberg*), Birger Malmsten (*Thomas*), Eva Henning (*Sofi, his wife*), Hasse Ekman (*Martin Grandé*), Stig Olin (*Peter*), Irma Christensson (*Linnéa, Birgitta-Carolina's sister*), Anders Henrikson (*Paul, professor of mathematics*), Marianne Löfgren (*Signe Bohlin*), Curt Masreliez (*Alf*), Birgit "Bibi" Lindqvist (*Anna Bohlin*), Arne Ragnebom (*postman*), Carl-Henrik Fant (*Arne, an actor*), Inger Juel (*Greta, an actress*), Torsten Lilliecrona (*cinematographer*), Segol Mann (*lighting technician*), Börje Mellvig (*commissioner*), Åke Engfeld (*policeman*), Åke Fridell (*Magnus*), Lasse Sarri (*Lasse*), Britta Brunius (*his mother*), Gunilla Klosterberg (*dark lady*), Ulf Palme (*man in dream*).

1949
TÖRST
(Thirst or Three Strange Loves)

Screenplay: Herbert Grevenius, from the collection of short stories, *Törst*, by Birgit Tengroth. Photography: Gunnar Fischer (assistant: Bengt Järnmark). Stills: Louis Huch. Sound: Lennart Unnerstad (assistant: Gustav Halldin). Music: Erik Nordgren, Olle Johnny (pseudonym for Olof Johansson), Georges Boulanger, George Botsford, Frédéric Burgmuller, Arthur Hedström, Ulf Peder Olrog, Erik Uppström, Henri Christiné, Den Berry. Choreography: Ellen Bergman. Art Direction: Nils Svenwall. Editing: Oscar Rosander. Main Titles: Alva Lundin. Production Manager: Helge Hagerman. Assistant Director: Hugo Bolander. Unit Managers: Gösta Ström, Hilmer Peters. Scriptgirl: Ingegerd Ericsson. Production Company: Svensk Filmindustri. 2,278 meters. 84 minutes. Swedish premiere: October 17, 1949.

Cast: Eva Henning (*Rut*), Birger Malmsten (*Bertil, her husband*), Birgit Tengroth (*Viola*), Mimi Nelson (*Valborg*), Hasse Ekman (*Rosengren*), Bengt Eklund (*Raoul*), Gaby Stenberg (*Astrid, his wife*), Naima Wifstrand (*Miss Henriksson, ballet teacher*), Sven-Eric Gamble (*worker in glass factory*), Gunnar Nielsen (*Rosengren's assistant*), Estrid Hesse (*patient*), Helge Hagerman (*Swedish priest*), Calle Flygare (*Danish priest*), Monica Weinzierl (*small girl on train*), Verner Arpe (*German conductor*), Else-Merete Heiberg (*Norwegian lady on train*), Sif Ruud (*garrulous widow*), Gerhard Beyer, Herman Greid (*newspaper sellers in Basel*), Oscar Rosander (*man in hotel*), Inga Gill (*lady in hotel*), Laila Jokimo, Inga Norin-Welton, Ingeborg Bergius (*ballet girls*), Peter Winner (*German policeman*), Britta Brunius (*nurse*), Wiktor Andersson (*porter*), Inga-Lill Åhlström (*pianist*), Gustaf A. Herzing (*policeman*), Ingmar Bergman (*passenger on train*), Erik Arrhenius (*man*).

1950
TILL GLÄDJE
(To Joy)

Screenplay: IB. Photography: Gunnar Fischer (assistant: Bengt Järnmark). Stills: Louis Huch. Editing: Oscar Rosander. Music: Beethoven, Mozart,

Mendelssohn, Smetana, Sam Samson, and Erik Johnsson. Art Direction: Nils Svenwall. Production Manager: Allan Ekelund. Unit Manager: Tor Borong. Scriptgirl: Ingegerd Ericsson. Production Company: Svensk Filmindustri. 2,700 meters. 98 minutes. Swedish premiere: February 20, 1950.

Cast: Maj-Britt Nilsson (*Marta*), Stig Olin (*Stig Eriksson*), Victor Sjöström (*Sönderby*), Birger Malmsten (*Marcel*), John Ekman (*Mikael Bro*), Margit Carlqvist (*Nelly Bro*), Sif Ruud (*Stina*), Erland Josephson (*Bertil*), Ernst Brunman (*janitor at concert house*), Allan Ekelund (*vicar at wedding*), Maud Hyttenberg (*toyshop assistant*), Berit Holmström (*Lisa*), Eva Fritz-Nilsson (*Lisa as a baby*), Björn Montin (*Lasse*), Staffan Axelsson (*Lasse as a baby*), George Skarstedt (*flautist*), Svea Holst (*nurse*), Ingmar Bergman (*himself*), Tor Borong (*man waiting in hospital*), Astrid Bodin, Marianne Schüler, Marrit Ohlsson (*guests at Marta's party*), Rune Stylander (*Persson*), Carin Swensson (*Anna*), Svea Holm (*Märta*), Agda Helin (*another nurse*), Dagny Lind (*Grannie*), Gunnar Rystedt (*man*).

1950
SÅNT HÄNDER INTE HÄR
(*High Tension* or *This Doesn't Happen Here*)

Screenplay: Herbert Grevenius, from the novel *I løpet av tolv timer*, by Waldemar Brøgger. Photography: Gunnar Fischer (assistant: Bengt Järnmark). Stills: Louis Huch. Editing: Lennart Wallén. Music: Erik Nordgren (music in export version by Herbert Stéen-Östling). Art Direction: Nils Svenwall. Production Manager: Helge Hagerman. Scriptgirl: Sol-Britt Norlander. Production Company: Svensk Filmindustri. 2,310 meters. 84 minutes. Swedish premiere: October 18, 1950.

Cast: Signe Hasso (*Vera*), Alf Kjellin (*Björn Almkvist*), Ulf Palme (*Atkä Natas*), Gösta Cederlund (*doctor*), Yngve Nordwall (*Lindell*), Hannu Kompus (*priest*), Els Vaarman (*female refugee*), Sylvia Tael (*Vanja*), Edmar Kuus (*Leino*), Helena Kuus (*another refugee*), Rudolf Lipp ("*the Shadow*"), Segol Mann, Willy Koblanck, Gregor Dahlman, Gösta Holmström, Ivan Bousé (*Liquidatzia agents*), Stig Olin (*young man*), Magnus Kesster (*houseowner*), Alexander von Baumgarten (*ship's captain*), Ragnar Klange (*motorist*), Lillie Wästfelt (*his wife*), Hanny Schedin (*lady*), Gunwer Bergkvist (*radio operator*), Mona Geijer-Falkner (*woman in apartment building*), Erik Forslund (*porter*), Akke Carlsson (*young man in car*), Helga Brofeldt (*elderly shocked woman*), Georg Skarstedt (*worker with hangover*), Tor Borong (*lab supervisor/theater manager*), Maud Hyttenberg (*student*), Wera Lindby (*shocked woman*), Mona Åstrand (*young girl*), Fritjof Hellberg (*ship's mate*), Eddy Andersson (*projectionist*), Harald Björling (*second projectionist*), Sten Hansson (*cook*), Eddie Ploman (*forensic official*), Ingemar Jacobsson (*policeman*).

1951
SOMMARLEK
(Summer Interlude or Illicit Interlude)

Screenplay: IB, Herbert Grevenius, from a story by IB entitled "Mari." Photography: Gunnar Fischer (assistant: Bengt Järnmark). Stills: Louis Huch. Editing: Oscar Rosander. Art Direction: Nils Svenwall. Music: Erik Nordgren, Delibes, Chopin, and Tchaikovsky. Production Manager: Allan Ekelund. Unit Manager: Gösta Ström. Scriptgirl: Ingegerd Ericsson. Production Company: Svensk Filmindustri. 2,635 meters. 96 minutes. Swedish premiere: October 1, 1951.

Cast: Maj-Britt Nilsson (*Marie*), Birger Malmsten (*Henrik*), Alf Kjellin (*David Nyström*), Georg Funkquist (*Uncle Erland*), Renée Björling (*Aunt Elisabeth*), Mimi Pollak (*Henrik's aunt*), Annalisa Ericson (*Kaj, a ballerina*), Stig Olin (*ballet master*), Gunnar Olsson (*pastor*), John Botvid (*Karl, a janitor*), Julia Caesar (*Maja, a dresser*), Douglas Håge (*Nisse, a janitor*), Carl Ström (*Sandell, stage manager*), Torsten Lilliecrona (*lighting man*), Marianne Schuler (*Kerstin*), Ernst Brunman (*boat's captain*), Olav Riego (*doctor*), Fylgia Zadig (*nurse*), Sten Mattsson (*boat hand*), Carl-Axel Elfving (*man with flowers*), Eskil Eckert-Lundin (*orchestra conductor*).

1952
KVINNORS VÄNTAN
(Secrets of Women or Waiting Women)

Screenplay: IB. Photography: Gunnar Fischer. Music: Erik Nordgren. Art Direction: Nils Svenwall. Editing: Oscar Rosander. Production Company: Svensk Filmindustri. 2,945 meters. 107 minutes. Swedish premiere: November 3, 1952.

Cast: Anita Björk (*Rakel*), Jarl Kulle (*Kaj*), Karl-Arne Holmsten (*Eugen Lobelius*), Maj-Britt Nilsson (*Märta*), Birger Malmsten (*Martin Lobelius*), Eva Dahlbeck (*Karin*), Gunnar Björnstrand (*Fredrik Lobelius*), Gerd Andersson (*Maj*), Björn Bjelvenstam (*Henrik*), Aino Taube (*Anita*), Håkan Westergren (*Paul*), Naima Wifstrand (*Mrs. Lobelius*), Torsten Lilliecrona (*host at nightclub*), Douglas Håge (*porter*), Lena Brogren (*hospital worker*), Wiktor Andersson (*refuse man*), Lil Yunkers (*Compere*), Marta Arbiin (*Sister Rit*), Kjell Nordenskold (*Bob*), Carl Ström (*anaesthetist*), Ingmar Bergman.

1953
SOMMAREN MED MONIKA
(Monika or Summer with Monika)

Screenplay: IB, P. A. Fogelström, from a novel by Fogelström. Photography: Gunnar Fischer. Music: Erik Nordgren, with the waltz "Kärlekens hamn," by Filip Olsson. Art Direction: P. A. Lundgren, Nils Svenwall. Editing: Tage Holmberg, Gösta Lewin. Production Manager: Allan Ekelund. Production

Company: Svensk Filmindustri. 2,630 meters. 96 minutes. Swedish premiere: February 9, 1953.

Cast: Harriet Andersson (*Monika*), Lars Ekborg (*Harry*), John Harryson (*Lelle*), Georg Skarstedt (*Harry's father*), Dagmar Ebbesen (*Harry's aunt*), Naemi Briese (*Monika's mother*), Åke Fridell (*Monika's father*), Gösta Eriksson (*manager of glass shop*), Gösta Gustafsson, Sigge Fürst, Gösta Prüzelius (*employees in glass shop*), Arthur Fischer (*chief of greengrocery*), Torsten Lilliecrona (*driver*), Bengt Eklund (*first man*), Gustaf Färingborg (*second man*), Ivar Wahlgren (*villager*), Renée Björling (*his wife*), Catrin Westerlund (*his daughter*), Harry Ahlin (*other villager*), Wiktor Andersson and Birger Sahlberg (*two men in street*), Hanny Schedin (*Mrs. Bohman*), Åke Grönberg (*foreman*), Magnus Kesster and Carl-Axel Elfving (*workmen*), Anders Andelius, Gordon Löwenadler, Bengt Brunskog (*Sicke*), Astrid Bodin and Mona Geijer-Falkner (*women in window*), Ernst Brunman (*tobacconist*), Nils Hultgren (*vicar*), Nils Whitén, Tor Borong, Einar Söderback (*beer drinkers*).

1953
GYCKLARNAS AFTON
(*The Naked Night* or *Sawdust and Tinsel*)

Screenplay: IB. Photography: Hilding Bladh, Göran Strindberg, Sven Nykvist. Music: Karl-Birger Blomdahl. Art Direction: Bibi Lindström. Editing: Carl-Olov Skeppstedt. Costumes: Mago. Producer: Rune Waldekranz. Production Company: Sandrews. 2,520 meters. 92 minutes. Swedish premiere: September 14, 1953.

Cast: Harriet Andersson (*Anne*), Åke Grönberg (*Albert Johansson*), Hasse Ekman (*Frans*), Anders Ek (*Frost*), Gudrun Brost (*Alma*), Annika Tretow (*Agda, Albert's wife*), Gunnar Björnstrand (*Mr. Sjuberg*), Erik Strandmark (*Jens*), Kiki (*the dwarf*), Åke Fridell (*officer*), Majken Torkeli (*Mrs. Ekberg*), Vanjek Hedberg (*Ekberg's son*), Curt Löwgren (*Blom*).

1954
EN LEKTION I KÄRLEK
(*A Lesson in Love*).

Screenplay: IB. Photography: Martin Bodin. Music: Dag Wirén. Art Direction: P. A. Lundgren. Editing: Oscar Rosander. Production Manager: Allan Ekelund. Production Company: Svensk Filmindustri. 2,620 meters. 95 minutes. Swedish premiere: October 4, 1954.

Cast: Eva Dahlbeck (*Marianne Erneman*), Gunnar Björnstrand (*Dr. David Erneman, her husband*), Yvonne Lombard (*Suzanne*), Harriet Andersson (*Nix*), Åke Grönberg (*Carl Adam*), Olof Winnerstrand (*Professor Henrik Erneman*), Renée Björling (*Svea Erneman*), Birgitte Reimar (*Lise*), John Elfström (*Sam*), Dagmar Ebbesen (*nurse*), Helge Hagerman (*traveling salesman*), Sigge Fürst (*priest*), Gösta Prüzelius (*guard on train*), Carl

Ström (*Uncle Axel*), Arne Lindblad (*hotel manager*), Torsten Lilliecrona (*porter*), Yvonne Brosset (*ballerina*).

1955
KVINNODRÖM
(Dreams or Journey into Autumn)

Screenplay: IB. Photography: Hilding Bladh. Music: archive. Art Direction: Gittan Gustafsson. Editing: Carl-Olov Skeppstedt. Production Manager: Rune Waldekranz. Production Company: Sandrews. 2,385 meters. 86 minutes. Swedish premiere: August 22, 1955.

Cast: Eva Dahlbeck (*Susanne*), Harriet Andersson (*Doris*), Gunnar Björnstrand (*Consul Sönderby*), Ulf Palme (*Henrik Lobelius*), Inga Landgré (*Mrs. Lobelius*), Sven Lindberg (*Palle*), Naima Wifstrand (*Mrs. Arén*), Benkt-Åke Benktsson (*Magnus, salon director*), Git Gay (*lady in studio*), Ludde Gentzel (*Sundström, the photographer*), Kerstin Hedeby (*Marianne*), Gunhild Kjellqvist (*another lady in studio*), Renée Björling (*Professor Berger*), Gösta Prüzelius, Sigvard Törnqvist (*two men on the train*), Tord Ståhl (*Mr. Barse*), Richard Mattsson (*Månsson*), Inga Gill (*shopgirl*), Greta Stare, Millan Lyxell, Gerd Widestedt, Margareta Bergström, Elsa Hovgren (*women in café*), Per-Erik Åström (*driver*), Carl-Gustaf Lindstedt (*porter*), Asta Beckman (*waitress*), Jessie Flaws (*makeup artist*), Marianne Nielsen (*Fanny*), Siv Ericks (*Katja*), Bengt Schött (*costume expert in studio*), Axel Düberg (*photographer in Stockholm*), Maud Hyttenberg, Folke Åström, Curt Kärrby, Ingmar Bergman.

1955
SOMMARNATTENS LEENDE
(Smiles of a Summer Night)

Screenplay: IB. Photography: Gunnar Fischer. Sound: P. O. Pettersson. Music: Erik Nordgren. Art Direction: P. A. Lundgren. Costumes: Mago. Makeup: Carl M. Lundh. Editing: Oscar Rosander. Production Manager: Allan Ekelund. Assistant Director: Lennart Olsson. Production Company: Svensk Filmindustri. 2,975 meters. 108 minutes. Swedish premiere: December 26, 1955.

Cast: Eva Dahlbeck (*Desirée Armfeldt*), Ulla Jacobsson (*Anne Egerman*), Harriet Andersson (*Petra, the maid*), Margit Carlqvist (*Charlotte Malcolm*), Jarl Kulle (*Count Carl-Magnus Malcolm*), Åke Fridell (*Frid, the groom*), Björn Bjelvenstam (*Henrik Egerman*), Naima Wifstrand (*Madame Armfeldt*), Jullan Kindahl (*the cook*), Gull Natorp (*Malla, Desirée's maid*), Birgitta Valberg, Bibi Andersson (*actresses*), Anders Wulff (*Desirée's son*), Gunnar Nielsen (*Niklas*), Gösta Prüzelius (*footman*), Svea Holst (*dresser*), Hans Strååt (*Almgren, the photographer*), Lisa Lundholm (*Mrs. Almgren*), Sigge Fürst (*policeman*), Lena Söderblom, Mona Malm (*chambermaids*), Josef Norrman (*elderly dinner guest*), Arne Lindblad (*actor*),

Börje Mellvig, Georg Adelly, Carl-Gustaf Lindstedt (*lawyers*), Ulf Johansson (*assistant in solicitor's office*), Yngve Nordwall (*Ferdinand*), Sten Gester, Mille Schmidt (*servants*), Gunnar Björnstrand (*Fredrik Egerman*).

1957
DET SJUNDE INSEGLET
(*The Seventh Seal*)

Screenplay: IB. Photography: Gunnar Fischer (assistant: Ake Nilsson). Sound: Aaby Wedin, Lennart Wallin. Special Sound Effects: Evald Andersson. Music: Erik Nordgren. Music Direction: Sixten Ehrling. Art Direction: P. A. Lundgren. Editing: Lennart Wallén. Choreography: Else Fisher. Costumes: Manne Lindholm. Makeup: Carl M. Lundh (Nils Nittel). Production Manager: Allan Ekelund. Assistant Director: Lennart Olsson. Production Company: Svensk Filmindustri. 2,620 meters. 95 minutes. Swedish premiere: February 16, 1957.

Cast: Max von Sydow (*Knight, Antonius Block*), Gunnar Björnstrand (*Squire, Jöns*), Bengt Ekerot (*Death*), Nils Poppe (*Jof*), Bibi Andersson (*Mia*), Ake Fridell (*Plog, the blacksmith*), Inga Gill (*Lisa, Plog's wife*), Maud Hansson (*witch*), Inga Landgré (*Knight's wife*), Gunnel Lindblom (*girl*), Bertil Anderberg (*Raval*), Anders Ek (*Monk*), Gunnar Olsson (*painter*), Erik Strandmark (*Skat*), Benkt-Åke Benktsson (*merchant*), Ulf Johansson (*leader of the soldiers*), Lars Lind (*young monk*), Gudrun Brost (*woman in tavern*), Ove Svensson (*corpse on hillside*).

1957
SMULTRONSTÄLLET
(*Wild Strawberries*)

Screenplay: IB. Photography: Gunnar Fischer (assistant: Björn Thermenius). Sound: Aaby Wedin, Lennart Wallin. Music: Erik Nordgren. Music Direction: E. Eckert-Lundin. Art Direction: Gittan Gustafsson. Editing: Oscar Rosander. Costumes: Millie Ström. Makeup: Carl M. Lundh (Nils Nittel). Production Manager: Allan Ekelund. Assistant Director: Gösta Ekman. Production Company: Svensk Filmindustri. 2,490 meters. 90 minutes. Swedish premiere: December 26, 1957.

Cast: Victor Sjöström (*Professor Isak Borg*), Bibi Andersson (*Sara*), Ingrid Thulin (*Marianne*), Gunnar Björnstrand (*Evald*), Folke Sundquist (*Anders*), Björn Bjelvenstam (*Viktor*), Naima Wifstrand (*Isak's mother*), Jullan Kindahl (*Agda, the housekeeper*), Gunnar Sjöberg (*Alman*), Gunnel Broström (*Mrs. Alman*), Gertrud Fridh (*Isak's wife*), Ake Fridell (*her lover*), Max von Sydow (*Akerman*), Sif Ruud (*aunt*), Yngve Nordwall (*Uncle Aron*), Per Sjöstrand (*Sigfrid*), Gio Petré (*Sigbritt*), Gunnel Lindblom (*Charlotta*), Maud Hansson (*Angelica*), Anne-Marie Wiman (*Mrs. Akerman*), Eva Norée (*Anna*), Lena Bergman, Monica Ehrling (*twins*), Per Skogsberg (*Hagbart*), Göran Lundquist (*Benjamin*), Prof. Sigge Wulff (*rector, Lund University*), Gunnar Olsson (*bishop*), Josef Norman (*Professor Tiger*), Vendela Rönnbäck (*Sister Elisabeth*).

1958
NÄRA LIVET
(*Brink of Life* or *So Close to Life*)

Screenplay: IB, Ulla Isaksson, based on the short story, "Det vänliga, värdiga," in her book, *Dödens faster*. Photography: Max Wilén. Art Direction: Bibi Lindström. Medical Adviser: Dr. Lars Engström. Editing: Carl-Olov Skeppstedt. Production Company: Nordisk Tonefilm. 2,310 meters. 84 minutes. Swedish premiere: March 31, 1958.

Cast: Eva Dahlbeck (*Stina Andersson*), Ingrid Thulin (*Cecilia Ellius*), Bibi Andersson (*Hjördis*), Barbro Hiort af Ornäs (*Sister Brita*), Erland Josephson (*Anders Ellius*), Inga Landgré (*Greta Ellius*), Max von Sydow (*Harry Andersson*), Gunnar Sjöberg (*Dr. Nordlander*), Anne-Marie Gyllenspetz (*welfare worker*), Sissi Kaiser (*Sister Marit*), Margareta Krook (*Dr. Larsson*), Lars Lind (*Dr. Thylenius*), Monica Ekberg (*Hjördis's friend*), Gun Jönsson (*night nurse*), Inga Gill (*woman*), Gunnar Nielsen (*a doctor*), Maud Elfsiö (*trainee nurse*), Kristina Adolphson (*assistant*).

1958
ANSIKTET
(*The Magician* or *The Face*)

Screenplay: IB. Photography: Gunnar Fischer. Sound: Aaby Wedin, Åke Hansson. Music: Erik Nordgren. Music Direction: E. Eckert-Lundin. Art Direction: P. A. Lundgren. Editing: Oscar Rosander. Costumes: Manne Lindholm, Greta Johansson. Makeup: Börje Lundh, Nils Nittel. Production Manager: Allan Ekelund. Assistant Director: Gösta Ekman. Production Company: Svensk Filmindustri. 2,755 meters. 100 minutes. Swedish premiere: December 26, 1958.

Cast: Max von Sydow (*Albert Emanuel Vogler*), Ingrid Thulin (*Manda Vogler*), Åke Fridell (*Tubal*), Naima Wifstrand (*Vogler's grandmother*), Gunnar Björnstrand (*Dr. Vergérus*), Bengt Ekerot (*Spegel*), Bibi Andersson (*Sara Lindqvist*), Gertrud Fridh (*Ottilia Egerman*), Erland Josephson (*Consul Abraham Egerman*), Lars Ekborg (*Simson, the coachman*), Toivo Pawlo (*Starbeck*), Ulla Sjöblom (*Henrietta*), Axel Düberg (*Rustan, the butler*), Birgitta Pettersson (*Sanna, the maid*), Oscar Ljung (*Antonsson*), Sif Ruud (*Sofia Garp*), Tor Borong, Arne Mårtensson, Frithiof Bjärne (*customs officers*).

1960
JUNGFRUKÄLLAN
(*The Virgin Spring*)

Screenplay: Ulla Isaksson, based on a fourteenth-century legend, "Töres dotter i Wänge." Photography: Sven Nykvist (assistant: Rolf Holmqvist).

Sound: Aaby Wedin (assistant: Staffan Dalin). Music: Erik Nordgren. Art Direction: P. A. Lundgren. Production Buyer: Karl-Arne Bergman. Editing: Oscar Rosander. Costumes: Marik Vos. Makeup: Börje Lundh. Production Manager: Allan Ekelund. Assistant Director: Lenn Hjortzberg. Unit Manager: Carl-Henry Cagarp. Scriptgirl: Ulla Furås. Production Company: Svensk Filmindustri. 2,435 meters. 88 minutes. Swedish premiere: February 8, 1960.

Cast: Max von Sydow (*Töre*), Birgitta Valberg (*Märeta*), Birgitta Pettersson (*Karin*), Gunnel Lindblom (*Ingeri*), Axel Düberg (*thin herdsman*), Tor Isedal (*mute herdsman*), Allan Edwall (*beggar*), Ove Porath (*boy*), Axel Slangus (*old man at ford*), Gudrun Brost (*Frida*), Oscar Ljung (*Simon*), Tor Borong, Leif Forstenberg (*farm laborers*).

1960
DJÄVULENS ÖGA
(*The Devil's Eye*)

Screenplay: IB, based on the radio play, *Don Juan vender tilbage*, by Oluf Bang. Photography: Gunnar Fischer. Sound: Stig Flodin. Mixing: Olle Jakobsson. Music: Erik Nordgren, with extracts from Domenico Scarlatti, played by Käbi Laretei. Art Direction: P. A. Lundgren. Production Buyer: Karl-Arne Bergman. Editing: Oscar Rosander. Sound Effects: Evald Andersson. Costumes: Mago. Makeup: Börje Lundh. Production Manager: Allan Ekelund. Unit Manager: Lars-Owe Carlberg. Assistant Director: Lenn Hjortzberg. Scriptgirl: Ulla Furås. Production Company: Svensk Filmindustri. 2,385 meters. 86 minutes. Swedish premiere: October 17, 1960.

Cast: Jarl Kulle (*Don Juan*), Bibi Andersson (*Britt-Marie*), Stig Järrel (*Satan*), Nils Poppe (*pastor*), Gertrud Fridh (*Renata, the pastor's wife*), Sture Lagerwall (*Pablo, Don Juan's servant*), Georg Funkquist (*Count Armand de Rochefoucauld*), Gunnar Sjöberg (*Marquis Giuseppe Maria de Maccopazza*), Torsten Winge (*old man*), Axel Düberg (*Jonas*), Kristina Adolphson (*veiled woman*), Allan Edwall (*Ear Devil*), Ragnar Arvedson (*Devil in Attendance*), Gunnar Björnstrand (*actor and narrator*), John Melin (*beauty doctor*), Sten-Torsten Thuul (*tailor*), Arne Lindblad (*tailor's assistant*), Svend Bunch (*quick-change expert*), Börje Lundh (*hairdresser*), Lenn Hjortzberg (*enema-doctor*), Tom Olsson (*black masseur*), Inga Gill (*housemaid*).

1961
SÅSOM I EN SPEGEL
(*Through a Glass Darkly*)

Screenplay: IB. Photography: Sven Nykvist (assistants: Rolf Holmqvist, Peter Wester). Sound: Stig Flodin (assistant: Staffan Dalin). Music: Erik Nordgren, with extracts from Bach, played by Erling Blöndal Bengtsson. Art Direction: P. A. Lundgren. Editing: Ulla Ryghe. Production Buyer: Karl-Arne

Bergman. Costumes: Mago. Sound Effects: Evald Andersson. Production Manager: Allan Ekelund. Unit Manager: Lars-Owe Carlberg. Assistant Director: Lenn Hjortzberg. Scriptgirl: Ulla Furås. Production Company: Svensk Filmindustri. 2,445 meters. 89 minutes. Swedish premiere: October 16, 1961.

Cast: Harriet Andersson (*Karin*), Gunnar Björnstrand (*David, her father*), Max von Sydow (*Martin, Karin's husband*), Lars Passgård (*Fredrik, David's son, known as Minus*).

1963
NATTVARDSGÄSTERNA
(*Winter Light*)

Screenplay: IB. Photography: Sven Nykvist (assistants: Rolf Holmqvist, Peter Wester). Sound: Stig Flodin (assistant: Brian Wikström). Music: extracts from Swedish psalms. Art Direction: P. A. Lundgren. Production Buyer: Karl-Arne Bergman. Editing: Ulla Ryghe. Costumes: Mago. Makeup: Börje Lundh. Sound Effects: Evald Andersson. Production Manager: Allan Ekelund. Unit Manager: Lars-Owe Carlberg. Assistant Directors: Lenn Hjortzberg, Vilgot Sjöman. Scriptgirl: Katherina Faragó. Production Company: Svensk Filmindustri. 2,215 meters. 80 minutes. Swedish premiere: February 11, 1963.

Cast: Ingrid Thulin (*Märta Lundberg*), Gunnar Björnstrand (*Tomas Ericsson*), Gunnel Lindblom (*Karin Persson*), Max von Sydow (*Jonas Persson*), Allan Edwall (*Algot Frövik*), Kolbjörn Knudsen (*Knut Aronsson*), Olof Thunberg (*Fredrik Blom, organist*), Elsa Ebbesen-Thornblad (*Magdalena Ledfors*), Tor Borong (*Johan Åkerblom*), Bertha Sånnell (*Hanna Appelblad*), Helena Palmgren (*Doris*), Eddie Axberg (*Johan Strand*), Lars-Owe Carlberg (*local police officer*), Ingmari Hjort (*Persson's daughter*), Stefan Larsson (*Persson's son*), Johan Olafs (*man*), Lars-Olof Andersson, Christer Öhman (*two boys*).

1963
TYSTNADEN
(*The Silence*)

Screenplay: IB. Photography: Sven Nykvist (assistant: Rolf Holmqvist). Sound: Stig Flodin (assistants: Bo Levén, Tage Sjöborg). Music: Ivan Renliden, R. Mersey, Johann Sebastian Bach (*Goldberg Variations*). Art Direction: P. A. Lundgren. Production Buyer: Karl-Arne Bergman. Editing: Ulla Ryghe. Costumes: Marik Vos-Lundh, Bertha Sånnell. Makeup: Gullan Westfelt. Production Manager: Allan Ekelund. Unit Manager: Lars-Owe Carlberg. Assistant Directors: Lars-Erik Liedholm, Lenn Hjortzberg. Scriptgirl: Katherina Faragó. Production Company: Svensk Filmindustri. 2,610 meters. 95 minutes. Swedish premiere: September 23, 1963.

Cast: Ingrid Thulin (*Ester*), Gunnel Lindblom (*Anna*), Jörgen Lindström (*Johan, her son*), Håkan Jahnberg (*waiter in hotel*), Birger Malmsten (*waiter in bar*), the Eduardinis (*seven dwarfs*), Eduardo Gutierrez (*their impresario*), Lissi Alandh (*woman in cabaret*), Leif Forstenberg (*man in cabaret*), Nils Waldt (*cinema cashier*), Birger Lensander (*cinema doorman*), Eskil Kalling (*man in bar*), Karl-Arne Bergman (*newspaper seller in bar*), Olof Widgren (*old man in hotel corridor*), Kristina Olansson (*double for Gunnel Lindblom*).

1964
FÖR ATT INTE TALA OM ALLA DESSA KVINNOR
(All These Women or Now About These Women)

Screenplay: Erland Josephson and IB, under pseudonym, "Buntel Eriksson." Photography (Eastmancolor): Sven Nykvist (assistants: Peter Wester, Lars Johnsson). Stills: Harry Kampf. Sound: P. O. Pettersson (assistant: Tage Sjöborg). Mixing: Olle Jakobsson. Music: Erik Nordgren, with extracts from Bach. Art Direction: P. A. Lundgren. Production Buyer: Karl-Arne Bergman. Editing: Ulla Ryghe. Costumes: Mago. Makeup: Börje Lundh, Britt Falkemo, Cecilia Drott. Sound Effects: Evald Andersson. Production Manager: Allan Ekelund. Unit Manager: Lars-Owe Carlberg. Assistant Directors: Lenn Hjortzberg, Lars-Erik Liedholm. Scriptgirl: Katherina Faragó. Production Company: Svensk Filmindustri. 2,195 meters. 80 minutes. Swedish premiere: June 15, 1964.

   Cast: Jarl Kulle (*Cornelius*), Bibi Andersson (*Bumble Bee, Felix's mistress*), Harriet Andersson (*Isolde, Felix's chambermaid*), Eva Dahlbeck (*Adelaide, Felix's wife*), Karin Kavli (*Madame Tussaud*), Gertrud Fridh (*Traviata*), Mona Malm (*Cecilia*), Barbro Hiort af Ornäs (*Beatrice, Felix's accompanist*), Allan Edwall (*Jillker, Felix's impresario*), Georg Funkquist (*Tristan*), Carl Billquist (*young man*), Jan Blomberg (*English radio announcer*), Göran Graffman (*French radio announcer*), Jan-Olof Strandberg (*German radio announcer*), Gösta Prüzelius (*Swedish radio announcer*), Ulf Johansson, Axel Düberg, Lars-Erik Liedholm (*men in black*), Lars-Owe Carlberg (*chauffeur*), Doris Funcke (*first waitress*), Yvonne Igell (*second waitress*).

1966
PERSONA

Screenplay: IB. Photography: Sven Nykvist (assistants: Anders Bodin, Lars Johnsson). Sound: P. O. Pettersson (assistant: Lennart Engholm). Mixing: Olle Jakobsson. Music: Lars Johan Werle, with extract from Bach. Art Direction: Bibi Lindström. Production Buyer: Karl-Arne Bergman. Editing: Ulla Ryghe. Costumes: Mago. Makeup: Börje Lundh, Tina Johansson. Sound Effects: Evald Andersson. Production Manager: Lars-Owe Carlberg. Unit Manager: Bo Vibenius. Assistant Director: Lenn Hjortzberg. Scriptgirl: Kerstin Berg. Production Company: Svensk Filmindustri. 2,320 meters. 84 minutes. Swedish premiere: October 18, 1966.

Cast: Bibi Andersson (*Sister Alma*), Liv Ullmann (*Elisabet Vogler*), Margaretha Krook (*doctor*), Gunnar Björnstrand (*Mr. Vogler*), Jörgen Lindström (*Elisabet's young son*).

1967
STIMULANTIA

Film in eight episodes. Bergman's episode entitled *Daniel*. Direction, Idea, and Photography (Eastmancolor, 16 mm.): IB. Editing: Ulla Ryghe. Music: Käbi Laretei, playing piano. Other episodes directed by Hans Abramson, Jörn Donner, Lars Görling, Arne Arnbom, Hans Alfredson and Tage Danielsson, Gustaf Molander, and Vilgot Sjöman. Swedish premiere: March 28, 1967.

Cast: Daniel Sebastian Bergman, Käbi Laretei (*themselves*).

1968
VARGTIMMEN
(Hour of the Wolf)

Screenplay: IB. Photography: Sven Nykvist (assistants: Anders Bodin, Roland Lundin). Stills: Roland Lundin. Sound: P. O. Pettersson (assistant: Lennart Engholm). Mixing: Olle Jakobsson. Music: Lars Johan Werle, with extracts from Mozart and Bach. Art Direction: Marik Vos-Lundh. Production Buyer: Karl-Arne Bergman. Editing: Ulla Ryghe. Costumes: Mago, Eivor Kullberg. Makeup: Börje Lundh, Kjell Gustavsson, Tina Johansson. Sound Effects: Evald Andersson. Production Manager: Lars-Owe Carlberg. Assistant Director: Lenn Hjortzberg. Unit Director: Bo A. Vibenius. Scriptgirl: Ulla Ryghe. Production Company: Svensk Filmindustri. 2,395 meters. 89 minutes. Swedish premiere: February 19, 1968.

Cast: Max von Sydow (*Johan Borg*), Liv Ullmann (*Alma Borg, his wife*), Ingrid Thulin (*Veronica Vogler*), Georg Rydeberg (*Archivist Lindhorst*), Erland Josephson (*Baron von Merkens*), Gertrud Fridh (*Corinne von Merkens*), Naima Wifstrand (*lady with the hat*), Bertil Anderberg (*Ernst von Merkens*), Ulf Johansson (*Curator Heerbrand*), Lenn Hjortzberg (*Kapellmeister Kreisler*), Agda Helin (*maid at the von Merkens'*), Mikael Rundquist (*boy in jeans*), Folke Sundquist (*Tamino in puppet theater*), Mona Seilitz (*corpse in mortuary*).

1968
SKAMMEN
(Shame or The Shame)

Screenplay: IB. Photography: Sven Nykvist (assistant: Roland Lundin). Sound: Lennart Engholm (assistant: Bernth Frithiof). Mixing: Olle Jakobsson. Art Direction: P. A. Lundgren. Production Buyer: Karl-Arne Bergman.

Editing: Ulla Ryghe. Costumes: Mago (assistant: Eivor Kullberg). Sound Effects: Evald Andersson. Makeup: Cecilia Drott. Hairstyles: Börje Lundh. Military Adviser: Stig Lindberg. Production Manager: Lars-Owe Carlberg. Unit Manager: Brian Wikström. Assistant Director: Raymond Lundberg. Scriptgirl: Katherina Faragó. Production Company: Svensk Filmindustri/ Cinematograph. 2,820 meters. 102 minutes. Swedish premiere: September 29, 1968.

Cast: Liv Ullmann (*Eva*), Max von Sydow (*Jan*), Gunnar Björnstrand (*Jacobi*), Birgitta Valberg (*Mrs. Jacobi*), Sigge Fürst (*Filip*), Hans Alfredson (*Lobelius*), Ingvar Kjellson (*Oswald*), Frank Sundström (*interrogator*), Ulf Johansson (*doctor*), Frej Lindqvist (*stooped man*), Rune Lindström (*stout gentleman*), Willy Peters (*older officer*), Bengt Eklund (*orderly*), Åke Jörnfalk (*condemned man*), Vilgot Sjöman (*interviewer*), Lars Amble (*an officer*), Björn Thambert (*Johan*), Karl-Axel Forsberg (*secretary*), Gösta Prüzelius (*pastor*), Brita Öberg (*lady in interrogation room*), Agda Helin (*woman in shop*), Ellika Mann (*prison warden*), Monica Lindberg, Gregor Dahlman, Nils Whiten, Per Berglund, Stig Lindberg, Jan Bergman, Nils Fogeby, Brian Wikström, Barbro Hiort af Ornäs, Georg Skarstedt, Lilian Carlsson, Börje Lundh, Eivor Kullberg, Karl-Arne Bergman.

1969
RITEN
(*The Ritual* or *The Rite*)

Screenplay: IB. Photography: Sven Nykvist. Sound Recording: Olle Jakobsson. Art Direction: Lennart Blomkvist. Editing: Siv Kanälv. Costumes: Mago. Production Manager: Lars-Owe Carlberg. Production Company: Svensk Filmindustri/Sveriges TV/Cinematograph. 2,030 meters. 74 minutes. Swedish premiere (on Swedish television): March 25, 1969.

Cast: Ingrid Thulin (*Thea Winkelmann*), Anders Ek (*Albert Emmanuel Sebastian Fischer*), Gunnar Björnstrand (*Hans Winkelmann*), Erik Hell (*Judge Abrahamson*), Ingmar Bergman (*priest in confessional*).

1969
EN PASSION
(*The Passion of Anna* or *A Passion*)

Screenplay: IB. Photography (Eastmancolor): Sven Nykvist (assistant: Roland Lundin). Sound: Lennart Engholm. Mixing: Olle Jakobsson. Music: extracts from Bach, and Allan Gray's song, "Always Romantic." Art Direction: P. A. Lundgren. Production Buyer: Karl-Arne Bergman (assistant: Jan Söderkvist). Editing: Siv Kanälv. Costumes: Mago (assistant: Ethel Sjöholm). Makeup: Cecilia Drott. Hairstyles: Börje Lundh. Set Decoration: Lennart Blomkvist. Sound Effects: Ulf Nordholm. Production Manager: Lars-Owe Carlberg. Unit Manager: Brian Wikström. Assistant: Arne Carlsson. Scriptgirl: Katherina Faragó. Production Company: Svensk Filmin-dustri/Cinematograph. 2,770 meters. 101 minutes. Swedish premiere: No-vember 10, 1969.

Cast: Liv Ullmann (*Anna Fromm*), Bibi Andersson (*Eva Vergérus*), Max von Sydow (*Andreas Winkelmann*), Erland Josephson (*Elis Vergérus*), Erik Hell (*Johan Andersson*), Sigge Fürst (*Verner*), Svea Holst (*Verner's wife*), Annika Kronberg (*Katarina*), Hjördis Pettersson (*Johan's sister*), Lars-Owe Carlberg, Brian Wikström (*policemen*), Barbro Hiort af Ornäs, Malin Ek, Britta Brunius, Brita Öberg, Marianne Karlbeck, Lennart Blomkvist.

1969
FÅRÖ-DOKUMENT
(*The Fårö Document*)

Photography (part Eastmancolor): Sven Nykvist. Editing: Siv Kanälv. Pro-duction Manager: Lars-Owe Carlberg. Production Company: Cinemato-graph. Narrator: IB. 78 minutes. Swedish premiere (on Swedish television): January 1, 1970.

1971
THE TOUCH or *BERÖRINGEN*

Screenplay: IB. Photography (Eastmancolor): Sven Nykvist. Sound: Len-nart Engholm, Harry Engholm, Bernt Frithiof. Music: Jan Johansson. Art Direction: P. A. Lungren. Editing: Siv Kanälv-Lundgren. Title Sequence Photography: Gunnar Fischer. Production Manager: Lars-Owe Carlberg. Assistant Director: Arne Carlsson. Production Company: ABC Pictures (New York)/Cinematograph (Stockholm). 3,102 meters. 113 minutes. Swedish premiere: August 30, 1971.

Cast: Elliott Gould (*David Kovac*), Bibi Andersson (*Karin Vergérus*), Max von Sydow (*Dr. Andreas Vergérus*), Sheila Reid (*Sara Kovac*), Barbro Hiort af Ornäs (*Karin's mother*), Staffan Hallerstam (*Anders Vergérus*), Maria Nolgård (*Agnes Vergérus*), Åke Lindström (*doctor*), Mimmi Wahl-ander (*nurse*), Else Ebbesen (*matron*), Anna von Rosen, Karin Nilsson (*neighbors*), Erik Nyhlen (*archeologist*), Margareta Byström (*Dr. Vergérus's secretary*), Alan Simon (*museum curator*), Per Sjöstrand (*another curator*), Aino Taube (*woman on staircase*), Ann-Christin Lobraten (*museum worker*), Dennis Gotobed (*British immigration officer*), Bengt Ottekil (*London bell-boy*), Harry Schein, Stig Björkman (*guests at party*).

1973
VISKNINGAR OCH ROP
(*Cries and Whispers*)

Screenplay: IB. Photography (Eastmancolor): Sven Nykvist. Sound: Owe Svensson. Music: Chopin, played by Käbi Laretei. Bach, played by Pierre

Fournier. Art Direction: Marik Vos. Editing: Siv Lundgren. Production Manager: Lars-Owe Carlberg. Production Company: Cinematograph, in association with Svenska Filminstitutet. 2,496 meters. 91 minutes. Swedish premiere: March 5, 1973.

Cast: Harriet Andersson (*Agnes*), Kari Sylwan (*Anna*), Ingrid Thulin (*Karin*), Liv Ullmann (*Maria*), Erland Josephson (*doctor*), Henning Moritzen (*Joakim*), Georg Åhlin (*Fredrik*), Anders Ek (*Pastor Isak*), Inga Gill (*Aunt Olga*), Malin Gjörup, Rosanna Mariano, Lena Bergman, Monika Priede, Greta Johanson, Karin Johanson.

1973
SCENER UR ETT ÄKTENSKAP
(Scenes from a Marriage)

Screenplay: IB. Photography (Eastmancolor, 16 mm.): Sven Nykvist. Sound: Owe Svensson. Art Direction: Björn Thulin. Editing: Siv Lundgren. Production Manager: Lars-Owe Carlberg. Executive Producer: Lars-Owe Carlberg. Production Company: Cinematograph. 4,609 meters. 168 minutes (theatrical version). Swedish premiere (on television, in 6 weekly parts): April 11 through May 16, 1973.

Cast: Liv Ullmann (*Marianne*), Erland Josephson (*Johan*), Bibi Andersson (*Katarina*), Jan Malmsjö (*Peter*), Anita Wall (*interviewer*), Gunnel Lindblom (*Eva*), Barbro Hiort af Ornäs (*Mrs. Jacobi*), Bertil Norström (*Arne*), Arne Carlsson. (Wenche Foss plays Marianne's mother in the TV version.)

1975
TROLLFLÖJTEN
(The Magic Flute)

Screenplay: IB, based on the opera by Mozart, libretto by Schikaneder. Photography (Eastmancolor): Sven Nykvist. Sound: Helmut Mühle, Peter Hennix. Musical Direction: Eric Ericson. Art Direction: Henny Noremark. Editing: Siv Lundgren. Costumes: Karin Erskine. Choreography: Donya Feuer. Production Manager. Måns Reuterswärd. Assistant Director: Kerstin Forsmark. Production Company: Sveriges TV 2. 3, 691 meters. 135 minutes. Swedish premiere (on television): January 1, 1975.

Cast: Josef Köstlinger (*Tamino*), Irma Urrila (*Pamina*), Håkan Hagegård (*Papageno*), Elisabeth Eriksson (*Papagena*), Ulrik Cold (*Sarastro*), Birgit Nordin (*Queen of the Night*), Ragnar Ulfung (*Monostatos*), Erik Saeden (*speaker*), Britt-Marie Aruhn, Birgitta Smiding, and Kirsten Vaupel (*ladies*), Gösta Prüzelius and Ulf Johanson (*priests*), Urban Malmberg, Ansgar Krook, and Erland von Heijne (*boys*), Hans Johansson, Jerker Arvidsson (*armed men*).

1976

ANSIKTE MOT ANSIKTE

(*Face to Face*)

Screenplay: IB. Photography (Eastmancolor): Sven Nykvist. Sound: Owe Svensson. Music: Mozart, played by Käbi Laretei. Art Direction: Anne Terselius-Hagegård, Anna Asp, Maggie Strindberg. Set Decoration: Peter Krupenin. Editing: Siv Lundgren. Producers: IB, Lars-Owe Carlberg. Production Manager: Katinka Faragó. Production Company: Cinematograph. English-language version: Paulette Rubinstein. 3,738 meters. 136 minutes. Swedish premiere (on television, in four weekly parts): April 28 through May 19, 1976.

Cast: Liv Ullmann (*Dr. Jenny Isaksson*), Erland Josephson (*Dr. Tomas Jacobi*), Gunnar Björnstrand (*grandfather*), Aino Taube-Henrikson (*grandmother*), Kari Sylwan (*Maria*), Sif Ruud (*Elisabeth Wankel*), Sven Lindberg (*Dr. Erik Isaksson*), Tore Segelcke (*lady*), Ulf Johanson (*Dr. Helmuth Wankel*), Helene Friberg (*Anna*), Kristina Adolphson (*Veronica*), Gösta Ekman (*Mikael Strömberg*), Käbi Laretei (*concert pianist*), Birger Malmsten (*rapist*), Göran Stangertz (*second rapist*), Marianne Aminoff (*Jenny's mother*), Gösta Prüzelius (*clergyman*), Rebecca Pawlo, Lena Ohlin (*boutique girls*).

1977

DAS SCHLANGENEI

(*The Serpent's Egg. Swedish title, Örmens ägg*)

Screenplay: IB. Photography (Eastmancolor): Sven Nykvist (assistants: Norbert Friedländer, Alexander Witt, Gerhard Fromm, Gunther Adlmuller, Hermann Fahr, Gernot Koehler, Werner Lühring, Bernd Heinl). Additional Photography: Peter Rohe, Dieter Lohmann. Sound: Karsten Ullrich (assistants: Theo Müller, Armin Münch, Daniel Nebenzal). Music: Rolf Wilhelm. Production Designer: Rolf Zehetbauer. Art Direction: Erner Achmann, Herbert Strabel. Editing: Jutta Hering, Petra von Oelffen. Scenic Artist: Friedrich Thaler. Special Effects: Karl Baumgartner, Dieter Ortmaier, Willi Hörmandinger. Choreography: Heino Hallhuber. Costumes: Charlotte Flemming (assistants: Egon Strasser, Ute Klimke). Makeup, Wigs, Hairstyles: Raimund Stangl, Susi Krause, Franz Göbel, Babette Juli, Hedi Polenski, Theodor Maier, Georg Rasche, Aloïs Steckermeier, Evelyn Döhring, Ariane Döhmel, Dagmar Friedrich, Marta Basedow, Marie-Luise Hantsch, Ute Hanow, Gerda Bublitz, Helga Kempke, Erika König, Mathile Kulanek, Albin Löw, Ursula Schaffert, Eva Uhl, Naksiye Prenović. Unit Managers: Rudolf Geiger, Franz Achter, Harry Wilbert, Horst Schneerbarth. Assistant Director: Wieland Liebske. Producer: Dino De Laurentiis. Executive Producer: Horst Wendlandt. Production Manager: Georg Föcking. Production Executive: Harold Nebenzal. Production Company: Rialto Film (West Berlin)/ Dino De Laurentiis Corporation (Los Angeles). 3,264 meters. 119 minutes. Filmed in English. German premiere: October 26, 1977.

Cast: Liv Ullmann (*Manuela Rosenberg*), David Carradine (*Abel Rosenberg*), Gert Froebe (*Inspector Bauer*), Heinz Bennent (*Hans Vergérus*), James Whitmore (*priest*), Glynn Turman (*Monroe*), Georg Hartmann (*Hollinger*), Edith Heerdegen (*Mrs. Holle*), Kyra Mladeck (*Miss Dorst*), Fritz Strassner (*Dr. Soltermann*), Hans Quest (*Dr. Silbermann*), Wolfgang Weiser (*civil servant*), Paula Braend (*Mrs. Hemse*), Walter Schmidinger (*Solomon*), Lisi Mangold (*Mikaela*), Grischa Huber (*Stella*), Paul Bürks (*cabaret comedian*), Isolde Barth, Rosemarie Heinikel, Andrea L'Arronge, and Beverly McNeely (*girls in guard uniform*), Toni Berger (*Mr. Rosenberg*), Erna Brunell (*Mrs. Rosenberg*), Hans Eichler (*Max Rosenberg*), Harry Kalenberg (*court's doctor*), Gaby Dohm (*woman with baby*), Christian Berkel (*student*), Paul Burian (*person in experiment*), Charles Regnier (*doctor*), Gunter Meisner (*prisoner*), Heida Picha (*wife*), Gunther Malzacher (*husband*), Hubert Mittendorf (*Balmer*), Hertha von Walther (*woman in street*), Ellen Umlauf (*landlady*), Renate Grosser and Hildegard Busse (*prostitutes*), Richard Bohne (*policeman*), Emil Feist (*cupid in cabaret*), Heino Hallhuber (*bride in cabaret*), Irene Steinbeisser (*groom in cabaret*).

1978
HERBSTSONAT
(*Autumn Sonata. Swedish title, Höstsonat*)

Screenplay: IB. Photography (Eastmancolor): Sven Nykvist. Sound: Owe Svensson (assistant: Tommy Persson). Music: Chopin, played by Käbi Laretei. Bach, performed by Claude Genetay; and Handel, performed by Frans Brüggen, Gustav Leonhardt, and Anne Bylsma. Set Design: Anna Asp. Editing: Sylvia Ingemarsson. Costumes: Inger Pehrsson. Makeup: Cecilia Drott. Production Supervisors: Ingrid Bergman, Lars-Owe Carlberg. Production Manager: Katinka Faragó. Unit Manager: Hans Lindgren. Assistant Director: Peder Langenskiöld. Production Assistant: Lena Hansson. Collaborators: Bo Andersson, Knut Andersen, Jon Arvesen, Jo Banoun, Daniel Bergman, Gunnar Bovollen, Demetrios Glavas, Jarle Hole, Bjarne Kjos, Per Mork, Percy Nilsson, Tom Olsen, Rolf Persson, Ulf Pramfors, Gunnar Sakshaug, Ase Seim, Ragnar Waarenperä. Production Company: Personafilm for ITC. 2,534 meters. 92 minutes. Swedish premiere: October 8, 1978.

Cast: Ingrid Bergman (*Charlotte*), Liv Ullmann (*Eva*), Lena Nyman (*Helena*), Halvar Björk (*Viktor*), Arne Bang-Hansen (*Uncle Otto*), Gunnar Björnstrand (*Paul*), Erland Josephson (*Josef*), Georg Løkkeberg (*Leonardo*), Linn Ullmann (*Eva, as a child*), Knut Wigert (*professor*), Eva von Hanno (*nurse*), Marianne Aminoff, Mimi Pollak.

1979
FÅRÖ-DOKUMENT 1979
(Fårö 1979)

Screenplay: IB. Photography (color): Arne Carlsson. Sound: Thomas Sam-
uelsson, Lars Persson. Sound Rerecording: Owe Svensson, Conrad Weyns.
Music: Svante Pettersson, Sigvard Huldt, Dag and Lena, Ingmar Nord-
ströms, Strix Q, Rock de Luxe, Ola and the Janglers. Editing: Sylvia Ingemarsson. Production Manager: Lars-Owe Carlberg. Production Assistants: Peder
Langenskiöld, Robert Herlitz, Siv Lundgren, Daniel Bergman. Narrator:
Ingmar Bergman. 1,132 meters (16 mm.). 103 minutes. Swedish premiere
(on television): December 24, 1979.
    Cast (themselves): Richard Östman, Ulla Silvergren, Annelie Nyström,
Per Broman, Irena Broman, Inge Nordström, Annika Liljegren, Arne Erik-
sson, Adolf Ekström, Victoria Ekström, Anton Ekström, Valter Broman,
Erik Ekström, Ingrid Ekman, Per Nordberg, Gunilla Johannesson, Herbert
Olsson, Rune Nilsson, Joe Nordenberg, Jan Nordberg.

1980
AUS DEM LEBEN DER MARIONETTEN
(From the Life of the Marionettes)

Screenplay: IB. Photography (part Eastmancolor): Sven Nykvist (assistants:
Lars Karlsson, Karl-Heinz Hoffmann). Sound: Peter Beil, Norbert Lill.
Sound rerecording: Milan Bor. Music: Rolf Wilhelm; Song, "Touch Me,
Take Me" (in English, singer uncredited). Production Design: Rolf Zehet-
bauer. Art Direction: Herbert Strabel. Set Decoration: Rolf Zehetbauer.
Editing: Petra von Oelffen (English-language version: Geri Ashur). Cos-
tumes: Charlotte Flemming, Egon Strasser. Fashion Show: Heinz A. Schulze-
Varell Couture. Wardrobe: Emmi Horoschenkoff, Anton Eder. Makeup:
Mathilde Basedow. English-language version: Paulette Rubinstein. Production Managers: Paulette Hufnagel, Irmgard Kelpinski. Unit Managers:
Michael Juncker, Franz Achter. Assistant Directors: Trudy von Trotha,
Johannes Kaetzler. Producers: Horst Wendlandt, Ingrid Bergman, (English-
language version) Richard Brick. Production Company: Personafilm (Munich) in collaboration with the Bayerische Staatsschauspiel. 2,842 meters.
104 minutes.
    Cast: Robert Atzorn *(Peter Egermann)*, Martin Benrath *(Professor Mo-
gens Jensen)*, Christine Buchegger *(Katarina Egermann)*, Rita Russek *(Katarina Krafft, known as Ka)*, Lola Müthel *(Cordelia Egermann)*, Walter
Schmidinger *(Tomas Isidor Mandelbaum, known as Tim)*, Heinz Bennent
(Arthur Brenner), Ruth Olafs *(nurse)*, Karl-Heinz Pelser *(police investigator)*, Gaby Dohm *(Frau Anders, Peter Egermann's secretary)*, Toni Berger
(peepshow doorman), Erwin Faber, Doris Jensen.

1982
FANNY OCH ALEXANDER
(Fanny and Alexander)

Screenplay: IB. Photography (Eastmancolor): Sven Nykvist (assistants: Lars Karlsson, Dan Myhrman). Stills: Arne Carlsson. Music: Daniel Bell. Sound: Owe Svensson, Bo Persson. Sync: Sylvia Ingemarsson. Art Direction: Anna Asp (assistants: Ulrika Rindegård, Annmargret Fyregård). Set Decoration: Kaj Larsen (assistants: Jan Andersson, Susanne Lingheim). Editing: Sylvia Ingemarsson. Wardrobe: Marik Vos-Lundh (assistants: Kristina Makroff, Lenamari Wallström, Maria Lindmark, Anne Marie Broms, Annchristin Lobråten-Hjelm, Ingabritt Adriansson, Ann Katrin Edmark, Wiveca Dahlström, Niclas Svartengren, Solveig Eriksson, Robert Nordlund, Kjell Sundqvist, Carolin von Rosen, Elsiebritt Lindström). Makeup: Leif Qviström, Anna-Lena Melin, Barbro Holmberg-Haugen. Production Manager: Katinka Faragó. Assistant Director: Peter Schildt. Unit Manager: Eva Ivarsson, Brita Werkmäster. Administration: Lars-Owe Carlberg, Ingrid Bergman, Fredrik von Rosen, Hellen Igler. Executive Producer: Jörn Donner. Production Company: Svenska Filminstitutet (Stockholm)/Sveriges TV 1 (Stockholm)/Personafilm (Munich)/Gaumont (Paris). Swedish premiere: Christmas 1982.

Cast: Gunn Wållgren (*Helena Ekdahl*), Allan Edwall (*Oscar Ekdahl*), Ewa Fröling (*Emilie Ekdahl*), Bertil Guve (*Alexander*), Pernilla Allwin (*Fanny*), Börje Ahlstedt (*Carl Ekdahl*), Christina Schollin (*Lydia Ekdahl*), Jarl Kulle (*Gustav Adolf Ekdahl*), Mona Malm (*Alma Ekdahl*), Maria Granlund (*Petra*), Emelie Werkö (*Jenny*), Kristian Almgren (*Putte*), Angelica Wallgren (*Eva*), Majlis Granlund (*Miss Vega*), Svea Holst-Widén (*Miss Ester*), Siv Ericks (*Alida*), Inga Ålenius (*Lisen*), Kristina Adolphson (*Siri*), Eva von Hanno (*Berta*), Pernilla Wallgren (*Maj*), Käbi Laretei (*Aunt Anna*), Sonya Hedenbratt (*Aunt Emma*), Erland Josephson (*Isak Jacobi*), Mats Bergman (*Aron*), Stina Ekblad (*Ismael*), Gunnar Björnstrand (*Mr. Filip Landahl*), Anna Bergman (*Miss Hanna Schwartz*), Per Mattson (*Mr. Mikael Bergman*), Nils Brandt (*Mr. Morsing*), Heinz Hopf (*Tomas Graal*), Åke Lagergren (*Johan Armfeldt*), Lickå Sjöman (*Grete Holm*), Sune Mangs, (*Mr. Salenius*), Maud Hyttenberg (*Mrs. Sinclair*), Kerstin Karte (*prompter*), Tore Karte (*administrative director*), Marianne Karlbeck (*Mrs. Palmgren*), Gus Dahlström (*set decorator*), Gösta Prüzelius (*Dr. Fürstenberg*), Georg Årlin (*colonel*), Ernst Günther (*dean of the university*), Jan Malmsjö (*Bishop Edvard Vergérus*), Kerstin Tidelius (*Henrietta Vergérus*), Marianne Aminoff (*Mrs. Blenda Vergérus*), Marrit Olsson (*Malla Tander*), Brita Billsten (*Karna*), Harriet Andersson (*Justina*), Krister Hell (*young man 1*), Peter Stormare (*young man 2*), Linda Krüger (*Pauline*), Pernilla Wahlgren (*Esmeralda*), Carl Billquist (*police inspector*), Anna Rydberg (*Rosa*).

Bergman's Principal Stage Productions

1944

Aschebergskan på Widtskövle (Brita von Horn and Elsa Collin). Helsingborg City Theater.
Fan ger ett anbud (Soya). Helsingborg City Theater.
Macbeth (Shakespeare). Helsingborg City Theater.

1945

Kriss-krass-filibom ("Scapin, Pimpel, and Kasper"). Helsingborg City Theater.
Reducera moralen (Sune Bergström). Helsingborg City Theater.
Jacobowsky och översten (Franz Werfel). Helsingborg City Theater.
Rabies (Olle Hedberg). Helsingborg City Theater.
Pelikanen (Strindberg). Helsingborg City Theater.

1946

Rekviem (Björn-Erik Höijer). Helsingborg City Theater.
Caligula (Albert Camus). Gothenburg Civic Theater.
Rakel och biografvaktmästaren (Ingmar Bergman). Malmö Municipal Theater.

1947

Macbeth (Shakespeare). Gothenburg Civic Theater.
Magic (G. K. Chesterton). Gothenburg Civic Theater.
Dagen slutar tidigt (Ingmar Bergman). Gothenburg Civic Theater.
Mig till skräck (Ingmar Bergman). Gothenburg Civic Theater.

1948

Dans på bryggan (Björn-Erik Höijer). Gothenburg Civic Theater.
Thieves' Carnival (Jean Anouilh). Gothenburg Civic Theater.
Kamma noll (Ingmar Bergman). Helsingborg City Theater.

1949

Le Sauvage (Jean Anouilh). Gothenburg Civic Theater.
A Streetcar Named Desire (Tennessee Williams). Gothenburg Civic Theater.

1950

Divine Words (Don Ramón de Valle-Inclán). Gothenburg Civic Theater.
The Threepenny Opera (Brecht). Intima Theater, Stockholm.
En skugga (Hjalmar Bergman). Intima Theater, Stockholm.
Medea (Jean Anouilh). Intima Theater, Stockholm.

1951

Det lyser i kåken (Björn-Erik Höijer). Royal Dramatic Theater, Stockholm.
The Rose Tattoo (Tennessee Williams). Norrköping Municipal Theater.

1952

Mordet i Barjärna (Ingmar Bergman). Malmö Municipal Theater.
Kronbruden (Strindberg). Malmö Municipal Theater.

1953

Six Characters in Search of an Author (Pirandello). Malmö Municipal
    Theater.
The Castle (Max Brod/Franz Kafka). Malmö Municipal Theater.

1954

Spöksonaten (Strindberg). Malmö Municipal Theater.
The Merry Widow (Léhar). Malmö Municipal Theater.

1955

Don Juan (Molière). Malmö Municipal Theater.
The Teahouse of the August Moon (John Patrick). Malmö Municipal
    Theater.
Lea och Rakel (Vilhelm Moberg). Malmö Municipal Theater.

1956

The Poor Bride (Alexander Ostrovsky). Malmö Municipal Theater.
Cat on a Hot Tin Roof (Tennessee Williams). Malmö Municipal Theater.
Erik XIV (Strindberg). Malmö Municipal Theater.

1957

Peer Gynt (Ibsen). Malmö Municipal Theater.
Le Misanthrope (Molière). Malmö Municipal Theater.

1958

Sagan (Hjalmar Bergman). Malmö Municipal Theater.
Urfaust (Goethe). Malmö Municipal Theater.
Värmlänningarna (F. A. Dahlgren). Malmö Municipal Theater.

1961

The Sea Gull (Chekhov). Royal Dramatic Theater, Stockholm.
The Rake's Progress (Stravinsky). Royal Opera, Stockholm.

1963

Who's Afraid of Virginia Woolf? (Edward Albee). Royal Dramatic Theater,
    Stockholm.
Sagan (Hjalmar Bergman). Royal Dramatic Theater, Stockholm.

1964

Tre knivar från Wei (Harry Martinson). Royal Dramatic Theater, Stock-
    holm.
Hedda Gabler (Ibsen). Royal Dramatic Theater, Stockholm.

1965

Tiny Alice (Edward Albee). Royal Dramatic Theater, Stockholm.

1966

The Investigation (Peter Weiss). Royal Dramatic Theater, Stockholm.
L'Ecole de femmes (Molière). Royal Dramatic Theater, Stockholm.

1967

Six Characters in Search of an Author (Pirandello). National Theater, Oslo.

1969

Woyzeck (Büchner). Royal Dramatic Theater, Stockholm.

1970

Drömspelet (Strindberg). Royal Dramatic Theater, Stockholm.

1971

Show (Lars Forssell). Royal Dramatic Theater, Stockholm.

1972

The Wild Duck (Ibsen). Royal Dramatic Theater, Stockholm.

1973

Spöksonaten (Strindberg). Royal Dramatic Theater, Stockholm.
Le Misanthrope (Molière). Danish Royal Theater.

1974

Till Damascus (Strindberg). Royal Dramatic Theater, Stockholm.

1975

Twelfth Night (Shakespeare). Royal Dramatic Theater, Stockholm.

1977

Drömspelet (Strindberg). Residenztheater, Munich.

1978

Three Sisters (Chekhov). Residenztheater, Munich.

1979

Tartuffe (Molière). Residenztheater, Munich.
Hedda Gabler (Ibsen). Residenztheater, Munich.

1980

Yvonne, Princess of Burgundy (Witold Gombrowicz). Residenztheater,
    Munich.

1981

A Doll's House (Ibsen), Fröken Julie (Strindberg), and Scener ur ett äktenskap (Ingmar Bergman). Residenztheater, Munich (in one program, at
two adjacent theaters).

Index